EMPIRE OF SELF

Also by Jay Parini

Fiction

The Love Run
The Patch Boys
The Last Station
Bay of Arrows
Benjamin's Crossing
The Apprentice Lover
The Passages of H.M.

Poetry

Singing in Time
Anthracite Country
Town Life
House of Days
The Art of Subtraction: New and Selected Poems

Nonfiction and Criticism

Theodore Roethke: An American Romantic
An Invitation to Poetry
Gore Vidal: Writer Against the Grain (edited by)
John Steinbeck: A Biography
Some Necessary Angels: Essays on Writing and Politics
Robert Frost: A Life
One Matchless Time: A Life of William Faulkner
The Art of Teaching
Why Poetry Matters
Promised Land: Thirteen Books That Changed America
The Selected Essays of Gore Vidal (edited by)
Jesus: The Human Face of God

EMPIRE OF SELF

A Life of Gore Vidal

JAY PARINI

Doubleday

New York · London · Toronto · Sydney · Auckland

www.doubleday.com

Jacket design by John Fontana
Jacket photograph © Arnold Newman/Getty Images

Parini, Jay.
Empire of self : a life of Gore Vidal / by Jay Parini.
pages cm
ISBN 978-0-385-53756-8 (hardcover) — ISBN 978-0-385-53757-5 (eBook) 1. Vidal, Gore,
1925–2012. 2. Authors, American—20th century—Biography. I. Title.
PS3543.I26Z85 2015
813'.54—dc23
[B]
2015004719

MANUFACTURED IN THE UNITED STATES OF AMERICA

1 3 5 7 9 10 8 6 4 2

First Edition

For Devon, always

Contents

EMPIRE OF SELF

Introduction

My friendship with Gore Vidal began in the mid-eighties, when I lived for a period on sabbatical with my wife and young children in Atrani, a village on the coast of southern Italy. We rented a small stone villa on a cliff overlooking the sea, with a view to Salerno to the south and Capri just out of sight to the north. The bay glistened below us, almost too bright to bear, with fishing vessels departing each morning in search of mullet, mussels, mackerel, tuna, and squid that would be unloaded in the afternoon and sold in wooden barrels by the dock. I went in the mornings to a café in Amalfi, walking into town along a stony footpath where a thousand cats seemed to prowl, where sturdy women carried groceries slowly up hundreds of steps and children kicked footballs in back alleys. The smells of laundry soap, cat piss, and wildflowers were ubiquitous.

We had a rooftop terrace, above which rose a lemon grove and limestone cliffs. A massive villa—alabaster white, clinging to the rocks like a swallow's nest—loomed above us, and we wondered who lived there in such opulence. Some Italian nobleman? A local Mafia don? A film star? When I asked the tobacconist in town about its resident, he said, "*Ah, lo scrittore!* Gore Vidal. *Americano.*" He explained that the writer stopped by his shop almost every afternoon for a newspaper, then retired to the bar next door for a drink, where he would sit and read for an hour or so before taking the bus up the hill to Ravello.

I knew the work of Gore Vidal moderately well already. Having been an antiwar activist during the Vietnam era, I admired his political commentaries in *Esquire* and *The New York Review of Books.*

I never forgot his fiery debates with William F. Buckley during the presidential conventions of 1968, especially during the siege of Chicago. He had held his ground, driving Buckley mad with his relentless logic and unflappable manner. I had read half a dozen of his novels, including *Julian*, *Myra Breckinridge*, *Burr*, and *Lincoln*. Needless to say, I wanted to meet him.

Responding to a note I'd sent, Gore pounded on my door one afternoon not long after our arrival, inviting my wife and me to dinner. I was terrified, as his reputation preceded him, and thought he might be tricky. But a friendship soon blossomed. I often met him for a drink or dinner, and a series of conversations began that lasted until his death in 2012. It would be fair to say, in a crude way, that I was looking for a father, and he seemed in search of a son. We had a good deal in common, including a passion for liberal politics, American history, and books. We both loved Henry James, Mark Twain, Anthony Trollope, and Henry Adams—and we invariably found we had more to talk about than time allowed. We also shared a love of both Italy and Britain. By that time I had spent seven years in the British Isles, and it turned out we knew many of the same people. The literary world is, in fact, quite small—especially in Britain and Italy, where writers and editors often converge at parties and literary events.

In the decades that followed, we spoke on the phone every week—for periods on a daily basis. And I would stay with him in Ravello or, later, Los Angeles, meeting him often when he traveled. I have strong memories of our time together in such places as Rome, Naples, Edinburgh, Oxford, London, New York, Boston, even Salzburg and Key West. He proved more than helpful to me as a younger writer, reading drafts of my books, offering frank critiques and encouragement. We discussed his work at length, too—he would frequently send a typescript or galley for me to read.

His phone calls, in later years, often began: "What are they saying about me?" To a somewhat frightening degree, he depended on the world's opinion. Once, in one of those memories that stands in for many others, my wife and I were sitting in his study in Ravello when he came in with drinks. On the wall behind his desk were twenty or so framed magazine covers, with Gore's face on each one. I asked,

"What's that all about, those covers?" He said, "When I come into this room in the morning to work, I like to be reminded who I am."

Over many decades he had built a huge empire of self, sending out colonies in various languages. "They love me in Brazil," he would say. Or Bulgaria, or Turkey, or Hong Kong. I took his rampant egotism with a grain of salt. It was part of him, but only part. The narcissism was, at times, an exhausting and debilitating thing for Gore, as it proved impossible to get enough satisfying responses. He required a hall of mirrors for adequate reflection, and there was never enough. The nature of the narcissistic hole is such that it can't be filled. At times, I wondered about how much money and time I spent in winging off to various far-flung cities to spend a few days with him, and my transatlantic phone bills reflected my own mania. But his flame was very bright and warm, and I was drawn to it.

He was usually kind to me, and to others in his surprisingly discrete circle of friends. He listened to my ideas for books and essays carefully, eager to respond in useful ways. He liked to know every detail in the lives of my children. He took an interest in my wife's work as a psychotherapist and asked about this frequently. When we met in various cities, we had lavish dinners in good restaurants, and there was never any question about who would pay. "I'm very rich," he would say, picking up the tab.

In the early nineties, Gore asked me to take over the biography that Walter Clemons was writing—or not writing because of writer's block and diabetes (among other things that seemed to delay Clemons). My wife, perceptively, insisted that I decline, saying that I would have to choose between the biography and my friendship. I couldn't have both. She understood that he would try to control what I wrote at every turn, driving us both insane. So I decided then to write a book that could only be published after his death, a frank yet fond look at a man I admired, even loved, and who had preoccupied me for such a long time. In the mid-nineties, I did edit a book about him, enlisting a number of critics to discuss phases of his career. I interviewed him then, and frequently in the years that followed, making it clear that one day I would write a book about him. He encouraged this Boswellian vein, and would sometimes say, "I hope you're writing this down!"

In fact, I did. And over the years, I interviewed people he knew, such as Anthony Burgess, Graham Greene, Alberto Moravia, Paul Newman, Richard Poirier, Frederic Prokosch, and many others. On several occasions I interviewed his companion, Howard Austen, a wry and congenial man with a big heart.

On one of my last visits with Gore, in the Hollywood Hills, he wondered if I would follow through and write a book about him. I said that I would. "So write the book," he said, "and do notice the potholes. But, for God's sake, keep your eyes on the main road!" In the course of bringing together thinking of nearly three decades about this complicated and gifted man, I've tried to take this advice seriously, emulating Gore himself, a writer who rarely lost sight of the road before him.

The reader will find brief first-person vignettes between the chapters, recollections of moments in our friendship that stuck in my head. In writing them, I thought of the suggestive vignettes between the stories of Ernest Hemingway's *In Our Time* and how each positioned the reader to enter the next story. My vignettes were culled from my journals, in each case written soon after the event described. This is as far as I go in making this a memoir of a friendship. It's not that. It's the story of Gore Vidal's extraordinary life and writing.

A passage from Gore's 1959 essay on Suetonius, the father of biographical writing, comes to mind. He praised this great Roman biographer who, "in holding up a mirror to those Caesars of diverting legend, reflects not only them but ourselves: half-tamed creatures, whose great moral task it is to hold in balance the angel and the monster within—for we are both, and to ignore this duality is to invite disaster." Gore certainly embodied both the angel and the monster, and he knew it. Over the decades, I witnessed more of the angel than the monster, although I saw him lash out at friends, and several times he said hurtful things to me, as when I got a fellowship at an Oxford college and Gore remarked, "They don't let in wops like you, do they really?" I would always come back at him, saying he had insulted me, but he would usually pretend that nothing had happened, and I let it pass. I allowed him to speak rudely to me to maintain a sense of equilibrium between us—a fault of mine, no doubt. But one usually had a choice with Gore: Agree with him or leave. I valued our friendship for a variety of reasons, including his mentorship, and—perhaps more than most—have a lot of patience. I made the decision to hang in there.

My goal in writing this book has been to look at the angel and the monster alike, offering a candid portrait of a gifted, difficult, influential man who remained in the foreground of his times. Gore gave me full access to his life: his letters and papers, his friends. He told me to say what I saw whenever I wrote about him, not pulling my punches. That is, of course, how he lived his life. I'd like to think he would appreciate my efforts, although I'm not looking forward to our meeting on the other side.

Rock Creek Ramble

Gore gives a talk at the National Press Club in Washington, D.C., in 1991: a rousing "State of the Union" address. But in the morning, at his request, I drive him to the old house in Rock Creek Park that had belonged to his grandparents. "I haven't seen it in a while," he says as we enter the drive at 1500 Broad Branch Road. "It's now the Malaysian embassy, but they know we're coming."

The circular drive has a fountain in the middle. "That wasn't there," he says, annoyed. "You could look across the street to the woods and see what we called the flags, pale irises. There was a rose garden somewhere, and it didn't belong to the president. The creek itself was often orange-brown, and I used to wade there with my trousers rolled up to the knees. You'd never know a city lay nearby, on the other side of the park."

It's a large and lovely house on a hill, built of gray-yellow Baltimore stone, much larger than I'd imagined. A Malaysian secretary meets us at the door. "Mr. Vidal, this is an honor," she says, bowing. She shows us to a white sofa in a room nearby, and two servants in white jackets bring tea and coconut macaroons. We talk with her for a while, and she apologizes for the absence of the ambassador, who apparently lives here. But Gore is itching to wander. "We'll just have a look upstairs," he says.

The woman seems unsure about this, but doesn't interfere. Suddenly the decades fall away—and Gore is eight or nine years old, stepping into the hallway outside of his grandfather's study. "He had so many books, which was an irony, because he was blind. In the attic were thousands of volumes, old yellow copies of the Congressional Record. My grandmother said to pay no attention to my grandfather when he grumbled. But he rarely grumbled. I was the child of their dreams, as I was quiet and liked to read. I read aloud to my grandfather in his study. We sat there night after night, working our way through Roman or American history. He would stop me, ask questions, making sure I understood what I read. Could there be a luckier boy in the world?"

He shows me a favorite place, this tiny alcove where he spent hours. "I would hear voices downstairs, and I would close my book and crouch on the stairs, hiding, listening. I could hear the voice of Huey Long—a low Southern drawl—or some other senator or congressional aide. I knew the sorts of thing they were saying, even if I couldn't hear the words. My grandfather was the master of ceremonies, but he always convinced everyone in the room that he was right and, no doubt, Franklin Roosevelt was wrong."

We step to the back door. "My grandfather kept chickens in the yards, so we had fresh eggs," he says. "My job was to fetch the eggs. They seemed the most precious and wonderful things in the world to a boy of seven or eight. I didn't eat chicken for a long time because I would think of those chickens, and it worried me that they had to lose their lives to feed us."

Gore stands in the driveway for a long time, looking across the road to the park. Then he shakes his head and steps into my car. "It never pays to go back," he says. "And you misremember it anyway."

Chapter One

> The genius of our ruling class is that it has kept a majority of the people from ever questioning the inequity of a system where most people drudge along paying heavy taxes for which they get nothing in return.
>
> —Gore Vidal

1. A Silver-Plated Mug

On a visit to Gore in Los Angeles, I watched as he poured himself a glass of Scotch in his favorite mug, which seemed to be flaking. "I always thought it was silver," he said. "It seems it was silver plate."

This was a mug given to him as a newborn by the football team of West Point, the United States Military Academy, a legendary institution on the Hudson River in New York where generations of officers have been trained since Thomas Jefferson signed legislation establishing it in 1802. The mug is engraved: Eugene L. Vidal Jr., October 3, 1925. At this time, Gore's father, also Eugene L. Vidal, was a football and track coach at West Point.

Known as Gene, Gore's father was a member of the West Point Class of 1918, a former star quarterback on the football team who had stood out in basketball, baseball, and track as well. (One of his classmates was the future general Mark Clark, who led the Allied invasion of Italy in 1943.) Born in 1895, Gene was a farm boy who had excelled in sports during his first two years at the University of South Dakota, where a local congressman noticed his prowess on the field and found him a place in West Point's illustrious Corps of Cadets. "This ended my father's dream of becoming a barber," recalled his son. "Barbers in those days had masses of free time, and that's mainly what my father wished for."

After a period in the army, Gene went on to play professional football for the Washington Senators and to compete in the 1920 Antwerp Olympics, finishing seventh in the decathlon—a grueling sequence of ten track-and-field events. In early January 1922, he married Nina Gore, the flamboyant daughter of a senator whom he had met at a party. "My mother loved athletes, famous men, and booze," says her son, "not necessarily in that order." It was a furious rise for a mild-mannered boy from South Dakota. "I don't think my father quite knew what hit him," said Gore.

Gene never felt especially comfortable among the elite political classes in Washington, but as Gore recalled, his father "came by his insecurity honestly." Gene's grandfather—Eugen Fidel Vidal—was a con artist, born in Feldkirch, Austria, of Romansh stock, a Swiss ethnic group that spoke German, Italian, and a native tongue of their own. Grandfather Vidal, whose family had been pharmacists, merchants, and doctors, later faked a medical degree and worked as a pharmacist after marrying Emma Traxler von Hartmann of Lucerne. She was, according to Gore, "an heiress, though her marriage to Dr. Vidal got her disinherited." They moved to Wisconsin in 1849, the year after all of Europe was in political revolt. In 1870, the undependable Dr. Vidal abandoned his wife and children, wandering off into parts unknown.

The former "heiress"—her status mattered to Gore, although she seems not to have been especially well-born or wealthy—earned a living as a seamstress and by her gift for languages, translating American stories for various newspapers into French, German, and Italian—a true Swiss polyglot. She was also a Roman Catholic, like Eugen, though Gene remained indifferent to the religious heritage of the Vidal and Traxler families. "He was pure pagan," said his son.

Gore's paternal grandparents, Felix and Margaret Ann Vidal, were recalled by him as being from "an indifferent low-middle-class prairie background." Felix was a machinist by trade, and there was little money or status in that occupation. This vaguely annoyed Gore, who had a profound sense of his aristocratic lineage. Fortunately for him, his father married well, at least with regard to family circumstances if not pedigree.

Gore's maternal grandfather was Senator Thomas Pryor Gore, born in Embry, a small town in Mississippi. As the historian Monroe Billington wrote: "Tom Gore had lived eight years of normal boyhood on a Mississippi farm when, one day while he and a young friend were playing near where the family's work oxen were grazing, Tom was struck in the left eye by a stick thrown by his playmate. The vision of his eye was partially impaired, but his parents were hardly aware of the fact at the time, and no medical attention was given after the accident. Three years later Tom purchased a toy crossbow for his brother's birthday. Before making the presentation, Tom decided to shoot the bow once to be sure that it would work. The arrow lodged in the bow and when he tried to get it out, it came loose and struck him in the right eye." It was a bizarre, unlucky coincidence, with lightning striking twice. But Senator Gore possessed an iron will that would not be subdued.

He graduated from a normal school, or teachers college, in Walthall, Mississippi, in 1890—a sign of his own middle-class roots. He taught for a while, then studied for a law degree at Cumberland University in Tennessee. He was admitted to the Tennessee bar soon after graduation, and in 1900 married Nina Belle Kay, usually called "Tot" by the family, and described by her grandson as "the woman who raised me. She was my real mother, a quiet woman with infinite patience, a shrewd sense of the world, and a dry wit." (Grandfather Gore was always "Dah.")

Senator Gore loomed massively in his grandson's imagination. "I sat beside him in the Senate," Gore recalled, "and, as he was blind—the result of two accidents in his boyhood—I served as his pair of eyes." One can see the origins of Gore's politics in those of his grandfather, a combination of populist and reactionary who ran unsuccessfully for Congress on the Populist Party ticket in Mississippi in 1898. After his marriage to Tot, Thomas moved to Oklahoma, where he quickly found that his oratorical skills served him well. He famously said, "I would rather be a humble private in the ranks of those who struggle for justice and equality than to be a minion of plutocracy, though adorned with purple and gold."

One can see Gore's affection for his blind grandfather in a poem written as a schoolboy:

Unyielding to adversity,
Conqueror of misfortune,
He served Oklahoma with
Indomitable will
For two decades.

First United States Senator
From Oklahoma,
He bequeathed us
Treasures of eloquence,
Wit and learning.
Great is the memory of his character.

Thomas P. Gore was indeed one of the first of two U.S. Senators elected in 1907, when Oklahoma became the forty-sixth state to join the Union, after protracted wrangling. The senator later attracted the attention of President Woodrow Wilson, who tried to lure him into his cabinet, without luck. This feisty and independent man preferred the Senate. "He admired its lore, its traditions," his grandson recalled. "It was the air he breathed."

An unapologetic isolationist, Senator Gore opposed American entry into World War I, annoying President Wilson, who cut off relations with his former ally and friend over their differences. "It was painful for him, as he liked access to the White House. And his antiwar attitudes didn't sit well with bellicose constituents back in Oklahoma," Gore said. "They remembered his radical views when it was time for reelection. And my grandfather lost." That was in 1920, and the former senator Gore turned to the practice of law in Washington, D.C., where he moved into a large, graceful house at 1500 Broad Branch Road on Rock Creek Park with his wife and two children—the eldest being Nina, Gore's mother, who was born in 1903.

"My parents' marriage was a major point of gossip in Washington in 1922," Gore recalled. The dashing young officer turned professional football player found the beautiful daughter of the blind senator irresistible. "He liked women, especially beautiful women." For her part, how could Nina, only eighteen, resist a handsome Olympic athlete who had recently qualified as a pilot and been hired to teach aeronautics at West Point? The potentially boring texture of her daily life as a faculty wife at West Point probably didn't occur to her.

It was, perhaps, with relief that—after three years of marriage—she found herself pregnant. Gore was named after his father: Big Gene and Little Gene, as they were called. He was christened Eugene Luther Gore Vidal by the headmaster of St. Albans, the Episcopal prep school in Washington, D.C., that he would later attend, giving him the plausible option of dropping the first two names when he decided to reinvent himself during his late teens.

Gene accepted a job as assistant football coach at the University of Oregon in 1926, taking his wife and child. "It was a job," his son recalled, "and God knows he needed one." But life in Oregon proved even more tedious for Nina than life at West Point, and she moved back to Washington with baby Gene. She quickly resumed her life as a socialite, although Big Gene must have sensed trouble and rejoined his wife soon, taking a job with the fledgling airline Transcontinental Air Transport.

Little Gene found himself largely in the care of his grandparents, especially Tot. "I would call her my real mother," he said, remembering that as a baby he slept in the drawer of a bureau. Whatever nurturing he experienced as a child came from that source. And the house on Rock Creek Park became not only his actual home but—in a sense—his Platonic ideal of a home. It would become the model for Gore's later dwellings: Edgewater on the Hudson River; La Rondinaia, his palatial villa in Ravello overlooking the Amalfi coast; and the cavernous home on Outpost Drive in the Hollywood Hills, where he spent his last decade.

II. Capitol Steps

Gore had free run of his grandfather's library, and Thomas P. Gore became a mentor, discussing books, suggesting that he read Edward Gibbon's history of the Roman Empire or Herodotus. The boy was especially fond of Henry Adams, whose multivolume history of the early American republic was among his favorite possessions—a resource that would become important to Gore in later years, when writing novels of American history. "My grandfather knew a great deal about everything. I don't know how or when he learned it all, but he had an enviable store of knowledge. He was encyclopedic, especially about classical history or American history. For me, it was an example. Learn things, and remember them."

Being out of office proved difficult for Gore's grandfather, who found the practice of law unrewarding. He missed the tug-of-war in the Senate, with its opportunities for oratory. He had strong opinions that needed expression, and the upper chamber offered a splendid bully pulpit. So he put a good deal of energy into getting elected again in 1930, hitching his wagon to that of the popular and controversial Oklahoma politician William H. "Alfalfa Bill" Murray, who rode into the governor's mansion in Oklahoma at the outset of the Great Depression, when the collapse of oil revenue combined with tanking agricultural prices to gut the state's economy. The populist streak of Senator Gore dovetailed with Murray's agrarian rhetoric. "He was suddenly back in the limelight, where he felt he belonged, sitting in the Senate beside Huey Long and the 'Lion of Idaho,' William Borah, who were both good friends."

Young Gore became the eyes for his blind grandfather—a role he often recalled with deep nostalgia. He would read to him in the evening from an assortment of books or newspapers. He also read from the *Congressional Record* along with briefs from the influential Finance Committee, where the newly reelected Senator Gore had landed a spot. "I always say that I was the only nine-year-old in the United States who knew the concept of bimetallism," his grandson recalled, referring to the monetary policy that is based on both gold and silver, and which stirred populist politicians, such as three-time presidential candidate William Jennings Bryan. Gore often sat in the Senate beside his grandfather, listening to speeches that would influence his own style as a politician and activist in decades to come. "They were distinguished and gifted actors. If you studied them, it was like studying at the Old Vic."

In his later years, Gore increasingly looked and sounded like a Roman elder statesman. One could hear the stentorian voice of Thomas P. Gore breaking out in his grandson's rhetoric, which leaned toward the oracular. The impression would be enhanced by Gore's increasingly senatorial girth and his preference for conservative pin-striped suits and starched shirts with gold cuff links (he had an impressive collection of cuff links, which he prized). When his knees seized up in later decades, he made use of an ornate cane that he waved like a scepter to emphasize a point.

One of Gore's few chores as a boy at home with his grandparents was to feed the chickens, which the blind senator kept in the backyard in deference to his own rural boyhood. "A visitor would arrive, and my grandfather would take the guest into the back garden to see the chickens. It was one of his favorite ploys. How could you mistrust a man with chickens?"

Indeed, the future writer's first memory reached back to these chickens. Judith Harris, a diplomat and journalist, and one of Gore's closest friends in Rome in later years, says, "Gore liked to recall his first memory. He had been playing with the chickens in the back of the house one afternoon. Then he sat down to dinner that evening. His grandmother served chicken. He started eating, then he realized that he was eating one of the birds from the back of the house. It shook him up. And he rarely again ate chicken, if he could help it."

Gore attended a couple of private schools in his earliest years. First there was the Potomac School, which he could barely recall except for its strong smell of disinfectant. Then came the Landon School for Boys, which he entered in the second grade. Things must have gone poorly, because his parents switched him to the Sidwell Friends School, where he remained for a few years, although his mother worried that he didn't "mix" with other children. He seemed withdrawn, moody, and bookish—unlike his exuberant and athletic father and socially minded mother. And his mother worried that he spent too much time reading.

Among several authors the boy especially enjoyed was L. Frank Baum, whose prose he later described as "the plain American style at its best." Baum's books about the mythical Land of Oz enchanted the impressionable child. Armed with silver dollars handed over by his grandfather (as payment for reading aloud to him), Little Gene bought any number of books, including the Tarzan series by Edgar Rice Burroughs. "I read all twenty-three of those," he later wrote in a thoughtful article about the attractions of Burroughs. "In its naïve way, the Tarzan legend returns us to that Eden where, free of clothes and the inhibitions of an oppressive society, a man can achieve in reverie his continuing need, which is, as William Faulkner put it in his high Confederate style, to prevail as well as to endure."

Gore also went to see movies, fascinated by such popular films as *The Last Days of Pompeii* and *The Mummy*. (On the latter, he said he recalled Boris Karloff as the somewhat revived Egyptian priest, calling him "Richard Nixon in drag.") He saw his first film at the age of four, then fell in love with fourteen-year-old Mickey Rooney as Puck in *A Midsummer Night's Dream* (1935). In the second of his two memoirs he writes of this film: "Bewitched, I read the play, guessing at half the words; then, addicted to this strange new language, I managed to read most of Shakespeare before I was sixteen." He would not, in fact, have been the only child of his generation attracted by Rooney into the depths of that Athenian forest.

Gore's boyhood dreams were shaped by films, and he preferred to live in a world of fantasies, as life at home was hardly ideal: His parents fought constantly and would eventually divorce, and his mother drank herself to sleep most nights, blithely ignoring her needy son. "My life seemed like some kind of hallucination," he said.

But reality sometimes intruded, as it did one afternoon in late May 1932 when he drove with his grandfather to the Capitol, where tens of thousands of veterans of the Great War with their friends and family members had formed an encampment in tents and cardboard shanties to protest their ill treatment by the federal government, which had refused to redeem their service certificates—cash bonuses that they felt were theirs by right. The press called them the Bonus Army, and they were in poor physical and emotional condition, many of them undernourished and ill.

"My grandfather and I drove to the edge of the bewildering encampment," Gore recalled. "I had never seen anything like this before. When a few of the marchers recognized Senator Gore, who had spoken against their movement on the Senate floor, they threw a rock through the open window. 'Shut the window!' my grandfather shouted, and I did." Senator Gore's populist rhetoric in fact belied a deep conservatism—a combination of contradictory impulses that his grandson would inherit.

Two months later, in July, General Douglas MacArthur, Chief of Staff of the U.S. Army, routed the encampment with Major George S. Patton at his side, killing a number of veterans and pursuing the protestors to their main location east of the Anacostia River. As *The New York Times* reported on July 28, 1932: "Flames rose high over the desolate Anacostia flats at midnight tonight, and a pitiful stream of refugee veterans of the World War walked out of their home of the past two months, going they knew not where." Gore recalled that, a day or so after the routing of the Bonus Army, his father flew him over the devastated area. The shanties still smoked, but the area had been cleared of protestors.

Herbert Hoover was driven from the White House within months by an aristocratic upstart from New York, Franklin Delano Roosevelt, a politician who figured hugely in the imagination of Gore Vidal, who (much like his grandfather) both admired and disliked him. Little Gene, only eight, watched the inaugural parade from a window of the famous Willard Hotel, where Abraham Lincoln had hidden out of public view in the weeks leading up to his inauguration in 1861—a scene beautifully dramatized by Gore in his 1984 novel, *Lincoln*.

Big Gene had, by now, established himself as an aviation pioneer, first at Transcontinental Air Transport, then by helping to found the Ludington Line, a profitable airline that was eventually absorbed into TWA. In 1930, he had hired a gorgeous and gifted young pilot named Amelia Earhart as vice president in charge of public relations and traffic management. She had, of course, made her name a couple of years earlier by crossing the Atlantic (a year after Charles Lindbergh's famous solo flight), becoming the first woman to do so, and was dubbed "Queen of the Air" by the press—even though she had not actually piloted the plane.

That the Ludington Line prospered surprised everyone. Aviation was a ramshackle affair in those early days, and flying was not for the faint of heart. Gore remembered that those with a particular fear of flying were encouraged to bring booze on board. They would open the window and toss out their empty bottles, which of course would splatter against the plane's fuselage. These were, indeed, the innocent early days of commercial aviation, which the prescient Gene Vidal recognized as an industry of importance for the economic revival that must, in due course, begin.

Yet success in aviation didn't help Gene and Nina's marriage. It was a disaster, and both pursued independent sexual lives. Nina's wild behavior—she never met a party she didn't like—terrified her parents, who had no way to restrain her. Gene, for his part, had adventures with any number of women, including Earhart. "She and my father were lovers, briefly, before her marriage to George Putnam, the publisher," Gore recalled. "Nobody thought much about this dalliance, although she apparently cared a great deal about my father. I found her charming, and more pleasant than my mother. Any woman in the world was more pleasant than my mother."

Along with FDR's son, Franklin Roosevelt Jr., Earhart helped to persuade the president to appoint Gene Vidal to a newly formed post as the director of air commerce. Once again, Gene found himself in the news. Indeed, *Time* magazine put him on their December 1933 cover, celebrating his success with the Ludington Line and dwelling on his fantasy that two-passenger airplanes would proliferate among middle-class Americans. In later life, Gore would recall that his father, in his government role, "systematized commercial aviation, issuing the first pilot's licenses (thoughtfully giving himself number one)." He also "standardized the national system of airports."

Gore's first exposure in the media occurred at his father's side in a

Hammond flivver-type plane on May 13, 1936, when—as an innocent blond eleven-year-old in white shorts and white polo shirt—he took control of the aircraft to demonstrate that even a kid could learn to pilot this plane. He was perhaps the youngest person ever to fly (he took the controls with his father beside him), and a Pathé newsreel of this adventure played in movie theaters around the country.

But Gore's high-flying life was bumpy, even unnerving. So he spent as much of his time as he could in the reading alcove at the top of his grandparents' house, alone with a book. He did his best to ignore his parents, who had become thoroughly estranged and unhappy. His mother rushed about town in pursuit of various men, including John Hay Whitney, known as Jock. A wealthy man by inheritance, and a publishing and business tycoon, he had married Liz Altemus, a Pennsylvania socialite, in 1930. But that fell apart within a couple of years, and soon Jock and Nina were having an affair, while at the same time Liz was sleeping with Gene Vidal. "I liked Liz more than my mother," Gore said. "She was like an Indian princess, slender and cheerful, full of money. She was Daisy Buchanan, only darker in complexion and less intelligent. But just as spoiled."

In the summer of 1934, Gore was sent to the William Lawrence Camp in New Hampshire, where swimming, canoeing, and archery mixed with baseball and overnight hiking—the sort of activities that Gore would hate for the rest of his life. The camp had been hastily chosen, and Gore knew why he was sent into the wilderness: to get him out of his parents' way while they wrangled.

The inevitable divorce came in 1935, when Gore traveled with Nina to Reno, Nevada, to await the outcome. They spent several weeks at a dude ranch, and it was there that Gore first met another of her boyfriends, Hugh D. Auchincloss—known to everyone in the family as Hughdie—who had already fallen hard for Nina. He determined to marry her immediately. This was fortunate for her, as she had been left with almost no money from the divorce settlement: 40 percent of her husband's meager salary with the government. Auchincloss, by contrast, was a very rich man, an heir to Standard Oil.

In later years, Gore reflected on his stepfather: "Early in life, at Yale, in fact, Hughdie's originality was revealed; he was unable to do work of any kind. Since the American ruling class, then and now, likes to give the impression that it is always hard at work, or at least very busy, Hughdie's sloth was something of a breakthrough. The word 'aristocrat' is never used by our rulers, but he acted suspiciously like one; certainly he was inert in a foreign way." Needless to say, this view of Auchincloss comes from an ambivalent stepson, who would nevertheless find some good things to say about him in a fictionalized portrait in *The Season of Comfort*, a later novel.

Though left a lot of money by his father, Auchincloss had been successful in his own right as a stockbroker, founding (with family money, to be sure) a firm in Washington called Auchincloss, Parker & Redpath. This was, in its way, real work. Having recently divorced an aristocratic Russian, he fell in love with Nina "at first glance." But she didn't love him. She didn't even like him, according to Gore, who often referred to this mismatch. But they married anyway, soon after Gore's tenth birthday, and moved into a mansion on the Potomac River on the road to Manassas, Virginia. It was called Merrywood, and Gore loved to describe it: "All of Merrywood's downstairs French windows were open onto the lawn and the woods beyond the lawn and the milk-chocolate-brown Potomac River far below." His novel *Washington, D.C.* opens with sixteen-year-old Peter Sanford standing in a storm outside of the house as "rain fell in dark diagonals across the summer lawn." Under a tall elm, he "pressed hard against the bole of the tree and through narrowed eyes watched the mock-Georgian façade of the house appear and disappear in rapid flashes like an old movie print, jerky and overexposed."

Gore later observed drily that "money hedged us all round. At the height of the Depression there were five servants in the house, white servants, a sign of wealth unique for Washington in those years. My stepfather was an heir to Standard Oil, the nemesis of T. P. Gore and Huey Long. Although I now lived the life of a very rich prince, I was still unconscious of class differences other than the relation between black and white." He would return to Merrywood often, in his fiction and nonfiction alike.

One can't help seeing young Gore in Peter Sanford: "Peter admired his father without liking him, just as he liked his mother without admiring her. But then, ever since June when school let out, he had been playing God, studying those about him as if through the wrong end of a telescope. But though they were properly diminished by his scrutiny, he still found the adult world puzzling; he was particularly confused by those who gathered in his father's drawing room. They seemed to be engaged in some sort of charade, known to them but not to him." And so Gore found himself at the margins of life at Merrywood, puzzled and unhappy, never fully at home.

Almost at once after the move to Merrywood, in October 1935, Nina wished to return to Gene Vidal, though he wasn't remotely interested. It seems the sexual side of the marriage to Hughdie had failed to ignite, and Nina moped around the big house in her silk dressing gown, smoking and drinking. Gore later recalled that "we rarely got into a conversation. It was pointless. She didn't see me. I wished I didn't see her." Not having the kind of mirroring that a young boy needs to affirm his sense of the world, he simply drifted—out of touch with the daily world. His constant wish to inflate himself, to see himself reflected in the world around him, started here. As with many adult narcissists, Gore's affliction could be traced back to a sense of rage at his mother's early defection. "I had no mother," Gore said, when I once asked him about Nina. "I prefer not to talk about her."

As was typical of this social class in the thirties, children were brought up by servants, and Gore's chief allies at Merrywood were Annie, a black nurse, and Maria, "a kind woman from Bavaria who kept me laughing, even when I didn't feel like laughing." There was also a French governess called Marguerite, whom Gore liked a great deal—so much so that his mother (with characteristic cruelty) fired her. A hurtful rivalry soon developed between Gore and Hughdie's son by his first marriage, called Yusha. "I try not to think back to that time in my life," Gore said. "Everything that could go wrong went wrong."

Understandably, he much preferred the less opulent but more emotionally comforting life at the home of his grandparents. Yet—in his own vague way—Hughdie was kind to his new stepson, lavishing gifts at Christmas and on birthdays. The Great Depression had not dampened life for Auchincloss, as his income and assets were impregnable. Not surprisingly, his politics were, according to Gore, "those of a Neanderthal." He spent a good deal of time bad-mouthing FDR, socialism, and most Jews. All Democrats were suspect, but he liked Senator Gore, whose anti–New Deal rhetoric played well around the dinner table at Merrywood, where important guests came and went, "helping themselves to Hughdie's liquor cabinet." Gore largely stayed away, in his bedroom, where he played with a small army of toy soldiers.

The summer of 1936 was mostly spent in Newport with members of the Auchincloss family, and it went poorly. Gore had tasted the first fruits of fame during his flying adventure with his father—and had yet to land. Only eleven, he was already (his own words) "a pain in the ass: sassy, belligerent, unhappy." Nobody wanted his company, and he was sent for the second time to the William Lawrence Camp, where he kept to himself, "hiding behind a thorn bush, reading Sir Walter Scott, desperate for the new school year to begin."

At the suggestion of Tot, "who didn't know one school from another but had her ear to the ground," Gore was sent to St. Albans—a boarding school in Washington that also had day students. At first, owing to his age—he was in the lower form, in the sixth grade—Gore was only an occasional boarder. But his mother's firm intention was to place him at a distance from Merrywood, and by the seventh grade he moved into a dormitory, relieved to get away from her, though he longed for the comforts of nearby Rock Creek Park, where Tot would spoil him with sweets and take him to the movies.

However, life at Rock Creek Park wasn't perfect. Gore's grandfather lost his reelection bid that summer in the Oklahoma primaries, and this upset the old man horribly. The mood back home had shifted, and Senator Gore's reactionary populism and anti–New Deal speeches went down badly. His opponents put forward the idea that relief checks would disappear if they returned Gore to the Senate. "He was the only senator from Oklahoma not to die rich," his grandson would say in later years. Indeed, his grandfather left office at the age of sixty-six with little in the way of savings, forced to resume his work as a lawyer, keeping a relatively brisk schedule until his death in the spring of 1949, a year after his grandson's third novel and first major best seller—*The City and the Pillar*—appeared. "I don't think we ever spoke of the book," Gore recalled. "He would not have approved—or even understood."

Meanwhile, life at St. Albans proved happier than Gore anticipated. A white Anglo-Saxon Protestant enclave, it had opened in 1909 as a school for choirboys who would sing at the National Cathedral, at that point still under construction. By Gore's time, the grand cathedral stood to the north of the school on a promontory known as Mount St. Albans. To the south lay the Capitol. "It was a traditional sort of place, then as now," says E. Barrett Prettyman, Gore's classmate and lifelong friend. "Boys came from good families. They had plenty of money, connections. This was a prep school in the New England tradition, though not actually in New England. They were competing in the same market, and sometimes—as in Gore's case—a boy would disappear from the upper school, head off to Exeter or Choate or Andover. I think Gore was fairly happy at St. Albans—he was a natural leader. People paid attention when he spoke in class. He wasn't an especially good student, but he was obviously very bright."

The main buildings of the school, like the cathedral itself, had been built of stone in the neo-Gothic style, and it was an impressive campus. The headmaster was Reverend Albert Hawley Lucas, "a former Marine who kept the place in good discipline," Prettyman recalls. "I think he understood his audience, the prominent families of Washington and surrounding areas. He knew what they wanted: a cheerful but well-regulated school with traditional courses. Gore could see the Washington Monument from the window of his dorm, and he liked that."

Midway through his first term at St. Albans, Gore met Jimmy Trimble ("Jimmie" in Gore's idiosyncratic spelling of his name). He was the boy who would, in Gore's erotic memory, occupy a unique position. In *Palimpsest*, his first memoir, Gore sentimentally calls Trimble "my other half," alluding to a remark by Aristophanes in Plato's *Symposium*, the origin of the idea of one's "other half" as the person who makes one complete. "We were friends immediately. I was one week older than he. We were the same height and weight. He had pale blue eyes; mine were pale brown." And so forth. Photographs confirm that Trimble was indeed handsome, with pouty lips, a full but straight nose, and tight curly blond hair: a younger version of Paul Newman. He was also muscular, an athlete who later had offers to play baseball for a couple of major league teams.

A boy from the Maryland suburbs, Trimble was the son of a formidable woman—Ruth Trimble—who had divorced Jimmie's father and married a man who, according to Gore, "took liberties with his stepson," which may have been why Ruth sent Jimmie to St. Albans as a boarder. "It was a very uncomfortable place, the Trimble household. Jimmie was relieved to get away," Gore recalled. "And as a star athlete—baseball was his best sport—he was a hero at the school."

The legend of Trimble's prowess on the athletic field has lived on. As Dave McKenna, writing in *Washington City Paper* observed, he "was a multi-sport superstar for the school in the early 1940s. In May, Trimble hurled successive no-hitters, including a perfect game against St. James of Hagerstown. Trimble was going to be the next Bob Feller and Walter Johnson, all in one. Legend holds that Clark Griffith tried to convince Trimble to turn pro right after graduating high school in 1943—but the two instead agreed that the Washington Senators would give Trimble a $5,000 signing bonus and the kid, being a St. Albans product, would put off his baseball career until after he'd graduated from Duke."

Gore writes in *Palimpsest* about the initiation of his erotic friendship with Trimble. It happened in an upstairs bathroom at Merrywood, on the white tile floor. Gore and Jimmie moved "belly to belly, in the act of becoming one." They "simply came together," he says. He recalled another vivid scene on the banks of the Potomac, probably at Merrywood, where they had sex in a natural setting, having gone for a swim. Naked in summer, they sunned themselves on "a special large gold-brown glacial rock." In this pristine setting, they lay side by side, and Gore imagined they would do this sort of thing for the rest of their lives, even as the war approached and their lives would move in separate ways.

If, that is, these encounters occurred. "What nonsense all of that is. I suspect none of that sexual business ever happened," says Prettyman, more than seven decades later. "Jimmie wasn't that kind of fellow. He would have hit Gore in the nose, hard. Everything in Gore's memories of Jimmie fits into the category of fantasy."

Did Gore remember or imagine this encounter with Trimble? It's plausible, of course, that a sensitive and sexually ambivalent boy of that age, barely post-puberty, could have wished to experiment with another boy. Even the most confirmed of heterosexual males will have homoerotic feelings, however fleeting. Gore may or may not have created these memories from whole cloth, but a distance will exist between the dream-figure "Jimmie Trimble" and Jimmy Trimble the young athlete and friend. Gore had a crush on this boy, and their "affair"—whatever form it took—no doubt became magnified in memory. Certainly it played a huge part in Gore's inner life from an early age—his 1948 novel, *The City and the Pillar*, was dedicated to "J.T." Indeed, this was one of the first explicitly gay novels of American fiction to find a mainstream outlet, as Jim Willard—the character who stands in for Gore—has sex with his straight "lover," Bob Ford (with his name alone seeming to typify an all-American boy), an obvious substitute for Jimmie Trimble.

Yet, as Gore said, "One must always be careful not to make easy connections between characters in novels and so-called real life," adding: "But of course the unconscious does its work, and one draws on personal sources. Bob is certainly like Jimmie in a lot of ways." In the original version of this novel, Jim actually strangles Bob when he won't have sex with him after a reunion many years after their adolescent encounters. " 'You're a queer,' he [Bob] said, 'you're nothing but a damned queer! Go on and get your ass out of here!' " In many ways, Bob resembles the Trimble that Prettyman recalled more than the eagerly sexual Trimble of *Palimpsest*. (When Gore revised *The City and the Pillar* in 1965, he changed the ending. In this version, Jim rapes Bob when he resists him, but doesn't kill him.)

It's possible that Gore wished, on some level, to take revenge on Jimmie for some resistance along these lines, that he felt rejected by his adolescent friend. However, the heterosexual protagonist of Gore's 1952 novel, *The Judgment of Paris*, encounters Bill and Stephen, a pair of male lovers from America in postwar Paris, who represent a kind of serene fulfillment of the writer's dream for himself and Jimmie, had Jimmie survived the war: "They were both twenty-five, robust, and charmingly simple. The following June, when they graduated from college, they were to be married to two girls they had known for a long time in their home town, Spartanburg, South Carolina, and their future was to be as simple and well directed as their past, living next door to one another, working in the same business. They would even, they confided to Philip, name their children for one another."

A careful reader will find versions of Trimble in several of Gore's future novels, but he barely mentioned him again until *Palimpsest*—written more than half a century after their naked afternoon on the banks of the Potomac in 1939. "It was like he came out of nowhere when Gore was writing *Palimpsest*," said Howard Austen, Gore's partner of fifty-three years. Yet by this time Gore's fleeting encounter with Jimmie had acquired an exalted place in sacred memory.

As Gore says at the outset of *Palimpsest*: "A memoir is how one remembers one's own life." Had Trimble not been blown apart in a foxhole in the Pacific in 1945, he may never have had anything like the same place in Gore's lively imagination. Trimble was probably more preoccupied with thoughts of his girlfriend Christine White, who believed she was "engaged" to him at the time of his death, than with Gore, an old classmate. Even Gore understood the overwhelming role that fantasy plays in these matters, as he wrote in 1997 to Val Holley, an inquiring correspondent, referring to Christine and her relations with Jimmie: "She saw poor Jimmie a half dozen times—she has now (thanks to me?) built this up into a major fantasy. But he was crazy about her & wrote her letters up until the end."

For all his outward aplomb and wit, Gore slipped through St. Albans without arousing much notice from his peers. Prettyman recalls: "He was something of an ordinary student, not terribly interested in sports or school activities. He said clever things, like in later years, but kept to himself, somewhat aloof. I went back to his house in Virginia one weekend, and had a perfectly good time. There was nothing unusual about him—you didn't think he was a homosexual in those days. You didn't have much sense of that, not then. I liked him, though, and we remained friends throughout our lives. I would visit him now and again, and we stayed in touch."

Only one schoolmaster at St. Albans, a heavyset young man named Stanley Sofield, made a lasting impression on Gore and Jimmie. They liked his gentle manner and his reasonable tone. He was affectionate with the boys, and he called Gore "Gene'y with the Light Brown Hair." According to *Palimpsest*, Gore and Jimmie would signal each other in Sofield's class whenever either got an erection, and soon this merriment caught on with the other boys, as adolescent flags rose around the room. Gore later said, "I can't think of a happier time in my life. St. Albans was an idyll of sorts." But his mother, unhappy with his mediocre grades, decided to send him elsewhere—first to a boys' school in New Mexico, then to Phillips Exeter Academy in New Hampshire.

III. A Wider World

Gore, who went to the movies at various theaters around Washington throughout the late thirties, had seen a number of films set in ancient Rome and dreamed of going to Italy one day. It would, in due course, become his home. Now an opportunity for European travel arose, and in June 1939 he crossed the Atlantic for the first time with two teachers from St. Albans and a small group of boys, mostly from St. Albans. It was not the obvious moment for a school trip, as the black clouds of fascism were amassing over Europe.

"We ignored the political winds and sailed from New York to Le Havre," Gore recalled. "It was the most beautiful ship of its time, the *Île de France*, with a famous Art Deco dining room. I spent most of my time in a canvas deck chair talking to Hammy Fish," the son of a well-known Republican congressman. (Hamilton "Hammy" Fish had lately become Gore's friend at St. Albans.) "We both thought the U.S. would never get involved in another European war. His father and my grandfather agreed on this. We had too much to lose."

The boys disembarked in France, making their way to Paris, then on to a school near Versailles, where a few weeks of daily French lessons and excursions were to be followed by the much-anticipated trip to Rome. Signs of trouble on the political front, however, prompted an early departure for Italy in late July.

George Armstrong, a journalist and close friend of Gore's from his decades in Italy, later recalled: "Rome lay at the center of Gore's literary imagination. He had read all the major books about the republic and empire, and characters such as Julius Caesar and Mark Antony felt to him like old friends. He referred easily and often to Cicero. He knew his Livy backwards and forwards—and Suetonius, too. So it meant everything to him when, as an adolescent boy, he stood on the Capitoline Hill above the Forum. I'm sure he was making speeches in his head. The fact that Mussolini's muscle men in black shirts were strutting in the Piazza Navona hardly fazed him."

This was no time to be anywhere in Europe, and the news grew more terrifying by the day. The Nazi invasion of Poland was imminent when a frantic message from home to the chaperons of the traveling party from St. Albans urged them to make a beeline to London, where they were encouraged to find an early passage back to the United States. Departing from Saint-Malo on the coast of Brittany, they crossed the English Channel in heavy fog, arriving at Dover on a chilly afternoon. "The white cliffs had what seemed like a rueful smile," Gore remembered.

They proceeded to London by train, taking rooms at a hotel in Russell Square. "I had tea with a friend of my mother's, in the somewhat dilapidated Russell Hotel. Scones like pieces of rock. She took me, with some of the other boys, to meet Joe Kennedy, then ambassador from the U.S. to Britain. One morning I caught a glimpse of Neville Chamberlain on his way to Parliament where, after the invasion of Poland, he was caught in a vise. War was inevitable. London braced for the worst, though even their pessimism couldn't match what actually happened."

Britain declared war on September 3, 1939, two days after the invasion of Poland and the very day that the St. Albans entourage set sail from Liverpool on a British liner. In *Palimpsest*, Gore writes: "In the Irish Sea we see our sister ship, *Athenia*, torpedoed by a Nazi sub. Longboats carrying passengers to the dull, misty green Irish shore . . .

Some wanted to turn back. Captain did not. We zigzagged across the North Atlantic. Canteen ran out of chocolate. No other hardship. I did not know fear because I knew that true history—life and death, too—only existed in books and this wasn't a book that I'd read—just a gray ship in a dark sea."

Back in America, Gore learned from his mother that he would attend a new school in Los Alamos, New Mexico. A friend had told her about this school, where forty or so boys came under the tutelage of A. J. Connell, a militaristic headmaster who stressed the outdoor life and scouting. It was a place where "the spindly sons of the rich could be transformed into manly specimens." (Among the well-known former pupils was William S. Burroughs, the Beat novelist who later became Gore's friend.) "Our parents wanted us remade into healthy heterosexual hunters," Gore recalled. Apparently rumors soon spread that Connell was himself not strictly beyond question. "Hating it there, loathing it, I revealed to my mother over the Christmas break that Mr. Connell was a degenerate." This caused a huge kerfuffle, and soon the rumors traced back to Gore, who was politely asked not to return after a depressing year of riding horses, hiking in the desert, and doing a little bit of schoolwork. "I missed Jimmie," Gore said. "That was the long and short of it."

Soon Los Alamos became the site where the atom bomb was developed, and the school where Gore spent this miserable year vanished. Gore's mother, meanwhile, managed to get him a place at Hughdie's old school, Phillips Exeter Academy in New Hampshire. Because he had mediocre grades, Exeter insisted that the young man attend a five-week prep course in Latin, math, and English in the summer of 1940. "I had a bad time," Gore said. In fact, he was nearly kicked out when a classmate peered over his shoulder at his work and Gore brushed him aside. Nothing came of this incident, however, and Gore entered the freshman class in September without high expectations for academic success. On the other hand, he was almost eerily self-confident. "I remember him walking serenely around the halls, quietly cheerful, self-contained, convinced of his prospects," one schoolmate recalled. "Everyone assumed he had high connections in Washington. He gave that impression, mentioning this senator or that one. He said to me once in a dining hall—I happened to sit next to him—that his grandfather knew the president. But aloofness was the main impression. A boy who didn't want to mix."

By now Big Gene had remarried a much younger woman. Kit Roberts was only twenty, more like an older sister for Gore than a plausible mother substitute. Gene had recently taken a consulting position with the Bendix Corporation, and he also served on the board of Eastern Airlines, which had purchased the Ludington Line. In his private time he tinkered with various aeronautical projects, trying to devise light wooden parts for airplanes. This became almost an obsession, and he sought investments wherever he could. For the most part, Gore didn't fight with his father as he did with Nina, so he much preferred staying with Gene and Kit, even if it meant spending weeks at a time in their cramped apartment in Washington, where he slept on a sofa in his father's study. He nevertheless eyed Kit with suspicion. What was his father doing with a woman of this age?

With some relief, Gore settled into his life at Exeter. It was a breeding ground for future politicians, journalists, scholars, and business leaders, and Gore sensed that he had landed in a good place, where his gifts would be nurtured. He showed an early interest in literary matters, writing poems and short stories, even drafting parts of a novel that he filed "where it belonged, in the waste basket." Among the many future authors who attended the school during Gore's years were the socialite and man of letters George Plimpton, the jazz writer Whitney Balliett, and John Knowles, a novelist who also touched on homosexuality in his fiction. Of these, only Knowles became a friend. Indeed, in his popular school novel about Exeter, *A Separate Peace*, Knowles based the figure of the school cynic on Gore. Brinker Hadley, a verbally precocious and pretentious figure, is known as "Brinker the Lawgiver," a boy who makes rules for others and yet suffers from "a faintly self-pitying resentment against millions of people he did not know." This sounds very much like Gore, who stood apart from his schoolmates yet could light up in their company, dropping witty asides. "He dropped names right, left, and center, speaking in a deep voice," a classmate recalls. He was a natural leader, too, though an indifferent student. "I never liked to read books assigned to me," Gore said. "I read everything else. My teachers, of course, found this less than thrilling."

He made few close friends at Exeter, and one gets a sense of his personal frustrations in *Palimpsest*, as when he talks about the lack of sexual opportunities, at least for him, at the school: "On the rare occasions when sex was a possibility, he who made the first move would be forever in the power of the moved upon, no matter what happened. This made for a certain guarded irritability in all relations. Later, I was told that 'the boys,' as we called the athletes, were somewhat freer with each other. One, a lanky baseball pitcher, swung his leg against mine in English class. I gave him a startled look. He grinned. I suspected a trap and pulled away."

Gore's best conversations took place with his teachers, especially Tom Riggs—a twenty-five-year-old Princeton graduate who in later years joined the faculty at his old university. "Tom and I were strong America Firsters," Gore remembered. "He organized a group called Veterans of Future Wars. Not a popular group. I would happily debate those who favored intervention—I was an orator in those days. We all, of course, went to war. Tom fought in Italy and survived Anzio." With his sharp tongue and antiestablishment attitudes, Riggs provided a model for Gore: the first adult rebel he encountered and could respect. "Lewis Perry, our head of school, hated him," said Gore. By now he had stopped calling himself Eugene Vidal, preferring his grandfather's surname. It had a vaguely Olympian ring: Gore Vidal.

One can only imagine how the faculty at Exeter felt about young Gore. One of them wrote after his sophomore year that he might well become "a credit to the school if we can stand him for another two years." Another said to a colleague: "I wish that I were a bull. So that I could gore Vidal."

Among his acquaintances at Exeter was Bob Bingham, known as "Hacker." Bingham was a large, oval-faced boy with pink cheeks and curly russet hair, rather fastidious in manner, and a capable editor who ran the school literary magazine, where Gore managed to get a place on the editorial committee. Even half a century later, Gore recalled him with a kind of pity. Bingham, "like several of our contemporaries who had seen heavy combat in the infantry," never quite recovered his balance and self-composure, as Gore wrote in *Palimpsest.* Yet they tangled over the publication of Gore's stories in the school magazine, as Bingham wasn't impressed with the work. This was, perhaps, an early instance of Gore's fierce sense of competition with potential rivals who might threaten his career.

At a party while he was home for Christmas in 1940, Gore took up with sixteen-year-old Rosalind Rust—a tall, slender girl whom he had met at dancing classes a few years earlier. She was boyish, with short hair and small breasts, a low voice; this appealed to Gore, who—given his homoerotic disposition—always preferred this type of girl. The romance blossomed, and it continued over several years, with Gore in due course thinking he might marry her. "My grandfather warned me away from early marriage," he later said.

They had sex the next summer, at his father's summer cottage, and she wrote in her diary in January 1941 that Gore was "my first beau and the best man I ever had . . . The best man I ever had in bed." One must wonder, of course, how much experience she actually had; nevertheless, her comment suggests that Gore was at least somewhat bisexual in his youth, given that he slept with a number of women during his early years. He certainly liked the idea of being bisexual, as the notion of being exclusively gay had very little appeal, pushing him too far into the margins of society, and it interfered with his theories about sexuality, which he developed in later decades. A note of self-hatred is, indeed, hard to miss in his novels that touch on homosexual themes, and throughout his life he spoke of gay men as "fags" and "degenerates," although he claimed to do so affectionately.

In his spare time at Exeter, he busied himself with short stories and poems. "I always wanted to be a poet," he said, "but the Muse passed over my doorstep." In the fall issue of *The Philips Exeter Review,* however, was a decent schoolboy poem, "To R.K.B.'s Lost Generation," dedicated to Bob Bingham, his friend and classmate. In lines that echo the loftiness of Victorian poets such as Matthew Arnold and William Ernest Henley, Gore ends on a note of elevated despair:

Night, night black as the wills of men;
We are lost to hope and God;
For the chosen, we the chosen, there is no start, no end;
Evil spirits that shall never yield nor bend
Save for the soul of night, not the rod.
For the night is black,
No light but night,
No God.

This is not immortal verse, but for a young poet, it shows a firm control of the line, a clarity of thought, and a keen ear for the music of language. In his early stories, too, Gore brought a poet's gift for clear images and concrete diction to his prose, and this remained a signal aspect of his work. "I discovered early that I had a facility," he said. "I wrote quickly, almost too easily. Pages piled in drawers. Much of this work was forgettable, and I've forgotten it."

Most holidays were spent at Rock Creek Park, where Gore sank into the motherly embrace of Tot, who protected him from his mother as best she could. "More than once, she threw Nina out of the house, calling her a drunk. I belonged to my grandparents, and they didn't want her interfering. I didn't either."

The Japanese attack on Pearl Harbor on December 7, 1941, both shocked and dismayed young Gore, a conspiratorial sort who never quite accepted the popular view of this pivotal event in American history: "Roosevelt knew about the attack in advance, and he needed it to happen. It was the only obvious way to get a Declaration of War from Congress." Gore had, of course, been one of the most vocal students at Exeter to oppose America entering the war, and it upset him that history refused to conform to his ideas. "Exeter commences to be very warlike," he wrote to his grandfather, who shared his isolationist views. More than ever, he felt out of place among his peers, who joined the patriotic pro-war chorus. "I knew there was nothing to be done. That the war would overwhelm us. And it did."

By now his mother had left Auchincloss and moved into a fashionable Georgetown house with her new beau, Robert Olds, a brigadier general who had won a Distinguished Flying Cross in World War I. At forty-four, Olds was a well-placed man in military and political circles, and many believed he would be tapped to run the Army Air Corps. Like Gene Vidal, he was handsome and tall. But he was even more outgoing, described as "explosive and dynamic" by one comrade. Another said, "He had energy to burn, on and off the job. He loved high living, and he loved women, too."

Gore found the rampant anti-Semitism of Olds and his friends distasteful. "They often referred to FDR as Franklin D. Rosenfeld," Gore recalled. "It was more frank and vicious than anything I'd overheard at Merrywood. I disliked Olds, but knew my mother wished to marry him, and I understood it would end badly." It did, with Olds succumbing to a heart attack only ten months after marrying Nina. By a grim coincidence, "It was about the same time my mother married [Olds] that my father had a heart attack," he said.

The athletic Gene, an Olympic hero, brought down by a heart attack? Young Gore felt that his world had become even less stable—if such a thing was possible—as he sat in a chair beside his father at St. Luke's Hospital in New York. It turned out that "marrying a barely post-adolescent girl had not proved the elixir of eternal life," and Gene lay in a daze, glassy-eyed, frail. Father and son exchanged awkward words, with Gene urging his offspring to study hard and focus. "He was full of platitudes," Gore said. This health crisis did not, however, lead to his death, and Gene lived until 1969.

Back at Exeter, Gore struggled with his studies, doing poorly in Latin and math, barely ticking over in English, almost failing in French—and this despite harangues from his grandparents and mother, who reminded him during the holidays that he was not doing well, as if he didn't know. His attention focused on the debating hall, where he soon made a name for himself as a quick-witted and knowledgeable speaker. A schoolmate says, "His debating skills struck us as remarkable, even if you didn't like what he said. He had strong views, and they weren't always popular ones. Nobody doubted his intelligence or verbal facility. It seemed obvious he would go into politics."

His mind was drawn toward the idea of a political future, as his family expected this of him. "My grandmother would say, 'When you're in the Senate,' and I assumed she knew my fate," he said. "It seemed best to settle into a district where I could get elected. I thought of Oklahoma, but my grandfather put that notion to rest." His grandson, with his eastern liberal breeding, would find the political climate inhospitable. He urged Gore to graduate from Exeter before thinking about the life to come. After that, he could attend Harvard or the University of Virginia or some other distinguished university. The army would sweep him up before long, of course. No young man could avoid induction. During his last year at school, Gore understood that indeed he must graduate in order to get into the army's training program for officers, and he didn't want to go into the service as a foot soldier. As it happened, his grades improved markedly in English, rising to a B+. To pass his math courses, he simply cheated. "After all, it was their honor system, not mine," he said.

Meanwhile, Gore continued to develop as an orator, relishing debate with his peers. *The Exonian*, his school newspaper, often reported his colorful speeches, as when in late October 1942 he was reported to have declared that President Roosevelt was "trying to use the war to make himself a dictator." His schoolmates widely considered him bombastic, but "he never failed to hold our attention," as one of them said. "He seemed to tease and blast away at the same time." In fact, he addressed a crowded room one evening in 1940, attacking FDR with a gusto gleaned from his grandfather's table talk. "In this last election the American people were duped," he intoned. "This nation has at last come under the regime that has been foretold by our forefathers as the Armageddon of American democracy and freedom. The light of democracy burns low and our sacred birthrights are in jeopardy due to the ambition of one man. In the past there have been many such men who have betrayed their people for gain. Christ had his Judas; Republican Rome had its Caesar; Russia had its Stalin—will future generations say that America had its Roosevelt?"

He sent a copy of his address to his grandfather, who wrote back with admiration for his grandson, telling him that he had "a lucky ticket in the Lottery of Talents. A talent for writing and a talent for speaking or for Oratory, if you please. I own that was my vaulting ambition in my youth." To say that Gore was a chip off the old block is putting it mildly: He and his grandfather's ambitions, interests, politics, even their oratorical skills, dovetailed in ways that gave pride to Senator Gore and, in fact, continued to the end to influence his grandson's manner and thought.

Gore's acquaintances at Exeter included Wilcomb "Wid" Washburn, who would go to Dartmouth, and A. K. Lewis, who went on to Harvard. Bingham continued as a kind of friendly rival, even in later years, when in the mid-fifties he briefly worked as a managing editor at *The Reporter* and got Gore a temporary job as the paper's drama reviewer. The rivalry between Bingham and Gore was noted by the writer John McPhee, who worked with Bingham at *The New Yorker*: "Within the first two years [at *The New Yorker*], Bob goes out to lunch with his old high-school friend Gore Vidal. And Gore says, What are you doing as an editor, Bobby? What happened to Bob Bingham the writer? And Bingham says, Well, I decided that I would rather be a first-rate editor than a second-rate writer. And Gore Vidal draws himself up and says, And what is wrong with a second-rate writer?"

One can almost see the glint in Gore's eyes as he said that. His relationship with his friends was oddly self-deprecating while, at the same time, self-inflating. He could not help but celebrate and sing himself. But his own egotistical displays troubled him as well. "I never talk about myself," he told me, talking about himself. What he meant, in fact, was that he rarely wrote about his own writing, preferring to adopt the stance of critic.

One event that stood out in Gore's memory was a final encounter with Jimmie Trimble at a dance over Christmas break at the elegant Sulgrave Club on Massachusetts Avenue in Washington. Gore accompanied Rosalind, whom he still thought he would marry, and he told Jimmie about their secret engagement. Jimmie replied, "You're crazy!" Soon Gore and Jimmie excused themselves and went downstairs to the men's room, with its icy marble floors and roomy toilet stalls, where—in Gore's recollection—they entered the same cubicle and stood belly to belly, pants down, coming together in a climax that, for Gore, remained vivid in his imagination after half a century. (Whether or not Gore should have kissed and told is another matter, and we can assume that—if this encounter actually happened—Trimble would not have been overjoyed to think the news of this tentative adolescent foray into homosexuality would be made public.)

In June 1943, Gore graduated from Exeter, having scraped through by a narrow margin. In a class poll, he was named the class "politician" as well as class "hypocrite." Lewis was named the class "wit." Washburn was the class "grind." Bingham, as class poet, read his work at the graduation. Only Gore's father and Kit attended the ceremony, as Nina, having recently lost her third husband to a heart attack, had moved to California, where she lived extravagantly in a cottage at the Beverly Hills Hotel with Tommy and Nini, her children by Auchincloss. By now, Gore understood that his boyhood had come to an end. "From the day I left Exeter, it was all war, all the time," Gore recalled. "I can't say I minded."

Truman and Gore at the Plaza

"So this is where you often had lunch with Capote, in the late forties?" I ask Gore. We're eating in the Oak Bar of the Plaza Hotel in New York in the spring of 1988. He calls this his "favorite time of the year in the city," and insists on a particular table. For him, it's a holy place, a chapel of memories.

"So he told everyone. By his account, you'd think we had lunch every week. I doubt we met more than a few times. I wasn't counting. But he was counting everything. Numbers of copies sold, mentions in the press. What a tedious creature, and a creature he was, much less than human."

"Can you recall your first meeting?"

"Can I forget it? That's the real question. He came to a party that Anaïs Nin threw at her apartment. I remember him extending his tiny little paw. It wasn't a hand, it was a kitten's paw. He was obsequious, light as a feather, almost nonexistent. He stole everything from the Southern girls, Eudora Welty and Carson McCullers. Nobody minded, as Southern literature is a quilting bee. Writers come and go, adding stitches. It's the same old quilt and so boring. We had something in common, of course: Our mothers were drunks. But that was it. He would say, 'Oh Gore, you're so mean,' in that creepy voice of his. I wish it would go away. But it hangs there, in my head."

We eat club sandwiches after Manhattan clam chowder. Gore drinks Scotch, but I stick with a glass of white wine.

"I love it here," says Gore. "Nothing ever changes. I've been coming to the Plaza for decades, since the thirties. It's perfect. Scott and Zelda liked it, in the early twenties. Hemingway stayed here. Now it's tourists. I don't know why I come back, but I live in the past, in my own past. The future doesn't look like a safe place, I fear."

Chapter Two

Class is the most difficult subject for American writers to deal with and the most difficult for the English to avoid.

—Gore Vidal

1. Not a Lovely War

Gore enlisted in the army in New York City on July 29, 1943. After Exeter, he had moved into his father's apartment overlooking Central Park on Fifth Avenue, where he slept in a tiny room once used by a maid. "It was the best of many bad options," he said. His half brother Vance, a child, slept in the next room. This arrangement soon proved claustrophobic, and Gore moved into his grandparents' home on Rock Creek Park: "As the house was for sale, this was my last time there." (His grandparents moved to an apartment in Washington, which was less expensive and required less work for an elderly couple to maintain.) His grandmother welcomed him with enthusiasm, as ever, but the joy of this homecoming was short-lived.

"I was soon off to VMI, for officer's training," he recalled. "But it was all engineers." The Army Special Training Program at the Virginia Military Institute in Blacksburg had been initially created for well-educated young men who might pursue a technical path in the military: building bridges and roads, repairing dams, viaducts, and trestles. As he had never been good at math, however, this course proved a disaster for Gore, and he wrote in desperation to his father, asking Big Gene to find him a commission. A bout of appendicitis followed by failing grades in physics and math led to a quick exit from VMI, and soon he found himself on KP duty at Fort Meade, near Washington. His mother wrote to him from the Beverly Hills Hotel, where she was living in considerable luxury. Addressing him as "Dearest Gene," she complained to him: "I couldn't be more upset over your plans not to go through with the schooling. For I think it a great mistake not to go through with this course even though you don't like it. This other way there is no telling what may happen to you. You'd probably end up in a gunnery school or something equally as unprofitable."

Gore's father and his uncle Pick (Felix Vidal, Big Gene's younger brother, who also attended West Point and later rose to the rank of brigadier general) quickly managed to get him transferred to an air base in Colorado Springs, where Pick was the officer in charge. As ever, pulling strings worked, and Gore felt relieved to join the Army Air Corps, where—after a brief period of training at Fort Dix in New Jersey—he was billeted in a Quonset hut in Colorado. "We had a splendid view of the Rockies, and the brisk November weather suited me." Probably because his uncle was the commander of the base, he was assigned duty as the base historian, and he spent much of his time in a pleasant library, writing a novel in the manner of Somerset Maugham, to be called *The Deserter*. "Exactly who was deserting what remained in doubt," he later admitted.

Life in Colorado Springs had appealing aspects. Uncle Pick and Aunt Sally often took him for Sunday lunches at the opulent Broadmoor Hotel, and he began what would become a lifelong pursuit: cruising for sex. "It all started in Colorado," he recalled. "There were lots of men willing to turn a trick." He was eager for sexual encounters. As Matt Tyrnauer (later an editor at *Vanity Fair* and a good friend) says, "It's hard to imagine how different the world was then, for gay men. It was relatively easy to find young partners, 'trade,' and yet this was hardly on the radar of mainstream society. Gore rushed into his sex life headlong."

Still restless about his role in the war, Gore decided to apply for Officer Candidate School, a course that would make him a very young officer, as he remarked to his father. Meanwhile, his parents were happy to have him in Colorado, safe and sound, especially since the army had actually dispersed the Army Special Training Program, shipping most of those young men to the European front. Military bureaucracy moved slowly, however, and Gore felt no need to rush things in his own case.

With Uncle Pick he traveled on leave to his father's childhood home in Madison, South Dakota—another privilege that came with being the nephew of the base commander. He was struck by the fact that Madison was hardly a backwater of the sort his father often described but a "pleasant if very small city." He also went to Hollywood for the first time, visiting his mother at the Beverly Hills Hotel, where she occupied a guest bungalow. Nina had made some important Hollywood friends, such as Jules and Doris Stein. Jules had founded Music Corporation of America (MCA), which in the thirties moved from New York to Los Angeles and became a talent agency, representing Bette Davis, Betty Grable, Joan Crawford, and Frank Sinatra, among their list of stars. At a party in Beverly Hills, Gore met the Steins' daughter Jean, who would become a lifelong friend. Jean recalls: "I met him when I was a child, and I knew him from then on. He was like an older brother to me. When I was older, he would tease me unmercifully, but he was always there for me."

Gore recalled meeting Orson Welles during this visit, only a couple of years after the debut of *Citizen Kane*, which Welles had co-written and directed. "Of course I loved that film," said Gore. They met at the Beverly Hills Hotel. "On his arm was Rita Hayworth, his wife," said Gore. "He has it all, I remember thinking in a state of perfect awe untouched by pity. Little did I know—did he know?—that just as I was observing him in triumph, the great career was already going off the rails, while the Gilda of all our dreams [Hayworth] was being supplanted by the even more beautiful Dolores del Rio. Well, Rita never had any luck." He also met Sinatra, Clark Gable, and the writer Leslie Charteris, known for his popular series of mystery novels about Simon Templar, "the Saint." Gore called Charteris "the first successful screenwriter I knew. I realized that gold lay in them hills." He wrote to his father, dropping names of the famous people he met, including Jack Warner (the president of Warner Brothers) and Dorothy Lamour, who had just made *Road to Morocco* with Bob Hope and Bing Crosby—the third in a popular series of movies that took this zany trio on the road to somewhere exotic.

Months passed until, in the summer of 1944, Gore landed a spot in the Second Air Force Rescue Boat Squadron in New Orleans, where he crewed on "crash boats" designed to rescue men from Lake Pontchartrain, where they often parachuted into the water during training exercises. One day another soldier suggested that Gore take a test to qualify for the sea transport division of the army. To Gore's amazement, he passed the test and, on November 8, 1944, he became a temporary warrant officer, junior grade. Orders soon arrived for him to proceed by ship to the Aleutian Islands, a daisy chain of icy volcanic islands on the westward edge of Alaska.

Stopping over briefly in Seattle, he found himself among men hungry for sex. "I was in the Snakepit Bar of the Olympia Hotel in Seattle," he recalled. "It was full of lean, sinewy, sweaty" men who were energized by the fear of death, which Gore called "the ultimate aphrodisiac." Afraid that he himself might die in the coming months (although this seemed unlikely in the Aleutians), Gore propositioned a merchant marine who wore a wedding ring. The man, in his mid-twenties, eagerly agreed to rent a room in a nearby hotel. "Once in bed," says Gore, "I realized I had no plan; this proved to be an error. Suddenly, he was on my back. I tried to push him off. He used an expert half nelson in order to shove partway in. I bucked like a horse from the pain, and threw us both off the bed. We rolled across the floor, slugging at each other. Then, exhausted, we separated. He cursed; dressed; left. That was my first and last experience of being nearly fucked." This encounter may, in fact, have inspired the revised ending of *The City and the Pillar*, where the "straight" man gets raped, not murdered.

By now Gore was firmly on the gay side of the bisexual equation, and he was clearly a "top," never a "bottom." He hated the idea of being submissive, in fact. He never acted like a gay man, never adopted gay mannerisms, and preferred anonymity when possible—he didn't even want to know the identity of the person he slept with. Sex was always furtive for him. He never denied being attracted to men—it wasn't that he would hide it—but he didn't like to think about it, even to acknowledge it to himself. He thought of himself as a heterosexual man who liked to "mess around" with men. It was a mental game he played, and it contributed to an aura of manliness that surrounded him, marking his public behavior.

From Seattle, Gore made his way on a troop ship to Anchorage, Alaska, where he spent a rowdy New Year's Eve, getting an official reprimand for drunkenness. But he did, in fact, like Alaska, with its bright cold and blue skies, and he hoped that he might have time to begin a novel there. He was writing poems as well as stories, filling brown folders with new work, sending out manuscripts to magazines in New York. At one point, he received an encouraging note from the editor of *Esquire*, who admired one of his stories but couldn't see his way toward publishing it.

Within a month, Gore had his orders: He must sail to the far western end of the Aleutian Islands, more than a thousand miles from Anchorage. The prospect of serving as first mate aboard a transport ship of about thirty sailors excited him, and he arrived in Umnak Island at the end of January, "amazed" by its desolation and remoteness. "I thought I'd come to the end of civilization," he recalled. "My focus was the run between Dutch Harbor and Chernowski Bay—a strangely beautiful run. There was a silence in the air, and the sky seemed bigger than anything I'd known before."

To his relief, there was a small library on Umnak that contained most of the novels of Frederic Prokosch—at the time a hugely popular and admired writer—and he read them avidly, moving through *The Seven Who Fled* (a fantastic adventure story concerning six men and one woman in the deserts of western China) with admiration for its narrative compulsion and sensuous, evocative prose. (When Gore introduced me to Prokosch in the late eighties, in southern France, I mentioned Gore's early admiration for *The Seven Who Fled*. Prokosch replied, "So he was the one.")

Gore enjoyed the prospect of life at sea, and he joked to his father in one letter: "I think perhaps I'll be a seaman for the rest of my life." But the navigation of these icy waters could be difficult, and Gore relied on his captain, who was only twenty-five but competent. As Gore later said, "There was so much fog in the run, and I had very little experience of setting a course. We relied on point to point navigation—getting from point A to point B without the benefit of a compass." The idea of navigating in this dangerous fashion so intrigued him that in 2007 he called the final installment of his memoirs *Point to Point Navigation.*

One time, while still in port, a "williwaw" or sudden storm blew in from the Bering Sea. The word (of unknown origin, according to the *Oxford English Dictionary*, although Gore insisted it was a Native American word) was one that he heard for the first time in the Aleutians, and in 1946 he would attach it to his first novel, *Williwaw*, set on a transport ship very like the one he served on. He had hardly gone to sea when he thought about "the idea of writing a brief novel about men against nature, a kind of Jack London rip-off that might be just the thing for me. I'd been casting about for a good subject. And here it came." The novel would owe more to Stephen Crane and Ernest Hemingway than to London, especially with its clipped narrative style. As Gore would write to his good friend Elaine Dundy years later: "Hemingway was the only writer that I ever dreamed of kicking the shit out of." This seems ironic, given that in the seventies and eighties he would dismiss Hemingway whenever he could. Meanwhile he was writing a thousand words a day, and soon the manuscript filled a file drawer in his tiny cabin aboard ship.

It was "not a lovely war, not for me," Gore said. "It was strange, in fact," and made even stranger by its remoteness from the main theaters of action in Europe and the South Pacific. All went smoothly enough until one morning, as the ship approached Dutch Harbor, a misty storm blew in from the south. "Everything turned white," Gore recalled, "including me. I froze like a statue." He returned to his cabin in a state of near immobility. "All night I shivered in my bunk, and I knew it was not normal." The next day, as they pulled into the harbor, he tried to leap onto the dock but his knee failed to bend. A deckhand assisted, jumping to the wharf and attaching a spring line, and Gore was taken to the tiny base hospital, where soon enough he had a diagnosis: acute rheumatoid arthritis. "And that was it: The war was over, for me." The army shipped him back to Anchorage for observation at Fort Richardson, where a series of tests confirmed the initial diagnosis.

Gore lay in a hospital bed, listening to the radio, when he learned on April 13, 1945, that Franklin Roosevelt had died. "I don't think it's possible to explain it, but the nation went into a kind of shock. In some ways I was delighted," Gore said. "He had become a dictator, and had made life for my grandfather awkward and difficult. I was glad my grandfather outlasted him." Writing in *Screening History* about the death of Roosevelt, Gore put it frankly: "I was relieved. We were done with him."

Gore had lived under the grand rainbow of FDR for most of his life, and his later rudeness about him was based on a long-held series of grievances that combined with a touch of envy as well as admiration. FDR had, of course, elevated Big Gene soon after his first election in 1932 to a sub-cabinet position. One hears a good deal about Roosevelt in Gore's historical novels, as in the following passage from *The Golden Age*: "Franklin goes on and on about how he hates wars because he has seen war. As usual, he lies. He toured a battlefield or two after Germany had surrendered. And that was that. He saw no war." Several sentences later, Gore's fictional Herbert Hoover quips: "Franklin claims to have written the Haitian constitution. As if he's ever read ours!" That note of dismissal arises whenever FDR comes near, in Gore's novels and essays alike.

He wrote eagerly to his grandfather about FDR's demise: "The king is dead—long live the president." It was a memorable remark, and his grandfather wrote back approvingly: "I thought your comment on the tragedy was classic. If it had got to the lips of the newspapermen it would have gone the rounds." Gore recalled that he and his grandfather "shared a sense of Roosevelt's overweening pride, and the way he had taken a nation into war because he wanted it. It was a point of intimacy between us."

Soon Gore managed to get the army to place him in a hospital in Van Nuys, California, where he would be near his mother ("not what I wanted") and near Hollywood, which had caught his fancy on his recent visit. In hand he carried about thirty thousand words of *Williwaw*, his novel about a three-day journey in the Aleutians, when the transport ship meets a violent storm, although the greater violence occurs in the lives of the characters, who struggle more with their shipmates than with the forces of nature.

As he expected, Van Nuys proved entertaining, and Gore would often hitch a ride into Beverly Hills, where he met up with his mother and, sometimes, the Steins. Jules Stein saw at once that Gore had an immense intelligence, and he credited himself with being the first to recognize Gore's talents. He got Gore entry passes for the major studios, and Gore meandered happily from lot to lot, watching films being made at first hand. It was enthralling for the young man who had spent a lot of his childhood in darkened movie houses. "I would stand around on the sets for hours, just listening, making notes in my head," Gore remembered. He longed to get back there, to have a hand in the business of filmmaking.

A quick visit to his father in Manhattan occurred in June. Gore stayed with Gene and Kit at the apartment on Fifth Avenue, once again crowding in. There was a new baby now, another half brother, yet the scene depressed Gore, as he no longer fit in. A chance encounter proved invaluable to him now, however. Janet Mabie, a journalist who had collaborated on a book with Amelia Earhart, turned up one afternoon to interview Big Gene about his relationship with Earhart before her mysterious disappearance in 1937. Gene mentioned in passing that his son had written a volume of poems, and she suggested that Gore meet her editor, Nicholas Wreden, at E. P. Dutton, a major literary house.

Gore leaped at the chance. A meeting over lunch in midtown Manhattan led to his first job offer: not quite what Gore expected. With the end of the war in view—victory in the European theater had recently been declared, and surely the Pacific war would conclude favorably as well—Dutton hoped to attract a number of young authors who might represent the new generation of writers and readers. Gore's presence on their staff was thought to be somehow useful in this regard, as he could fish for manuscripts from young writers, who might like to be in touch with someone their own age. It was unclear how long it would take for Gore to get a discharge, however. He was certainly in no shape to go back overseas. In fact, a board of physicians in Van Nuys decided that he required a warm, dry climate for full recovery, and he was assigned to a base on the west coast of Florida.

He set off eastward by train, with a trunk full of manuscripts and books, stopping in Michigan to visit some of his father's family. It was in Ann Arbor that by chance he met a woman from the Washington area who told him that Jimmie Trimble had been killed at Iwo Jima, the bloody battle that happened while Gore was in the Aleutians. "I wandered in a daze for hours, unable to take it in—a casual remark that ruined my life for a while," Gore recalled. "It was a moment that stayed with me."

It's worth noting, however, that he and Trimble had lost track of each other. The relationship could not actually have meant nearly as much to Trimble as it did to Gore. "Jimmie was more like a symbol," Howard Austen later said to me. "I don't think you can take it at face value." In other words, Trimble stood in for something. He represented all that was gentle, handsome, innocent, and masculine in some idealized sense. When Gore thought back to Trimble, he was trying to repossess his own lost innocence. But this was never a relationship that would or could have had any materiality, not in the real world. Whatever happened between them in their brief encounters—if indeed they happened at all—belongs to a kind of perpetual fantasy of perfect adolescence: boys being boys, out of the range of their mothers, without the responsibilities or consequences of adult sexuality. "I don't even believe it, not so much," said Austen.

Still en route to Florida, Gore spent a weekend at his father's summer house in the Hamptons, where he met Frederic Prokosch for the first time. Prokosch later recalled "a sudden unexpected introduction to this bright young man, Gore Vidal. He had read my novels, and brimmed with energy and ideas. He told me about a novel of his, set in the Pacific theater. I had no doubt: Here was a fresh voice. It seemed terribly obvious. He had such confidence, and a rare wit that he could only just contain. We exchanged addresses, and would remain in touch over the years. I marveled, mostly from a distance."

There seemed no rush to get to the base in Florida, and Gore managed to spend much of July and August in the Hamptons and New York. It was at his father's apartment that he heard on the radio about the release of atomic bombs over Hiroshima. The bombing of Nagasaki followed three days later. On August 14, Gore joined the victory parade in Times Square—a spontaneous celebration of Japan's surrender, which had been announced by President Harry S. Truman at seven in the evening and memorialized by Alfred Eisenstaedt in the classic photograph of a sailor kissing a girl in Times Square. And of course, Gore was there.

That summer, he spent many sensuous evenings at major gay hangouts, such as the former Hotel Astor bar on West Forty-Fourth Street or the Everard Baths on West Twenty-Eighth Street near Broadway. The Everard was among his favorite cruising places. Known as the "Ever Hard," it attracted men from many backgrounds. Howard recalled, "Nobody had inhibitions there. The steam rooms were full of sailors, businessmen, actors, you name it. I used to see W. H. Auden there, hiding in the mist. It was a carnival." He added: "That was pure sex and without the frills. No violins."

That he still had to report to a base in western Florida seemed impossible, but there it was. Gore set off in late August, arriving at Camp Gordon in an exhausted state. But as there was little to do, he could put the last touches on the manuscript of *Williwaw.* "I was on night duty, and I had plenty of time. I finished the book in a matter of weeks. My life as a writer started," he recalled. "I read it over carefully one night, and I thought it was good. Better than I expected, not as Hemingway as I feared." To Bill Gray, a young fan with whom he struck up a friendship, he recalled that the book had been started aboard ship in the Aleutians "just before New Year's in 1944" and completed in Southampton, "shortly after Hiroshima" in 1945. Yet he kept revising for several months, well into the autumn.

Again using Uncle Pick's influence, he transferred back to Mitchell Field on Long Island. Pick got him a job, once again, as the base historian, a position that required no real work. The process of discharging millions of men was now under way—a mammoth logistical task for the military—and Gore had to wait his turn. But he found himself remarkably free and spent a great deal of time in New York, often staying in cheap hotels in lower Manhattan, within easy reach of the Everard Baths.

Meeting up again with Wreden, the editor from Dutton, he mentioned in passing that he had just completed a novel titled *Williwaw*. Wreden asked to read it, and within a week, Gore had an offer for the book. Dutton would print five thousand copies, and the author would receive an advance of $250. The novel would appear in June 1946. Dutton also agreed to publish his poems at some point. (Nothing would come of the poetry volume, as Gore knew he lacked talent as a poet, and he mostly stopped writing poems at this time. "I lost interest in the art," he said, "as a writer, but I kept reading poetry.")

The offer of an editorial job at Dutton remained in place, and Gore agreed to come into the office each Thursday for meetings. His work as an associate editor had begun, and he would join the firm in a full-time capacity as soon as he was discharged. "They paid me once a week now, handing over a fat envelope. Cash on the barrel," Gore said. His pay was $35 per week. "It kept me in cocktails."

It was convivial work—the one and only time Gore had a "real" job—and Wreden proved good company. A large, sharp-tongued man who drank double Scotches for lunch and enjoyed his life hugely, he often took Gore to the Players Club on Gramercy Park. There Gore rapidly expanded his circle, meeting a number of the local literati, including the poet James Merrill, still an undergraduate at Amherst, who had come under the protective wing of Kimon Friar, a poet and translator whom Gore described as a "queen bee at the center of a literary nest in New York." A new postwar generation of writers that included John Horne Burns, Truman Capote, and Norman Mailer was just beginning to emerge. They had come through the Great Depression as children and through the war as young adults. These twin catastrophes would inform their work and preoccupations in the decades to come.

II. Two Roads Diverging

The New York scene appealed to Gore, who continued for some time to wear the uniform of a warrant officer because it drew congratulatory nods from strangers. It was a sign of patriotism, perhaps heroism, and Gore looked dashing in khakis: tall, slender, cool-eyed. He spoke in a clipped way with the accent of his class, a transatlantic accent in which the word "rather" rhymed with "bother." Alastair Reid, the Scottish poet and journalist who moved to New York after the war, recalls, "The city was coming alive again, and Gore was a glittering presence, a wit, a young man who caught the eye and ear of a generation."

A life in politics still seemed possible for Gore, yet he guessed it would never work to be seen as "queer" by the electorate. This was the United States, after all. And the great population rushed toward marriage and children, toward a "normalization" of the workforce, with the women retreating from factories into the home, with men pounding the streets in search of occupations, not gay one-night stands.

Gore went out conspicuously in public with women, such as Cornelia Phelps Claiborne, a Vassar dropout who had been a member of his Washington dancing class. (She was a friend of Rosalind Rust, now pushed to Gore's social back burner.) Claiborne had deep political roots—one of her ancestors had been Thomas Jefferson's close friend, whom Jefferson appointed as the governor of the Mississippi Territory. As ever, Gore liked radiant connections, however distant or peripheral. But this was all cover, a way to hide his true or, at least, dominant sexuality.

One of the complicating figures in his life now was Anaïs Nin, a former lover of Henry Miller and, later, widely known as the author of *The Diary of Anaïs Nin*, a key document in the history of sexual liberation in America. Gore met her at the end of 1945, during a lecture given by Friar at the 92nd Street Y. By chance, Nin occupied a seat next to Gore in the cavernous auditorium, and they began to chat. A slender woman with dark hair, she wore a tight black dress. Gore joked with her about her hat, saying that Mary Queen of Scots used to wear one like it. Nin's husband, a banker named Hugh Guiler, sat behind her, out of sight but eyeing Gore with suspicion.

Nin struck Gore as exotic. Raised in France, she was the daughter of a Cuban composer. Her mother was part French, part Danish, and she had trained as a singer. She had already, at forty-two, moved through a series of high-profile lovers, including Miller, the psychologist Otto

Rank, and the literary critic Edmund Wilson. As Gore would learn, she had been molested by her father, Joaquín Nin. "She usually looked for versions of her father," Gore said, "but, in me, she was looking for a son." For his part, Gore was looking for a mother, as Nina had been such a disaster. Nin would stand in, painfully, for Nina.

In her diaries, Nin would describe Gore as "clear and bright" as well as "luminous and manly." His worldly manner and knowledge of current political affairs impressed her, and he no doubt talked about his soon-to-be-published first novel and his work at Dutton as an editor. Her diaries tell only a bit of the story, but—as the writer Kim Krizan has shown—the voluminous unpublished diaries reveal a great deal about Gore as a young man and Nin's reactions to him. With good reason, Gore remained suspicious of Nin and her work as a diarist. "She constantly reworked the diaries to absorb new grudges."

That evening at the 92nd Street Y, Gore agreed to meet her again at her apartment in Greenwich Village, and within weeks the two had become close friends (but not lovers). Their mutual attraction, according to Nin's unpublished diary, was "undeniable, inescapable." Yet she understood that her young friend was predominantly homosexual, and that this would make sustained relations difficult, even impossible. She urged Gore to seek therapy as she had done (rather catastrophically with Rank, who seduced her). He didn't want to, and he warned Nin that if the therapy succeeded he might "become normal" and take her away from Guiler. She considered her friendship with Gore "the most painful of all relationships" she had ever had—and that is saying something. For his part, Gore's frantic letters suggest a deep attachment to Nin. He had, briefly, found a mother substitute, and this was eroticized: an Oedipal dream of sorts, nearly fully realized, although it seems unlikely that they never went to bed together. Gore was not one to hold back, nor was Nin.

Meanwhile, Gore assumed his job at Dutton. "Nick Wreden was his big supporter," recalls Jack Macrae, whose uncle owned the firm. "It was such a conservative publishing house, you didn't expect to see anyone like Gore there. I remember stepping into the office and seeing him with a shawl around his neck in a kind of languid way. It was so odd. But everyone accepted him. In those days, being gay wasn't easy.

And everything about Gore was so surprising, what he might say or do. He cultivated the unexpected and seemed to take pleasure in that." His complex sexuality confused his officemates, as he couldn't be easily pigeonholed. "One Monday morning Gore didn't appear as usual. Neither did a young lady in the office. It seems they had run off to the Caribbean for a week together. Nobody knew quite how to process this. Was it just show?"

It wasn't easy being around him. "I think he had a very difficult time of it, and this made everything so awkward," says Macrae. "He couldn't take a compliment. He was suspicious of everyone. But I myself had never seen anyone so advanced in thought, so unusual. He was both confident and suspicious: an odd combination but one dictated by the times, by his sexuality. You never for a moment lost sight of his intelligence. It was almost piercing."

Gore tried to get Dutton to publish some of Nin's fiction, but they were not interested. This was a manly house, and they shied away from anyone like Nin, who exuded both femininity and exoticism.

Nin herself took a broad liberal view of her new friend. "What I see in the homosexual is different from what others see," she wrote. "I never see perversion, but rather a childlike quality, a pause in childhood or adolescence when one hesitates to enter the adult world." In truth, this explains a good deal about Gore: his narcissism, in particular. It often had a childlike quality about it, including an adolescent irritability and uncertainty. His sexuality had been locked into place quite early, and he never shifted beyond it, although his quasi-erotic feelings toward the opposite sex focused on older women, mother figures such as Nin. Yet even this seems reductive, however useful, in attempts to understand Gore's sexuality. He did appear to have a genuine attraction to both Rosalind Rust and Cornelia Claiborne. Perhaps a later comment by Howard helps to explain this: "Gore wanted to be straight. It would have made his public life a lot easier. When he tried to go straight, he found girls who were boyish." Austen speculates further: "Maybe Rosalind Rust became Rusty Godowsky, the straight man in *Myra Breckinridge*? Gore often said that."

Gore's post-army life in New York was energetically social when he was not working on his second novel, initially called *Myriad Faces* but eventually published as *In a Yellow Wood*. He awaited with some anxiety the publication of *Williwaw*, hoping it might provide enough royalties to liberate him from the publishing job, even though his duties at Dutton still only consumed a day or two each week. The work had, however, begun to irritate him, especially because his tastes rubbed against those of Wreden and Macrae. (For instance, they refused to publish an early version of James Baldwin's *Go Tell It on the Mountain*.) But where would he get enough money to quit his day job for good? "After Exeter, I didn't want to go to Harvard, as I might have," he recalled. "My father had saved some money for my education, but I wanted the money. I'd have a small but tidy sum to launch me in the world." He would actually receive about $10,000 from his father—a substantial amount in those days and worth roughly $120,000 today.

Gore shifted from place to place, often staying at his father's apartment, although he spent a lot of time with Nin, who—with her conversational talent and thirsty ego—drew artists and journalists to her in droves. Among those Gore met at this time were the gay magazine editor Leo Lerman, who held court at a brownstone on the Upper East Side, inviting the likes of Marlene Dietrich, Maria Callas, William Faulkner, and others to his campy quarters. (Lerman's posthumous journals offer a vivid portrait of this world.) Gore soon met prominent figures from the worlds of ballet, theater, and literature, including Dawn Powell, the novelist from Ohio, who was two decades his senior, a warm and witty person who had lived in Greenwich Village since the twenties. Her postwar New York novel *The Locusts Have No King* had been popular, especially among Gore's friends, and he admired it. "I adored her as much as the novel," Gore later said.

Another writer whom Gore met after the war was Truman Capote, the feline young novelist from New Orleans and Alabama whose fiction was suddenly attracting a good deal of attention—a situation that naturally unnerved Gore, who didn't suffer rivals gladly. He later recalled (one of several versions of their first meeting): "I first met Truman at Anaïs Nin's apartment. My first impression—as I wasn't wearing my glasses—was that it was a colorful ottoman. When I sat down on it, it squealed. It was Truman."

Nin also brought him to the sumptuously furnished town house of the heiress Peggy Guggenheim, whom Gore described as "the last of Henry James' transatlantic heroines, Daisy Miller with rather more balls." Guggenheim was the daughter of Benjamin Guggenheim, a financier who died on the *Titanic*. She had a large fortune at her disposal, which she spent mainly on modern art, collecting works by Picasso, Kandinsky, Braque, Duchamp, and many others, including her former husband, Max Ernst, the surrealist painter. "People wanted to meet Peggy just to see her art," recalls Edmund White, a younger gay writer who later met Guggenheim through Gore.

As ever, Gore relished these meetings with the great and the good, and he knew instinctively how to work his contacts, widening his circle at every turn. Soon the avant-garde filmmaker Maya Deren, the poet Theodore Roethke, and the novelist Paul Bowles could be numbered among his acquaintances. He also caught a glimpse for the first time of Jack Kennedy, the future senator and president who would later marry Jacqueline Bouvier, Gore's stepsister by way of his mother's marriage to Hugh Auchincloss. In *Palimpsest*, Gore recalls:

> It is 1946. I am twenty years old, riding in a taxi down Park Avenue on my way to the publisher, E. P. Dutton. My first novel, *Williwaw*, is about to appear. In the left-over-from-the-war khakis that we all wore, skinny, yellow-faced Jack Kennedy is wandering down the west side of the avenue. In a blaze of publicity, he is now running for Congress. Our fathers are friends, but we've never met.

There is so much of Gore in those few sentences: the memory (real or imagined) of place, his own trajectory as a writer, the deprecatory put-down of some famous person, his association with someone famous. He envies the "blaze of publicity" around Kennedy and wonders if he has himself chosen the right path in the fork of the yellow wood.

III. Storm at Sea

Williwaw is the story of men at sea during a storm in the Aleutians, and the strange aftermath of the squall, centered on a death that may or may not have been a murder. As noted, this book owes something to Stephen Crane, particularly to his story "The Open Boat," that elegantly compressed allegorical tale in which the sea stands in for the surge of time. "A singular disadvantage of the sea lies in the fact that after successfully surmounting one wave you discover that there is another behind it just as important and just as nervously anxious to do something effective in the way of swamping boats," Crane wrote. That laconic note undergirds Gore's clever first novel, in which the sea curls under the freighter as it makes its way through dangerous weather in a bleak northern world.

Gore shows a fine grasp of the sea as symbol, as *paysage moralisé*, such as when Evans, the skipper, steps onto the bridge: "The air was cool and moist. There was no wind and no sign of wind. Dark clouds hung motionless in the air. He felt the vastness of the sea and the loneliness of one small boat on the dividing line between gray sky and gray water. They were quite alone out here and he was the only one who realized it. This was very sad, and feeling sad and lonely he went back into the wheelhouse."

The inescapable echo of Hemingway can be heard in a simple phrase: "This was very sad," an almost childlike statement, shorn of complication or nuance. But it's important to note here that, despite its imitative surfaces, the novel has a deeply Vidalian center. A wild anarchic feeling underlies this book. The war is on, but it's in the hearts of his characters. The lonely men aboard this transport ship seem wholly disconnected, isolated, and suffused with bellicose feelings that can't quite fit in their skins.

The plot is simple, occupying six days in which the mysterious death of Duval, the ship's chief engineer and a man disliked by others aboard the ship, becomes a source of narrative energy. The eponymous storm strikes suddenly, skimming down from coastal distances, and the captain loses control of the ship, which is driven to shore and wedged between rocks. The next day, while helping his rival Berwick repair a ventilator, Duval tumbles overboard to his death. Murder or accident? It hardly matters, as the small crew prefers not to face the truth. A convenient cover-up is the order of the day.

Gore's cynicism about human nature, and his natural posture of bemused detachment in the face of immorality and madness, were missed by reviewers who rushed to praise the young novelist for his promise and self-evident narrative skill. There was an eagerness afoot to locate the voices of this new literary generation, and Gore Vidal had stepped forward with a credible war novel, although one that hardly celebrated American values in the usual ways. Orville Prescott, a major reviewer for *The New York Times*, patted the author politely on the head, noting his "sound craftsmanship." He considered *Williwaw* "a good start toward more substantial accomplishments."

At Dutton, Gore retreated to a back office to read a thick folder of first reviews, and—like all writers—he focused on the few negative notes. He would never, in fact, accept praise of any kind without a wry instinctual dismissal of the person who offered a compliment. Macrae says, "You couldn't praise him. It was impossible. He would turn away."

But praise came, in the form of letters from friends such as Claiborne or, more surprisingly, Nin's former lover Henry Miller, who wrote to express his amazement for what Gore had accomplished at such a young age. Miller even encouraged Gore to quit his job at Dutton and take up a full-time career as a writer. Gore recalled that "Miller seemed to know exactly what I was thinking. I had to get out of New York. It was a black hole, and I couldn't take it much longer. Not then. I needed a remote place to live and work, as I had not one but two novels under way, some poems, and a play, too. I needed to work, without the distractions of city life."

More approval came from Big Gene, who listened carefully to his son's case for following Miller's advice, and happily turned over the railway bonds he had put away for Gore's education. Gore cashed them in, banking the money, planning his escape. He had some royalties, too: *Williwaw* was hardly a best seller, but nearly three thousand copies sold within a few months. And Gore also had more than a thousand dollars saved from his time in the army. In all, this was enough to give him a few years of independence, especially if he found somewhere cheap to live.

It's important to note that Gore was not a rich young man. Indeed, sometimes he didn't know where the next bottle of champagne might come from. But he was resourceful and knew how to manage whatever resources he could muster. Living well meant a great deal to him, even at this tender age.

IV. Hearts of Darkness

"On a visit south of the border, I more or less stumbled on Guatemala City," he later recalled. "It was more developed than I expected. The old quarter, especially, caught my eye." So in September 1946, Gore decided to settle in this colonial city in Central America, far from the distractions of New York, D.C., or California. "It was, in those days, an exciting place, inexpensive, livelier than you would guess. And good things were happening on the political front. We all liked Arévalo."

Juan José Arévalo had been the Guatemalan president since 1944, having returned from exile in Argentina to head a reformist government led by the military. In office, he established a system of social security that would provide a retirement income for all classes, built public hospitals, encouraged freedom of the press, and instituted agricultural reforms. Calling himself "a spiritual socialist," Arévalo infused this little country with a huge optimism, although he could not overcome the power of the United Fruit Company, which would manage—with the help of the U.S. government—to overthrow this fragile democracy. "American tax dollars paid for the overthrow of democracy in Guatemala," said Gore. "What else is new? We would soon do the same thing in Iran, in the early fifties, and later in Chile."

Of course Gore benefited from being an American of the elite class, with political and social associations that he could exploit. Soon he joined the upper crust of Guatemalan society at parties and restaurants—an early example of a disconnect between his democratic impulses and his need to enjoy the pleasures that come with wealth and connections. "The nice thing about such a small country is the fact that everyone knows everyone else," he wrote to his father, with boyish enthusiasm. He seemed quite thrilled about the "delightful ruling class" that he found himself among, and he imagined staying in Guatemala for some years. "Time stood still" in that climate, he said.

At a bar in Guatemala City where American and European expats drank rum and sodas in a cat-infested garden under tall palm trees, Gore met a young man named Pat Crocker, a would-be painter, who (like Gore) had moved to Guatemala in search of an inexpensive place to work. Crocker was a short fellow with a slight paunch and blond hair like flax, which he let grow over his forehead in girlish bangs. He was a lively person, too, and told raucous jokes as he drank. Soon he and Gore became sexual partners, although Gore never thought of him as more than a friend and quickly found other sexual playmates, usually transitory ones.

The easy homosexual milieu in Guatemala at this time made life agreeable for gay men—much happier than back in the States, as Gore noted with a twang of irony: "Degenerates were always welcome under the big sun, under the palm trees." Perhaps for this reason, any number of gay men from America and Europe gravitated to Guatemala, where they mixed with the sons of wealthy businessmen and landowners, who had the immunity of class privilege.

Of Crocker, Tyrnauer says, "Pat became the earliest version of Howard Austen: Someone who would provide companionship, shop and cook, help with the household chores." Crocker was not someone who would make any effort to compete with Gore, intellectually or socially, and he provided a kind of uncritical echo chamber that Gore, as a narcissist, enjoyed. It was a simple, fun-loving friendship, and each took pleasure in the other's company.

Both Crocker and Gore had rooms in a boardinghouse in Guatemala City, "an old, somewhat decrepit building with floors that tipped to the east and windows that wouldn't shut. As the screens were ratty, flies became our roommates. I wrote at a wobbly table pushed against a wall blackened with mold, working every morning for three hours, trying for two thousand words a day. This was a draft of *The City and the Pillar.*" He wrote, as usual, in longhand on yellow legal-size pads, rarely backtracking to revise. More so than ever, the writing came quickly. He later wrote to a friend: "I recall celebrating my twenty-first birthday shortly before the last chapters, in Guatemala City."

The City and the Pillar was a remarkable novel, his best work in fiction so far: the story of Jim Willard and Bob Ford and their ill-fated sexual and emotional relations. Jim stood in, to a degree, for Gore. Bob is a version of Jimmie Trimble, a dreamy-headed teenage tennis player who moves beyond his early relations with Jim. Bob enlists as a merchant marine and goes his separate way, while Jim pursues a number of unsatisfactory homosexual affairs. Far from being fixated on Jim, Bob has found a footing in the world of adult heterosexuality and married his high-school girlfriend. When Bob and Jim meet again, years later, Jim's sexual overtures are met with shock and disgust. Harshly rejected, Jim kills Bob—a rather extreme, unrealistic conclusion to what is not an unrealistic novel but a fairly straightforward and plausible story. That Gore would feel compelled two decades later to revise the ending, where Jim murders Bob, was a good move on his part, strengthening the novel.

Gore recalled his work on this novel, with its ominous title from the Genesis story of Sodom, which was destroyed by fire and brimstone because of its sinfulness as a warning to future generations. As Claude J. Summers notes, the title reflects the "central myth of homosexuality in Judeo-Christian culture." "I wanted to take risks," Gore said, in an afterword to the 1965 edition, "to try something no American had done before." He would examine the homosexual underworld in a bravely matter-of-fact way, as it had arisen in Hollywood and New Orleans, and in New York, which Gore described as "a new Sodom" where a gay man "could be unnoticed by the enemy and yet known to one another."

This was not quite as new as Gore imagined. Homoerotic themes had long figured in the mainstream of American literature, though usually disguised if not totally repressed, as in *Huckleberry Finn* or *The Last of the Mohicans*, to say nothing of Walt Whitman's *Leaves of Grass*. (This point was made forcefully by Leslie Fiedler in *Love and Death in the American Novel*, a classic survey of American fiction and sexuality.) Rather than a major departure, Gore's work should be regarded as an ironic comment on a very old theme, on a world of narrative where men commonly fled the reach of women, facing into the winds of homoerotic feeling, lighting out for wild territories, trying to repossess an Eden that probably never existed. To its credit, *The City and the Pillar* is a novel that confronts this commonplace idealization, subverting the idea that homoerotic impulses derive from an innocent sense of Edenic longing—Hemingway's world of men without women. Gore's novel troubles those waters severely.

Gore felt pleased by the initial response to the novel, especially from his friends at Dutton, who must have felt some anxiety about publishing an explicitly gay novel. Some relief came when early signs pointed in the direction of success. "It appears on January 9th," Gore wrote to Crocker with unbridled excitement, "and the advance sale is fabulous. The Book of the Month Club, of all places, has called it one of the three best American novels the reviewer has read. *Harper's* magazine has declared me the leader of the new generation of writers." Only a few months later, he would add: "The book is now the #5 bestseller and I'm flooded with letters from happy queers wanting to meet me . . . no pictures included, alas."

In the meantime, his not-quite-sizzling second novel, *In a Yellow Wood*, neared publication. It had been written hastily in the wake of *Williwaw*. "I couldn't stop writing books," he said. "My head was a swirl in those days. I had in mind more books than I could possibly write, and often had two or three things under way. This rather promiscuous writing frightened my friends at Dutton, who wanted only one book at a time, with a respectable few years between each publication."

In a Yellow Wood appeared in March 1947, offering a laconic portrait of postwar New York, focused on Robert Holton, a feckless young veteran who takes a job with a Wall Street firm. It's also a novel about repressed homosexuality, serving as a bridge in Gore's progression from *Williwaw* to *The City and the Pillar*. This brief, unaffected story centers on a day of crisis and choice in this uninspired character's life, and it found relatively few readers. It was dismissed by the handful of reviewers who bothered to read it. The city, in Gore's portrait, radiates despair and unrealized erotic impulse, although the streets glitter in a kind of noir fashion. The dialogue is stiff, unreal. Robert has to choose between a life of security in his brokerage firm or love (in the broadest sense). Among the roads diverging in the yellow wood are heterosexuality and homosexuality, although this is left vague. Yet Gore allowed himself to write (but not as explicitly as he would in later years) about same-sex impulses. Even so, one reviewer found Gore's minor divagation into the homosexual underworld scandalous: "Twenty-two pages of homosexualism have nothing to do with the case, and could well have been left in the gutter where they were found without affecting the plot one way or another."

At the turn of the year, in early 1947, Gore and Crocker visited Antigua, a colonial city in the central highlands of Guatemala, an hour or so by car from Guatemala City, and fell immediately under its spell. In the middle distance the tips of ancient volcanoes thrust into the cobalt sky. The dusty wide streets and crumbling houses, with their mossy stone façades, appealed to them. The air tingled with odors of green papaya, dust, and damp plaster. Gore sat on the steps of the white cathedral in the central square, and it felt, he said, "very Italian." He especially admired the porticos of formerly elegant buildings: This was once the capital of a vast region under the control of the Spanish, a colonial tract extending from southern Mexico to Costa Rica. A lush fountain in the center of the square held his gaze. "I've always been attracted to the ruins of empire," Gore said (revealing a great deal about himself as well as Guatemala).

He heard about a ruined convent for sale nearby, only two blocks from the main square on the quiet Avenida Norte. It had once been connected to the dilapidated colonial church, Our Lady of El Carmen. They examined it, and Crocker was especially eager for Gore to buy it, so he did, spending a portion of the money his father had given him. It cost only $2,500, which was cheap for a large house with a walled garden, a tropical patio, and an attached sixteenth-century chapel with a fine old bell tower.

A local American architect, a "friend of a friend," was engaged to make the place livable, and—as labor was shockingly cheap—Gore managed within a month to get the house into good shape, with lots of solid antique furniture purchased from a vendor just off the main square. "The empty bedrooms were like rooms in my mind," Gore said. "I could fill them as I pleased, when I pleased."

He wrote to Nin that he "must construct this home as a symbol, whether I live in it or not is not important, it is enough that it is here." He was putting the last touches on *The City and the Pillar* when he wasn't busy with moving into the convent. "I have sometimes the feeling," he wrote to Nin, with unusual self-reflection, "that too much of me was left in the womb, it is not a matter of development, rather of what never was—was not born at all. I can never be too long bemused by dreams. I feel a stranger passing through, the books are only shadows I cast before the sun." As ever, he had a fragile sense of his own reality, though he would erect a vast empire of self on this slender foundation.

Never one to stay put for long, Gore flew to New York to visit his publishers, see his father, and reconnect with Nin. Their relationship, as viewed from her journals, was passionate but unfocused. An unlikely mate for Gore, she regarded him as a silly, innocent boy who, with his homoerotic impulses, posed a challenge. (She was not used to having men hold their physical distance.) She later bragged that Gore begged her to marry him, to return to Guatemala as his wife. He may have suggested this, but she doubtless understood he wasn't serious. How could he be?

She soon took off for the American West, leaving Gore to return to Antigua by himself. He wrote to her from Guatemala:

> Your sad Denver letter received and discounted. I was bitterly disappointed that you did not come down. You are quite necessary to me as you know. As for your fear that you would keep me from having a complete relationship, have no fear; I am quite alone here . . . I have adjusted myself to the fact that I shall never have a satisfying homosexual relationship. I am attracted to youth, to beauty, and separately, unphysically, to you, to the spiritual emotional rapport

> we have had. I need that more than the other. I cannot, and this is strange, do without women. I like to think that it is not necessarily the mother in women that I want.

Like Jim Willard, the young Gore Vidal found it difficult to be gay and to see his possibilities for a robust "normal" life fading and probably damaging his prospects for a career in politics. To the end of his life, Gore wrestled with his sexual identity, unhappy about it, never quite willing to acknowledge that he was "gay," a term he despised, preferring to call himself with a certain degree of self-loathing irony "a degenerate." He mostly stood aside during the AIDS crisis, afraid to find himself implicated in some way, although he spoke up in private, and in the 1990s mourned the loss of a beloved nephew from the disease.

Restless as ever, Gore began writing another novel in Guatemala that had, in a vague way, been dawning in his head (with miscellaneous notes) for some time. He originally called it *The Womb*, though it would be published in 1949 as *The Season of Comfort*. It remains the best of his early novels, a lucid story about the growth of a young man who is abused by his arrogant, alcoholic mother. Its first-person voice is crisp and fierce as the narrative proceeds through a series of significant moments in the life of William Hawkins Giraud, culminating in an almost hallucinatory fusillade of recriminations between mother and son: A nightmare come true some years later when he told his mother he never wished to see her again. This confessional novel emerged from long contemplation; it seemed to shudder into being, taking its author by surprise. "I never reread it," Gore told me in 2010. "That would have been too painful."

That he was writing too furiously, even compulsively, should be evident: four novels in four years or less. And two more would follow in quick succession, a blizzard of publication that established the name of Gore Vidal as one of the most productive and exotic of the postwar novelists. Indeed, an article appeared in *Life* celebrating the new writers, calling them "a refreshing group of newcomers." Unfortunately, Capote got the largest picture, with Thomas Heggen, Calder

Willingham, Jean Stafford, and Gore given lesser billing and smaller pictures—a slight that hardly passed without notice.

Back in his Antiguan house, Gore wrote at a wrought-iron table on the patio, with Crocker in the kitchen preparing for lavish dinner parties that would draw an array of friends and acquaintances: expat painters and writers, shell-shocked veterans of the recent war, even a few Guatemalan playboys from wealthy local families. Nevertheless, Gore felt lonely. The relationship with Crocker wasn't a durable one, but Gore was evolving a model for domestic relations that would carry over into his fifty-three-year partnership with Howard. The idea was that Gore's partner would provide companionship, cooking skills, and moral support of the kind that a man in an old-fashioned marriage usually got from his wife: Everything but the sex.

Nin eventually responded to Gore's endless requests for her company, joining him in Guatemala. She found the young man in terrible shape. "She thought I was dying," Gore recalled. "I should not have eaten from pots in the village square. Street food is almost always fatal. In my case, whatever I ate nearly killed me. I grew thinner and thinner. Jaundiced and dizzy. Anaïs came to create the role of Nurse Ratched."

A chance visitor that summer was the future writer Dominick Dunne, then an undergraduate at Williams College who had come to Guatemala with Andres Devendorf, an army buddy from Long Island. Devendorf's father knew Gene, and Gore had met Andres in the Hamptons the previous summer, so there were easy connections. Dunne later recalled Gore's "self-assurance, which was dazzling for a boy of that age, twenty-one. He seemed to know everyone in Guatemala. Often he wore linen jackets and trousers, colorful silk scarves, and large sunglasses. You could have mistaken him for a movie star trying to avoid being recognized—or the son of a gangster or South American dictator."

Dunne found Nin as amusing as Gore, and he remembered her "red hair in braids entwined in brightly colored yarn, magenta-and-lavender shawls, and the kind of jewelry made by artists in Greenwich Village." They all went swimming one night, in the nude, in a neighbor's pool, and there was a good deal of drinking and gossiping. But Gore's heart and mind were not happily in Guatemala. He felt desperately ill, and the relationship with Nin troubled him in ways he could not understand. As a man who lacked proper mothering, and who had just written a furious novel about mothers and sons, Gore was probably the last person in the world who could abide for long the overzealous ministrations of Nin, who wished to add him to her list of sexual acquisitions.

Gore's illness worsened, with night fevers and loose bowels, and he decided to go back to the States for medical care, accompanied by Nin, via Acapulco. For several weeks, he languished in a state of exhaustion, his skin a sulfurous yellow. He lost thirty pounds within two weeks. In need of serious medical attention, he went with Nin to Mexico City in the back of a rattling hired car. Blood tests soon revealed that he was suffering from hepatitis. "I have only the dimmest memory of that time," Gore later said. "I think I was dying. I may have died and come back."

Although Gore would return to Guatemala briefly, he had already lost interest in the place. Antigua had proved less productive than desired as a place for picking up men, and signs of intellectual life were even rarer than sexual opportunities. In short, Gore was bored. Leaving Crocker in charge of the house, which he planned to sell when he could, he hurried back to New York, anticipating the response to *The City and the Pillar*, thinking about various projects that lay ahead.

Edgewater Recalled

It is cold in the city, and Gore seems restless as we have coffee with toast in his suite at the Plaza. "Let me show you Edgewater?"

I've never been to Edgewater, and welcome the chance to see it, especially in Gore's company. I had an image of Gore's early life there with Howard, both of them in their twenties, young and ambitious, the world opening before them. It was what Gore calls "the golden time," and he says he often misses it.

We drive along the Hudson into Dutchess County, to Barrytown, a few miles north of Rhinebeck. It takes about two hours, and Gore is full of memories even before we set foot on the property. "I got it so cheap," he recalls, always interested in the details of money. "But I sold it to Dick Jenrette, a businessman, in 1969. He paid about $125,000. I had paid $35,000 for the place. Better than stocks or bonds! Never buy stocks or bonds! Buy houses!"

We park nearby on gravel. The river is locked in ice, the sky like a cobalt lid. The gentle slope to the water is white with snow, but a hard crust covers it. "I can see Dick Wilbur and his wife, Mary, running naked down this slope. They arrived in the early afternoon, had a drink or two, then ran to the river. Both of them naked, hand in hand! He was the most beautiful young man. Glorious. And a great poet. Even Wystan thought so."

There are six white pillars, making this a stately home of sorts. "Doric pillars—I loved them on first sight. These pillars sold the house. I pictured myself on this veranda, sipping a mint julep. My Southern genes activated. I was suddenly the owner of a plantation house in

Mississippi, my grandfather's home state. I had overseas investments. I didn't have to lift a finger to live. A fantasy."

We looked through the window into an octagonal room. "That was my study," says Gore. "It's more elegant now. Jenrette has filled it with period furniture. He has a great library. I had one, too, but it was a working library, the books I needed around me to convince myself that I was a writer. A writer needs books for support. You see what everyone else has done, and it gives you courage."

He tries the door. Of course it's locked. "I should have called ahead. He would have let us in."

I watch him as he looks out to the river toward a little island. I can't imagine how many ghosts are crossing the lawn in his mind, running toward the river. They make no footprints in the snow, but they are there, lightly running.

Chapter Three

> Actually, there is no such thing as a homosexual person, any more than there is such a thing as a heterosexual person. The words are adjectives describing sexual acts, not people.
>
> —Gore Vidal

I. Portrait of the Artist as Balletomane

After the war, Gore developed a passion for ballet, practicing a sequence of ballet exercises in the walled garden in Antigua, where a wooden rail was attached to the old stone wall of the ruined chapel. There he could be seen doing his demi-plié in various positions from the patio, and he seemed indifferent to the scrutiny of guests, who watched with bemused interest as he moved through his routine. Having suffered during the war from severe arthritis, he found this was good exercise for him. It loosened him up. "And God knows, he needed loosening," said Howard Austen. "After a certain age, he couldn't do the exercises, so he turned to booze."

Returning to New York, he at first stayed with his father or—like so many artists and writers from Mark Twain through Dylan Thomas and Arthur Miller—at the Chelsea Hotel on West Twenty-Third Street. He had an unerring instinct for what he considered the "right" hotel. In every city in the world, or so it seemed, he had a hotel that was "his," such as the Connaught in London, the Chelsea or Plaza in New York, the Oriental in Bangkok (which, indeed, dedicated a suite to

Gore as well as to Somerset Maugham and Graham Greene, other frequent literary guests and devotees of the brothel culture that has made Thailand a prime destination for sexual tourism for at least a century).

Gore had an instinct for meeting people with influence in the literary world, and soon he befriended Victor Weybright, the young publisher of New American Library, a mass-market house. In 1952, at a friend's apartment on East Twenty-Seventh Street, Weybright introduced Gore to Norman Mailer, who in 1948 had made a huge splash with his own war novel, *The Naked and the Dead*. Weybright recalled that "Mailer had obviously suffered from some social ostracism as a Jew at Harvard, which left scars on his personality that were deeper than any cruelties endured in active service in the war. It was apparent that drink and possibly drugs as well were involved in his insatiable quest for every sort of experience, physical and mental. He was disdainful of most of his contemporaries with the exception of Gore Vidal, whose grace and wit and incredible sense of learning—although he had never gone beyond prep school—baffled Norman as too sophisticated for anyone not a Jew." A complicated friendship began, one that would oscillate in dramatic ways over the next five decades or more.

Gore continued to see Cornelia Claiborne, who adored him (as her eager notes and letters suggest), but the needle of his erotic compass veered firmly toward the gay world, which for him was true north. For almost a year, he pursued Harold Lang, a slender dancer who moved between the Ballet Theatre (later called the American Ballet Theatre) and Broadway, where he had leading roles in musical comedies, such as *Kiss Me, Kate*, a popular takeoff by Cole Porter on Shakespeare's *Taming of the Shrew*, and *Look, Ma, I'm Dancin'!*, a comedy about a rich woman who finances a ballet troupe just so she can dance with them. "Harold had a very nice ass," Gore recalled with pleasure. "Lenny Bernstein called it the seventh or maybe the eighth wonder of the world." Lang was promiscuous on a scale that startled Gore, who later remarked: "That wasn't sex, it was hydraulics." Lang often slept with the author of the musical he was currently in and "with the leading lady as well." One hears Gore trying to rationalize all of this in *Palimpsest*: "This hardly bothered me, since I was almost as promiscuous as Harold. But during our short time together I was obliged to face the fact that I was never going to make the journey from homoerotic to homosexual."

Never? This is, of course, nonsense, a kind of Jesuitical argumentation. (For obvious reasons, Gore loved *Greek Homosexuality*, a groundbreaking if controversial 1978 book by K. J. Dover that showed, with dispassionate scholarly thoroughness, that the Athenians had often been bisexual, attaching no stigma to homosexual relations.) Gore in fact suffered what seems an unusual degree of anguish about Lang, undermining his pretense that he really didn't care about anyone. Lang inexplicably left New York one time, without bothering to tell Gore where he was going. "I suppose you're with your mother since someone said you'd gone to California," Gore wrote, trying to establish contact. "I hope you continue the analysis. I haven't talked to your analyst since that's unethical, but I gather from Ephron [a mutual friend] that all was going fairly well." He added: "Analysis is quite a frightening experience. I think we've reached a similar impasse: when our careers don't give the same satisfaction, the same forgetfulness as they once did; it's not a pleasant thing to see oneself but it must be faced sometime."

For the first and only time, Gore went into therapy, though he didn't really consider himself a suitable subject for psychoanalysis and would often disparage psychiatry in later years. "I have no unconscious," he said. "This upset my therapist, who was left to pick whatever fruits hung in my conscious mind."

Gore had obviously begun to make the journey—however tentatively—from homoerotic to homosexual, although he still felt a need to cling to some image of himself as bisexual, at least *in potentia*. "It was an idea he held on to dearly," said Howard, speaking from half a century of experience with Gore. "I didn't want to argue about it. What did I know? But if he's straight or even bisexual, I'm Genghis Khan."

Worship of the male figure drew Gore to the ballet, and in the immediate postwar years, he attended performances at New York theaters almost reverently, savoring the techniques of his favorite dancers, intrigued by the social dynamics of the troupe. He loved getting the gossip firsthand from dancers, many of whom became close friends. In *Palimpsest*, he explains: "In the late forties, balletomania hit New York City. For years there had been the Ballet Russes de Monte Carlo, a spin-off of the prewar Diaghilev company with a small but loyal audience." Among the stars in this resurgent world of ballet were Lang, Leon Danielian, and John Kriza (who later starred in Eugene Loring's *Billy the Kid*, one of Gore's favorite legends, which he would in due course adapt as a film).

New York ballet was a somewhat inbred world where Gore felt comfortable, a gay enclave with many glittering names, and weekends were often spent at house parties in the Hamptons with one or more of the ballet stars on view. It was a claustrophobic scene, too, with considerable intrigue, sexual and otherwise, and it would provide Gore with a good setting for *Death in the Fifth Position*, his first mystery, written under the pseudonym of Edgar Box in 1952—the best of three novels written under this name.

II. Pillars of Salt

As 1948 approached, Gore braced himself for the publication of *The City and the Pillar.* He knew that, from this point on, nobody would wonder about his sexual preferences; it was a grand if risky "coming out" party, a novel that explored gay life in America in courageous ways, opening him to criticism of a kind that he seems not to have anticipated. He had sent the galleys to Anaïs Nin, who met him for a drink one afternoon at the Oak Bar of the Plaza Hotel to talk about it. She had recognized herself in the unflattering portrait of one character, the vampy Maria Verlaine, and she didn't like it one bit, considering this caricature an act of betrayal. Gore recalled this meeting in *Palimpsest*, suggesting that it was his description of the age lines around Maria's eyes that upset Nin, quoting her objection from memory: "You say that she—that she—that she has lines about her eyes!" But Nin was smarter than this, and Gore was being unfair, as he often was to those who upset him in some way, in reality or in his imagination.

The City and the Pillar arrived in bookstores in January, with advance orders for five thousand copies. That was good for a literary novel in 1948, though less than he had expected. And there was a sale to John Lehmann in England, which gave the publication an international aura. Within weeks of its arrival in bookstores, it was evident to Nicholas Wreden, Gore's editor, that a commercial if not a critical success lay at hand, and he doubled the print run and authorized a major ad campaign. Soon Gore saw his name on best-seller lists around the country, and this cheered him. "That I might actually make a living from this business of writing seemed possible now," he said.

Always an inspired strategist when it came to marketing himself, Gore mailed signed copies to well-known older authors, including Thomas Mann and Christopher Isherwood, both of whom responded with respect. And the reviews came thick and fast, though most were bad, with a few exceptions. C. V. Terry, a prim but popular novelist, typically hammered Gore in a dismissive piece in *The New York Times Book Review*, describing *The City and the Pillar* as "coldly clinical," a novel that added little to the subject of homosexuality. The daily *Times* decided to pass altogether, which Gore imagined was an act of rejection purposefully designed to ruin his career. Reviewers in the daily paper did turn away from Gore for a stretch of seven years, and he invariably described this period as "the dark ages" or "the seven lean years," somewhat exaggerating the influence of *The New York Times*. A survey of the reviews that actually occurred during the years in question confirms that the daily *Times* ignored Gore for a long time as a novelist, although he was never ignored in the pages of the Sunday *Book Review*, the most important of publications at the time. The real problem was that reviewers didn't especially like the novels that followed *The City and the Pillar*. It wasn't until *Julian* arrived, in 1964, that critics once again discovered—and began to appreciate—Gore as novelist.

The public fuss over Gore's gay novel actually helped to sell the book—any publicity was good publicity and a book that dealt openly with sexual ambiguities and revealed a world that many Americans only vaguely knew about was perhaps bound to find an audience. Yet the lack of critical affirmation proved too much for the young author.

"My nerves were bad," he said, "and I needed to get away. Far away was best." In pursuit of "far away," he set sail for Naples in February 1948 on the *Neue Helena*, this young man who had already lived more life in two decades than many live in eight or nine. In his first-class stateroom, he had in hand chapters of a novel about the twelfth-century troubadour Blondel de Neel, who had rushed off to rescue King Richard the Lionheart in 1192. The English king was being held prisoner by Duke Leopold V of Austria after the Third Crusade, which had been an attempt to rescue Jerusalem from Saladin, the Muslim leader. (Richard had failed to capture Jerusalem, the symbolic endpoint of their mission.) Richard's imprisonment was a story from history that Gore had loved since childhood, and he thought he could write a short, accessible novel on the subject that would attract a wide readership.

While crossing the Atlantic, he kept a diary that has been shielded from public eyes in his papers at Harvard's Houghton Library—the only material in the Gore Vidal Papers that is locked from view for fifty years after the author's death. ("Post-adolescent despair is never pretty," he replied, when I asked him about this mysterious journal.) What its pages contain can't be known for sure, but it seems obvious that Gore's sense of self had been shattered by reviewers. He had somehow counted on an easy climb up the steps of Parnassus, but the stairway felt steep and treacherous now. He kept recalling phrases from the reviews: "sordid novel" or "tragedy of perversion" or "abnormality revealed." Even the liberal critic Leslie Fiedler, who considered homosexuality a matter of unresolved adolescent feelings but was otherwise unaffected by the sexual content of the novel, dismissed *The City and the Pillar* in *The Kenyon Review*, considering it full of "long artificial speeches" that would only bore readers.

This whirl of criticism was exactly what Gore needed to escape, and Europe was good for that. He disembarked in Naples but took the first train he could get to Rome, always the city of his dreams. With some grandiosity, he checked in to the Hotel Eden on Via Ludovisi, near the Spanish Steps: a turn-of-the-century palace with a dramatic rooftop terrace overlooking the Eternal City. The Eden was then, as now, a prestigious Roman address, and Gore thought he had arrived where he belonged. "A long view of Rome is a long view of life," he would often say.

But Italy had yet to recover from the war. Even at the Eden, the food was hardly up to former Italian standards. Gore walked the streets in awe, nevertheless, feeling the presence of the past in the back alleys and tiny piazzas of the Old City. "It's one of the things about Rome," he later said, "that you always hear the footsteps of earlier generations. It's a kind of noiseless thunder."

"I found Gore surprisingly quiet, unsettled," said Frederic Prokosch, who called on the young man at the Eden and offered to give him a walking tour of his favorite districts. "I introduced him to Tennessee Williams at a party thrown by Samuel Barber [the American composer] and they seemed almost to recognize each other, even though they'd never met. Williams was in his mid-thirties, so quite a bit older than Gore. He thought Gore was gorgeous and winked at me, and Gore really was. He was just a kid, but he had the self-composure of a mature man. And he already seemed to know everybody in the universe. I don't know how he managed that."

At thirty-six, Williams was already well established, enjoying the afterglow of a great success on Broadway. *A Streetcar Named Desire* had swept the theater world like a hurricane, with Marlon Brando and Jessica Tandy in the leading roles of Stanley Kowalski and Blanche DuBois. Gore was both impressed and fiercely jealous; for his part, Williams wrote to a friend in New York that he had just met "that unhappy young egotist Gore Vidal." The cause of the unhappiness was, in part, related to Gore's recent novel. He had expected a huge reception for *The City and the Pillar*, which sold well for several months but then faded from view. The testy response of critics had further upset Gore, and he began to think about writing plays instead of novels. Perhaps this was his true métier?

Prokosch recalled: "Gore kept talking about writing a play. It was a fantasy—at that time. But he saw the kind of acclaim that had come to Tennessee, and he understood that a successful play on Broadway was a money-spinner like nothing else. You could make a killing. And Gore liked the good life, and could barely pay for his suite at the Eden. I could sense a kind of coiled ambition, a drive that was almost frightening in a boy of that age. Tennessee enjoyed the adulation, of course. Gore was like a puppy around him, barking questions."

Postwar Rome was freer than New York or London for gay men, who flocked there. The streets teemed with unemployed young Italians desperate for money, and they had few scruples about trading sex for cash, "although they never liked anal sex," says Edmund White. "That was the only no-no, as it threatened their masculinity." For a thousand lire (less than two dollars at the time) a "street boy" (that was the common phrase) would return to your room for a night. "I was a chickenhawk," said Gore, "and so was Tennessee. We liked boys about eighteen or nineteen: what we called the Golden Age." "The idea put forward in some circles, that Gore would go for younger boys, boys in their early or mid-teens, is preposterous," said Scotty Bowers, a hustler and pimp who met Gore in 1948 in Los Angeles and often procured sexual partners for him, so he would know the truth about this sensitive topic. "He actually disliked children. For sex, he preferred men in their twenties, even thirties were fine with him."

Photographs of Gore from this period capture an incredibly good-looking young man with angular features and a focused gaze, and those who encountered him rarely forgot the experience. "I first met Gore Vidal in 1947," recalled Stephen Spender. "He was very young and looked spruce and golden. He had tawny hair and eyes that made me think of bees' abdomens drenched in pollen. The center of each eye, perhaps its iris, held a sting." Williams struck a similar note in his memoirs: "Gore was a handsome kid, about twenty-four, and I was quite taken by his wit as well as his appearance. We found that we had interests in common and we spent a lot of time together. Please don't imagine that I am suggesting a romance. We merely enjoyed conversation and a lot of laughter together." Prokosch, in fact, thought that Williams "would certainly have liked a physical relationship with Gore, but that didn't happen."

As Williams noted, he hadn't read Gore's book when they first met, although word of the young man's scandalous novel had reached him. Later, when he read the book—the only one of Gore's he read with any interest—he objected to the violent ending, saying, "I don't think you realized what a good book you had written." That he found the ending "melodramatic" struck Gore as a marvelous irony, coming from this particular playwright. "The most melodramatic of writers accused me of being melodramatic?"

Gore considered Williams "one of the best people to talk to that I'd met at this point in my life," someone with a "perverse sense of humor, which we shared. His mimicking of Roosevelt exceeded mine, and I mean Mrs. Roosevelt."

Within a few weeks of their initial meeting, Williams bought an old army jeep, with a canvas roof that neither of them could put up, and set off for the Amalfi coast—the place that would, in due course, become Gore's home for many decades. They spent happy hours in cafés, drinking wine and ogling Italian boys, who struck them both as exceptionally beautiful. "It was all spring flowers and corrosive but strong white wine and sunshine. And amusing conversation," Gore remembered. "We both had difficult mothers, and that became a subject we could develop at length, each in his own sordid way." They stayed in Amalfi in the Hotel Luna, but this naturally gorgeous region had suffered badly during the war. As Gore later wrote to his close friend Gianfranco Corsini, a Roman journalist, "Tennessee and I drove his jeep from Rome to Naples to Amalfi and up into the hills to Ravello. Naples harbor still torn up from the war. Villages in ruins. People poor but busy. Tennessee was the world's worst driver: 'I am, for all practical purposes, blind in one eye' he would say, serenely making his way down the middle of the Amalfi Drive, the last flash of beauty many a tourist ever sees as he falls into the sea or upon the rocks."

Gore visited Ravello for the first time, wandering its broad, stone-paved piazza, peering from the edge of town to the panoramic view he would in due course make his own. He adored the sweeping view of the Amalfi coast, one of the finest views in the world. The turquoise waters of the Tyrrhenian Sea almost blinded him, with a million coins of light glittering on the water. The limestone cliffs thrilled him as he and Tennessee climbed a path through lush pine and lemon groves to the Villa Cimbrone, an eleventh-century structure that was rebuilt by the Victorian British aristocrat Lord Grimthorpe, who would also construct La Rondinaia (Swallow's Nest), the handsome five-story villa that Gore would purchase in 1972 and occupy for nearly four decades. He considered Ravello "a fragment of heaven," and vowed to return.

Back in Rome again, Gore paid a respectful call on George Santayana, the onetime Harvard philosopher, essayist, and poet whose writing he admired. (It was Santayana who famously said, "Those who cannot remember the past are doomed to repeat it.") This eminent sage was celebrated by Wallace Stevens in "To an Old Philosopher in Rome," where Stevens remarked on "the bed, the books, the chair, the moving nuns" in the candlelit room where Santayana worked in quiet isolation at the Convent of the Blue Nuns on the Celian Hill. There Santayana had hidden himself when the German army invaded Rome a few years earlier, and it proved a quiet place to remain.

There is something touching about this visit, Gore's effort to make contact with a philosopher and writer long past his prime. Santayana represented, for him, the life of the mind, a man committed to his ideas and ideals. Gore knew that Santayana had once been a hugely important and influential figure, but that history had passed him over. Santayana, for his part, had no interest in worldly fame, and Gore found their conversation calming and inspirational. "He kissed me on the forehead when I left the room," Gore said. "It was a kind of priestly act."

During the spring, Gore also spent several weeks in Cairo, often sitting in the bar of Shepheard Hotel, a legendary watering hole for spies, diplomats, foreign traders, writers, and rakes. It was there he saw the overweight King Farouk in his trademark dark glasses surrounded by henchmen and young Egyptian women in search of patronage. In the postwar era, Cairo's bars and smoky restaurants thronged with dethroned royalty and their dazed offspring, who wandered in a mist of confusion (often addled by opium). Among these "wonderfully shady characters" was Mehmed Abib, a local playboy aristocrat, "who wooed me sadly and hopelessly beside the pool at Mena House. He looked like a sensitive dentist."

By contrast, Williams's work ethic had impressed Gore on their tour of the Amalfi coast, as the playwright never missed a few hours of writing after breakfast. In imitation of his new hero, Gore spent at least three or four hours each morning on his novel, usually in cafés, finishing it within days of his arrival. Then he turned to a play version of *The City and the Pillar* that featured a terrifying mother very like his own. "It wasn't any good, and I felt the air leaking out of its tires as I drove it down the dusty streets of Cairo."

Moving on to Paris, Gore checked in to the Hôtel Pont-Royal on rue Montalembert. "My room," he recalled, "faced Saint Thomas d'Aquin. The latest version of Thomas Aquinas, Jean-Paul Sartre, smoked his pipe in the downstairs bar. I watched him from the side of the room as he talked to Simone de Beauvoir. A crowd of would-be existentialists hovered behind them, listening in, full of excitement. This was a world unlike our own. In France, literature and writers mattered a good deal. A writer lived and worked at the center of the culture."

Soon Williams arrived in Paris, attracting a group of writers and intellectuals who gathered around him eagerly. For the first time Gore met his English publisher John Lehmann, as well as Christopher Isherwood, who had been a person of interest to Gore for several years as an openly gay writer with a good deal of critical acclaim. They liked each other at once. Indeed, Gore later wrote to Lehmann: "I don't know when I've met anyone I liked so much in such a short time," and praised Isherwood's "wit and conversation." Isherwood's lover at that time was the photographer Bill Caskey, who regarded Gore with some contempt as a spoiled preppie who sought out the company of Isherwood for advice about his literary career. For his part, Isherwood (as his diaries suggest) considered young Gore a resentful, unhappy creature. Their friendship, however, would lead to mutual book dedications and visits over the next few decades.

Coincidentally, Truman Capote came to Paris that month. It was Johnny Nicholson, a mutual friend, who brought them together over lunch at Les Deux Magots, the café where Hemingway, Fitzgerald, Pound, and Picasso had passed time in earlier years. Gore had been quietly at odds with Capote for a few years, and Capote was surely a peculiar young man to encounter face-to-face: a squeaky-voiced albino dwarf, with mannerisms of the kind that Gore found highly irritating. "Sissy boys are not my thing," he would often say. And yet Capote attracted large quantities of gossip and publicity, and Gore envied this. The two would meet again occasionally over the years, but friendship eluded them. Their relationship ended, in the mid-seventies, with bitter name-calling and well-publicized lawsuits.

Lehmann took Gore to meet an elder statesman of world literature, André Gide, at his "cluttered and dark book-lined apartment in the seventh arrondissement," as Gore recalled. Gide, who had won the Nobel Prize in Literature only a year before, was at the peak of his fame, a celebrated writer and public intellectual who represented, for Gore, an ideal of sorts. That Gide was also gay intrigued him, and he gratefully accepted from the seventy-nine-year-old writer an inscribed copy of *Corydon*, a volume of four dialogues on homosexuality that had been written between 1911 and 1920 and which now existed in an English-language version. Like Gore, Gide considered homosexuality utterly natural, noting that it could be found in most of the advanced cultural moments in time, from Greece in the age of Pericles through Italy during the Renaissance and England in the age of Elizabeth. As the English writer John Weightman said, "When I was a student in France before the war, Gide was very popular with most young people. They read him as a kind of prophet calling on them to revolt against the religious and moral conventions of French bourgeois society, and to achieve the fullest possible expression of their individual temperaments."

Gore admired Gide's severe manner, and recalled his large bald head with a dent in the forehead, skin like rice paper, and eyes that glistened with a combination of "lust and intelligence." Gide smoked, talking in mandarin French about Oscar Wilde and Henry James as if he were giving a lecture. When Gore heard that Capote had been there a couple of days before him, he asked the old master how he found Capote. "Is he in Paris?" he wondered, provocatively. "I would like to meet him." Gide obviously had Gore's number, amusing himself by teasing the younger writer when he detected an unhealthy sense of rivalry.

Another writer Gore met in Paris, not for the first time, was Paul Bowles, who was en route to Morocco from New York. Bowles had come to visit Williams, and Gore joined them for dinner one night. Bowles warmed to Gore, and the feeling was mutual. The following day Bowles called on Gore at his hotel, and they strolled through the Left Bank for several hours. Bowles was tall and slender, blond, well-dressed, and eager to talk about music as well as literature. Fifteen years older than Gore, on the verge of success with his 1949 novel, *The Sheltering Sky*, Bowles talked about his work as a composer and writer. He had just agreed to write some incidental music for *Summer and Smoke*, a new play by Williams slated for its New York premiere in the fall. He also told Gore about his life in Morocco, where he had a wife, Jane, although he explained that he slept with a variety of young men. All of this appealed to Gore, and Bowles would become a lifelong friend.

After a week, Gore and Williams crossed the English Channel at the playwright's suggestion: He wanted to attend rehearsals of *The Glass Menagerie* in the West End. Lehmann served as their genial host, introducing Gore to several well-known British writers, including Graham Greene and V. S. Pritchett. Isherwood was in Cheshire at the time, at his family home, and he came into London to see Gore and Williams at the party given by Lehmann, as did E. M. Forster, the great novelist himself, who wished to meet Williams, not Gore Vidal. But Forster liked the young man, and invited him to call on him in Cambridge: an invitation Gore could hardly refuse.

Gore had read everything by Forster, and often spoke of Forster's early Cambridge novel, *The Longest Journey*, as a portrait of English university life at its best—an experience Gore longed for but never had. (He never much liked Forster's early Italian novels, such as *A Room with a View* or *Where Angels Fear to Tread*, which he considered sentimental, even shallow.) Rather typically, Williams had little idea who Forster was and, according to Gore, confused him with C. S. Forester, the popular creator of novels about Captain Horatio Hornblower.

Judy Montagu was another new acquaintance who would, over the years, grow close to Gore, often engineering meetings with prominent figures. A smart, witty society lady with aristocratic connections, she had a good deal of money, too, being the granddaughter of a wealthy merchant banker. She was a close friend of Princess Margaret, who would in turn become Gore's friend. And Gore could count on Montagu, whenever he came to London, to strike up the band.

British society appealed to Gore, with its upper-class circles within circles. He fit in well there, as a kind of socialist Tory, a snob who nevertheless objected to people in power using their leverage in ways detrimental to working people. The strong populist streak he had inherited from his grandfather continued to bleed through his elitism. Having gone to Exeter, he identified with public-school boys who went to Eton and Harrow. In the coming decades he would make London a regular port of call, expanding his connections in its interlocking literary, political, and social worlds, feeling at home there. At his club in Pall Mall, the Athenaeum, he would hold court in the bar under the portraits of Matthew Arnold and Charles Dickens, sometimes writing in the hushed library where Thackeray liked to write. Or he would entertain visitors in a suite at Claridge's or, in later years, at the Connaught in Mayfair.

For the sake of his prospects in Britain, Gore cultivated Lehmann, who was widely known in London's literary circles and much admired by many as a publisher; but Gore never liked him. The feeling was certainly mutual. They exchanged testy letters when Gore returned to Paris, with Gore feeling hurt by the rumor that Lehmann had made snide remarks about him and his pursuit of "trade," meaning rent boys. Gore felt that Lehmann had misunderstood him, and wrote caustically: "American is not English even though it has a familiar ring." But Lehmann demurred, telling Gore: "I'm fond of you, and believe in you." He added that he looked forward to Gore's next novel, though in fact he didn't.

Paris in July proved hot and sticky, and Gore lost interest in living like a vagabond. He wanted to get back to the States to see his elderly grandparents in Washington. He also needed to finish *A Search for the King*, which had failed to unfold with the speed he expected as he shifted from hotel to hotel. He believed this novel would find a wide audience and bolster his bank account, which had grown perilously thin. He still planned to return to Guatemala, which remained his home base. But Williams urged him to move to New York, the center of American literary life, and Gore thought this a sensible idea—if he could unload the house in Antigua. Gore referred to Williams as "the Bird," as he flew over the heads of lesser mortals, sometimes calling him "the Golden Bird." And Gore planned to do a little soaring of his own.

III. Stateside

For a couple of weeks, Gore stayed at his father's house in East Hampton, finishing the novel, which Dutton agreed to publish in the winter. Although he was tired of living out of suitcases, he nevertheless spent much of the fall at the Chelsea Hotel or, briefly, at Williams's apartment. He eyed the New York scene with some fear—it was full of emotional pitfalls—but he continued to play the game. In a note to Capote, he suggested that they meet for a drink at the Plaza one day soon. They did, and Gore observed Capote's eccentric mannerisms and pretensions with some horror, though he saw that his rival's reputation only seemed to grow. *Other Voices, Other Rooms* had lofted Capote's name onto best-seller lists in 1948, and it stayed there for months. By contrast, *The City and the Pillar* had flashed, then faded. It further irritated Gore that Orville Prescott—the influential daily reviewer for *The New York Times* who he assumed was homophobic because of his response to *The City and the Pillar*—had written glowingly about Capote's debut novel, calling it "artistically exciting" and announcing "the arrival of a new writer of substantial talent." Even more annoying was the fact that Williams paid close attention to Capote, whom he cattily described as "a sweetly vicious old lady."

This was a heady time in New York for writers, as recorded in an iconic *Life* magazine photograph taken at the Gotham Book Mart in November 1948. Among those present were W. H. Auden, Stephen Spender, Marianne Moore, Delmore Schwartz, Elizabeth Bishop, Richard Eberhart, and Williams, as well as Sir Osbert and Dame Edith Sitwell, whom Gore had met through Alice Bouverie. Eberhart later recalled: "Everybody who was anybody in the poetry world gathered in that bookstore. The Sitwells were the great draw, of course, and this gathering was in their honor. The war was really over, and American literary life had started up again with a bang. There was a huge optimism." With his unerring capacity to arrive in time for the right photographic moment, Gore—the true Zelig of his age—stood eagerly beside these stars of the current Pleiades, even though he had written only a handful of poems.

Capote was furious that Gore, not he, had been included in this picture. "You're not a poet!" he complained to Gore. Like children, they picked and jabbed at each other about their individual styles, bobbing and weaving for notice in the press. Gore accused Capote of imitating the prose of Carson McCullers with "a bit of Eudora Welty." Capote in turn suggested that Gore's main literary influence was the New York *Daily News*. Overhearing this particular exchange, Williams rolled his eyes: "Please! You are making your mother ill."

Gore used Williams as a calling card, taking him to parties and dinners, such as those hosted by the socialites Mona and Harrison Williams, who occupied a Gilded Age mansion on Fifth Avenue and Ninety-Fourth Street. Mona's secretary and companion was Eddie von Bismarck, a grandson of the legendary German leader Otto von Bismarck. (The pansexual and party-loving Eddie proved to be a reliable friend to Gore, and they would often socialize in later years, especially at Eddie's villa on Capri.) Mona and Eddie lived at the decadent center of a swirl of European aristocrats in exile in New York. Everyone, it seemed, wanted to meet Williams, and they usually admired Gore, the young man who never lacked for a witty remark and quick smile.

Among those closest to Gore in the fall of 1948 was John Latouche, a Broadway lyricist who had become a fixture in gay society. In *The Golden Age*, Gore describes him (not flatteringly) as "a short, barrel-chested, barrel-stomached man with a large head, bushy dark hair, bright blue eyes." Latouche's biggest hit, "Taking a Chance on Love," had appeared in *Cabin in the Sky*, a popular 1940 musical, and he had a string of minor successes, all of which pointed to a brilliant career that never quite materialized. In any case, Gore loved his madcap humor and verbal gymnastics, and didn't mind his heavy drinking. Although too chaotic to harness his own gifts, Latouche was a welcome guest at dinner parties, and Gore tagged along for the fun, continually expanding his circle of acquaintances.

In December, Gore returned to Guatemala for what would be his last lengthy visit. He found the place "seedier than ever, and boring," so used his time to finish the very rough draft of *Dark Green, Bright Red*, a thriller about Guatemala that had been brewing in his mind for some time. It's the story of a military dictator, General Jorge Alvarez, who hopes to regain control of Guatemala (unnamed in the novel) by enlisting the help of "the Company," a shadowy organization based on the United Fruit Company, and a gang of sleazy hangers-on that includes a West Point graduate and a washed-up French novelist. The story is briskly paced, staccato in its dialogue, and relatively clichéd in overall design, as reviewers noted. Yet the minor characters, especially Charles de Cluny (the failed novelist turned speechwriter and court jester), are sympathetically drawn, and they stay in the mind. (Gore would rewrite this novel for a later edition, convinced that it had been terribly underrated.)

Gore's friendship with Pat Crocker had stalled—in his frequent letters, Crocker sounds needy and underappreciated—and the opportunities for sex were limited in Antigua. Gore picked up a number of local boys, but this proved unsatisfactory in various ways. In a few weeks, he caught a nasty case of the clap from one of them, and this prompted him to return to New York for treatment in late February 1949. The experience of living in Central America had served its purpose and given him the setting for a novel, but he was an American writer and needed to immerse himself in the culture back home, for better or worse.

Shortly after Gore returned to the United States, his beloved grandfather suffered a stroke while eating breakfast with his wife, the faithful Tot. At seventy-eight, Thomas P. Gore was a man who had lost his sense of purpose, having been out of office for some years. Tot called her grandson within the hour, and he immediately called his father, who had always remained on good terms with his in-laws, who continued to admire him even though their daughter had left him years ago. Father and son traveled together by train to Washington.

"He was the single most influential being in my life," said Gore of his grandfather. "I couldn't believe he was actually mortal."

One can look back over Gore's life and see the indelible imprint of his grandfather: the shrewd analytical turn of mind, the love for and detailed knowledge of history, and the fondness for oratory laced with apt and unusual quotations and unexpected analogies. In his later years, Senator Gore was asked by a reporter why he had once been a radical but had become very conservative. He responded by using the analogy of a cannonball fired at night that would appear to stand still if a flash of lightning should illumine the sky at the moment of its firing. "I am going as fast as the cannon ball," he said, "but I am not going as fast as lightning."

In the meantime, reviewers yawned loudly at Gore's *The Season of Comfort*. Even the sympathetic John W. Aldridge, who also wrote novels, observed in the *Saturday Review*: "Vidal apparently intended to write a story of a son's struggle 'to sever the psychological umbilical cord which ties him to a selfish and possessive mother.' We are informed that this is so by the jacket blurb, but at no time up to the concluding sections is it demonstrated to us in the novel." What Aldridge noticed was that the resolution of the novel breaks on the reader unexpectedly; the plot has not been well constructed. And so the finale, which features vigorous (and fresh) interior monologues by both mother and son, arrives without much thought to anything that went before. The novel fails to satisfy the reader's natural wish for cohesion.

Gore read his notices with petulance, deciding that he had alienated reviewers with *The City and the Pillar.* "They hated me for many years after that novel, and I couldn't buy a good review, not in any respectable journal," Gore said. "The Great Eraser had begun its deadly work."

The real problem lay in the fact that Gore had written half a dozen novels in less than five years, and none—not even *The City and the Pillar*—was more than the work of a brilliant apprentice, a young novelist searching for his voice. As 1950 approached, his fifth and sixth novels were finished and ready for publication by Dutton. Most novelists publish their first titles around the age of twenty-five or thirty, and they often throw away several books, thus sparing themselves the bad reviews they would otherwise get. Hemingway, for instance, was twenty-seven when he published *The Sun Also Rises*. Even more typically, Virginia Woolf was in her mid-thirties when *The Voyage Out* appeared. The novel is a demanding form best suited to a writer of some maturity, and Gore had not quite achieved that, despite an uncanny facility for language and a firsthand knowledge of the world that was unusual in one so young.

He wrote to Crocker that the critics regarded him as "a variety of poison oak," and wondered out loud about finding an easier way to make a living. He tried his best to show some interest in the house in Antigua, asking "How is the house? Has it weathered the various storms of faction and nature which, one hears, have been convulsing the proud republic ever since my departure." He counted himself lucky that Wreden, his editor, continued to support him, however lackluster the sales of *In a Yellow Wood* and *The Season of Comfort*. The publisher had hoped that either *A Search for the King* or *Dark Green, Bright Red* might reignite interest in the young author. *The City and the Pillar* had been a modest commercial success, although Gore wasn't happy with the numbers. But its notoriety and sales showed enough promise to inspire hope at Dutton that Gore might one day write truly popular books. "There was terrific enthusiasm for Gore at the firm," recalls Macrae. And Dutton would remain Gore's American publisher through *Messiah* in 1954.

IV. More Dolce Vita

Gore's response to the reception of *The Season of Comfort* was, as usual, to get out of town. The impending British publication of *The City and the Pillar* gave him a good excuse to cross the ocean, this time traveling in May with Leon Danielian, who had become a friend. On arrival in London, Gore and Danielian went straight to Lehmann's house. A round of parties followed, and the British reviews were reasonably good, without the faux horror of certain American headlines. Thus began a long relationship between Gore and the British, who reveled in his caustic wit, his elegance of style, his quick intelligence, and his blistering critiques of American power.

Gore and Danielian also traveled to Paris, where they met up with Capote as well as Bowles, who was about to publish the first English edition of *The Sheltering Sky*, his haunting novel of an American couple in North Africa. The book had been warmly received at home. Indeed, Williams had reviewed it in *The New York Times* on December 4, 1949, hailing Bowles as "a talent of true maturity and sophistication of a sort that I had begun to fear was to be found nowadays only among the insurgent novelists of France, such as Jean Genet and Albert Camus and Jean-Paul Sartre."

Such praise from Williams caught Gore's attention, and probably Capote's as well. Bowles intrigued them both: Here was a mysterious American with a worldly manner. He wrote music as well as novels, and lived with his gifted wife, Jane, in Morocco, where they enjoyed a kind of easy bisexuality—the ideal to which Gore himself aspired. There was a distinctly cosmopolitan hipness about Tangier, the Bowleses' main base, a city that would in due course attract stars of the Beat generation, including William S. Burroughs and Jack Kerouac. Yet Bowles had somehow made the country his own ahead of the pack. "Paul was a Beat before there were Beats," said Gore.

During long walks in the Left Bank, Bowles enthused to Gore about the Moroccan boys, how gentle and beautiful they were. Within weeks they were strolling the narrow labyrinthine streets of Tangier as well. "I hadn't seen anything quite so interesting before," Gore recalled. "Queens from around the world gathered there, and I don't mean the royal kind. There were poets and painters and musicians, too. Jane was rather suspicious of my friendship with Paul. They each pursued separate lives; but they were a couple as well."

When Bowles explained that Capote planned to come to Tangier for the summer, Gore cooked up a kind of practical joke. He thought it would be amusing for Capote to step off the boat and see Bowles there with Gore at his side. The Capote-Vidal rivalry had already reached an intensity that made such a joke possible. And it worked. Bowles met Capote at the dock, and Capote looked behind him to see Gore with his hands in his jacket pockets, as if casually in permanent residence. Gore told him, "I plan to spend a few months here," though in fact he intended to stay only a week or so. Capote's face fell "like a soufflé that had been stuck into a freezer," recalls Daniel Rondeau, a French diplomat who happened to be standing next to them.

Although Gore would visit Morocco on several occasions in the future, drawn mostly by his admiration for Bowles, there was something a little too seedy about this French colonial backwater. "Fleas and scorpions make unpleasant bedmates," he said. The vaguely mystical aura of the desert had no allure for him, nor did he like Moroccan boys, despite Bowles's enthusiasm. "They were too dirty," he said. "The country was primitive, without electricity much of the time, bad toilets." He preferred European cities, or the Amalfi coast. That Paul and Jane Bowles lived in what struck Gore as a run-down tenement inspired no desire in him to decamp there for long. Having lived in Guatemala, he had already had enough of remote backwaters.

To his family, Gore seemed lost, and his homosexuality upset his mother, who urged him to seek therapy with a good psychiatrist. When he wrote to say he might actually prefer to live in Europe, she wrote back annoyingly: "It would be a good idea if you put off Europe as long as you can and take advantage of becoming comfortable with yourself—Europe will still be there! We come from pretty tough stock, and you will—with luck—have fifty years more of living with yourself—and those providence puts in your circle—sweetie, you have too much ability to permit letting the ropes be fouled. It is awfully tough on super-sensitive folk like us: I've always wanted the moon, and it is usually cheese, and you are young enough to orient—so DO!" She actually gave him the name of a psychoanalyst and urged him to make an appointment. Typically, Gore ignored her advice, regarding it as merely her selfish attempt to refashion him in ways that might please her. "I needed to get as far away from her as I could," he said.

A peculiar mix-up brought 1949 to a close. "At the end of the year I planned a trip to Ceylon to meet Bowles there—another exotic holiday. But I missed the boat, quite literally. Instead, I went to New Orleans." Furious, Bowles wrote to Gore in February: "What nonsense! Missed the boat, indeed! How was I to know that? I was literally expecting you from one day to the next, put off trips in order to make them with you when you came. I wrote to you in Rome." After a catalogue of his misadventures in the East, he says, "Perhaps it's just as well for your own peace of soul that you stayed in God's country." "But Jane Bowles somehow believed I was in Ceylon with Paul, and I was surprised to read her letters, to see how jealous she had become of our friendship. It rose to the level of an obsession, though there was never anything between us. We just liked each other." In *Palimpsest*, Gore quotes a letter of February 15, 1950, from Jane to Paul: "Now that Gore is with you I suppose you are less lonely and you may even put off your return." Apparently Bowles never bothered to mention that Gore wasn't there.

V. Finding Dutchess County

Gore considered New York an ideal hub for his frenetic activities, and he spent much of the fall of 1949 at the Chelsea Hotel. His association with the ballet world continued through his friendship with Kriza, now a principal at the American Ballet Theatre, and often attended performances. In the mornings he busily corrected galleys of *A Search for the King* and continued to revise *Dark Green, Bright Red*, which Lehmann had expressed interest in publishing after the modest British success of *The City and the Pillar.*

As the midcentury point approached, Gore had reason to feel hopeful about his writing career. *The City and the Pillar*, which had sold almost thirty thousand copies by 1949 and earned Gore about $9,000, had put his name into play as one of the writers of his generation to watch. "But I had much less money than everyone imagined," said Gore. "This meant I had to keep thinking of ways to earn a living." The idea of writing under a pseudonym appealed greatly, as he had the ability to write quickly, and he could master a new (and possibly lucrative) genre—murder mystery or romance—without straining.

With the aid of a Dictaphone, Gore wrote a pulp novel called *A Star's Progress* in the course of an intense week in May 1949. "I thought I'd make a lot of money," he said, "though I was wrong." It was the story of Graziella Serrano, an exotic beauty from Mexico who wishes to become a movie star. She rises through the ranks as a dancer in New Orleans and Hollywood, where she finds stardom as an actress under the name Grace Carter. Soon she is dazzled by one of her co-stars, Eric, a bisexual man with considerable charm. This soon leads to misery for Grace, as it must. Indeed, death follows: as the genre demanded. In 1950, a Grace Carter could not have her cake and eat it. She simply had to die.

This trashy but entertaining and sparkling novel (Gore couldn't write a genuinely bad sentence, even when he tried) appeared under the pseudonym of Katherine Everard—her name taken from the gay baths. "Miss Kitty had a little romp," Gore said, "but she did not amount to much." For many years the existence of Gore-as-Everard was a closely held secret. "A confidante I had at the time was Alice Bouverie, and she thought I should keep Miss Kitty—my pseudonymous lady—alive. But I doubted this." In later years, in fact, he could flatly deny writing this book to innocent inquiries.

Gore adored Bouverie, who would crop up repeatedly in various guises in his later novels: the heiress with a court of admirers around her. She was the only daughter of John Jacob Astor, the wealthy investor, and had recently married her fourth husband, William Pleydell-Bouverie, who was the grandson of an English earl. Twenty-three years older than Gore, she was—like him—something of a diva, and their friendship flourished, as she liked gay men (and often married them). Gore had been introduced to her in the spring of 1949 by one of her former lovers, the dancer and later celebrated choreographer Frederick Ashton.

One weekend Gore joined a party at Rhinebeck, her expansive country house (named after the town itself) in Dutchess County. Among the many guests was Judy Montagu, whom Gore had already met in London. Circles moved within circles, and it was a lively time. Gore experienced for the first time the pretty towns along the Hudson River that had long been attractive to the upper crust of New York. It was also an area associated with FDR, and Eleanor Roosevelt now lived at Hyde Park, the presiding spirit of Dutchess County.

Gore first saw Edgewater—the house he would soon buy—on this visit, taken there by Bouverie. The stately 1820 Greek Federal Revival mansion, with six white columns at the front of a pinkish-brown façade that featured an octagonal library, appealed to him at once. It was in Barrytown, some ten miles from Rhinebeck, overlooking the Hudson. As Gore would write in 1995, in an essay about FDR, this part of the country was rich in historical associations:

> The area entered our American history when the Dutch patroons, centered upon New Amsterdam, began to build neat stone houses north of their island city. Of the Dutch families, the grandest was called Beekman. Then, in war, the Dutch gave way to the English, some of whom were actually gentry though most were not. But the river proved to be a common leveler—or raiser up. The newcomers were headed by one Robert Livingston, who had received from James II the "Livingston Manor" grant that included most of today's Dutchess and Columbia counties. Other wealthy families began to build great houses on the east bank of the river, making sure that their Greek Revival porticoes or mock Gothic towers would make a fine impression on those traveling up or down river.

The house he now coveted was spacious and grand, in a parklike setting. On the downside, it backed onto the main railway line, which lessened its value. And it needed work. "The house had not been looked after properly, which was good for me. It should have been well beyond my reach, but the price was right: $16,000," Gore recalled. To assemble this kind of money, he would have to sell the house in Antigua and scrape for money among his relatives, but at this price the property was hardly out of reach. (He sent petulant letters to Crocker, who was now serving as his agent for the house in Guatemala, asking about rental arrangements. "I should be thrilled from time to time, preferably once a month," he wrote, "to receive a check from the tenants.")

It would take several months to organize the financing of Edgewater, with help mainly from his grandmother (who contributed $6,000, leaving $10,000 to mortgage). Gore had set his mind on this project and had the necessary connections to make it happen. He loved houses, and a grand address with a view was irresistible. A house, for him, was like his soul: an expansive version of himself. He prized the view from Edgewater: the lawn that sloped to the edge of the Hudson (somewhat reminiscent of Merrywood) through a bay of willows, with a small island not far from the shore. He correctly assumed that the money required to fix up Edgewater would come from the sale of the Guatemalan house.

That winter, dreaming of Edgewater, he shifted restlessly about the country, spending several weeks near Williams in Key West—a winter base since 1941 for Williams, who lived not far from the so-called Winter White House, where President Truman found quiet and comfort by the sea. Gore took immediately to the island and found rooms at a boardinghouse, where he set to work on a sequence of stories, hoping he could sell them to major publications for a lot of money. "I knew I had to add some ballast to my bank account," he said. In February 1950, he traveled to New Orleans for Mardi Gras: a good place for sexual cruising and adventure. And he had various contacts in the city, including an old friend from Exeter, who took him on a tour of Mississippi, Gore's grandfather's home state. "The Delta seemed exotic but somehow perfectly natural. I was putting the world together," Gore said, "seeing places my grandparents had known, getting a sense of this patchwork nation, which is really many different countries under a single banner."

Back in New York by April, Gore once again shifted from hotel to hotel, sometimes staying with his father or with friends. His mother, in fact, grew annoyed with him for preferring Gene to herself, although declaring that she "thoroughly understood why"; but she lamented their broken relations, "all the years we could have had closeness and friendship." She added: "Please remember you are quite a steam roller when you want and it really does not get the results you want and really yearn for. I am most sad for you. You are my child and I love you. I know you much better than you think." As he would, Gore angrily dismissed her efforts to play a role she had long ago forfeited.

Yet the nomad life had lost its allure, and he wanted a place of his own, a house equal to his sense of self. This would require lots of money, of course, so he urged Crocker to find a buyer for the Antigua house. "I need this to happen!" he wrote urgently. The feeling of homelessness had grown old, even disconcerting. By midsummer, however, Edgewater was his, and he would not turn twenty-five until the following October. It was a surpassingly grand residence for one so young, but it suited him.

Bouverie liked having her adoring young consort nearby, and helped him furnish the house, rummaging in her attic for lamps, chests of drawers, beds, chairs, and rugs. Gore was settled in by late July, turning the octagonal library into a magnificent study. "When a writer moves into a house that he most wants or needs," he wrote in *Palimpsest*, "the result is often a sudden release of new energy." He thought of Henry James, who in 1897 took possession of Lamb House in Rye, England, where he wrote his magnificent last novels. (Of course, James was fifty-five by the time he occupied a house of his own, and Lamb House was simply leased.)

With James heavily on his mind, Gore acquired the New York Edition of the novels, a set of twenty-four volumes, which he began to read in earnest, and which would become a touchstone for him, showing him possibilities for what might be considered his own mature style. Within fairly short order, he jettisoned the terse masculine style of his earlier novels and began, with some excitement, to move toward a more languorous manner. He also began to read widely in European, especially French, literature. "It was as if my education were beginning. I don't think I'd ever before read so much, in such a concentrated way. I read Montaigne, and began to think about writing essays. I learned that John Jay Chapman, a very good if obscure American essayist, had lived at Edgewater, and I could feel his presence in the house. Two of his essay collections lay at hand, and I began to think about the possibilities of the essay."

Gore began to try his hand at the genre that he would remake in his own image, writing an (unpublished) essay on homosexuality as well as a kind of Platonic dialogue (in imitation of Gide) where he would begin to explore and formulate his ideas on this taboo subject. In essence, he set in motion what would become a lifetime of asserting that there were no homosexuals, only homosexual acts. He would continue to refer to himself as bisexual, and to a degree this may have been true. Yet his primary attachment to men, and to "trade," puts him mainly in the gay camp, however much he protested against such categorizing.

In the midst of this assertion of bisexuality, somewhat ironically but happily indeed, he met the man with whom he would share his life.

VI. Loving Howard

Gore met Howard Austen (then Auster) on Labor Day in 1950, at the Everard Baths. "I liked him a lot, right away," Howard recalled. "Who wouldn't? Gore was handsome, tall, muscular but thin. He had the attitude that's in his books: smarty-pants, knowing. He and I had sex, but it wasn't what attracted us. We could talk to each other. Gore was staying at the Plaza during the week, and we had lunch there the next day. Let me tell you, he looked even better with his clothes on. I never looked back. This was it."

Howard was a carrot-topped Jewish boy from the Bronx. His mother had changed her name to Ann Austen from Hannah Auster: The idea was that a non-Jewish name might play better in the American marketplace, where she was trying for different jobs. His father, Harry Auster, drove a taxi during the day and gambled in the evenings. Howard was an only child for his first twelve years, and then his parents had a daughter, Howard's only sibling. "It was the typical formerly Yiddish working-class stuff," said Howard. "We lived in an apartment in the Bronx, went to the Catskills once in the summer. Otherwise, everybody kept their head down." Gore would later suggest that Ann was right, and that Howard should use the name Austen, not Auster, as he aspired to a career in music. This was a period in American history when Jewish performers often changed their names: Benjamin Kubelsky became Jack Benny, Nathan Birnbaum became George Burns, Bernard Schwartz became Tony Curtis, and Isadore Demsky became Kirk Douglas, for instance.

In junior high, Howard realized he was gay, and he was "quite promiscuous" in high school and beyond: "I made waves, but I rode over the waves." At twenty-one, he worked in a mail room in lower

Manhattan but dreamed of becoming a singer. "Frank Sinatra was my hero," he said. Howard had red hair, lots of freckles, and a barrel chest. A short fellow, he looked up to Gore in every way. But he was not unsophisticated, having worked his way through New York University. For Gore, he was an ideal companion: frank, unpretentious, bright. He knew the streets of New York, and he knew the gay world inside out, being another regular at the Everard Baths. A childlike aspect of Howard appealed to Gore's fatherly instincts, and he would often refer to him as his "child."

Howard's chief role in the relationship was that of the deflating voice. Gore's ego had a tendency to swell like a balloon, and his grandiose side could make him, to the outside world, appear self-regarding, even embarrassingly so. But Howard helped Gore control this. A key memory of their relationship (for me) dates to the late eighties, when Gore and Howard sat after dinner, as usual, in Gore's study in Ravello, overlooking the Amalfi coast. Gore had launched into a soliloquy of some kind, while Howard, behind him, winked at me and began to slide his hand up and down, as if to say: "There he goes, jerking off again." Often Gore would make an outrageous assertion, and it would float in the air for a little while, then Howard would simply say, "Oh, Gore. Stop it. Just stop it!" And Gore would.

"I'm not as smart as Gore," Howard said, "but maybe Gore's not as smart as he thinks he is. Gore lectures, I kibitz." Another time, Howard said, "Nobody knows more than Gore, not even God. That's why Gore's an atheist. He couldn't believe in an inferior God." Howard oscillated between a kind of florid (but genuine) admiration and a jokey deflationary manner. He really loved Gore, who loved him in return.

They both swore that sex quickly became a thing of the past for them as a couple, and this seems largely true. But sexual relations continued for a while. One witness at the time was Marion Holt, a scholarly young man from South Carolina. "I had read *The City and the Pillar* in 1950 and wrote Gore a fan letter. It finally reached him and he answered with an invitation to visit him if I was in New York at any time." It's interesting to read the letter from Gore that arrived within days:

> Letters such as yours are always a pleasure, and a rare one. I have very often the feeling that I am dropping book after book into an abyss (to use Henry James' phrase) and that that is the end of them. Reminders that they were not lost entirely are heartening, and I thank you. I wish that I could at this point say something very wise and memorable, like those postcards Mr. Shaw used to send out, but I'm afraid that I need at least eight thousand words in which to turn around and you would be drowned in the attempt if I tried.

Gore continued at length, answering questions. Holt had asked to meet him, and Gore thought it might be awkward:

> Such meetings make me nervous because I feel usually inadequate to the occasion. The books don't seem very close to me once they're done and I am not much like them as far as I know: writers are usually a severe disappointment. I once was invited to have lunch with Forster down at Cambridge. I admired him enormously; I thought, if only in our attitude toward humanism, we had a great deal in common. To my horror I found a nervous maiden lady who had very nearly forgotten those books composed, most of them, thirty to forty years ago. We lunched on squares of cabbage which squirted jets of tepid water and, after a steamed Lemon Curd Roll, we wandered uneasily about the lovely grounds of Kings College.

As usual, Gore reverted to the role of gracious grandee, despite his youth. Holt recalls: "Gore invited me to visit him in the country, and I spent about five weeks at Edgewater, typing for him. Gore had just met Howard, and I saw them together—so playful, the two of them. They were like kids, wrestling in the grass, swimming in the river, joking, so delighted that they had found each other. After dinner, they would retreat as quickly as possible to Gore's bedroom, where they stayed together. That they had a sexual relationship at that time wasn't in doubt. I was there."

Holt recalled the illustrious visitors who would come and go: "Samuel Barber, John Latouche, and Leo Lerman—important figures in the arts—showed up for weekends. Alice Bouverie played mother hen to Gore and Howard. Gore had quickly gotten to know all sorts of people in the county, and he brought them to the house." Howard had recently moved out of his parents' home in the Bronx, taking a room at the YMCA in Manhattan, but he came out to Edgewater every weekend. For his part, Gore traveled into New York quite often during the week, usually for meetings with editors or friends. "I was amazed by the level of social energy," says Holt.

That Howard now occupied a special place in Gore's life was announced symbolically at Christmas, when he arrived in Washington to visit his mother and Tot with his new partner in tow. Apart from the fact that Nina got wildly drunk, the visit went well. Nina and Tot had by now abandoned the idea that Gore might become heterosexual, and they wanted him to be happy. And Howard could help on that front. Their early correspondence is touching, with Howard looking up to Gore as a kind of benevolent father figure, constantly telling him how handsome and intelligent he was. A typical letter, written on February 10, 1953, when Gore was away on a trip, ends: "I miss you and I love you very very much. I miss you. I love you." As ever, it's signed "Tinker." Often he adopts a babyish tone, as when he writes to "Mr. Me," his pet name for Gore: "A little bird came through the window last night and said, 'Tinkerbell, Mr. Me really wants to write but he's so busy having such a good time, while you have nothing to do, that he's just forgotten all about his Tinkerat. Of course he claims it's all part of the double standard and of course that makes it all right."

Between Gore and Howard there remained, and would always remain, a defining double standard. Gore was the star, and Howard was the suffering servant, the intimate, the counselor in times of need. He would wax the floors and manage household affairs. Gore would keep his invented name to the end, and it would say on his tombstone Gore Vidal, not Eugene L. Vidal. On Howard's gravestone in Rock Creek Park, it would say: Howard Auster. He would take his old name back. But Gore would continue into eternity as a self-created figure. "Is Mr. Me selfish?" asked Howard in this same letter. "No," he writes. "Is Mr. Me nasty? Yes!"

Gore continued to crave the social scene at Rhinebeck, the Bouverie estate. "All the lights in the house lit up when Alice called," Howard said. It helped that she often entertained various English aristocrats, including Osbert and Edith Sitwell, whom Gore would occasionally visit in Britain in later years. "Edith interested me more than her brother," Gore said. "She had long Gothic bones, sharp features. Her nose never stopped lengthening. She drank martinis in large glasses, and when she stood—if she could stand—she seemed to reach the ceiling, she was so tall. We would have lunch in later years at her club in London, where she was queen bee. I read her poetry and liked it, even memorizing bits and pieces, which I could recite to her for effect."

Writers and academics had begun to find the northwest part of Dutchess County appealing, and it was a heady time there, with the novelists Saul Bellow and Ralph Ellison sharing a house for a period near Barrytown. Bellow came to Edgewater in those days, liking Gore's company. Mary McCarthy taught at Bard, which was not far away, and Gore admired her wry, biting humor. There was the poet Ted Weiss, who also taught at Bard and invited Gore to the campus to hear poetry readings and introduced him to the poet Richard Wilbur, who came to visit at Edgewater. Richard Rovere, a political journalist, lived in Rhinebeck, and he and Gore quickly became friends, as did F. W. Dupee (known as Fred), a genteel and erudite professor of English at Columbia University who commuted into the city from a house near Edgewater. "Fred had written on Henry James, and he had read everything worth reading," said Gore. "Nobody else could talk about literature in quite the same way, with such passion and clarity. He had been a Marxist in the thirties, a fan of Trotsky, but that had settled into a clear-eyed humanism, somewhat apolitical, very shrewd. He edited *The Partisan Review* for a period when it was actually readable—not a long period."

"I'd never seen anything like this," Howard said. "Gore put on a banquet of the gods, and I got to listen."

The years at Edgewater, Gore's "seat" through the fifties and sixties (he sold the house in 1969), might be considered his prime time. He read and talked about books and ideas with a handful of the finest minds in America and Britain, and his table was "a place where lively talk and interesting ideas flowed," according to Jason Epstein, his friend and future editor, who once arrived at Edgewater on his motor launch. Despite an intense social life, Gore usually wrote in the morning for at least three hours, producing a shelf of novels, plays, essays, and television and film scripts during this busy and productive period. But it was with *The Judgment of Paris* that he began to find his true voice as a novelist.

Beverly Hills Blues

"Take me to the Beverly Hills Hotel," says Gore. "We'll have dinner in the Polo Lounge."

We've been driving around this famous suburb, not far from Gore's house in the Hollywood Hills. He asks me to stop in front of some mansion: tall palm trees, an immense, well-manicured garden, fountains. "Rock Hudson took me to a party at this house, in the fifties. I got a blow job from some young actor, not Rock, behind the most beautiful flowering bush in the world, under a spray of stars. Hollywood stars."

He seems wistful today. We park at the hotel, walk behind the main building where the bungalows huddle under palms. "My horrible mother lived in one of these. She was having an affair with this or that leading man. Clark Gable was among them. I don't know where she got the money. But she always knew where to find it. It was her great gift in life, apart from holding her liquor. No amount of alcohol toppled her. Then again, it wasn't hard to topple her into bed, if that's what you wanted."

Sitting by the pool, Gore orders a cocktail. "I rarely drink cocktails, as they make me sick. But here, it's different. The years fall away. I came here after the war. Mother introduced me to Jules Stein, who owned Hollywood in those days. He got me passes to all the lots. I met stars and more stars. I understood, from Jules, that there was money in these Beverly Hills, and that I should learn to write scripts. So I did. Very carefully I read scripts and saw what had to be done.

Not much, as it turned out. Good dialogue, movement, some plot. Not too much plot. It's been the death of films, all of this plotting."

At the Polo Lounge, the head waiter knows Gore by name. He bows and scrapes. "I've been eating here for half a century," Gore says. "I like the formality. They once kicked out Marlene Dietrich, who dared to step into the room in pants. Women didn't wear pants in those days. Her partner was Hemingway that night. He was probably wearing a skirt. You know Hem. Boys will be girls."

He sips another cocktail, a sidecar. It's something Howard likes to make. "I shouldn't be drinking this," he says, then tells me that the Watergate scandal started here, with a call from G. Gordon Liddy to Jeb Magruder, a ranking officer on the Committee to Re-Elect the President. "I associate this room with Nixon's downfall, so it makes me happy. On the other hand, my mother ate over there." He points to a corner table. "It was always empty when she was around. It was her table."

Gore doesn't seem happy, and I ask what's wrong. "I get the blues here. I don't know why. Something about the history, my history. Or American history. Isn't that enough to make anyone sad?"

Chapter Four

A narcissist is someone better-looking than you are.

—Gore Vidal

1. Detecting Life

In 1952, Gore published two radically different novels, both of which involve the act of detection: *The Judgment of Paris* and *Death in the Fifth Position* (the latter using his pen name Edgar Box, a clever pseudonym that pays homage to Edgar Allan Poe, the American inventor of detective fiction, not the English writer Edgar Wallace, as his editor Victor Weybright imagined). In the former, he found a voice that felt very true to himself. "It was the first time I heard myself as myself," he said. The hero at the center of this mythic narrative is Philip Warren, a wry young man of twenty-eight who seems a bit lost, more bemused than dismayed by his lack of worldly success. A veteran of the Pacific war, he had graduated from Harvard Law School; he is heterosexual, with a variety of paths opening before him. The three sections of the novel correspond (roughly) to the three choices that the Greek god Hermes offered to Paris. He could choose among three goddesses: Hera (representing worldly power), Athena (representing wisdom as well as the skills of a warrior), and Aphrodite (representing love). But the mythic dimension is deceptive, as Philip learns; there are really no choices, only the illusion of choices. That is, each choice plays to a certain self-conception, but none of them has the energy to activate a life or inform its true contours.

The novel involves a journey, a *Wanderjahr* in which Gore's hero migrates from Italy to Egypt to France. "He was here at last: Italy, Europe, a year of leisure, a time for decision, a prelude to the distinguished fugue his life was sure to be, once he got really to it, once the delightful prelude had been played to its conclusion among the foreign cities." We're at once in the hands of a knowing, worldly, chatty narrator: a successor to such English novelists as Laurence Sterne, Henry Fielding, or, more recently, Aldous Huxley. (As Gore noted: "It was Huxley, in fact, who got me moving in certain directions: *Crome Yellow* and *Antic Hay*, the earliest and best of his books. These were novels of 'types,' lightly satirized, always part of a larger fugue of ideas.")

In Rome, Regina Durham dangles before Philip's gaze the possibility of a career in politics: a choice that had been set before Gore by his family. She is a power broker who wants his body as well as the pleasure of stage-managing his career. In Egypt he meets Sophia Oliver, representing wisdom (as in the Greek roots of her name). She issues the call to intellect: here lies the "real" life, the life of the mind. But in Cairo Philip meets Anna Morris, the wife of a businessman; he finds her irresistible, and follows her to Paris, choosing love over power and wisdom. But this proves a false choice, as he comes to see. In the last paragraph of the novel, Philip looks at her smile and sees "the silver mirror dissolve before his eyes." The narcissistic image that she offers is broken, and he looks beyond her to "a promise at the present's farthest edge."

The plot, however, is little more than a shelf upon which the author will stack his many insights, his caricatures of various types, his lovingly rendered scenes of European life. Philip indeed is not a double for Gore. He is far too innocent, naïve, and easily led. He gazes wide-eyed at the various figures who loom before him, as in a dream, including a couple of gay dilettantes in Rome who want to restore the old monarchy: a parody of certain themes in Gothic fiction. Philip at one point carries a secret for his friends—the message is a single word in Greek: *asebia*, a term that connotes an inability to worship the gods. None of the choices that lay before his hero (or Gore himself, for that matter) proved truly satisfying.

Among the vivid minor characters in *The Judgment of Paris* is Mrs. Fay Peabody, a "famous mystery-story writer" based on Agatha Christie, whom she of course derides. She tries to bring her novelistic inventiveness to "real life," conjuring various plots to murder a poor fellow called Briggs Willys, who lacks the competence required to commit suicide, his only goal. "I came to Egypt to die," he explains. "I was afraid I wouldn't have the courage to kill myself so I decided to come up the Nile to the hottest town with a decent hotel and there, if I failed to kill myself, I should die of the heat."

The final section of the novel is set (as promised by the title) in Paris. Any number of outlandish subplots erupt, one of them involving a bizarre cult dedicated to the idea of the androgyne—a notion that would, in the late sixties, erupt in the gender-bending figure of Myra/Myron Breckinridge. Another plotline centers on Zoe Helotius, a crass socialite with designs on the House of Windsor. Elsewhere in the book, three characters from Gore's earlier novels—Robert Holton, Jim Willard, and Charles de Cluny—spin across the pages in a parody of William Faulkner's sage style, in which characters introduced in previous novels or stories show up in later ones. One reads in vain hoping for a firm sense of resolution, which seems to elude Gore's protagonist, who remains a cipher. But Gore had begun to find a real voice, and the novel has vivid passages that reveal a world of wan sophistication. Here was a young writer who had seen a great deal and could suggest as much.

The Judgment of Paris sold nearly ten thousand copies, attracting decent reviews, including a mostly positive one by John W. Aldridge in *The New York Times Book Review*. Much to Gore's fury, Aldridge compared him unfavorably to Truman Capote, regarding Capote as a young writer who arrived on the scene "with a subject and a manner distinctly his own." Gore, by contrast, he saw as someone throwing "badly balanced darts" at a moving target, trying desperately to find a subject and a voice. To a degree, Aldridge was right: Gore had been searching without obvious success for a subject and a manner, working in an obliquely autobiographical vein, although Philip Warren is certainly not Gore—he is too feckless, and the world pushes him around, leads him this way and that. If he finally chooses love in Anna, as Aldridge mistakenly imagines, this is not much. In creating Philip, Gore was exploring the difficulties of selfhood, contemplating the lack of emotional and psychological coherence in a world that looks and feels more like a fun house, or a hall of mirrors, than a place where anyone could establish a firm identity. And Philip seems, ultimately, like a narcissist: a young man (like the author) in desperate need of reflection.

In a letter to a friend, Norman Mailer writes interestingly about Gore's "narcissism" in relation to this novel: "When I implied that Gore's worst vice as a writer might be narcissism I was not talking about homosexuality. He has written very well about that particular subject, modestly, soberly and with instinctive good taste." He noted that it was "precisely in his more ambitious books like *The Judgment of Paris*, some of which I did read and did like, that this narcissism is most present and most defeating to the potential reach of his talents which are considerable. The difficulty of writing in a narcissistic vein is that one's heroes are hermetically sealed in upon themselves. They may rant, rage and roar, or stand aside burnishing their wit, but either way nothing dramatic passes between them and other persons in the novel. The result is inevitably a study of lonely decomposition."

The charge of narcissism would dog Gore (and his fictional protagonists) for decades to come, though he always denied the charge as unworthy of consideration. "A narcissist is someone better-looking than you are," he famously said. But the young Philip does, more or less, evoke the young Gore in his search for identity, his difficulty in making choices.

In an effort to market his work, Gore traveled about the country, giving lectures and readings, although this aspect of the literary life never appealed to him. "Gore's reputation was beginning to expand in academic circles," said Richard Poirier, a literary scholar who met Gore in the early fifties when he came to lecture at Williams College. "But he never actually liked colleges or universities, and they didn't like him back. As an autodidact, he didn't approve of those who didn't fit that mold." It was obvious to Poirier and others who met Gore that he didn't admire or wish to emulate those novelists who were adored in the academic village, such as William Faulkner or, in later years, Thomas Pynchon, Toni Morrison, or Don DeLillo. "Gore kept his eye on New York, on Broadway, on Hollywood—always looking for what he believed was the main chance," Poirier noted. "He didn't especially like being among 'teachers,' as he called us."

In truth, Gore also moved uncomfortably among his fellow writers, especially when he felt competitive with them. His chief rivals among the younger novelists and story writers were Capote, Mailer, and William Styron, none of whom he liked. In each case, the feeling was mutual. In a letter of 1953, Styron called Gore "a talentless, self-promoting, spineless snob." As for Mailer, his biographer J. Michael Lennon writes: "The two met at Millie Brower's apartment on East 27th Street in 1952. In slightly different ways, they both recalled that at their first meeting Vidal was eager to know at what age Mailer's grandparents had died. Mailer said around seventy. Vidal announced that his grandparents had died much older and, therefore, he told Mailer, 'I've got you.' He went on, saying that the one who lived the longest would have the best purchase on literary fame. Brower remembered that Mailer told her that Vidal was 'gornisht,' the Yiddish word for nothing."

On August 23, 1953, Gore got a call from Jack Kerouac, a good-looking young writer he had first met at the Metropolitan Opera in 1949, soon after *The City and the Pillar* had appeared. Kerouac (soon to write *On the Road*) was not yet the heroic rebel-novelist of the Beat generation, a literary movement that never much interested Gore, though he knew many of the key figures in this group fairly well. Kerouac had recently finished his first, highly autobiographical novel, *The Town and the City*, which was yet to be published. "This time," Gore recalled, "he asked me to meet him with Bill Burroughs. It was a hot night, with the air thick and smoky. We met at a bar, the San Remo, in the Village. He reminded me of the young Brando in a T-shirt. Burroughs wore a wrinkled suit, and he seemed drunk or drugged. You expected that. Kerouac was drunk, too. He flirted the whole time, and Burroughs left us alone after a while. We checked into the Chelsea Hotel, where I often stayed, and spent the night in an uncomfortable, damp bed. I think I got a blow job. It wasn't memorable. Certainly Jack had a terrible hangover in the morning."

Perhaps the most affable of Gore's allies among writers was Louis Auchincloss, a relative of Hughdie's and therefore, in Gore's mind, somehow a "cousin." "Of all our novelists," Gore wrote, "Auchincloss is the only one who tells us how our rulers behave in their banks and their boardrooms, their law offices and their clubs." Revealing a snobbery inherited from his mother, Gore recalled: "My cousin became my lawyer. I trusted him. He had a fine intellect, a real understanding of the way money works. We talked about books, writers, about politics, New York. He was an heir of Edith Wharton and Henry James, and he knew it. Only the dumb-dumb public didn't know it."

Gore had made a fair amount of money as a young writer, but not enough to live as grandly as he wished. At the suggestion of his publishing friend Victor Weybright, he wrote a mystery novel "in perhaps a week or two." He dictated the first draft, then revised a typed version with care. The book was *Death in the Fifth Position*, and it proved entertaining. "I had read Agatha Christie, S. S. Van Dine, John Dickson Carr, and Edgar Wallace. The genre made sense," he said, "in that all you had to do was establish a particular world, create some disequilibrium, and take it from there."

As a writer, Gore invariably drew on material that interested him, and ballet had been much on his mind in recent years. So the scene of the murder—murders, in this case—is a ballet troupe. They occur onstage, as well they should. The hero in this novel, and in all three mysteries by Gore under the name of Edgar Box, is Peter Cutler Sargeant II, a Harvard man (like Philip Warren) and heterosexual sleuth who makes his living in public relations. Much like in the novels of Christie, the police pursue various red herrings, having no real gift for solving crimes; so Sargeant outwits them, though it's not hard to manage this. An ex-journalist, Sargeant also gets to report on the crimes in the *New York Globe*.

The author's wit comes through repeatedly, as when a ballerina plunges to her death onstage while maintaining "the fifth position," a ballet pose. Vidal writes that she was "a dedicated artist to the very end." Another important feature of this first Box novel is the portrait of Louis Giraud, based partly on Harold Lang, Gore's recent lover. Gore portrays Giraud as a sexually voracious gay man: quite "advanced" for 1952, when the general public had very little sense of the gay underworld. Perhaps the aesthetic weakness of this novel, not unlike the others in this series, hinges on the fact that satire upstages intrigue at every point. Gore didn't quite adhere to the models before him, and this was genre fiction.

Sargeant may well represent Gore's ideal version of himself at this age. Although he didn't go to Harvard, many of his characters did, and Gore would ultimately leave his entire estate to Harvard in a sign that he valued this gold standard for American intellectual achievement. In the three Box novels that Gore wrote for New American Library (without ever revealing his name to readers), Sargeant sounds very like Gore: witty and clear-eyed, a cool customer. One can read these books as campy sexual farces, with Gore wearing a disguise (heterosexual sleuth) that is almost a kind of reverse drag. Indeed, Sargeant at one point resists the sexual advances of Giraud, though he wonders if there is much difference between sleeping with men and women. "It's all very confusing," Sargeant notes.

While this novel and its successors, which followed in short order in 1953 and 1954, didn't make Gore a lot of money, they added something to the coffers. "I got an advance of $1,000 for *Death in the Fifth Position*. Bits and pieces of income arrived, and I could meet my mortgage, but it wasn't easy in these years. I kept trying to think how I could 'solve' the problem of money," he said. At the same time, Howard kept trying to get a better job in New York, hoping to contribute to household expenses. He found a job at an ad agency—Batten, Barton, Durstine and Osborne—a respectable firm, but the position didn't pay much, and Howard lost interest. "Gore made money, more than I could, in any case, and he needed my help with everything," Howard said. "It just wasn't worth it, after a while, to trudge into Manhattan."

But Howard had become indispensable in another way. Whereas Gore remained awkward in company, Howard showed an easy affability. "He could get people laughing and joking," remembers George Armstrong, "and Gore understood how useful this was." Howard's warmth proved especially useful on long weekends at Edgewater, when visitors arrived with expectations and needs. In general, Howard had a practical side that would save Gore a great deal of time in years to come; he could order plane tickets, make reservations at restaurants, call taxis, ensure that supplies were delivered to Edgewater, hire and fire cleaning ladies and gardeners. He knew how to mix drinks, specializing in ice-cold sidecars. He saw to it that guests found clean sheets and towels in their bedrooms upon arrival. Local plumbers and carpenters came to know him, and he sorted out what had to be done: windows replaced or frames painted, a step on the porch mended, a section of the roof retiled. He assumed these duties without having to be asked.

But Gore went away by himself to Key West in the coldest months, once with his grandmother. One day just off Duval Street, in a hamburger joint, he met a slender young woman, a waitress, with whom he spent a couple of weeks "in the sack," as he put it. "She claimed that I had knocked her up. It was possible. She asked for money for an abortion," and so Gore provided it: $780, sent via a money order from New York that could not easily be traced. "I was never cut out for fatherhood," Gore said. On this matter, Howard suggested that "the whole thing was a scam. She was never pregnant. Gore bought her a new Frigidaire." This episode suggests, of course, that Gore still felt uncertain about his sexual identity, or at least determined to tell himself that he was bisexual. If he could impregnate this young woman, he must be!

Gore so liked working on the original Box novel that he dashed off another in the spring of 1953. *Death Before Bedtime* centered on the mysterious death of a senator, which Sargeant helps to solve. Only a year later came *Death Likes It Hot*, which again features the debonair Sargeant, who helps to solve a murder that occurs at a summer party filled with New York socialites. Indeed, Gore often spent time in the Hamptons in the summer, and in 1953 he spent a long weekend with Francis Markoe, whom he described as "an old-fashioned queen who produced plays on his lawn. People sat on blankets and watched them and swatted mosquitoes." One of these lawn dramas was by

Vance Bourjaily, a well-known novelist and creative-writing professor at the University of Iowa. It concerned a visitor from outer space, and it planted in Gore's head the idea for *Visit to a Small Planet*, his first Broadway hit, which was based on his own teleplay by the same name.

The need for money pressed on him, however, as Edgewater proved very expensive to maintain. His pulp novels from this era—all paperback originals—included one called *Thieves Fall Out* written under the pseudonym of Cameron Kay (Kay was his grandmother's maiden name, and Cameron Kay was, indeed, Gore's great-uncle, an attorney general in Texas). This vein of writing never earned enough to ease Gore's way in the world, however. And he was already working on *Messiah*, a dystopian satire on religion. But it grew clear to him that pseudonymous novels, however amusing to write, would not "solve" the problem of his finances. Playwriting and screenwriting seemed the obvious move. As he later remarked, "I am a novelist turned temporary adventurer; and I chose to write television, movies and plays for much the same reason that Henry Morgan selected the Spanish Main for his peculiar—and not dissimilar—sphere of operations."

II. The Spanish Main

It's not that Gore hadn't already tried to write a play. *The Different Journey* was written in Egypt and revised in Paris, with input from Tennessee Williams. It centered on a young gay man at a loss to make his way. Most who read it thought the homosexual theme made it difficult to produce in New York. But Gore persisted, trying to get Audrey Wood, Tennessee's agent, to support the project. She and Gore corresponded for several years, and she encouraged him to keep trying. "Ideally you need that ugly word a 'dramatist collaborator,'" she told him. With the right kind of assistance, she thought he might fashion a workable play. She added that, given the "depressed book market," he might think of drama as a way of adding to his income. Wood never managed to place anything of Gore's on the stage, however, so he turned to television, having been advised by his mother's old friend

Jules Stein that this new medium would soon blossom into a major industry. At Stein's suggestion, Gore called on Harold Franklin, an agent at the respected William Morris Agency.

Franklin introduced him to Florence Britton, who was looking for stories for *Studio One*, an early CBS program of original live dramas. Gore pitched *Dark Possession*, a Jekyll-and-Hyde concoction about a woman with a split personality who murders her husband but doesn't know it until her notes are revealed to her, at which point she commits suicide. Britton commissioned the piece, and Gore wrote it—as ever, quickly. It aired nationally on February 15, 1954, on what was then a major venue, with millions of viewers. At twenty-eight, Gore had finally found a large audience, and he would never turn back.

This was the so-called golden age of television, with only three networks—CBS, NBC, and ABC—controlling what the public could watch. The growth of the medium over only a few years was staggering. Well over half of American households had a television set by 1954, and the audience grew terrifically month by month. Live drama became an important feature of network programming, complementing an array of game and variety shows, westerns, and soap operas. It was obvious to corporations that TV offered a captive audience for promoting their products, so the race was on for appealing content.

The television industry was based in New York, where empty warehouses suddenly transformed into full production studios for live drama. With millions ready to watch, the networks swung into action, and such programs as *Studio One*, *Kraft Television Theatre*, and *Playhouse 90* became staples of American television, offering original dramas. According to the cultural critic Neil Postman, "between the years 1948 and 1958, approximately 1,500 fifty-two-minute plays were performed 'live' on American television." It really was a new gold rush, and after the success of *Dark Possession*, Gore found himself in demand as a writer for the booming medium.

Many of these were adaptations, starting with Royall Tyler's *The Contrast*, a late-eighteenth-century play by an American imitator of the British Restoration drama. Other assignments followed, including two episodes of *The Telltale Clue*, a police drama. Gore worked on several projects that had been long-running obsessions, including a teleplay about Billy the Kid, the legendary rogue who remained loyal to friends and insisted on his own freedom at any cost. (Gore had admired Aaron Copland's magical *Billy the Kid*, commissioned in 1938 by Lincoln Kirstein for Ballet Caravan and choreographed by Eugene Loring.) Gore's script, in different versions, would continue to hold his interest over many decades. He also adapted a couple of famous stories by William Faulkner—"Smoke" and "Barn Burning"—for Martin Manulis, a director at CBS who became a close friend.

Gore's facility was exactly what the TV market required, and he found he could complete an adaptation over a long weekend; an original hour-length drama would occupy him for a week or ten days. He adapted *The Turn of the Screw* by Henry James and Stephen Crane's "The Blue Hotel"—both classic stories he had long admired. He wrote *Summer Pavilion*, a melodrama about a Southern family that was reminiscent of Tennessee Williams, though without the rhetorical flourishes. Soon Gore's name appeared on the A-list of television dramatists beside writers like Rod Serling, Paddy Chayefsky, and Horton Foote.

The money—he earned $7,000 from television work in 1954—helped to oil the machinery of his life, though it was hardly a fortune. Once again, however, the promise of riches outstripped the reality. He confessed to Pat Crocker: "I have developed an insatiable love of money in the last four years as a result largely of keeping that huge house going. I always thought I was beyond such things because I was not competent in money matters. I have now discovered that I love money but am still incompetent." Nevertheless, the work he was doing in television opened doors while adding to his bank account. "I am king of television," he bragged to Crocker, who still lived in Antigua and hadn't caught up with the new technology. "Television is a thing which has happened since your last visit to this cultural paradise we call America," he said, adding: "I myself did a dozen plays this year, adapting Faulkner, Sophocles, H. James and some original plays of my own spurious invention. I drift enigmatically through rehearsal halls; I undercut my directors; I am treacherous in all things; I sign contracts

I have no intention of fulfilling; I give dishonorable and incoherent interviews to the press." This was not, it seemed, the happiest occupation for a man who preferred the freedom of writing novels.

"There was a lot of busyness during those television years," Gore recalled. And he often neglected his family, even his beloved grandmother, Tot, who complained to him on April 15, 1954: "My dear Mr. Vidal: I used to have a very dear grandson by your name. I have been wondering if you might know him and see him some time, if you should please tell him I should like very much to hear from him." Gore paid a quick call on Tot in response, of course, but his mind was elsewhere. He had the scent of glory in his nostrils, and he was on the move, hunting for fame and fortune in whatever forms they might take.

III. Media as Messages

"Never lose an opportunity to have sex or be on television," Gore famously quipped, always following his own advice. Encouraged by the success of his TV plays, Gore proposed a special program—narrated by himself—about his grandfather. It had been conceived as something for *Playhouse 90*, a kind of biopic, with Gore acting in a role like that of the Stage Manager in *Our Town*. The project stalled, however, while Gore shifted among producers, eventually getting a shortened version of *The Indestructible Mr. Gore* on NBC's *Sunday Showcase* aired on December 13, 1959. William Shatner played Senator Gore, with Gore as the on-screen narrator: "I'm Gore Vidal," he began, "and this is the town of Corsicana, Texas, in the year 1892." The handsome, baritone-voiced author soon became a familiar face on American television, seen on talk shows hosted by Jack Paar, David Susskind, Les Crane, and Steve Allen, even on popular game shows, such as *What's My Line?* "You've got to keep popping up, out of the rabbit hole, in different places. It's the only way," Gore said. By 1960, after three years of incessant popping up out of various holes, Richard H. Rovere could write in *The New Yorker*: "Nothing is easier nowadays than to get a feeling of being entirely surrounded by Gore Vidal."

Rovere added: "Stay at home at night, and like as not you'll be assailed by Mr. Vidal on television."

It's easy to overestimate how often Gore got his face on the small screen, but in those days—with only three networks—any appearance got more attention than is possible now, with countless channels pushing content around the world. Gore Vidal became a name to reckon with in the mid-fifties, as he grew into his fame, combining work on Broadway with TV plays as well as incidental appearances here and there. In addition, he kept at work on his novel-writing, although with less compulsiveness.

In the meantime, his novel *Messiah* appeared in 1954, attracting a small but devoted readership. Thomas Powers, a friend of Gore's from Rome in the 1960s, recalled, "I was maybe fifteen or sixteen when that came out. I read it not once but three or four times. I kept going back to it. What an astonishing book, and really one of the best things Gore ever wrote." It was, in fact, a kind of prologue to one of his finest novels, *Julian* (1964)—the two novels are best read in tandem. "That early novel was an attack on the church, not on the teachings of Jesus," Gore said. "One can't displace the ethical teaching of Christianity. They are rarely followed, of course. Turning the other cheek has never been a popular notion." Like his later hero, the apostate Roman emperor Julian, Gore's narrator in *Messiah* is yet another version of himself: Eugene Luther (as in his "real" name: Eugene Luther Gore Vidal). And Luther's complicity in helping to create the new religion of Cavism (perhaps a play on Calvinism, a severe sixteenth-century version of Protestantism) is central to this novel-as-memoir.

A mortician by training, John Cave is a latter-day Christ figure. His characterization combines features of the Los Angeles evangelist Aimee Semple McPherson (1890–1944) with Evelyn Waugh's 1948 novel *The Loved One*, a satire on the California funeral industry. A visionary and born salesman, Cave is destined to unite his occupation and preoccupation. He has discerned a great truth: death trumps life. In a decade devoted to the fear of death (with bomb shelters being built at a rapid speed around the country) and hooked on TV evangelism, what better way to satirize the moment than to create a lurid version of Christianity, one that celebrates not resurrection but death?

In later years, Gore often suggested that Catholic homes should ditch their pictures of Christ on the cross and hang in their place paintings of the Resurrection. This is helpful in thinking about Cavism, a pseudo-religion that leads to the ultimate act of obedience: suicide. (Indeed, Cavism anticipates any number of cults, such as the group suicide in Guyana in 1978 led by Jim Jones, a charismatic if diabolical preacher.)

In *Messiah*, Gore doesn't so much dismiss Christianity as explore its misuses, which are largely institutional. The novel offers an anatomy of cultic imperialism and its propagandists. In this case, the religion is spread by Paul Himmell (a parody of the Apostle Paul, a man despised by Gore), who knows how to maximize the effects of television appearances by Cave and promote Cavesword, the authorized "Bible" of the new religion Cavesway. And who understood the use of television for self-promotion better than Gore Vidal? An impishness shimmers through this novel, as when Luther meets with Paul to discuss his assignment to write the official Testament of Cavism: "I faced the efficient vulgarity of Paul Himmell across the portable bar which reflected so brightly in its crystal his competence."

Cave knows far too much about this history of the religion founded in his name, so Himmell kills him. Luther—a writer who stands in coyly for Gore—is forced to disappear into Egypt, where he hopes to resume writing his book about Julian the Apostate, the emperor who renounced Christianity and briefly restored the old gods. And Luther has much to hide from, as the fanatical votaries of Cave (having killed the messiah himself) wish to control the meaning of their religion without fear of exposure. Luther's contribution to Cavesword must not be revealed, lest it shake the foundations and trouble the faithful. The final version of the Testament must be orthodox truth, with earlier versions eradicated, as contradictions will only confuse true believers. Heretics need reprogramming, of course. That this new faith depends on confession as a kind of near-sacrament parodies Christianity, which soon after the death of Jesus began to struggle toward its own orthodoxy, with Paul winning the argument on many grounds, and with competing strains of Christianity (such as the Jerusalem group led by James, the brother of Jesus, and Peter) suppressed.

This is a genuine novel of ideas, at once recalling visionary religious figures such as Joseph Smith and L. Ron Hubbard (whose *Dianetics* hit the bookshelves only four years before Gore's novel appeared) but also anticipating Jim Jones, David Koresh, and a range of future "messiahs." It seems prescient in its understanding of the media, and how the manipulations by quasi-religious figures would figure importantly in American culture. Before Marshall McLuhan, Gore understood that "the medium is the message."

Messiah received only brief, though fairly kind, notices, as in the *Saturday Review*, where Jerome Stone noted that "the prolific Mr. Vidal writes with a facility and an easy authority unusual in one so young." The book dropped into a generic niche in paperback format as a "sci-fi" novel and—except among a small coterie of fans—disappeared. One feels Gore's sense of despair and self-doubt in a letter he wrote to Crocker just after the novel's publication: "*Messiah* is rather a bore," he told him. But *Messiah* pointed a way forward in many directions, to *Julian* and *Kalki* (1978) and other future works, such as *Live from Golgotha*, published thirty-eight years later. Any number of false, even half-baked, messiahs would appear in Gore's novels, plays, and screenplays in years to come, and he would continue to ponder the use and misuse of religion, the production of messiah figures, and their amplifications by the media.

IV. Silvery Screens

The failure of *Messiah* to reach an especially wide audience—it sold the usual ten thousand copies—upset Gore. "I thought I'd done something unusual," he said, "and that readers would find me." He noted that here and there enthusiasm had flared, as in *The Boston Globe*, where Lucien Price, an Exeter graduate, recommended the novel highly. Price saw that Gore had managed to put his finger on a key problem with America, where the mainstream media pushed their vision of a Christian, anti-Communist utopia. To Kimon Friar, Gore wrote that the book had been "a noble failure," but the novel as a genre remained the most prestigious and arguably influential form of human expression in the mid-twentieth century, and Gore would never abandon it. He regarded playwriting as simply a form of cleverness, a craft one developed. In "Writing Plays for Television," an autobiographical essay, Gore mused: "A novel is all one's own, a world fashioned by a single intelligence, its reality in no way dependent upon the collective excellence of others." But he also understood that, with the dwindling of fiction as a cultural medium, he had no choice if he didn't want to teach or get a nine-to-five job in the corporate world: He had to keep writing for television and Broadway.

At this point Gore's career as a screenwriter began in earnest. He had overseen the production in New York of *The Death of Billy the Kid*, his most accomplished teleplay, for NBC's *Philco Television Playhouse*, one of the premier venues for live drama. Billy's independence, as well as his ruthless qualities, appealed to Gore, and he wanted to make a full-length movie from the story. As sometimes happens, the pieces fell together suddenly, and it was fortunate that Robert Mulligan, the director, opted for young Paul Newman to play Billy.

"I was just getting into my life as an actor, on the stage, in films," Newman recalled. "Gore seemed so alive, so funny. He was always pushing things as far as they would go. We were friends within days, and we never let go of that." A small, intense, blue-eyed young man, Newman looked very like Jimmie Trimble, with an astounding (and vaguely feminine) beauty. Newman appealed to Gore at once. "To be frank, Gore loved him," Howard said. "He was Gore's type: all boy." Newman had come from Ohio, the son of a Jewish businessman (his father owned a sporting goods store). Like Gore and Jimmie, he had served in the Pacific theater during the war. But he graduated from Kenyon College and attended Yale for a year before going to New York to study at the Actors Studio under the legendary instructor Lee Strasberg (the pioneer of so-called method acting). With his good looks and raw talent, Newman made a quick success on Broadway in 1953 in William Inge's *Picnic*, followed by a role in Joseph Hayes's hostage melodrama, *The Desperate Hours*.

Newman moved to Hollywood to act in a second-rate epic set in Jerusalem and Rome at the time of Christ, *The Silver Chalice* (1954), his first major film; while there, he lived for a period at the legendary

Chateau Marmont on Sunset Boulevard. Gore was beginning to get regular work from MGM at this time, and he also took a room at the Marmont. Howard soon followed, and so did Joanne Woodward, Newman's girlfriend, who had been an understudy for *Picnic*. "We got along so well," recalled Howard, "almost like a family. Those were beautiful days, though everybody drank too much." In 1973, Gore would write: "I knew Joanne since television's self-proclaimed Golden Age, when she acted and I wrote. I watched the Hollywood studio system try to change her into a standard blonde sex symbol; and the Hollywood studio system was the first to collapse. Joanne survived as herself, which is whatever a given role requires." The rumor, long circulated, that Gore and Joanne were at one time engaged remains, as Gore said, "a piece of fiction."

Money began to flow, and Gore soon had a contract with MGM to adapt *The Catered Affair*, a teleplay by Paddy Chayefsky—the hugely admired TV writer in New York—for the silver screen at a salary of $2,000 per week. He also received $2,500 for the film rights to his teleplay about Billy the Kid. "I was determined," said Gore, "to make as much money as quickly as I could, and to put money concerns behind me."

Occasionally Gore found himself at the writers' table in Culver City. In essays and interviews, he recalled being surrounded by any number of "hacks" as well as Christopher Isherwood, Aldous Huxley, and others. There was, of course, a tradition of well-established novelists working for the studios to support their writing habits. Scott Fitzgerald and William Faulkner spent a good deal of time in Hollywood. And Gore didn't really disdain this work, agreeing with the Wise Hack (a kind of composite figure based on many journeymen screenwriters that Gore met) who said to him one day, "Shit has its own integrity." Before long, Gore was offered a permanent contract with MGM, one that required him to be "in residence" for four months a year; the rest of the time he could live wherever he chose, which of course would be Edgewater. According to this new contract, he would make $2,000 a week, increasing to $2,750 by 1959. This was well over $100,000 per year—an impressive sum in the fifties.

Howard recalled: "We would meet Paul and Joanne at the pool, and we'd run into all sorts of Hollywood people, hangers-on, stars, producers. We got invited to parties. It was such a creepy place, the Marmont. A run-down fake château, but perfect, too. We liked it there. After a while we moved up into Laurel Canyon, not far away, overlooking the city. What a view!"

"Gore liked the sexual possibilities in Hollywood," says Scotty Bowers, his pimp, who acted as a go-between among homosexual celebrities. "I remember meeting him after the war. He drove into the gas station where I worked in his '47 Chevy. He was very handsome, very kind. Word had got around that I could make introductions, and I introduced him to all sorts of stars, and lots of ordinary guys. He'd hook up for a night or two. He was always a gentleman, didn't want much. He slept with Rock Hudson, Tyrone Power, Charles Laughton, Fred Astaire, and other actors. This was a lively time for everybody, and nobody thought much about it. Gore liked clean-cut guys best. Guys like Paul Newman, only Newman wasn't gay. But that was the look he preferred. Sailors were perfect. And he never liked guys too young. His perfect boy was about twenty or twenty-two, crew cut, strong." Gore and Bowers became lifelong friends. "Scotty was always someone I could trust," Gore said. "And he didn't lie. He was a truth-teller. I admired that in him."

Meanwhile, opportunities for writing teleplays kept coming. Gore had adapted his first Edgar Box novel into *Portrait of a Ballerina*, which CBS broadcast on New Year's Day in 1956. There seemed to be no end of such work, and he and Howard decided to lease a spacious apartment in New York on East Fifty-Fifth Street, since Gore often had to meet producers and agents. In addition to the teleplays, Gore worked on a script for MGM based on the infamous Dreyfus Affair—it ultimately came out in 1958 as *I Accuse!* With its cozy bars and cheerful crowds, Manhattan appealed to Gore in the winter, but he preferred Edgewater in the summer, with its access to the river and its capacious lawns. "I would sit in the garden and write under a big elm, watching boats," he said.

With money from scripts pouring into his bank account, Gore could afford to fix up the house. "Everything needed doing," said Howard, "the roof had to be tiled again, the floors sanded. We got some new furniture and rugs." Newman and Woodward often came to visit on weekends, and there was the usual parade of poets and journalists, producers, dancers. Gore marked his thirtieth birthday there in October 1955 with a party that Howard threw for him. A few days later Gore wrote to Crocker: "We celebrated with much champagne and maudlin good will by some 75 people, ranging from Tennessee to [film actress] Ella Raines and back again." His sense of time passing seems almost terrifyingly premature: "I am increasingly aware of pains in the back and unusual occurrences in the respiratory system."

But sadness clouded their lives, too. Alice Bouverie died on July 19, 1956, only fifty-four years old. She stumbled and hit her head on the toilet, but the coroner determined it was a heart attack that precipitated the fall. Three weeks later, John Latouche died as well, also from a heart attack, though rumors of his mixing drugs and alcohol had long circulated among his friends. The effect of these two deaths on Gore was palpable. He languished for days, not working, preoccupied with the question of mortality.

v. More Visits to Small Planets

One teleplay by Gore called *Visit to a Small Planet* attracted more attention than others he had seen produced. "The audience loved it," Gore recalled. It had evolved from the simple skit he saw in Francis Markoe's garden in Southampton some years earlier into a fierce satire in the manner of George Bernard Shaw. Its plot was straightforward: A fellow from outer space named Kreton drops to Earth with the idea of creating global mayhem. Human beings at war offered a grand spectacle for his curiosity, and the fifties was a good period for this: The nuclear age had arrived, with the Cold War fueling the dark imagination of the masses, who had begun to build bomb shelters in their backyards. Children were drilled at school, taught to hide under their desks and cover their heads. Fear moved like the wind in a forest. In fact, the paranoia about Communism had been ramped up to new levels with the hearings led by Senator Joseph McCarthy. The Korean War had raged from 1950 through 1953, when an uncertain armistice was signed; indeed, nobody knew for sure if the peace would hold. This tense political setting was a perfect atmosphere for a drama that satirized the madness of war and the fear of outsiders.

Kreton arrives in the midst of the Spelding household in Manassas, Virginia, hoping to witness the Civil War. Something goes wrong with his time machine, however, and the Battle of Bull Run is long since over. But Kreton is undeterred, and with his penchant for mischief and otherworldly talents—such as reading minds or creating force fields—he begins causing trouble, hoping to precipitate a catastrophe, perhaps something as violent as the Civil War. He is no sweet little alien like E.T. "We're going to have such good times!" he declares, greedy for mayhem.

Gore satirizes middle America through the Spelding family and their friends as they come to understand that an alien has landed in their midst. In the course of this brief play, he excoriates the politics of the McCarthy era, with its hyped-up anti-Communist passion and paranoia, poking fun at popular culture in ways that made an impression on the audience on May 8, 1955, when the live drama aired on NBC's *Goodyear Television Playhouse*, with the Australian-born actor Cyril Ritchard playing Kreton. The broadcast attracted thirty million viewers—Gore's largest audience thus far. "We expected the worst," said Gore, "but the audience and reviews were good." After the broadcast, a huge party was thrown by Martin Manulis, and there Gore met for the first time John Steinbeck and his wife, Elaine, who years later remembered him as "a tense, smart, glittering young man" who got on well with her husband and seemed to admire him. "They shared a passion for politics, and it was a marvelous kind of encounter. John liked him very much. We all adored the play."

Soon enough, plans were afoot to turn this teleplay into a full-length Broadway drama, with Gore acting as a producer with help from various friends, including George Axelrod, the author of *The Seven Year Itch*, a 1952 Broadway hit (and later a film starring Marilyn Monroe). Gore's energy now seemed startling to those around him. "He couldn't sit still," said Howard, "but he was making money, getting a lot of attention. He liked all that."

During the summer of 1955, Gore worked to expand the teleplay.

Once again Ritchard was tapped to play Kreton as well as to direct, and Gore spent several weeks discussing the project with him at his home in Jamaica. "We worked in wicker chairs under a large palm tree in his garden, drinking lots of rum to smooth out our differences. He was a sharp, funny man from Sydney. His best part on stage was as Captain Hook in *Peter Pan*, in the Mary Martin production. But he was a brilliant Kreton. He understood the tone, and his timing was perfect."

The play worked very well in expanded form. Gore and Ritchard had created a sturdy theatrical vehicle, one full of merriment, mayhem, and satire. It underscored an American penchant for naïve self-destruction, though Gore had expanded the object of his satire beyond U.S. borders. His target was now humankind in general. As Kreton observes to Rosemary, a cat: "I simply dote on people. Why? Because of their primitive addiction to violence." It's a mad romp through the funhouse of the fifties, with its religiosity and fury, its transparent bellicosity, its willed innocence. Instead of religious faith, Ellen Spelding depends on telepathy to contact Delton 4—a creature from outer space—who swoops in (quite literally) to save the day, taking away the naughty Kreton before he manages to disrupt the entire planet.

Visit was a huge hit on Broadway in 1957, running for 388 performances at the Booth Theatre, and was described by Brooks Atkinson, the influential theater critic at *The New York Times*, as "uproarious." Gore held its success in sacred memory, as is evident in the opening of his essay on Dawn Powell:

> One evening back there in once upon a time (February 7, 1957, to be exact) my first play opened at the Booth Theatre. Traditionally, the playwright was invisible to the audience: One hid out in a nearby bar, listening to the sweet nasalities of Pat Boone's rendering of "Love Letters in the Sand" from a glowing jukebox. But when the curtain fell on this particular night, I went into the crowded lobby to collect someone. Overcoat collar high about my face, I moved invisibly through the crowd, or so I thought. Suddenly a voice boomed-tolled across the lobby. "Gore!" I stopped; everyone stopped. From the cloakroom a small round figure, rather like a Civil War cannon ball, hurtled toward me and collided. As I looked

> down into that familiar round face with its snub nose and shining bloodshot eyes, I heard, the entire crowded room heard: "How could you do this? How could you sell out like this? To Broadway! To Commercialism! How could you give up The Novel?"

In reality, Gore had been trying to sell out for years, and he had finally succeeded.

VI. Outlaws

Newman persuaded Warner Bros. to get behind Gore's film version of Billy the Kid, and Fred Coe, who had previously worked only in television, came aboard as the director. But he didn't like Gore's script and hired an acquaintance in Hollywood to rewrite it, causing resentment. "There is always a hack in the wings," said Gore. As so often happens with films, one misstep led to another, and soon Gore was divorced from the project and felt terribly betrayed by Coe. "It was my story," he said, "and I had interested Paul in the project. But I was cut out." With the help of his agent, he managed to regain control of his original television script, which he planned to remake one day on his own terms.

Meanwhile, Gore traveled, often to London, where he stayed in a suite at Claridge's, still fussing with his script on the Dreyfus Affair, which had proved challenging. One day he received a letter from his half sister, Nini, saying she was pregnant and seeking advice. They had seen little of each other in the past decade, but a warm relationship had developed between them, and Gore had been asked to serve as a groomsman at her wedding on June 8, 1957. Senator John F. Kennedy was another groomsman, as by now he had married Jacqueline Bouvier, another stepchild of Nini's father, Hugh D. Auchincloss. Gore wrote back promptly, dispensing avuncular wisdom: "You will be fortunate in having money so you won't have to face the burden of nursing and cooking and letting go bit by bit your own life. The difficulty, of course, in your case, is determining what you want your life to be. You have a first-class mind and energy . . . right there you are a leap ahead of most people. But if I may say so you picked up from your family (all sides, including me) a success-worship which is dangerous and destructive without an underlying purpose. Ambition and energy in a void is always disturbing." In the same letter he refers to Jack Kennedy as "a conscienceless opportunist who wants to be President just for the sake of being, of showing everybody: here is a man." This was, perhaps, the first sign that trouble lay ahead in Gore's relations with the Kennedy family.

By now, he was acutely conscious of spreading himself thin. "I'd come to not one but several crossroads," Gore recalled. "There was Hollywood, and there was Broadway. I wanted to write a better novel than anything I'd managed yet. The idea of a book about Julian, the emperor, wouldn't go away. I was writing reviews and essays, and this work intrigued me. I liked my house on the Hudson, but I could not suppress an urge to travel."

In the meantime, Newman had rented a beach house in Malibu from the actress Shirley MacLaine, who was in fact one of the first people in show biz whom Gore met when he went to work at MGM. In the late summer of 1957, Woodward moved in with Newman. At Newman's suggestion, Howard and Gore joined them. How could they resist? It was a cozy foursome, with lots of jokes and some serious conversation. "It was one of those perfect, unforgettable times," Howard said. Gore liked it too, as it was a large house, and one that seemed perfect for parties. With Newman and Woodward as draws, the social circle widened, and Gore met a great many actors, producers, directors, and screenwriters, some of whom became useful contacts in the years ahead. Gore had bright prospects everywhere, in fact; but the klieg lights of Hollywood had stunned him, and he worked more slowly than usual. As Howard wrote to Bill Gray: "Gore is doing well, but at a pace so slow that I can't believe it is Gore working." He noted that he and Woodward spent a good deal of their time lounging at the pool, and this worried him. He had lost a sense of having his own profession. "I can never see myself sitting around and being a kept boy." This self-doubt would continue to haunt Howard, whom Gore still called Tinker or just Tink, as in Tinker Bell. "It took some years for that to stop," recalled Howard. "I was a fairy, but I couldn't fly."

Most days, Newman was busy at Warner Bros., playing Billy the Kid in *The Left Handed Gun* (1958). It was still based on the teleplay by Gore, but had been adapted by another writer, much to Gore's annoyance. But he had other projects and worked mostly in Malibu, often at a table on the patio, though he checked in once in a while at the MGM writers' office. The studio farmed out various scripts to him, but nothing really amused him, and he had a strong sense that his life as a novelist had somehow been hijacked. Nonetheless, he enjoyed living on the West Coast, with its predictable good weather, in a house with lots of room for guests, who kept coming.

Woodward, who was the only woman in the group, soon felt like "the mother of them all," as she said, and found herself less than thrilled by her circumstances. (She was quite happy when this little commune came to an end.) Occasionally Gore's friend Claire Bloom, another budding actress, joined the group. (They had met in London nine years earlier, when Bloom was only seventeen.) This friendship developed nicely, with Gore introducing the beautiful young actress to many of his closest friends.

Christopher Isherwood lived nearby, and Gore enjoyed the time he spent with the fifty-three-year-old writer and his young boyfriend, the artist Don Bachardy. But the stresses of being a studio writer proved irksome, and Gore increasingly chafed at the demands made by MGM. He had begun working on both *Washington, D.C.* and *Julian*, two novels that would eventually appear. But these remained only half developed as miscellaneous notes, assorted scenes with bits of dialogue, raw outlines. "I needed to keep working on scripts to pay the tax man," Gore reflected.

To reduce his tax liabilities, he put $300,000 (he really had been doing well!) into a retirement account and bought a rental property in New York City: a four-story brownstone on East Fifty-Eighth Street. "I always believed in property," Gore said. "It was the only constant in a world of unstable economic value. One could never depend on stocks or other investments. I like bricks and mortar. I like to see my money in front of me. And buildings tend to appreciate in time. All you need is patience." As ever, Gore took the long view. Indeed, he was shrewd about money—an unusual trait for a novelist—and was determined to die a rich man, which he did.

When the lease ended on MacLaine's house in Malibu, Gore returned to Edgewater with some relief, getting back to the big desk in his octagonal study, where an array of projects lay before him. He had a play about the Civil War—an extension of a teleplay—that didn't seem to work. He had pieces of two novels and further assignments from MGM. The project on his grandfather hung in abeyance, never quite ready for production. Of course *Visit* still played to reasonably full houses on Broadway, so he consoled himself that the name of Gore Vidal would not fade too quickly. More and more, he found himself in demand on talk shows, such as Jack Paar's popular *Tonight Show*. But nothing felt quite right.

"Whenever I get out of sorts, I travel," he said. And so, in the fall of 1957, he took off for London on the *Queen Mary* with an MGM project in hand: a rewrite of *The Scapegoat*, a script adapted from a crime novel by Daphne du Maurier. It would star Alec Guinness and Bette Davis (whom Gore enlisted for the role, although her part was cut back in the final production, much to her annoyance). Gore checked in to a suite at Claridge's, all paid for by MGM. Kenneth Tynan—an influential theater critic at *The Observer*—had been a fellow passenger on the Atlantic crossing, and what had been a passing contact became a lasting friendship. "I loved Ken," said Gore, "who was probably one of the most intelligent critics ever." Gore also met Tynan's American wife, the actress and writer Elaine Dundy, who was working on her first novel and eagerly sought Gore's advice. They, too, became friends. Of Tynan's wives, Gore noted in 1988, "For decades now I have been a friend to the first as well as the second Widow Tynan. Each regards me with suspicion vis-à-vis the other but, as I liked to explain, I am extremely insensitive to the feelings of others, particularly when it comes to *amour propre*. Each widow agreed that my indifference was to be counted upon as safe haven in a stormy sea."

Gore now made his first strenuous effort to get *Visit to a Small*

Planet staged in the West End. "I was sabotaged at every turn by Binkie Beaumont, then and forever," he recalled bitterly. Hugh Beaumont was, indeed, a major impresario, one of the most powerful figures in British drama for many decades, and he disliked Gore and his plays, believing their humor was far too American for the West End. Another British actor of note, Robert Morley, considered taking on the role of Kreton, but he insisted on a portion of the royalties and Gore refused, thinking he could get Guinness or someone else to play Kreton. But American humor often fell flat in Britain, and offers failed to materialize.

The Christmas season in London brought no joy, as Nina arrived, expecting grande dame treatment. As usual, Howard—who had moved into a room at Claridge's near Gore's suite—took on the task of looking after her. But her alcoholism had become a problem beyond solution, and she made life miserable for Gore. He took some comfort in a brief visit by Newman and Woodward, who had recently married. But he missed the solace of Edgewater and felt desperate to work without interruption.

VII. *BEN-HUR*

New York seemed appealing again. Gore's apartment at 360 East Fifty-Fifth Street became an ideal pied-à-terre, so he didn't feel the financial need to rent it out. And Edgewater had, with recent improvements, become very comfortable at last. Gore settled in to work as spring arrived in 1957.

But what would he do next? He had in hand his hastily rewritten script of *Honor*, a Civil War play, which he retitled *On the March to the Sea*. He had hardly finished revising the first act when the producer Sam Zimbalist called about *Ben-Hur*—a major MGM production in the works, with a budget of $15 million, the largest of any film to date. Gore knew the novel well, having read it at his grandfather's house as a teenager. It had been one of the most popular novels in American history, an 1880 publication by Lew Wallace, a Civil War general and the onetime governor of the New Mexico Territory, where he had met Gore's hero, Billy the Kid. *Ben-Hur* had outsold everything but the Bible until 1936, when *Gone with the Wind* by Margaret Mitchell rushed like a tornado across the country.

Wallace's story of Rome in the time of Jesus had already been adapted twice for Hollywood, but this was going to be a major film, an event in itself, with William Wyler directing Charlton Heston, from a script by journeyman screenwriter Karl Tunberg, who had spent two decades working for major studios. Judah Ben-Hur is a wealthy prince in Jerusalem who runs afoul of the authorities when he refuses to provide his old friend Messala—a Roman tribune—with names of anti-Roman Jews. It's a vivid story, conceived on an epic scale. But there was script trouble, to put it mildly.

Gore recalled: "I was eager to get out of my contract with MGM. It felt like a life sentence. Having already worked with Sam on *The Catered Affair* and *I Accuse!*, I thought this might work. I liked the story well enough. But the original version by Tunberg lacked drama. The dialogue was flat, very American. Tunberg was a studio hack. Sam Behrman had been brought on, but the script still didn't work, and now they found themselves in a mess. The grand sets had been built in Rome. Money sluiced in the gutters."

Arriving in April in Rome, still his favorite city, Gore set to work on Tunberg's script. Zimbalist had also hired Christopher Fry, the British playwright, to work with Gore on the script. It was a peculiar arrangement, and Gore knew at once that trouble lay ahead. The sets had been constructed, the actors had assembled, but the script remained a mess. Dutifully Gore and Fry did their best, producing page after page for rehearsal, even shooting. Wyler, for his part, knew that the script still lacked a necessary tension.

Gore suggested to Wyler that a homoerotic subplot of sorts might help: assume that Messala had once loved Ben-Hur as a boy and hoped to reignite this passion (shades of Gore and Jimmie Trimble). Orthodox and obdurate Ben-Hur would want nothing of this, being—as Gore put it—"all boy." He hadn't the slightest interest in a dalliance with Messala: hence the vengefulness that arises. What else could explain the sadistic lengths to which Messala was willing to go to humiliate his former friend by imprisoning his family and sending him into slavery on a galley ship?

Wyler showed some skepticism about this plot twist, but he finally agreed, as long as nobody told Heston, who would never approve. Gore recalled: "Heston was not a good actor, and Willy Wyler knew it. He said to me: 'It's one thing to try to inspire a wooden actor. It's another to animate an entire lumberyard.'" Stephen Boyd, who played Messala, was an intelligent actor, however, and he responded well to Gore's suggestions. "He got the idea right away and seemed to like it." (Heston, for his part, furiously denied that the plot had any homosexual overtones and said that Gore's claims infuriated him.) The early rushes, with scenes mostly written by Gore, surprised everyone with their high quality. Wyler felt relieved, and the film proceeded, with Gore on the set every day for five weeks. Zimbalist kept Gore abreast of the filming, and said that his only regret was that Gore "couldn't stay longer." This would have allowed him to "work a bit more slowly." But Gore had other fish to fry, and he found the atmosphere on the set of the film poisonous.

On cue, a battle for screenplay credit ensued and Tunberg, as a former head of the Screen Writers Guild, won. This judgment appalled both Fry and Gore. *Ben-Hur* was not only a film; it was a major cultural event. Being attached to it, formally or informally, provided a good deal of street credit for everyone involved, especially when it won eleven Academy Awards—the first film ever so lavishly honored.

Gore rushed back to Edgewater to try to get his play *On the March to the Sea* into production. But this work attracted no interest from producers, who thought it flat and dull, without the Oscar Wilde–like quips that had made *Visit to a Small Planet* soar on Broadway. He sent the script to several of his actor friends, but nobody showed the slightest interest. So he returned to his novel about Julian, trying to recall what it felt like to write novels. To Paul Bowles, he wrote that he had really had it with script-writing and the distractions that came with it: "No more movies for some time."

Promises, promises. After only five months of work on *Julian*, he received a call from Sam Spiegel, the film producer who had, four years earlier, scored a major artistic and commercial success with *On the Waterfront*. Spiegel wanted to know if Gore might adapt *Suddenly, Last Summer*, a play by Tennessee Williams that had opened Off-Broadway on January 7, 1958, as part of a duo of one-act plays called *Garden District*. This stark, melodramatic play about homosexuality and cannibalism drew heavily on Greek tragedy, especially *The Bacchae* of Euripides. Given his friendship with Williams and the nature of the material, Gore could hardly resist.

But the plot was ludicrous. A strangely remote young brain surgeon (Montgomery Clift) tries to understand why a peculiar and overwrought dowager from New Orleans (Katharine Hepburn) wishes to lobotomize her gorgeous young niece (Elizabeth Taylor). After an oppressive amount of conversation, it becomes clear to the moviegoer that the dowager's son was killed while on a trip to Europe with her niece. It takes a strong dose of "truth serum" to get the niece to reveal the bizarre circumstances. It turns out the young man was overwhelmed, then eaten, by young boys—"urchins." Presumably he had sexual designs on them, and had used his cousin as a lure.

Really?

The Gothic imagination of Williams had begun to descend in a downdraft of madness, and this lurid plot was an unlikely vehicle for big-name Hollywood stars. But Spiegel knew what he was doing, and the film—despite terrible reviews—found a receptive audience. Perhaps in the fiercely repressed atmosphere of the late fifties, it made a kind of peculiar sense that audiences would respond to a film that conflated homosexuality, madness, and cannibalism. The fact that Clift, himself a gay man who battled alcoholism, fit the part so well may have helped. But it's a weak film, nevertheless, and not one of Gore's better moments as a writer in any medium.

Nevertheless, the fact that it did well at the box office and garnered Academy Award nominations for both Hepburn and Taylor certainly helped to float the name of Gore Vidal, a banner that now rippled in the cultural winds even more prominently.

There was the added benefit, for Gore, of spending more time with Williams, who had to a degree fallen off his radar, because Frank Merlo, Williams's partner, never liked or trusted Gore. Out of loyalty,

Gore never missed a play by Williams, usually contriving to appear on its first night. Gore recalled the early discussions of his adaptation of *Suddenly, Last Summer*: "The Bird [Williams] and I had an initial script conference with Sam in Florida. Sam was a monster, but very bright, and he got things done. It was during this visit that I took him to meet Jack and Jackie Kennedy. They were staying at the old man's [Joseph Kennedy's] house in Palm Beach. The Bird had no idea who these people were. 'They must have money,' he said. I explained that Jack might be the next president, and this interested him. Jackie loved meeting Tennessee, and so did Jack. After lunch and cocktails, he took us onto the lawn to shoot skeet, and Tennessee showed him how it was really done. He was a much better shot than Jack. The Bird leaned to my ear: 'What a nice ass!' I told this to Jack, who loved it." Gore recalled that Jack praised *Summer and Smoke*, not *Streetcar* or *Glass Menagerie*. "Now that was a political move. It tells you what you need to know about why Jack became president."

VIII. A Place at the Round Table

Always attracted by power, Gore found the Kennedy aura both thrilling and disconcerting. He envied Kennedy's popularity and good looks, his grand prospects, and also liked his intelligence and charm, even the furious ambition. He began to wonder again if he might run for political office himself. Certainly he loved being in the public eye, and in appearances on chat shows—now a staple guest on late-afternoon and late-evening television—he felt surprisingly at ease. The camera liked him, and the feeling was mutual. And now his drama about his grandfather was scheduled, near the close of 1959, for a national airing on NBC's *Sunday Showcase*. This would ramp up his profile in a more sustained way than brief appearances on a talk show possibly could.

Meanwhile, another idea dawned. Why not write a play about politics? With the 1960 presidential election in view, it made sense to get a play on Broadway that would expose the backroom boys at their own game. He spent a few weeks in Provincetown with Howard in the late summer of 1959, and during this time he sketched the characters and possible action of *The Best Man.* Working with his usual speed, he had a full draft of the play by October. At the suggestion of Williams, he approached Roger L. Stevens, a prolific producer who had only a few years earlier put on *Cat on a Hot Tin Roof* as well as *West Side Story. The Best Man* struck Stevens as an obvious hit, and he moved ahead with arrangements for the play to open on Broadway in the spring of 1960, just as the presidential sweepstakes began in earnest.

In the fall of 1959 Gore called on Eleanor Roosevelt at Hyde Park, seeking her encouragement for him to run for Congress in Dutchess County. He wondered if he might represent the Twenty-Ninth Congressional District. At first she demurred. It was obvious that no Democrat could win in the county, which was heavily Republican and had been for the past half century. Mrs. Roosevelt probably also knew that Gore was gay and held radical views on any number of topics. She doubtless recalled that Senator Thomas P. Gore had been something of a thorn in her husband's political flesh for many years. Nevertheless, she weighed the idea carefully and, within weeks, told Gore she would support him if he ran. She also paved the way for him with Joseph Hawkins, the local head of the Democratic Party, who was glad to have a young man of some fame, even notoriety, to put forward.

"In 1960, I was seeing all sorts of things coming together," Gore recalled. "My political life, my writing life. It was a good moment, if only a moment."

At the Water's Edge—Hyannis

A sunny morning in spring, and Gore will be lecturing at Harvard in the evening. I pick him up at the Ritz, as he says he wants to "go driving." He rarely gets to see the countryside, and—since he never drives—it's amusing for him to see the country he writes about from Ravello.

"Take me to Hyannis," he says.

Hyannis?

"It will take an hour," he adds, sensing my skepticism. "Maybe a little more."

Gore seems moodier than usual, preoccupied with his lecture. He's been a friend for many years, and I admire him. But I can't help wondering if it's worth the effort. Does he give anything back?

"What are you working on?" he asks, looking up. It's as if he can read my thoughts.

I tell him about a life of Robert Frost that has occupied me for some time now.

"I saw Frost a couple of times at Exeter. He would come and read in the chapel. Everybody worshipped the old man, but I couldn't see the point. He was self-involved."

Coming from Gore, that sounds rich. I recite "Provide, Provide," and Gore listens keenly.

"I didn't know that one," he says. "That last stanza, saying it's better to go down dignified in the end, with paid help, than to die alone. I see his point."

After a while, Hyannis appears: a glistening port, with ferries to Nantucket and Martha's Vineyard.

"I was staying in Provincetown," he says. "It was soon after Jack's election, and I saw a few amusing souvenirs, images of Jack and Jackie. I sent them over to the house in Hyannis—a little joke. I didn't know they were there, but Jackie called. She came to my hotel the next afternoon. Like a teenage girl playing hooky from school. She jumped up and down on the bed. We went out on the town that night."

He grows silent and moody, and I know not to pummel him with questions.

We drive through Barnstable, and Gore says, "It was at the armory here that Jack gave his acceptance speech. Old Joe stood beside him, beaming. He was a gangster."

We park in Hyannis, one of seven villages that make up Barnstable.

"Hyannis Port is that way," says Gore, after we park on the street. We walk southwest of the village, along a street filled with gray-weathered clapboard houses. We stand at the railing overlooking Nantucket Bay.

"I came over for dinner," says Gore. "Jack loved it, being president. A gift from old Joe."

"Isn't that a myth?"

"It's a myth that it's a myth. I asked Jack about it. We sat in his living room, and I asked him. He said his father paid for part of the election, not all. It was the important part, I told him. He bought votes for him, too. Old Joe didn't care what it cost."

I wonder if we might walk to the compound itself, as I'd never been there.

"It's not public property. And I don't want to go there," says Gore. He grips the iron railing, looking at the water. A sailboat tilts into the sun, although it's too bright to see anything clearly: a dazzle. Gore is talking to himself now. "I might have been president, but it wasn't to be. My grandfather used to say I'd live in the White House one day. He didn't realize that it would be in Ravello."

Chapter Five

Each writer is born with a repertory company in his head.

—Gore Vidal

I. "You'll Get More with Gore"

Julian lay in a drawer in his desk at Edgewater. "I would look into the drawer now and then. I'd finished a couple of chapters, and I assumed—correctly—I would need a few years to finish it. The research was demanding. But so much else occupied me now, with Kennedy putting his hat into the big ring, with my decision to run for Congress, with *The Best Man* making its way toward Broadway. Politics was everything now," said Gore.

"This was in the day when political conventions meant something," Gore said. The plot of *The Best Man* capitalizes on the drama of an old-fashioned presidential convention, when the nominee was often in doubt until the last moment. We get coronations now, not deal-brokering in which successive waves of votes might or might not yield a nominee. In his play, an opportunistic young Southerner named Joseph Cantwell angles for attention. Not unlike Gore's father, he has attended a state college but climbed to considerable heights on his own long legs, though rumors of homosexuality have plagued him on the way up. Unlike Eugene Vidal, he is a cutthroat who will do anything to gain an advantage over his more privileged rivals. Cantwell's wife—a shrill creature with troubles of her own—seems to have wandered onto Gore's stage from Tennessee Williams's *Cat on a Hot Tin Roof*, where she would have found a comfortable home.

Cantwell's chief rival is William Russell, a former secretary of state who seems not unlike the Illinois governor Adlai Stevenson, whom Gore admired. Russell is a loyal Harvard man (Gore could never resist a Harvard man), prone to self-congratulatory intellectualism, dropping names like Bertrand Russell at news conferences, much to the dismay of his campaign manager. He has his frailties, too: rumors of psychiatric problems and marital problems abound. His reputation for philandering (shades of JFK) threatens to bring him down.

Both candidates seek the approval of Arthur ("Art") Hockstader, the outgoing president, modeled perhaps on Harry Truman. "Ronald Reagan auditioned for the part in the later film of the play," Gore recalls. "But nobody thought he was credible as a presidential figure."

Gore's dramatic pacing is perfect, and he brings several vivid minor characters into the mix, such as Sue-Ellen Gamadge, a cool-headed if clamorous national committee chairwoman who tends to expound on what "the female voter" wants or doesn't want. With each major candidate having secret ammunition against the other, it seems far from inevitable that either will ultimately triumph. Not surprisingly, the ambitions of both men are destined for deflation.

As so often before and after, Gore's timing was superb, with the play feeding off an election frenzy. The actors were well chosen, too, with Melvyn Douglas winning the Tony Award for Best Actor as Russell, playing him very much as an Adlai Stevenson type. Frank Lovejoy turned Cantwell into Nixon, with trembling jowls and shaking voice, although the audience could easily hear overtones of Joe McCarthy or Estes Kefauver or, indeed, John Kennedy, with his clear ambition. (Kennedy, as it happened, later explained to Gore that, in the midst of a campaign, there was hardly enough time for so much talk.)

The play racked up 520 performances in its initial Broadway run, and it has proved a durable drama, with periodic revivals from decade to decade—especially as presidential elections draw near. Brooks Atkinson wrote in *The New York Times* that the play was "both amusing and engrossing." It was Gore's best play so far, as Arthur Schlesinger Jr. noted to the author in a letter of March 16, 1960: "The play will be a great success. It is lively, sharp and arresting, and keeps the audience excited and absorbed." Honest to a fault, Schlesinger also wrote that "the second act curtain didn't seem quite right—I think because the bulk of the act is about the Russell-Cantwell conflict, and the reversion of focus to Hockstader and his illness is something the audience is not quite prepared for." He also faulted certain details of the production, which had not properly conveyed "the atmosphere of a convention." He suggested there should be more commotion, with buttons and balloons, reporters, clutter, noise, and music. (Later revivals would often work to create this commotion, and quite successfully.)

When Gore died in 2012, Jon Wiener reported in *The Nation* that the author of *The Best Man* had attracted the interest of J. Edgar Hoover and the FBI. It wasn't Gore's political activism that drew their attention. It was *The Best Man.* A New York City–based FBI agent sent a note to one of Hoover's assistants, telling him that this new play on Broadway contained "an unnecessary, quite unfunny and certainly unfair jibe at J. Edgar Hoover." The agent got his information from a gossip column and was immediately told to attend the play undercover. He filed a report, saying: "The only reference to the Director is when one play character—presumably Vice President Nixon—says to another—presumably Harry Truman, 'J. Edgar Hoover considers you to be one of the most moral and religious men ever to be in the White House.' The man replies with a sarcastic inflection, 'I'll reserve my opinion of J. Edgar Hoover for a posthumous memoir.' " The agent assured the director that, in fact, the joke "fell very flat." From this point on, the FBI kept a file on Gore, although it mostly contained letters from angry right-wingers demanding that the agency do something about this loud-mouthed Communist homosexual. (Nothing came of any of this, and the file amounts only to thirty-five pages.)

One minor distraction for Gore at this moment was the release of *Visit to a Small Planet* as a film by Paramount on February 4, 1960. "It was possibly the worst adaptation ever perpetrated," Gore said. "My luck with Hollywood was never good." The film starred Jerry Lewis as a barely credible version of Kreton. "It was all gimmicks and silly farce," Gore complained, "with all the trappings of satire stripped away." The critics, as they would, hated it, and it bombed at the box office.

In 1956, Gore had been an enthusiastic supporter of Stevenson for president, and it was thought that Jack Kennedy would be a good second man on the ticket. But JFK had not managed to get the nod, losing out by a narrow margin to Estes Kefauver at the convention. The leaders of the Democratic Party in Dutchess County knew that Gore had political connections in high places, and that JFK was a friend. Indeed, Gore had consulted with Jackie about his possible run, inviting the future First Lady to dinner in New York one evening, where he introduced her to Kenneth Tynan and Elaine Dundy. "In those days I could introduce her to the kinds of people she didn't often meet," he said.

Gore enjoyed talking about his relationship with JFK, and in a review of Seymour Hersh's 1997 biography of Kennedy, he recalled a scene from December 1959:

> Jackie asked me to a charity costume ball at the Plaza. "I'll put you at Jack's table, so he'll have someone to talk to. Just ignore what I'm placing between you. She's very beautiful. Very stupid. She's also just arrived from England, so Jack will have first crack at it." "It," not "her."
>
> We sat at a round table with eight or so other guests. Jack's costume was a holster with two six-shooters and a bandanna around his neck. He puffed a cigar and gazed intently at the blond girl between us. She was very beautiful. "You're in politics, aren't you?" Thus she broke the ice. I was curious to see Jack in action. "Uh . . . well, yes. I am. I'm . . . uh, running for President."
>
> "That's so fascinating!" she exclaimed. "And will you win?"
>
> "Well, it won't be easy . . ."
>
> "Why not?"
>
> "Well, you see, I'm . . . uh, Catholic . . ."
>
> "But what's that got to do with anything?"
>
> "Oh, Gore, you tell her." I did, and then he and I talked politics across her: not a woman's court, Camelot.

Needless to say, Gore worried that his robustly unorthodox sex life might intrude on his political career. If word about any of this got out to the press, he could be attacked in vengeful ways. But this was an age when sexual peccadilloes were usually overlooked by the press: JFK himself was a case in point. Yet one does wonder how a man who had written an openly homosexual novel, who moved among movie stars and scripted *Suddenly, Last Summer*, and who had noticeably radical views on a wide variety of subjects could possibly have imagined he could win a seat in the U.S. Congress.

A young man named L. Jay Oliva was hired by Gore as his driver and assistant during the campaign. "Imagine a guy in those days who didn't drive," says Oliva, who later became the president of New York University. They drove around the Twenty-Ninth Congressional District, "a huge area on both sides of the river," traveling in Oliva's sports car, an old MG. "Gore wondered about arriving in some fancy car like that," he said, "afraid people would think he was putting on airs."

Oliva recalls that Gore was asked directly by one reporter about being a homosexual as well as a candidate. Weren't these incompatible? "If that were the case," Gore said, "this would be the first election in American history where the electorate had its choice of perversions." He had turned the tables, drawing attention to the fact that his opponent had recently married a much younger woman. The gambit worked, and the reporter fell silent.

"Gore loved the politicking," Oliva says. "Howard hated it, on the other hand, and stayed out of it completely. I remember going up to Edgewater the first time, and it seemed Gore was surrounded by movie stars: Paul Newman, Joanne Woodward, some actors from Broadway. He knew these people as friends and never thought about them as celebrities. They wanted to help Gore, so they would appear at rallies, at picnics for firemen, church picnics, that sort of thing." Oliva remembers the red-white-and-blue bumper stickers and billboards that read YOU'LL GET MORE WITH GORE.

By now, Gore was an adroit public speaker, an articulate and unapologetic progressive. "In his stump speech," says Oliva, "he emphasized the need to put educational funding in the U.S. on a federal basis, leveling the playing ground for poorer school districts. He believed in recognizing Red China. He advocated for a small defense budget, noting that the U.S. spent more money on the military than most other countries combined, and he argued for the abolition of capital punishment, which he considered an American disgrace, and one that contributed to a culture of violence."

In June, Gore served as an alternate delegate to the Democratic National Convention in Los Angeles. He had not in his adulthood attended one of these circus-like events, though he had written about one in *The Best Man*. Suddenly he found his network of Hollywood connections useful, playing host to a large party at Romanoff's, a fashionable restaurant, on July 12, 1960. He brought together a range of politicians and Democratic operatives, with the likes of Gary Cooper, Charlton Heston, Bing Crosby, and others attending. Norman Mailer was there, too, looking warily around the room. Lyndon Johnson put in a brief appearance, but JFK stayed away, much to Gore's annoyance. (Gore later claimed that Kennedy had a date that night, and that sex for him always came first.)

"The college professors also turned up at the convention," Gore recalled. "They came out in force for Kennedy, a Harvard man." At one private party, he met John Kenneth Galbraith, the influential Harvard economist, and told him how much he admired his best-selling *The Affluent Society* (1958), a book in which Galbraith explained how the United States had become wealthy while neglecting the public sector. The main problem, he argued, was an economy based on luxury goods, on creating "needs" that were not reality-based. He disparaged the widespread idea that "production" was the most useful measure of success for a nation. "On the importance of production as a test of performance," Galbraith said, "there is no difference between Republicans and Democrats, right and left." In the coming years in his own writings Gore would draw a good deal on the thinking and research put forward by Galbraith.

Gore also spent an evening with Arthur Schlesinger Jr., the historian of the FDR era, whom he had met once before—during the Boston tryout of *The Best Man*, when Schlesinger had invited him to a dinner at his home in Cambridge with Reinhold Niebuhr, Edmund Wilson, and the British economist John Strachey, three of the most eminent of thinkers in their fields. According to Schlesinger, Gore (deeply in his cups) "dominated the evening, instructing Niebuhr in theology, Wilson in literary criticism and Strachey in economics and strategy. Next morning he called up and apologized for being tight."

For all his talk about connections to the Kennedys, Gore was hardly a member of the inner circle. "It rankled him," says Oliva, "that he didn't have easy access to the Kennedys, even though he had a vague familial relationship with Jackie as a kind of stepsister through marriage. Bobby Kennedy seemed to dislike Gore, probably because he was gay. Bobby was a fierce Catholic moralist, and he disapproved of Gore's ways. Gore, too, hated Bobby, who was a prig. He never had a good word to say about him." Indeed, Gore and RFK were already on a collision course.

In mid-August, Gore lured JFK into his own campaign orbit in upstate New York, however briefly. Kennedy wanted the approval of Eleanor Roosevelt, who had refused to support him at the convention, making it clear that her preference was for Stevenson. Since Gore knew Mrs. Roosevelt, however slightly, this was a way of getting to her. Serving as the intermediary, he arranged a private lunch at Hyde Park for Kennedy, although the timing proved awkward, as Mrs. Roosevelt's thirteen-year-old granddaughter had been killed in a fall from a horse only two days before. Kennedy reached out sympathetically to her in her grief, and this helped to repair a rift that had grown wide over the years. (Mrs. Roosevelt would write to a friend about this lunch: "I liked him better than I ever had before because he seemed so little cock-sure, and I think he has a mind that is open to new ideas.")

Later that day, at a rally hastily arranged by the Democrats of Dutchess County, Kennedy spoke out boldly for Gore: "He has the will and the vigor and he understands the need for action in this changing world," he said, according to a local newspaper. This was echoed in Eleanor Roosevelt's national column on October 10, 1960, when she pointed out that she stood strongly "behind Vidal in my neck of the woods."

"It was going very well, even in this Republican district. But the sharks began to circle," Gore recalled. In particular, a reporter from *The New York Times* interviewed this "bachelor . . . who lives in lonely splendor in an 1820 Greek Revival Mansion" on the Hudson. The description of Edgewater suggested opulence and decadence of an almost surreal kind, saying that during the conversation Gore "sprawled barefooted in a gilded fauteuil of his luxurious octagonal Empire study" while his cocker spaniel was allowed to "lick the Chateau d'Yquem off his fingers." This was homophobic journalism at its most unsubtle, and it added to Gore's already well-developed hatred for the Gray Lady, America's "newspaper of record."

Election night in November found Gore driving with his father (who wished to be supportive) and Howard to a party in Poughkeepsie, where the returns came in slowly throughout the night. Joe Hawkins hosted the celebration, though nobody expected Gore to win. In the end, he got 43 percent of the total, polling twenty thousand more votes than JFK in the Twenty-Ninth District: an impressive result. Oliva recalls that "Gore never tired of pointing out that he had bested John Kennedy in this district. That statistic always delighted him."

After the election, Gore felt at a loss. "I hadn't seen Gore so down, sort of confused," Howard recalled. Immediately Gore wrote to congratulate Kennedy, dropping a heavy hint that he would be willing to take some role in the new government: "If there is anything connected with education, foreign affairs, and, God help us, culture (both Kultur and Kitsch) that I might do, in a general or specific way, remember me." Jackie, instead of Jack, wrote back—somewhat to Gore's displeasure. But he liked the news that she and the president-elect had decided to see *The Best Man* on an upcoming visit to New York. Indeed, on December 6, 1960, the motorcade arrived at the Morosco Theatre on West Forty-Fifth, clogging the streets. Gore welcomed the Kennedys, who were greeted by cheers from the crowd on the streets and countless flashbulbs.

The thrill of this moment lingered in Gore's memory, and he often alluded to it, awed by the attention given by the public to any American head of state. Although friends urged Gore to begin to think about running for office again in 1962, possibly for the Senate, he shrugged off these suggestions, knowing in his heart that he was never going to win, not in a country that leaned (by his standards) to the far right.

Instead, Gore and Howard joined the Newmans for Christmas in Paris, where Paul was filming *Lady L* with Sophia Loren. They took a suite at the Plaza-Athénée, a luxurious hotel just off the Champs-

Élysées, where Gore spent his mornings working on early chapters of *Julian*, trying to revive his interest in the project. "What to do? That was always the big question," he said. The idea of writing another play appealed to him, though *On the March to the Sea*, his Civil War play, had failed to interest any Broadway producer. Yet royalties from *The Best Man* poured into his bank in New York, and he invested them wisely. "Real estate was the only safe place to put money, so we bought another brownstone on the Upper East Side," he recalled.

Back at Edgewater in February 1961, he resumed his weekend entertaining. Mailer, William Styron, and others came to stay, and he increasingly found Fred Dupee a convivial neighbor and dinner guest. "I think of Fred often," he later recalled. "Those years on the Hudson were made so much friendlier, more interesting, with Fred as a tutor. I read to keep up with him, to continue our conversations." He and Fred often talked about Roman history, especially as Gore began to think aloud about the directions he might take in *Julian*.

Gore soon began to think about the last of the Roman emperors, Romulus Augustulus. He had been the subject of a 1950 play by Friedrich Dürrenmatt, whom Gore had met in 1959. In the fantasy version of history put forward by Dürrenmatt in *Romulus the Great*, the hapless emperor spends his time raising chickens and dropping aphorisms while the Goths beat down his door. He dismisses the idea that these barbarians will overrun the empire, though he gratefully accepts the offer of a nice villa and a peaceful retirement as the king of Italy when push comes to shove. Gore decided to "adapt" this play. "How could I resist?" he said, thinking of Romulus Augustulus and his follies. "The story had everything except a story."

Gore worried that the subject was too elevated for a Broadway audience. In a retrospective piece in *Esquire* in 1962, he said, "I liked the play, though it was quite apparent why it had failed. Duerrenmatt had neglected to dramatize his situation. To paraphrase T. S. Eliot, to be effective in the theatre one must be very interesting. His play was interesting only in conception." Gore knew he would have to do some heavy lifting to create an entertainment onstage, one that bore any resemblance to the original. "In any case, the amount of thinking you can get audiences to do is negligible. But you must hold their attention for two hours if you want them to absorb a single thought or present them with a single unfamiliar attitude. This is done through the emotions. You tell a story."

Romulus, Gore's adaptation, opened on January 10, 1962, at the Music Box Theatre and closed after only sixty-nine performances—a disappointing run that upset him considerably. But Gore had a way of dismissing any failure, any bad review or cutting remark in the press, with a flippant gesture, blaming the audience. In this case, the Broadway crowd was not easily won over by toga dramas, and this one failed to catch dramatic fire.

II. Slouching Towards Camelot

Gore's relations with Norman Mailer had always been testy, and they rarely socialized. But the friendship got a boost in the spring of 1961, when Gore invited Mailer and his then-wife, Adele Morales, to Edgewater with their small daughter. This came after the well-known incident in 1960 when Mailer, drunk at a party where he planned to announce his candidacy for mayor of New York, stabbed Adele with a rusty penknife, nearly killing her, though she apparently forgave him quickly and refused to press charges. Mailer's friends largely closed ranks. Indeed, Lionel Trilling supposedly told his wife, Diana, that Mailer had engaged in "a Dostoevskyan ploy," whatever that is. Even Gore stood (rather quietly) behind him. "Gore and I were, in fact, good friends, though we argued, sometimes loudly," Mailer recalled. "Gore was hospitable, a good host, and cheerful." Dupee and his wife joined them for the weekend. "We talked about everything whenever we got together," Mailer said. "Politics, books, friends, enemies."

Mailer adored Provincetown, in later years making it his home, and during this visit he and Gore spoke fondly of this magical village at the tip of Cape Cod. Provincetown had long attracted gay men and women as well as artists and bohemians, and Gore decided to go there without Howard for a period in the summer of 1961. He hoped to work quietly on *Julian*, bringing a large suitcase full of books about the Roman Empire. One day he sent a cheap souvenir—a platter with the Kennedys drawn in caricature—over to the Kennedy compound in Hyannis Port. Much to his surprise, he got a call at his hotel from Jackie, who said she and Jack were actually staying at the compound and would he care to join them one night for dinner.

How could he, or anyone, resist such an invitation? He actually visited twice that week—the most sustained contact he ever had with JFK. These visits yielded any number of bright anecdotes, amplified in the gilded chambers of his memory, as in a piece for *Vanity Fair* written in 2000:

> In August 1961, I visited President Kennedy at Hyannis Port. The Berlin Wall was going up, and he was about to begin a huge military buildup—reluctantly, or so he said, as he puffed on a cigar liberated by a friend from Castro's Cuba. It should be noted that Jack hated liberals more than he did conservatives. "No one can ever be liberal enough for the *New York Post*," he said. "Well, the *Post* should be happy now. Berlin's going to cost us at least three and a half billion dollars. So, with this military buildup, we're going to have a $7 billion deficit for the year. That's a lot of pump priming." He scowled. "God, I hate the way they throw money around over there at the Pentagon."

Gore's relationship with Jackie reached a kind of peak when she donned a halfhearted disguise—"a scarf or hat," Gore recalled, "and the ubiquitous sunglasses"—and called on him in his hotel room, where she "bounced up and down on the bed like a child. She was free at last." They went to dinner and a play with a friend, then to a small club, where Jackie was recognized, and a crowd materialized. "We had to escape," Gore said. "I felt a little sad for her. The marriage was unpleasant for her, and now she had this big role on a big stage."

Relations between Robert F. Kennedy and Gore had, by contrast, always been uneasy, though Gore rarely saw him. They brushed against each other a few times, a brief period when Gore was welcome at the White House during the first year of the Kennedy administration. "Bobby was a self-righteous little prick," said Gore, who had begun to write for *Esquire* now, commentaries critical of the FBI, which seemed (under the heavy hand of J. Edgar Hoover) to ignore

Baby Gore with his mother, Nina.

Gore and his father, Gene.

Gore's parents, Rock Creek Park, 1927.

Senator Thomas P. Gore and his beloved grandson.

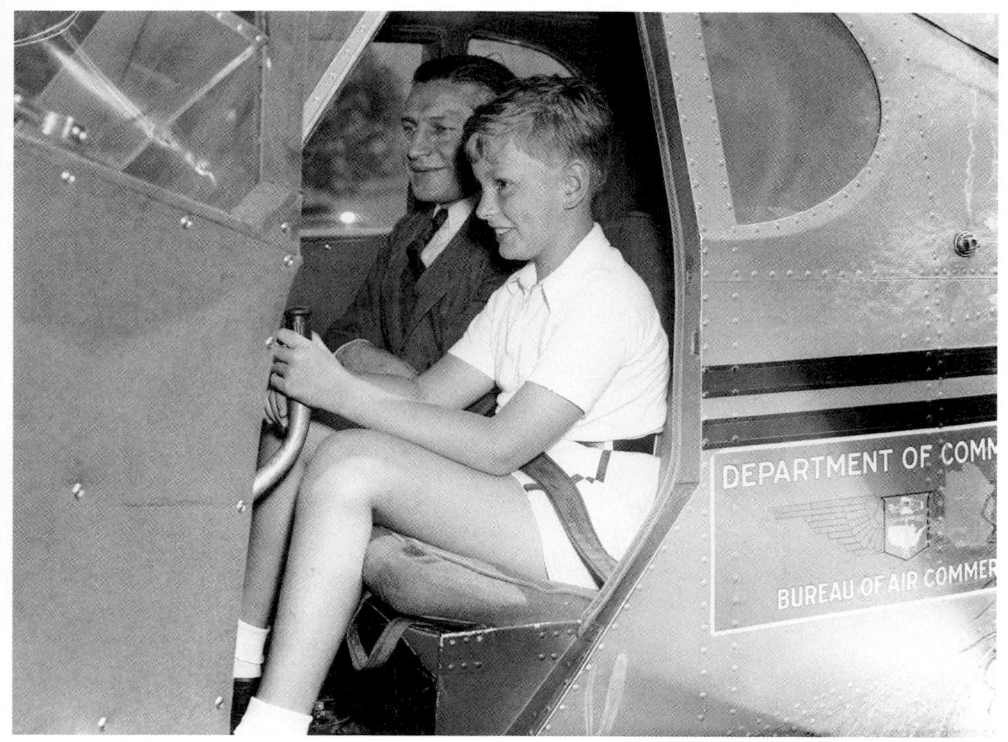

At twelve, Gore flies with his father and makes the news for doing it.

Gore adores Nina in her bathing suit. This will not last.

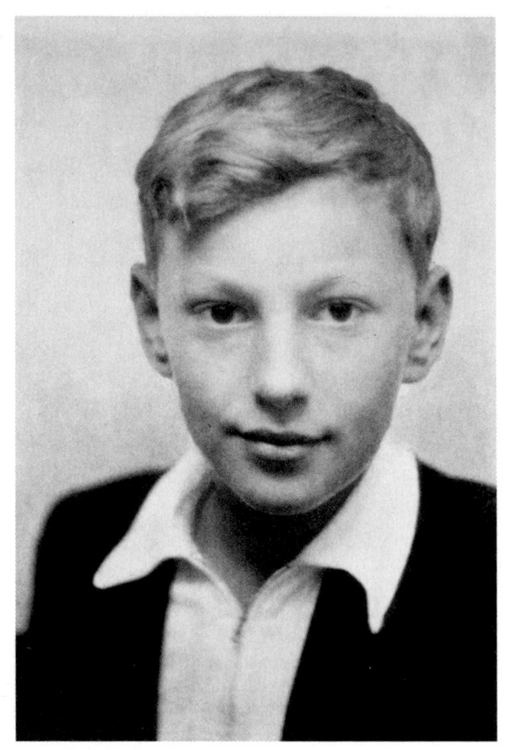

Gore enters his teenage years, 1937.

Gore at Merrywood, 1938.

Gore's childhood home in Rock Creek Park.

Gore goes scouting, Los Alamos Ranch School, 1941.

Gore at St. Albans, right behind Jimmie Trimble.

Jimmie Trimble, all boy and Gore's bliss.

Gore tells them off at Exeter, 1943. He'd do a lot of that in future years.

Gore's in the army now, in
Colorado Springs, 1944.

Another view from the bridge—this
time of the Navy freighter *USS FS-35*.

Gore and Anaïs Nin, an odd literary couple.

In Guatemala, 1947, during the first of his expatriations.

Life calls to Gore, 1947, on the occasion of his novel *Williwaw.*

Gore and Tennessee, 1950, in Florida.

Gore with the dancer Harold Lang in Bermuda.

Gore and Tennessee and an army surplus jeep on the Amalfi Coast, 1948.

Gore, an inexplicable bear, and dancer Johnny Kliza in Florida.

The legendary gathering of poets—and one novelist,
Gore Vidal—at the Gotham Book Mart in 1948.

Casual dining in New York at Johnny Nicolson's Café in 1949—
from left, the ballerina Tanaquil LeClercq, the novelist Donald Windham,
the painter Buffie Johnson, Tennessee Williams, and Gore.

Howard Austen, Gore's lifelong companion, in 1951.

Gore and Howard at their beloved Hudson Valley estate, Edgewater.

Lord of the Manor at his ease, Edgewater, 1958.

On the set of *Ben-Hur,* 1959: director William Wyler, Christopher Fry, Gore, and star Charlton Heston.

In Palm Beach with JFK and the Bird. Williams's admiration for JFK was more physical than political.

Gore's highly collectible campaign button.

Gore campaigns for Congress with JFK in Dutchess County.

In 1960 JFK arrives at *The Best Man* to meet the cast.

civil liberties. In one he mocked "Presidential cries for action, vigor, and moving-aheadness." He implied that a kind of police state existed, and that the FBI had informants everywhere. He even wrote to Bobby Kennedy to complain about the way the FBI ignored the activities of the Ku Klux Klan, receiving a perfunctory response from the attorney general.

Through Jackie's influence, Gore was offered and accepted a place on a new presidential committee on the arts, but such a minor appointment upset him. He had hoped for something more, and committees bored him. But he did accept an invitation to dinner at the White House in November 1961. The occasion was ostensibly to honor Gianni Agnelli, the Italian car magnate, as well as Lee Radziwill (Jackie's younger sister), whose husband, Stanislaw, had descended from the Polish aristocracy. "They gave royalty a bad name," Gore said. He drove to the White House that night with George Plimpton, Galbraith, and Schlesinger. It was an evening to forget.

Trouble started early, when an anxious Gore swept glass after glass of champagne from silver trays that whirled about the room. He may have felt a bit woozy when he saw Jackie sitting in the Blue Room, surrounded by admirers, and he decided to join them. There was no seat, so he crouched beside her, using her shoulder as a steadying point as he knelt. Suddenly a man appeared behind them, removing Gore's hand firmly from her shoulder, glaring at him fiercely. It was Bobby Kennedy.

Gore recalled: "I was furious. What right did he have to do that? I followed him into a corridor and told him never to do that again. He insulted me—the exact words aren't worth repeating—and I insulted him back. It was terrible, and the evening was ruined for me. I sat at the dinner with his wife, Ethel, and some other bores. It was one bad encounter after another, and I probably drank more than I should have. As I was leaving, I spoke briefly to Jack, telling him I wanted to wring his brother's neck. He just laughed. This was politics. Forget about it, he said. But some things are easier to forget than others." Bobby Kennedy's glare of distaste (as often recalled by Gore) upset him to such a degree that his growing reservations about the Kennedy clan turned venomous.

The aftershocks of this evening continued. In an interview in *Playgirl*, years later, Truman Capote remarked that Gore had been physically tossed out of the White House "for being drunk and obnoxious." He added: "It was the only time he had ever been invited to the White House and he got drunk." In a fit of pique that exposed his thin skin and vindictiveness, Gore sued Capote over his fairly bland comment, which only drew further attention to the incident. (The suit came to nothing but an apology by Capote.) But the effect of this was to emphasize Gore's vindictiveness. "We know what they are," Lee Radziwill said in one interview. "They are just two fags. It is really the most disgusting thing."

Not surprisingly, Gore received no further invitations to the Kennedy White House after this disquieting dinner, although it seems unlikely that his spat with Bobby had much to do with it. The Kennedys had other concerns, personal and political. Indeed, world events—the Cuban missile crisis in October 1962 being only the most vivid of these—preoccupied them. Still eager, however, to remain in touch with the presidential circle, Gore continued to write occasional notes to Jackie, and to send autographed books, which she rarely acknowledged.

III. Essaying the World

Almost by chance, Gore had begun to write book and theater reviews as well as political commentaries for a variety of journals and papers beginning in the early fifties, but these were occasional pieces, the by-products of a busy writing life. By 1959, however, he had launched into a full-blown sub-career, writing frequently for the biweekly news magazine *The Reporter*, for *Esquire*, and for other high-profile publications. On June 9, 1961, he published a droll conversation in *Life* with the ultra-conservative senator Barry Goldwater, the man most likely to run against Kennedy in 1964.

This profile is a stunning piece of journalism, which Gore begins loftily by invoking Julius Caesar, Alexander the Great, and Pascal—

names seldom seen in the pages of *Life*. In Goldwater's Senate office, Gore questions the former Arizona department store marketing executive, provoking a discussion of national and world affairs. It's fair and fresh, full of interesting things. Gore ends by quoting an anonymous critic who calls Goldwater "ignorant but shrewd." Gore disagrees: "I am not sure I would agree that Goldwater's ignorance of ideas is necessarily relevant to his ability or his capacity for growth." This leads to a canny overview:

> I was impressed by his charm, which, even for a politician, is considerable. More than that, in his simplifying of great issues Goldwater has a real appeal for a nation which is not at all certain about its future either as a society or as a world power. Up and down the land there are storm warnings. Many look nervously for shelter, and Goldwater, in the name of old-time virtue and ruggedness and self-reliance, offers them refuge beneath the venerable great roof of the Constitution. True or not, his simplifications are enormously appealing and, who knows, in a time of crisis he might seize the prize.

The balance here, syntactical and emotional, creates a strong impression, and the haughtiness, as in "even for a politician," doesn't go overboard. As usual, his command of detail impresses, and he reaches for a larger context, ending with a remark of warning by Cicero to a "fellow political adventurer."

Rocking the Boat (1962)—Gore's earliest collection of essays—came adorned with blurbs by Tynan, Mailer, and Schlesinger. The reviews were strong (especially those by friends, such as Dupee, who praised the book in *Commentary*). The essays glitter with bright shards of perception, as when he writes of the American theater:

> The cult of feeling has not only undone much of our theater writing, it has also peculiarly victimized those gentles, the actors. They have been taught that "truth" is everything. And what is "truth"? Feeling. And what is feeling? Their own secret core, to which the character they are to interpret must be related. To listen to actors

> talk about "truth" is a chilling experience. They employ a kind of solemn baby talk compounded of analysts' jargon and the arcane prose of the late Stanislavsky.

In 1990 Anthony Burgess, the English novelist and critic, said what many would say when comparing Gore's fiction to his essays: "Gore would hate to hear this, but his true gift was in the form of the essay. It was there that his intelligence and wide knowledge of the world got the best traction. He controlled the tone of those essays, and he brought in everything he had learned in his life, stories from his own life. He understood the genre, and its possibilities." Gore always chose to interpret such comments as put-downs, as he considered novels the primary form of literature in his time, hoping to secure a place for himself on the same shelf as Saul Bellow and Philip Roth, John Updike and Toni Morrison. This never happened, yet his essays—beginning with *Rocking the Boat*—form a body of work unrivaled for its variety, humor, elegant prose, and critical energy in essay-writing of the postwar era.

In *Rocking the Boat*, one sees in book form for the first time his early essay on his postwar rivals in "Ladders to Heaven: Novelists and Critics of the 1940s," writing with good humor, as when he compares the critical currents of the time to philosophical and theological arguments in the fourth century, a period when "a diphthong was able to break the civilized world in half and spin civilization into nearly a millennium of darkness." He draws hilarious analogies between the fourth and twentieth centuries: "F. R. Leavis and Saint Jerome are perfectly matched, while John Chrysostom and John Crowe Ransom suggest a possibility." He declared that Carson McCullers, Paul Bowles, and Tennessee Williams (all personal friends) were "the three most interesting writers in the United States," observing that each of these writers had gone "further into the rich interior of the human drama than any of our immediate predecessors with the possible exception of William Faulkner, whose recent work has unfortunately resembled bad translations from Pindar." As noted, he used the platform of the essay to deride enemies, such as John W. Aldridge, an influential critic (who had dismissed Gore's later novels, after initially being a supporter). He called Aldridge's critical survey *After the Lost Generation* "a novel" full of unlikely characters "with names like Truman Capote and Gore Vidal."

Julian still languished, in part because the author knew he needed to do more research, probably even to see the eastern part of the Roman Empire firsthand. So in the winter of 1962, he and Howard sailed to Italy on the *Leonardo da Vinci*—a beautiful Italian liner built only two years before (the company offered Gore free passage, as they often did for celebrities, who would earn their keep by simply mingling with the other guests). Newman and Woodward joined him, as did other New York friends. The foursome proceeded to Athens, where they met Dundy, then in the process of separating from Tynan—the marriage had been severely challenged for some years, although Gore remained friends with both. "This was all part of my *Julian* research, seeing with my own eyes again the landscape, the way the light fell, the color of the earth. I had seen a few of these places before, but I was looking with a kind of particular interest now, taking mental notes."

Athens in the sixties attracted any number of American writers, such as Kimon Friar and James Merrill. Merrill recalled: "He came to Athens several times and called on me. But Gore sucked all the air out of any room he entered. You couldn't breathe in his presence. I remember one of the local English gossip rags ran a story about one of his visits, calling him 'the American actor, Gore Vidal.' In a way they got it right." Gore enjoyed Athens, however, and wrote later in the year to Alexandros Matsas, a Greek poet and diplomat, "I have never felt more completely, atavistically at home than in Athens."

From Athens, he and Howard continued on. Egypt was always a major port of call. "Gore loved the look of Arab boys," Howard recalled. "But their hygiene bothered him. He didn't want to sleep with anybody who didn't take showers." The pair visited Jordan, traveling through the desert to Petra, an ancient city quarried from rose-colored stone, and went on to Jerusalem and Cyprus. Beirut, with its broad colonnades and Parisian atmosphere, was alluring. Then they went to Turkey, where so many of the ruins associated with *Julian* could be seen. "Julian, as a boy, had spent half a dozen years in a palace near Mount Argaeus and Caesarea, now called Kayseri, in Turkey," Gore recalled. He knew what he wanted to see, and it proved mildly irksome that Howard preferred the hotel bars to sightseeing.

Rome was their destination now, if not their destiny. "I felt at ease in Rome," Gore said. "It was always the city that settled things for me, and I started to think I must live there. No place else made any sense." He took a side trip to Capri, on the Amalfi coast, staying with Eddie von Bismarck and Mona Williams at their villa, Palazzo Fortina, with its staggering views of the Bay of Naples, with Vesuvius rising in the middle distance. Like Somerset Maugham before him, Gore loved Capri but thought it too far from civilized life. "I needed a city at this stage," he said. "And I knew it would be Rome, sooner rather than later. Rome and only Rome."

They returned to Edgewater in March, but had begun to think about spending part of each year in Rome. It seemed perfect for Gore's research, and Howard liked it, too, although he loved New York and had reservations about moving such a distance. In the meantime, they resumed life on the Hudson, where Gore turned back to his political novel, *Washington, D.C.* He had already written much of it, and it came together quickly. As summer approached, he began to work at a frenetic pace. "I often thought of Sir Walter Scott," Gore said. "He had a desk in his study with two sides, so that he could have two novels boiling at the same time. I was doing the same. Two historical novels, although *Washington, D.C.* was memory lane. It was my own history. *Julian* was mine, too, I suppose."

Toward the end of summer, Gore felt determined to move to Rome. He would never completely abandon the United States: that was never his plan. But he thought he could finish *Julian* more easily in Rome, working in the library of the American Academy, which had most of the materials he needed. He and Howard could take side trips to Greece and Egypt. "There was something about Rome at this time, in the early sixties. It had an allure," said the American poet and novelist Harry Mathews, a friend of Gore's who lived in France much of the time but now came to Rome quite often.

Howard had sacrificed a lot to live with Gore, even his aspiration to become a singer. He had genuine talent, with a lovely baritone and jazzy manner in the vein of Frank Sinatra and Tony Bennett. But the prospect of standing on a stage terrified him, and he never pushed his career. That fall, while singing for friends one weekend, he found himself getting raspy-voiced. The condition persisted, so he went to a doctor, who found a huge tumor growing on his thyroid. Gore sent him to Sloan Kettering—a hospital on the front lines of cancer treatment in New York.

By chance, Williams's partner, Frank Merlo, was in Sloan Kettering on a different floor. It was a bad time for Williams; Merlo—a Sicilian by heritage—was dying of lung cancer. Howard's diagnosis wasn't as frightening: He had a piece of his thyroid cut out, and it was benign. "Tennessee and I would ride the lift together," recalled Gore. "And Frank was dying, and the Bird knew it. The Bird was such a romantic. 'I shall love thee better after death,' that was his marching song. Of course he was quite forgetting that he'd already kicked Frank out."

Gore felt worried about Howard now, who seemed suddenly vulnerable. "His damn smoking," Gore said. "I always feared it would get him." Howard was the mainstay of his life, and it frightened him to think that anything could happen to his partner. With the health problem resolved, Howard now agreed to join Gore in Rome for an experimental year. They rented an apartment at 4 Via Giulia, near the Campo dei Fiori. Although to Gore it felt cramped, it was within easy reach of the American Academy.

Almost too eager to get this experiment in Roman life under way, Gore flew ahead of Howard, who stayed behind to close Edgewater and the apartment in New York. The brownstone was rented, and it would provide a good monthly income. "I'd been working very hard for a long time," Gore said, "and I had the money we needed to change our lives, and so we did."

IV. ROMAN SPRING

Gore's American life dropped out of sight behind him, and he had a sense of finally being "home." "I was a Roman," he said. "It was in my blood, in my ancestry." He was strangely convinced of this, although his actual Roman roots were more imagined than real. This was an emotional affiliation, and a deep one. Even before Howard arrived, Gore had settled into the new apartment, which was fully furnished, although he bought a few paintings that he put up to replace the "ghastly and sentimental ones" that hung on the "dull gray walls." To make the place more cheerful for Howard, he had his bedroom painted a brighter color.

Each morning he walked through the ancient streets to the library of the American Academy located on the Janiculum Hill. There he sat at a long table, surrounded by books on the Roman Empire. He liked the peacefulness of this research, which allowed him to wander in the imagination, to track the byways of history at his own pace. It was good to have New York behind him, as he had never felt wholly at ease there. It stirred his competitive juices in ways that upset him, even though he responded by working harder and striving mightily: always the empire builder. Not yet forty, he had a shelf of books to his credit, Broadway plays, countless teleplays and screenplays, dozens of essays and reviews, a few stories and poems. Yet he knew in his bones that better work lay ahead. "I didn't think of anything I'd yet accomplished as sufficient," he said.

Surrounded by echoes and images of the Roman Empire, he was now adding to his own, an empire of self he would continue to expand, pushing into farther and more foreign territories without fear. "One afternoon, alone, I went to visit Hadrian's Villa in Tivoli. I'd been reading the novel by Marguerite Yourcenar, *Memoirs of Hadrian*. I thought about his life, lived on a grand scale. He had traveled to the farthest outposts of empire: a large part of his adult life spent outside of Rome. He loved poetry. He was writing his own memoirs, now lost. He loved Antinous, a Greek boy who drowned on a trip to Egypt—a terrible moment in Hadrian's life. He found peace at the villa in Tivoli."

The manuscript of *Julian* grew, written on yellow pads in dark blue ink. He found himself writing more freely and happily than ever before. The decision not to run for public office again in 1962 felt right, and he liked being away from the hubbub of politics. He thought he might actually be able to write more easily about American history from Italy, often saying that this distance gave him a clarity he might not have up close.

Harold Hayes, a young editor whom Gore found responsive to his ideas for essays, asked him to write a piece about the American presidency for *Esquire*, which had been shape-shifting for a few years, moving from a men's service and pin-up magazine to more serious subjects. It attracted a number of first-rate writers, such as Gay Talese, Tom Wolfe, and Mailer—a cluster who formed a movement known as the New Journalism. One of the key articles in *Esquire* that set the tone for this movement was "Joe Louis at Fifty," a profile by Talese that brought to bear all of the creative tactics that a novelist would deploy, and it caught Gore's attention. Gore's own early journalism, such as his profile of Goldwater, also broke new ground: The lively and personal voice that becomes part of the story was something that Mailer, Talese, and Wolfe would build on. But Gore had been doing this, too, writing like an artist, not an "objective" and anonymous journalist. He cultivated a uniquely inflected voice, not the bland and telegraphic voice of newspaper writing.

Gore wrote "The Best Man, 1968" for Hayes in 1962. It was in essence an attack on Robert Kennedy, whom Gore derided at length. "How simpleminded should a President be might well be the issue," he asked, after a hilarious description of a "study group" that RFK and his wife attended that was addressed by A. J. Ayer, the Oxford philosopher. Gore assumed that Jack would continue as president until 1968, whereupon the main alternatives would be RFK or Nelson Rockefeller. He disliked them both, and didn't pull any punches. The response was one of delight or outrage, depending on the reader, and Hayes saw he had scored a major hit—the circulation of the magazine jumped, as Hayes reported to Gore.

With this controversial piece, Gore severed his ties with the Kennedy clan for good, leaving himself out on a limb in faraway Italy, where he felt safe, like the golden bird in Yeats's poem, to sing "Of what is past, or passing, or to come." "I didn't give a fuck what the Kennedys thought about it," Gore said. "I would tell the truth. It was always my Achilles' heel."

Meanwhile, a newspaper strike in New York shut down *The New York Times* for three months. A by-product of the strike proved important: the creation of *The New York Review of Books* by Jason and Barbara Epstein, with Elizabeth Hardwick and her husband, Robert Lowell, assisting as well. "We saw the opening," said Jason, "and we moved quickly." The first issue came out in February, with Gore among a stellar group of contributors that included W. H. Auden, Robert Penn Warren, Lowell, Mary McCarthy, Dupee, Alfred Kazin, Adrienne Rich, Paul Goodman, Mailer, Styron, and Hardwick.

Gore assumed the new periodical would collapse after a few issues, but *The New York Review* would prosper in time, becoming the chief outlet for Gore's explosive career as an essayist and a showcase for important writing from across the literary spectrum, "although the editors tended to favor elderly and claret-besotted dons from Oxford and Cambridge over Bright Young Things," Gore maintained.

Rome in the sixties was the center of "the sweet life," as depicted by Federico Fellini in *La Dolce Vita*. The eternal city had finally recovered from the war, and it was a lively scene for writers, especially those with an interest in film. "I would see Gore at parties," recalled the actor Anthony Quinn, who worked often in Rome and soon bought a house there. "He knew everybody, and everybody knew him. I saw him with Fellini, with actors, with writers. Alberto Moravia and he would have drinks in some piazza, and I sat with them a couple of times. Gore had a way of putting himself at the center of things." Moravia, a novelist and film critic who had first met Gore in 1948, introduced him to various friends in the burgeoning Italian film industry and to writers as well. To a friend, Gore wrote: "I always felt that, somehow, Italy was secure, as long as Moravia could be counted on to make his irritable judgments."

Then, as ever, Italy was a magnet for British writers, and Gore would in due course get to know many who lived there, such as Muriel Spark, whose work he admired. Others came through as visitors. Burgess, the author of *A Clockwork Orange*, recalled that "Rome was a kind of axis, and everyone touched base there. Some lived there for a while or moved to Tuscany or Venice. Gore was a port of call. I loved seeing him, as he loved gossip." Among those who dropped by were the English novelist Angus Wilson, and Tom Driberg, a witty member of the Labour Party and a journalist who managed to retain a seat in Parliament for many years despite his openly gay behavior. Christopher Hitchens, a younger English journalist who courted Gore for decades until their falling-out over the Iraq War, described Driberg and Gore cruising for "rugged young men recruited from the Via Veneto." He claims, indeed, that these young men would "be taken from the rear by Gore and then thrust, with any luck semi-erect, into the next-door room where Tom would suck them dry."

"I visited him often in Rome in the sixties," recalls the film agent Boaty Boatwright, a close and long-standing friend of Gore's. "He fit in. It was as if he had lived there forever. He quickly got to know everybody in Rome. He and Howard would find young men on the streets, of course. That's what they did for amusement. But Rome was much more than that. It was an easy place to find good conversation, and Gore was the best for that. He could talk about anything: books, movies, theater, politics. People were attracted to that, and they would call him, and he would take them to dinner or invite them to his apartment."

An important new friend was the journalist George Armstrong, who was a year older than Gore. "I was a kid from Arkansas who went to Harvard, then—after the war—studied in Florence. I loved Rome. In the early sixties, about the time Gore arrived, so did I. It cost nothing to live there, and I got work from the London papers, writing on Italian subjects. I called on Gore at the Via Giulia, and he and Howard just took me in. They became my closest friends, almost family. I liked helping Gore in any way I could and did a lot of typing for him. He was very generous and often just gave me cash. I don't think anyone quite knows how generous he was with friends. He didn't worry about money." Armstrong and Gore often went out late at night to Roman cafés, where they took to the street life. Indeed, Armstrong shared Gore's adventures in cruising.

A lean, good-looking man who relished Gore's quips, Armstrong combined a keen intelligence with a modest nature. This mixture of traits appealed strongly to Gore. "We would talk about books and politics, about movies," Armstrong remembered. "And we did, hour upon hour, over good wine." Howard, for all his kindness and warmth, was no match for Gore when it came to intellect and learning, so Gore had to find those where he could. Armstrong proved an ideal companion, someone who would remain close to Gore for the rest of his life, though they were never sexually involved. "It was rule number one," Gore said, "to never mix sex and friendship. That's fatal."

Gore was also lucky in the fact that Claire Bloom, whom he liked immensely, had moved to Rome with her husband Rod Steiger and their infant daughter. Howard loved film actors, and together, he and Gore would mingle with the film trade. "It was a good place for actors," Armstrong said. "The center of filmmaking had shifted from Hollywood, and they were making movies in the Mediterranean region, in Italy and Egypt, Tunisia, Morocco, Greece, France. The presence of Claire Bloom really lifted Gore's spirits." As usual, Gore had landed in the right place at the right time.

v. *Julian* Rising

The manuscript of *Julian* grew steadily month by month, and Gore found himself "caught in its flywheel, spinning" as he wrote the last chapters. When it was typed, he left it with Dupee, who happened to be visiting Rome. "Fred was the only critic I ever trusted with my own work in those days," he recalled.

During this break from work on his novel, he flew back to Los Angeles for the filming of *The Best Man*, based on his own screenplay adaptation of the stage play, for which he was paid $100,000. "It was always best to keep an eye on a production like this," he said. "I'd learned a sad lesson with *Visit to a Small Planet*. This time, I saw eye to eye with Frank Schaffner," a young director who had worked briefly with Gore in live television and would later direct such films as *Planet of the Apes*, *Patton*, and *The Boys from Brazil*. "He was alert to the pitfalls, and mostly avoided them."

The prospects for this production had improved considerably when Henry Fonda, one of Hollywood's luminous stars, agreed to play William Russell. "Gore had been working, off and on, in Hollywood for nearly a decade, and he really needed this film to work," said Gavin Lambert, an English screenwriter and novelist who had become a good friend. "I visited the set of *The Best Man* with Gore, and it was very tense. Frank Schaffner didn't work well with women, and Cliff Robertson as Joe Cantwell seemed distracted. Gore functioned as a kind of cheerleader, and the shoot went pretty well. Gore left at one point for a few weeks, then returned to look at the raw footage. He saw many problems." As it turned out, this well-paced film, starring Fonda, Robertson, and Lee Tracy as the president, is probably the most artfully realized of Gore's films.

Stopping by Edgewater on the way back to Rome, Gore met with Dupee, who had been carrying around the manuscript of *Julian*, which amounted to nearly two hundred thousand words. Gore was writing a piece for *Esquire* on Tarzan, one of his boyhood obsessions, another on the Kennedy presidency (which never appeared), as well as a long essay on John Kenneth Galbraith for *The New York Review of Books*. In the latter, with his usual candidness, he describes Galbraith as America's "economic apostle to the middlebrows." He met Barbara Epstein over lunch in Manhattan to talk about his work for *The New York Review*, and she encouraged him. "He was one of the best writers in our stable," she said, "and we gave him his head. He could do whatever he liked, but he had to fit in writing for us somewhere among his other projects."

Gore reunited happily with Howard in Rome, and they celebrated by taking a trip to the north, visiting Siena and Florence, Bologna and Ferrara. They were back in Rome on November 22, 1963, when the world ground to a chilling halt with the assassination of John Kennedy. Gore had gone to see a film that day. "I was in the audience, watching some film, when at intermission word spread through the crowd that Kennedy had been shot in Dallas. It was as he predicted, but I never saw it coming. Nobody did. This wasn't supposed to happen."

Although he flew to Washington for the funeral, Gore never got to attend the actual service and suspected the dark hand of Bobby Kennedy at work, once again pushing him out of the inner circle. But his relations with Jackie had never recovered from that embarrassing night at the White House two years earlier, and she had no impulse to bring him nearer. The Kennedys simply didn't want Gore around, and he was forced to watch the procession of the coffin through the streets with thousands of others, as a bystander.

Before he returned to Rome, he sent the final version of *Julian* to his new publisher, Little, Brown and Company, where they rightly guessed it would be a success. The Book-of-the-Month Club—a mighty engine of American publishing in those days—soon chose the novel as its Main Selection, paying $250,000 for the right to bring out their own edition of the novel for their subscribers. When the novel arrived in bookshops in May, Gore had an inkling that this one might go well. It had, after all, been ten years since he last published a novel. In the meantime, he had written or worked on countless scripts, had seen full-length plays produced on Broadway and elsewhere, had run for Congress and written numerous essays and reviews. He had traveled widely, appeared on television, and generally spent a good deal of time and imagination on the expansion of his personal empire. He had, as planned, made himself financially independent. But *Julian* was his biggest gamble yet: an ambitious work of fiction rivaled in his work only by *Burr* and *Lincoln*.

The film of *The Best Man* was released in the spring, and for once *The New York Times* applauded: "The head-on clash of two threatening character assassins that was made so engrossing on the stage is even more vivid, energetic and lacerating on the screen. And the drama of this confrontation, happening in the midst of a hot and howling but strangely oblivious convention, is even more shockingly intense," wrote Bosley Crowther—a view confirmed by others in the press. Yet Gore felt vaguely let down when he watched the initial screening. "He was disappointed by the results," recalled Lambert. "His deep conviction was that no work of his would ever translate well to the screen, and he was probably right, as there is very little room for voice in a film. It's all moving pictures, not wry asides or quotable aphorisms." Yet he enjoyed the fanfare, which landed him on many chat shows, including *The Tonight Show*—always a favorite venue. He forged a lasting connection with Johnny Carson, its new host and the successor to Jack Paar.

That summer, spent partly at Edgewater, he enjoyed the fanfare that greeted *Julian*, published on June 8, with an initial print run of twenty-five thousand. For the first time, he hit number one on the best-seller list of *The New York Times*. And the reviews, while expressing reservations here and there, were mostly positive. Even *The New York Times Book Review*, regarded by Gore as enemy territory, printed a grudgingly positive review by the classical translator and poet Dudley Fitts, who wrote: "The breathing actuality of *Julian* is not to be denied."

The novel is, indeed, a "breathing actuality," with the eponymous central figure an attractive creation, based on the emperor known as "the Apostate," a self-assured and intelligent man who reigned for only sixteen months and was killed, at thirty-two, in a battle that occurred in 363 CE. The novel takes the form of diary entries by the emperor, with framing letters and commentary by two older mentors who survived their star pupil. This web of texts shimmers in space, somewhat unattached to realities on the ground but ever quick and compelling, often posing the ultimate question that Pontius Pilate put before Jesus: "What is truth?"

One recalls that, in *Messiah*, Eugene Luther had nearly finished his memoir of Julian when he shifted gears, becoming a covert founder of John Cave's religion. "I kept being drawn back to this century," said Gore, "as it played such a role in shaping the modern world." During the half century that elapsed between the accession of Julian's uncle, Constantine, and the death of Julian, "Christianity was established," as Gore writes in his "Note" at the beginning of the novel. "For better or worse," he says, "we are today very much the result of what they were then."

Perhaps the most obvious influences on Gore in his new role as novelist of the Roman Empire are *I, Claudius* (1934), a fictional memoir by Robert Graves, and Thornton Wilder's epistolary novel *The Ides of March* (1948). Gore didn't simply read these books; he studied them carefully, noting their use of historical sources, their narrative strategies. In a sense, he merges these prototypes, finding his own unique, and highly complex, form. His apposite but sometimes contradictory narratives remind us that history is fiction (i.e., a narrative that is shaped), and that the truth is invariably difficult to access. In this, Gore anticipates the postmodern turn in fiction, with its mistrust of objectivity and its frequent reliance on multiple perspectives.

In his historical fiction, Gore often centers on the everyday life of men in power. As Julian proceeds to Constantinople, for example, he speaks frankly of the physical demands and discomforts of the journey:

> In a blizzard, we filed through the pass of Succi and descended into Thrace. From there we proceeded to the ancient city of Philippopolis where we stayed overnight. Then we moved south to Heraclea, a town fifty miles southwest of Constantinople where, shortly before midday, to my astonishment, most of the Senate and the Sacred Consistory were gathered in the main square.

Then comes *Julian*'s ironic aside: "I was hardly prepared for such a greeting. I was tired, dirty, and I desperately needed to relieve myself. Imagine then the new emperor, eyes twitching with fatigue, hands, legs, face streaked with dust, bladder full, receiving the slow, measured, stately acclamation of the Senate."

The radical subjectivity of *Julian*, with its competing voices, prefigures the new biographical novel—a movement described by Michael Lackey, who writes: "For many biographical novelists, developments in postmodernism made it possible to fuse biography and the novel." He cites half a dozen practitioners of the genre (myself included) who argue in various essays and interviews that "it is no longer possible to treat historical and/or biographical representations as any more truthful than narratives of fiction because historians and biographers use the same rhetorical strategies, devices, and techniques as creative writers in constructing their narratives."

In *Julian* Gore demonstrates a subtle command of his sources, an easy knowledge of Roman history and geography, and a grasp of the theological issues of the day (Julian had been raised with the Arian view of Christianity, which regards Jesus as secondary to God: a view later regarded as heretical by the church). But it can hardly be said that this emperor was without a sense of spirituality. He combines personal asceticism with a profound awareness of spiritual realities, mixing and matching various mythic traditions, taking pieces from Hellenistic cults, combining them with Mithraism and a devotion to God in the form of the One (in the terminology of Plotinus). Julian loved the sun, in fact: Helios. He worshipped this physical manifestation of a larger power, basking in its energies. Even the mysteries represented by the oracle at Delphi interest him, and he celebrates them, revering ancient rites that have fallen into disrepute.

The novel ends with the frank musings of Julian's old teacher, Libanius, as he reflects on his pupil's life and its meaning. He is, like Gore's grandfather, a blind man (or almost blind, in this case). He has just come from the funeral of a great bishop, and he has listened with considerable attention to the eulogy. The speaker was John Chrysostom, "the new deacon, appointed last month by Meletius." Of course, Chrysostom would become an archbishop and early Church Father, famous as a preacher and theologian. Suddenly Libanius recognizes the voice as that of a former pupil. "My best student!" he cries. "Stolen from me by Christians!" It's a sign that things have changed, and not necessarily for the better. Christianity, with an unrelenting orthodox tone that disturbs him, has triumphed. "The spirit of what we were has fled," he says. "So be it." He notes, in the last paragraph of the novel, that "With Julian, the light went, and now nothing remains but to let the darkness come, and hope for a new sun and another day, born of time's mystery and man's love of light." It's a resonant concluding note, and one that bathes the novel in a serene light as voice is layered against voice, and the magic lantern of this elegant novel glows in the falling dark.

Moravia and Gore on the Isola Tiberna

Alberto Moravia has been here with Gore before, back in the sixties, but it's been a long time. "This is the only island in Rome," Gore says as we cross a bridge, the Ponte Fabricio. He explains that it was constructed "half a century before Christ." For whatever reason, he can't stop playing tour guide. George Armstrong, walking beside him, says, "You don't get a big serving for the price at this place, so order carefully."

Moravia waits for us in the tiny restaurant. He is tall, stooped-shouldered, very old and pasty. He speaks in a whisper like some Mafia don. His English isn't terribly good, but Gore's Italian is no better. I have to listen close.

George whispers in my ear, "They speak something between English and Italian. Gore just adds a vowel to English words and thinks it's Italian. Alberto grunts, as if he's speaking German."

At Gore's insistence, everybody orders the pasta with sausage, eggs, walnuts, and cream, and I soon see why. "In the sixties" he says, "I would come with Fred."

Fred is Federico Fellini, and Gore adores this joke. Moravia asks Gore what he's writing. "It's a novel about Hollywood," says Gore.

"Like Myra Breckinridge*?" asks Moravia.*

"No, it's one of my historical novels. It's a novel about our rulers."

"They're your rulers, not mine," says Moravia.

"I'm going to show that Washington—the people who rule our country—suddenly realized that they could manipulate the masses.

If only they could get their hands on the film industry, they could do anything they wanted. They succeeded."

The waiter brings another bottle of wine, which Gore grabs eagerly, pouring himself a large glass.

"I don't like your conspiracy theories," says Moravia. "You always assume there is a plan, Gore. There is no plan."

"In Italy, if there were a plan, it would never work," Gore responds. "That's why nobody makes plans here. Whatever happens, well, happens. That's why I live here. But in my country—"

"Your country!" Moravia interrupts.

"In my country, yes, the people can say anything they want, as long as nobody is listening. They do as they are told. On the other hand, Hollywood makes them happy."

"The movies only make me sad," says Moravia. "That's why I go so often."

Chapter Six

> Happily for the busy lunatics who rule over us, we are permanently the United States of Amnesia.
>
> —Gore Vidal

I. Romanitas

What we often call "the sixties" is really the late sixties, when seismic shifts in social attitudes occurred, and when the aspirations of the younger generation (especially those of college age) began to shift. The fifties represented a repressive era, the hectoring voice of Joe McCarthy or the House Committee on Un-American Activities in Washington, men in crew cuts, "homemakers" in the kitchen. The sexual mores of the generation that fought in World War II seemed hypocritical to their children. It's not that sex didn't happen in the old days, and lots of it. The problem was the masking of sexual feelings, the pushing of eros into a corner marked "out of bounds." There was also the matter of foreign policy. The Cold War had divided nations as well as parents and children. The steady escalation of the Vietnam War by Lyndon Johnson and Richard Nixon only opened this divide further, especially as young men who might be drafted into the army and possibly killed increasingly regarded this far-off war as futile and immoral.

So *Julian* arrived at a moment when readers were ready to look for rebels, and the Apostate was a prime example. The novel was reprinted again and again, and Gore's future as a novelist seemed assured. With his bank account swelling, he and Howard decided to refurbish Edgewater, perhaps in advance of selling it one day—that uncomfortable notion had been in the air for some time. They improved the kitchen and repainted most of the rooms. Howard insisted on adding a swimming pool on the south lawn, as the Hudson had grown increasingly polluted. He also went forward with plans to carve out an apartment in the brownstone at 416 East Fifty-Eighth, sensing that Gore's mind was in Italy. He wanted a foothold in Manhattan, and this would work. "Gore kept tugging me to Italy," he said. "I had to be careful."

Gore had invitations now to appear on most major talk shows in an era when they flourished on American television. He could be found talking with Norman Mailer at the Cow Palace in San Francisco during the 1964 Republican National Convention or sitting opposite William F. Buckley (the conservative journalist and founding editor of *National Review*) on David Susskind's *Open End* in New York. Or dropping witty asides on *What's My Line?*—a silly game show. "I needed television as much as it needed me," Gore later recalled. "It was a way of talking directly to people, without my voice filtered—distorted—by reviewers."

The television confrontations between Gore and Buckley began in 1962 and peaked early—but hardly for the last time—at the Cow Palace in 1964, where the two of them hissed and snarled at each other, Buckley sticking out his tongue in reptilian fashion, and Gore seeming bored, annoyed, or petulant. They traded barbs and witticisms, and both proved adept at working with the camera. It was obvious that this was a pairing made in television heaven. Both were lean, clever, sharp-witted, and capable of retaining large quantities of information, which each could dispatch at the right moment to confound the other, at least temporarily.

Buckley was the quintessential American conservative of a certain stripe: Roman Catholic, Ivy League educated, wealthy, with a mid-Atlantic accent that seemed to parody itself at times. His *National Review* was a conservative semimonthly magazine, begun in 1955, and Buckley used it as a platform to make himself the spokesman for laissez-faire, pro-business economics at home and a hard-nosed, anti-Communist foreign policy. With his first book, a feisty memoir called

God and Man at Yale (1951), he had stepped onto the national stage. For more than a decade he worked tirelessly to knit the various and often contradictory strands in American conservatism into a coherent ideology. He admired Joe McCarthy and was willing to go to great lengths to isolate Communist-leaning enemies. Yet he had a libertarian strain that was hard to reconcile with status-quo "Country Club Republicanism," which remained largely statist. Somehow Buckley had managed to fuse elements of both. His Catholicism added another element: that of piety and traditionalism, which seemed at odds with the (often anti-Catholic) Midwestern Protestant conservatives, who had a strong voice in the conservative movement of the fifties.

To his credit, Buckley and his circle did a good job in the fifties and early sixties of separating themselves from segregationist and anti-Semitic voices in the American conservative movement. And Buckley himself disliked Ayn Rand (an atheist) and George Wallace (a racist, in his view—although it took him a while to come around to this attitude). He also—not unlike Gore—denounced the John Birch Society, an extreme right-wing organization headed by Robert W. Welch Jr. Buckley argued sanely that this version of conservatism was far removed from common sense.

Gore would never accept, of course, that he and Buckley had a great deal in common. In addition to a wry, even caustic manner and highly variable upper-class accents (Gore didn't always speak in this fashion, but he did during his debates with Buckley), they also shared a similar background, with roots in the South—Gore's grandfather came from Mississippi, while Buckley's father, Will Buckley, had struck it rich as an oil man in Texas. Both, to a degree, had inherited their political stances and shared a core Jeffersonian reversion from the liberal mean, as represented by FDR and the New Deal. Gore's grandfather, of course, disliked the big-government style of Roosevelt, and so did Buckley's father. While they took opposing stances on many aspects of foreign and domestic policy, they shared more than either would admit.

Mailer, by contrast, had very little in common with Gore as far as their social backgrounds went, yet he was a good sparring partner. "Norman imagined himself by nature a kind of boxer—though he wasn't, not really," says Gay Talese, a friend to both Gore and Mailer. "In reality, Norman was soft. But he put on this aggressive mask. Gore had another kind of mask: cool, suave, worldly-wise. It was a good contrast with Norman. They played well together, but it was always a kind of act. They both understood the publicity value of this contest, and they let it play out in different ways." Mailer and Gore were often pitted against each other in public venues, though they remained friendly if not true friends. They both feared a Goldwater victory in 1964, although Johnson won the election handily, raking in more than 60 percent of the vote: the largest plurality since James Monroe was reelected in 1820.

This was something of an idyllic time for Gore, the calm before the storm of the later sixties. And yet his work on *Washington, D.C.* progressed more slowly than usual because he found it difficult to find a satisfactory voice, and to picture his own past, with its fading images. It seemed hard to make this familiar world seem real. In fact, Gore had an easier time with daily life in ancient Antioch or Constantinople: The deflecting mirror of history provided a feeling of comfort, whereas he did not yet have quite enough emotional distance from his youth to get a solid purchase on it. Nor was it easy to refuse offers from Hollywood. In 1965, for instance, from January through to his fortieth birthday in October, he spent most days on several scripts, including *Is Paris Burning?* and *The Night of the Generals.* (He got a partial screen credit for the former, nothing for the latter.) "I had learned a trade," Gore explained. "If you're a plumber, and a pipe is broken, someone is sure to call."

George Armstrong recalled this period: "In the mid-sixties, it looked as though we had Gore and Howard back with us, in Rome, for good. They both talked about it as home, and Gore wanted to sell the place on the Hudson." Another friend of this period was Judith Harris, who worked in the cultural office at the American embassy. She met Gore at a party and they became close friends. As she recalled, "Over the next two decades, from the mid-sixties through the eighties, Rome was Gore's main residence. A few of us became family. His real family. And there was always George. Gore loved George and even supported him financially in later years. There was a left-wing

Italian journalist called Gianfranco Corsini, too. Quite often Bill Pepper, another journalist, and his wife, Beverly, a sculptor, were around and joined the party. Celebrities would come through, and Gore loved that. But this wasn't daily life. For him, daily life was writing. In the evenings he liked to drink and go out to dinner, often with a large crowd, at one of the restaurants near the Campo dei Fiori. But the next day he was back at the desk. He had enviable self-discipline."

Life in Rome had a sensuous aspect that fed Gore's imagination. He took long walks through the old city, lingering at favorite spots, sometimes jotting down ideas in a notebook. He wrote to Fred Dupee that all he needed to feel well was to catch a glimpse of the Campidoglio—the sixteenth-century piazza designed by Michelangelo. He felt happier now than ever before, and wondered if he could bear to leave Rome again. His aristocratic English friend Judy Montagu had an apartment in Rome now, too, and this added spice. At her bountiful table he soon met Katharine Graham, the owner of *The Washington Post*, and Princess Margaret, the younger sister of Queen Elizabeth II, who soon became an important figure in his mind if not his life—a bold reminder to himself that he was important, and that he moved in the highest social circles.

Rome attracted an endless rotation of friends and even enemies, such as Truman Capote, who arrived "wreathed in friendship" one day that Gore recalled ruefully. "I tried to stay away from him as much as I could," he said. "The creepiness was distressing." He remained suspicious of Capote, with good reason, as Capote had never liked him and lost no opportunity to deride him in public (and especially behind his back). "Gore thinks distance from them will make the American critics' hearts grow fonder," Capote once said, in a typical later remark. "I guess Gore left the country because he felt underappreciated here. I have news for him: people who actually read his books will underappreciate him everywhere."

Harry Mathews would see Gore in Rome on occasional visits from France, where he was based. "It was a good life in Rome for Gore and Howard, as in those days the city had a kind of ease and charm that's gone now. You could pick up younger men on the streets, and for very little money. Gore liked anonymous sex, and that was plentiful. He once asked me to join him for a threesome, but I wasn't interested." Armstrong said, "It's what we all liked, the street boys. We felt avuncular to them. They were mostly in their twenties, repeat customers, and friends in a way. We met them at the bars for a drink, once in a while. We joked. Howard had learned a lot of slang from them, though Gore rarely listened and didn't understand what anybody was saying. His Italian was atrocious."

Thomas Powers, a recent Yale graduate who had just arrived in Rome and worked for the *Rome Daily American*, met Gore through Armstrong. They soon became friends. Powers recalled that during this period "sex was hugely important to Gore. It was almost an addiction, a daily addiction. But it wasn't the most important thing in his life. It was something he did, and then moved on."

One day in the spring of 1966, Howard passed a building on the Via di Torre Argentina, not far from the Pantheon, off the Corso Vittorio Emanuele II. "I saw a sign saying an apartment was for rent and soon I called the landlady about it. She took me upstairs in this caged elevator, very Roman. She showed me this beautiful sixth-floor penthouse apartment, very large, with a double terrace that looked out over red-tiled rooftops, church spires. One of the best terraces, and that really sold the place. There were three good-sized bedrooms and a smaller bedroom for a child or servant or whatever. It was so cheap, too. We took a year's lease, and it remained our base in Rome, really our main home, for a long time. It was kind of accidental. But there it was."

The unimposing building—with a faded yellow façade with storefronts at ground level—was called the Palazzo Origo, "named after Iris Origo, who was something of a writer," Gore recalled. "I knew her a little. An astonishing woman who would hide Allied soldiers." It had a dank, gray lobby with worn tile floors. There was a language school on one floor, offices on others, and a number of apartments, with the penthouse at the top. The elevator was a tiny cage that often broke down, leaving Gore and Howard to climb the cement steps with wrought-iron rails that rose through a dim stairwell. "The place stank," said Howard, "but it was just cooking, bad cooking, and garbage. Maybe a little piss. But the view made up for everything, and it had empty walls for lots of books."

The drawing room was large and dark, with cold terra-cotta walls, but the wraparound terrace had staggering views of the Largo di Torre Argentina below, a square that had been the site of four temples during the Roman Republic and still held the remains of the Theatre of Pompey. From one angle, there was Francesco Borromini's Sant'Ivo alla Sapienzia, with a spiraling steeple. Other domes caught the sunlight and glistened on a bright day, and there were two hills nearby, the Janiculum and the Aventine. "With this view," said Gore, "I didn't need more."

This was the first apartment that Gore and Howard furnished for themselves in Rome, as the others had been sublets. Edgewater had receded from their lives over the last few years, and Gore's loss in his bid for Congress in 1960 had pretty much destined this move to a more permanent Roman apartment. "It was a good time to get out of America," Howard said, "with Vietnam and all of that. We felt alien there. This seemed right, and Rome had a lot more for us than the Hudson Valley." Gore later reflected on the Italian versus the American character, noting: "The Italian *character* has a good deal of strength of a sort that the American character lacks. The Italian means to survive, at any cost. The American survives, but there is often too high a cost. Left to themselves, the Italians work out a fine balance between anarchy and order. When times are bad—or good—the balance shifts this way or that. But the nice balance, sooner or later, is restored. Fundamentally, Italians hate both anarchy and order. This is very human."

Powers recalls: "I would stop by the Largo Argentina, where he had a penthouse apartment, with a sheaf of magazines to pass along to him, things like *The Nation* or *The Economist*—he liked to get those, to keep up with whatever was going on at home in the States. We would sit together with a glass of wine on his terrace—an acre of terrace—and talk. He paid such close attention to me. He didn't have to do that. But he did it with people, gave them his complete attention, asked questions, told stories with huge enthusiasm. You knew he'd told these stories many times, but it didn't matter. He told them over again, always with a fresh sense. He was very kind and responsive. We would sometimes meet in a restaurant—there is nothing like a Roman restaurant in midwinter—and we'd talk about politics and history, current happenings. Rome was such a fine place then."

II. Capitol Steps Revisited

Gore's labor on *Washington, D.C.* came to an end in the fall of 1966. He had been trying, he told his stepsister Nina, to capture the sense of a "republic becoming an empire" in this novel, but he fretted about the reviews. Holdovers from the Kennedy administration would dislike the not-so-blurry image of JFK in the character of Clay Overbury, a former senatorial aide turned war hero turned presidential aspirant. The character most like Gore is Peter Sanford, whose family will figure in several of the Narratives of Empire that would preoccupy him for decades, encompassing seven novels between 1967 and 2000. The first novel in the series begins in 1937 and unfolds over a decade, tracking events in the lives of Senator James Burden Day and the newspaper magnate Blaise Sanford. Not unlike Gore's grandfather, Senator Day opposes the New Deal and regards FDR warily as a potential tyrant—the conclusion reached by Thomas P. Gore during the late thirties.

It's a straightforward story, with the usual backroom machinations on view as the ambitious Overbury, a former aide to Burden Day, marries Enid, the tempestuous daughter of the senator. Gore skillfully tracks Peter Sanford's evolving sensibility as he tries to differentiate himself from his overbearing father and establish himself as a literary figure in the postwar moment. Senator Day closely resembles Senator Gore; indeed, his address on Rock Creek Park is actually adjacent to Senator Gore's, and Senator Day, like Gore's grandfather, led the isolationist wing of the Democratic Party that crumbled when the Japanese invaded Pearl Harbor. Laurel House—the estate of Blaise and Frederika Sanford—resembles Merrywood, the Auchincloss mansion where Gore spent some of his teenage years.

Senator Day has only one daughter, Diana, and he would like Clay to marry her, but Clay—who resembles John Kennedy in many particulars—believes that Enid Sanford is a much better prospect. As Enid says to her father: "After all, Clay will do anything to help his career." After she and Clay have separated, she suggests darkly that her father secretly loves Clay. Indeed, skeletons rattle in this sexual closet, as they often do in Gore's fiction.

But there is no love in *Washington, D.C.*, the novel or the city. The main players cavort, but their passion for power overwhelms their desire for sex. The author pauses to admire the fabric of these gossipy circles, where ambition drives nearly everyone to perdition, but no love survives. This is the new Rome, transmogrified. Gore brings to the material his experience of watching at close hand how politicians operate. He has observed his grandfather moving and shaking hands through the U.S. Senate. He has studied JFK at close quarters. He has met so many real players on the American political scene. Yet hardly a single character in this world is not—like Gore himself—a narcissist, in desperate need of reflection. This cynical attitude may owe something to Gore's own failure to thrive in this atmosphere, but his resentment, combined with a satirist's eye for human foibles, generates an entertaining plot despite its failure to reach the higher levels of political fiction, as in Trollope's Palliser novels, which Gore often reread and kept in view. "I also had in mind *Democracy*, one of the best things Henry Adams did," Gore said, referring to a sharply cynical novel of 1880.

The first edition of thirty-five thousand copies appeared on May 1, 1967, and it sold well, if not as well as *Julian*. In any case, Gore had stumbled on a kind of writing that would continue to interest him: the American political novel, a kind of family saga as well as roman-fleuve, with recurring characters. He could draw on his own deep knowledge of American political life and project his growing awareness of the American imperium. In *Julian*, of course, Gore portrays a real emperor who rejected Judeo-Christian norms and failed, whereas in *Washington, D.C.*, he depicts several would-be emperors playing cynically with American values, which he regards as shallow and hypocritical. With his exquisitely tuned cultural antennae,

Gore now began to revise American history in his own image, seeing hypocrisy everywhere. He took for granted that all who aspired to power had selfish reasons for behaving as they did. Sexuality itself, in Gore's radical understanding of this basic human drive, was fluid. He regarded bisexuality as the norm, with every attempt to isolate the erotic impulse on one side of the great divide (gay or straight, not male or female) destined to produce some form of distortion. As a consequence, duplicity ripples through *Washington, D.C.*, much as it would circulate through his future novels of American history and politics.

III. The Holy Family

In the Roman winter of 1967, Gore occupied himself with rewriting a major essay, "The Holy Family," which would appear in *Esquire* in April. With his sure instinct for self-marketing, he engineered its publication only a month before the release of his latest novel, making sure he would get maximum exposure. It had already been rejected by *The New York Review of Books*, whose editors, Barbara Epstein and Robert Silvers, considered its tone if not its content inflammatory. And it was. It was shocking that, only a few years after the traumatizing death of JFK, Gore could write: "Kennedy dead has infinitely more force than Kennedy living." In the "holy family" of the Kennedys, Jack had become the "the subject of a cult" that persisted through the machinery of publicity, which the Kennedy family had learned to operate. The murdered president is seen as a kind of Osiris-Adonis-Christ figure: the dying and reviving god who saves the world in ways that he had failed to do during his feeble presidency, which began with the Bay of Pigs fiasco and never really went anywhere. Kennedy's hagiographers called it the "thousand days"—the length of this sad presidency, now created, as Gore quips, in "a thousand books," which he ostensibly reviews here but really uses as the occasion for his own musings.

Gore had begun to enlarge and redefine the book-review essay in his own way, making it a personal essay, a confessional, a philosophical journey, a political rout, a college lecture, a close-up on history lived firsthand by Gore and now put forward less than modestly. "Mrs. Kennedy once said to me . . ." becomes the thin wedge with which Gore drives himself, with astonishing ease, into the middle of Camelot. As a writer, he takes his seat at the high table, where in real life he never found much of a welcome. And he uses the essay (cleverly, coolly) to get at Robert F. Kennedy, who dared to toss him (though not literally) from the White House. We get a number of personal quotes from JFK, too, as when he tells Gore that Eleanor Roosevelt hated his father because "she can't stand it that his children turned out so much better than hers." Did Kennedy really say that? Probably not. But I have no doubt Gore believed he heard it from the emperor's lips. In all, this is a tour de force, as much fiction as nonfiction, which is to say that it highlights certain aspects of the Kennedy story and represses others, an arrangement of facts designed to create an impression.

The essay asks a pressing question: "What sort of men ought we to be governed by in the coming years?" Not Robert Kennedy, for sure, is an underlying and (just barely) unspoken point here, as in: "Since Bobby is thought by some to be ruthless, he must therefore be photographed with children, smiling and happy and athletic, in every way a boy's ideal man." The sword rips quietly through the flesh of the as yet undead brother, although in a postscript to the essay published in 1968, shortly after RFK's assassination, Gore (unconvincingly) backtracks: "Although I certainly never wanted Bobby to be President, I had lately come to accept him as a useful figure on the scene—and now that he is gone I find that I genuinely miss him." That last phrase sounds an embarrassing false note—one of the few anywhere in Gore's essays.

Needless to say, the essay was a Molotov cocktail thrown at the Kennedys, albeit a small one. The family had other, more pressing things to worry about than a sniping near-relative who could write. "It was Gore's way of getting rid of the Kennedy thing," said Howard. "And it worked. He didn't have a close connection to Jackie in the first place; now he had none to speak of."

IV. MYRA

Essays became an absorbing passion now, and Gore continued to write for a variety of publications, including *Book Week*, *The New York Review of Books*, and *Esquire*. As he noted in an eloquent preface to *Reflections Upon a Sinking Ship* (1969), his second volume of essays, "I personally find myself vacillating between living in Rome and raging in New York, between silence and exhortation, between human despair and animal hope." The essay—as a literary genre—provided an outlet, a way of breaking the silence, and a mode of exhortation. And writing essays brought him, purposefully, into contact with a range of new writing. This was all part of his self-education, as book reviews became his very own Harvard.

One evening Kenneth Tynan telephoned to invite Gore to contribute to a new theatrical review to be called *Oh! Calcutta!* It was intended as a series of erotic sketches, and Tynan explained that he had already garnered commitments from the likes of Samuel Beckett, John Lennon, and Edna O'Brien, the Irish novelist who became Gore's friend in later years. Although nobody could have predicted it at the time, *Oh! Calcutta!* was one of the most successful Broadway shows of all time, running for 1,314 performances in its first incarnation. (It was equally successful in London's West End and elsewhere.) The playwright Harold Pinter had promised to direct, along with Tynan.

As Gore later recalled: "I just didn't want anything to do with Ken's project. I had no plans, and I liked it that way. But I recall sitting at my desk, on a warm spring day in Rome, staring into space, when a voice entered my head: 'I am Myra Breckinridge whom no man will ever possess.' I never quite had that experience, an otherworldly voice, one that took me over. I felt like a medium. The book poured out in a few weeks. The short chapters just unfurled. I felt I must find out what happened and watched the developing plot with interest." The novel "unfurls" its lavender flag as Gore assumes the campy bravura voice of Myra, which stands in contrast to some (appropriately) dull dictation by Myra's uncle, Buck Loner—an overweight former singing cowboy who runs an acting academy for Hollywood wannabes.

The novel might also be regarded as something that grew from Gore's recent plunge into avant-garde French literary theory. In February and March 1967, he wrote "French Letters: Theories of the New Novel," a sweeping essay that was turned down by *The New York Review of Books* because they considered the subject terminally boring; *Encounter*, an elite English journal of ideas and opinion, eagerly published it in December. In a critique of French theories of fiction as posed and practiced by such writers as Nathalie Sarraute and Alain Robbe-Grillet, Gore explores with superb mastery of the subject the directions in which the novel had veered as authors tried to come to terms with the loss of belief in language itself, in the failure of narrative to take readers on a significant journey. And so, in *Myra Breckinridge*, begun only weeks after he finished his essay on the New Novel, he invents his own "New Novel." Gore's sly surrogate declares: "The novel being dead, there is no point to writing made-up stories." She wryly meditates on the loss of conventional narrative structure: "I shall not begin at the beginning since there is no beginning, only a middle into which you, fortunate reader, have just strayed . . ."

In Gore's confection, Myra is supposedly the widow of one Myron Breckinridge, a gay film critic from New York whose abiding obsession is a real-life film critic called Parker Tyler, who focused on the films of the late thirties and forties. Myron was the nephew of Buck Loner, and Myra has come to claim her inheritance from Myron's mother, Gertrude (shades of *Hamlet*?). Buck Loner isn't sure what to do, so he temporizes, giving Myra a job as a teacher of Empathy and Posture. As it happens, Myra was once Myron, having been transformed from a man to a woman by a surgeon in Copenhagen. Myra is also a goddess, an embodiment of the feminine archetype, a kind of White Goddess figure as described by Robert Graves in a book by the same name. Riffing on Graves's theme, Myra creates her own highly subjective theology, suggesting that "the cock-worshipping Dorians enslaved the West, impiously replacing the Goddess with a god." Yet Myra hovers between sexes, having not quite made the transition to female. One thinks of the character of Tiresias in T. S. Eliot's *The Waste Land*, a hermaphroditic figure "throbbing between two lives" and therefore possessed of prophetic powers. This goddess wants revenge, however, especially on men who have (in her previous incarnation, perhaps as homophobes) treated her badly.

Overpopulation is a consistent problem in Gore's world. "Man plus woman equals baby equals famine," he wrote in 1966 in "On Pornography." "If the human race is to survive, population will have to be reduced drastically, if not by atomic war, by law, an unhappy prospect for civil liberties but better than starving to death." Yet men must be men, therefore aesthetically (if not sexually) virile. So Myra tells her therapist that one day men will go around masquerading as men, standing at the bar in cowboy hats, in boots and spurs, drinking whiskey.

Despite (or because of) its over-the-top violence and far-out sexuality, *Myra* was a best seller, landing Gore on the cover of glossy magazines and enhancing his presence to an astounding degree, although many reviewers looked askance at his flagrantly vulgar production. "Has literary decency fallen so low?" asked the reviewer in *Time*, echoing others. For *Newsweek*, the book was just "erotic propaganda," whatever that might be. But this novel was so much more than that. Gore had ushered in what might be considered the expressionistic postmodern pop-comic novel, a satire on sex and celebrity, so ruthless, so visionary, that it remains a jaw-dropping performance, on a par with John Updike's *Couples* (1968) and Philip Roth's *Portnoy's Complaint* (1969)—novels that signaled to the American reading public that the sexual revolution would be felt in major fiction.

Myra is a giddy celebration of bad taste, as embodied by the overblown Chateau Marmont, a glorious piece of architectural kitsch. Myra gazes out from her terrace in the opening scene, much as Gore did when he first moved to Hollywood, seeing "the midsection of the huge printed plaster chorus girl who holds a sombrero in one hand as she revolves slowly." Even the "straight" characters exhibit bad taste, especially Rusty Godowsky, a handsome masculine ideal who proves an ideal subject for Gore's dissolute satire. Rusty is in love with Mary-Ann Pringle, a matching cardboard cutout. Myra, in her perverse role as savior ("I alone can save the human race," she says), needs to recalibrate sexuality, forging a fresh new balance between the sexes. "It is plain that nature and I are on a collision course," she says.

Few reviewers fathomed what was on Gore Vidal's mind in *Myra*. Was he writing porn for the masses? Was he allowing his own camp sensibility to run wild? A climactic scene in the novel is the rape of Rusty by Myra, a lewd parody of pornographic scenes featuring a dominatrix and an innocent young man who seems to want, but doesn't really, what he gets. Myra uses a dildo to deflower him in an anal rape that still beggars the imagination as Gore mimics the language of gay porn: "The sphincter resembled a tiny pale pink tea rose, or perhaps a kitten's nose and mouth." It's a terrifying, unpleasant scene at best. Afterward Myra is "saddened and repelled" by the act of sodomy. But she's a goddess, after all, and guilt weighs lightly on her conscience. "I was one with the Bacchae," she reminds us, "with all the priestesses of the dark bloody cults, with the great goddess herself for whom Attis unmanned himself."

Part confession to her analyst/dentist, part self-dramatizing diary (in the mode of Anaïs Nin, Gore's supposed model for the voice), part Hollywood memoir, the book leaves almost no popular genre unmolested. This is an all-consuming narrative that fields every possibility as the speaker tries desperately "to capture the reality of Myra Breckinridge, despite the treachery and inadequacy of words." It is, indeed, a send-up of narrative in itself. "I knew a female impersonator called Myra," Gore recalled. "And her performance stuck with me. Then I imagined it. Hollywood creates our myths now, not our novelists. Myra smiles at the destruction of our culture, such as it was." The name Breckinridge had two possible sources: James Buchanan's vice president was John C. Breckinridge, and there was a famous transsexual in San Francisco called Bunny Breckinridge, who was "the biggest queen in the world," according to Gore. Yet there was a more mundane side to the name: Gore just liked the sound of it, how it rolls off the tongue.

Myra "understands" that Hollywood trumps religion, wondering if the "actual Christ" could have held a candle to the radiant figure in *The King of Kings*, the 1927 biblical epic produced by Cecil B. DeMille with H. B. Warner as Jesus. One of the running gags in the novel is a meditation on Tyler's *Magic and Myth of the Movies*, which becomes a kind of sacred text: Myra's "worn copy" is always open before her as she writes. She constantly searches the familiar book for guidance, as did the readers of the Testament of Cavesword in *Messiah*. "Sympathetic magic must be made," Myra exclaims. With her unchecked ambition, Myra wants to make this magic herself, to be a star (like Gore, she is a compulsive mimic of earlier stars) and to become a producer as well. She realizes that television now plays a major role in shaping culture and wants part of that, too. Her lust for life, for power, for all things bright and beautiful, suffuses her narrative. "She took joie de vivre to an unnatural summit," said Gore. "I gazed in admiration from well below her."

It's not easy to wrap one's mind around *Myra*. "I was thinking, of course, about *Orlando*, an earlier take on gender-shifting," Gore said of Virginia Woolf's 1928 novel, where she offers a witty meditation on gender, suggesting that the character of her hero/heroine transcends sex. *Myra Breckinridge* goes further, plunging us into contradictions of transsexual border-crossings, exploring the implications of gender (a cultural construct) and sex (a biological basis) in ways that anticipate later versions of queer theory. Myron becomes Myra becomes Myron. In each incarnation, he/she embodies some aspect of that gender, sometimes (as in the rape of Rusty) seeming unable to put aside certain male (homosexual) urges, preferring to lapse into the language of a female deity.

Gore's novel is darkly prophetic, envisioning a world of confused gender and sexual violence, exploring the as yet uncharted boundaries of feminist theory just as the movement was beginning to emerge. *Myra*'s prurience remains, to some readers, disturbing. In some ways, as in the rape of Rusty, Gore seems to enjoy the parody a little too much. It's entirely believable when he writes about Rusty's "healthy earthlike aroma," and one knows that Gore writes from experience. Yet readers flocked to bookstores, and *Myra* rode high on the best-seller lists, a success at home and abroad. In fact, three printings of the Little, Brown edition, published on February 29, 1968, sold out before it officially arrived in bookstores, with more than eighty-five thousand copies sold before publication. It remained on most best-seller lists for thirty-six weeks, two million copies of the Bantam paperback were sold within a month of its first printing in September 1968, and the novel appeared in more than fifteen languages.

v. Busy Weekends

After finishing the rough draft of *Myra*, Gore took an excursion with Howard, Paul Newman, and Joanne Woodward to the Greek islands, a two-week journey by sailboat that proved unpleasant. "Everybody was sick," Howard recalled. "Waves, waves, waves. The captain was an idiot who didn't seem to know how to sail. We got boarded by the Greek navy, who thought we were spies. Nobody was happy. And Gore just wanted to get back to work."

World tension was high, with the Six-Day War sweeping the Middle East in June 1967 and the Vietnam War so hot that a war with China seemed entirely possible. (The infamous Tet Offensive would occur in January 1968, making the situation for Americans in Southeast Asia even more perilous.) Back in the States, the antiwar movement had begun to gather momentum, and thousands surrounded the Pentagon on October 21, 1967, an event that Mailer would describe in *The Armies of the Night* (1968), perhaps his best work. "The old alliances, everywhere, seemed to break down," Gore said.

In July, Gore "finished *Myra*, in Rome. George [Armstrong] typed it. I knew I'd done something at the very least unusual." He mailed it to his editor at Little, Brown, and also sent a copy to its dedicatee, Christopher Isherwood, who wrote back coyly to say it was a "very subtle psychological self-portrait." In a way, it was: Gore had fully inhabited Myra/Myron, not the other way around. He was using her to express something in himself that was difficult to express, and that required the deflecting mirror of the novel. Her "dress shield," mentioned in the opening paragraph, might be regarded as the protective shield of Perseus, the mythical hero who decapitated the Gorgon Medusa (into whose eyes you could not look without turning into stone). Gore deflected his life, his dark passions, his rage and need for revenge, in Myra's glistening surfaces.

Feeling pleased with himself, Gore set off (this time, without Howard) to Sardinia for ten days at a seaside villa rented by Diana Phipps, a gifted interior designer whom Gore had met through Judy Montagu. Phipps had been born into a noble Czech family, the Sternbergs (who for hundreds of years occupied a castle in the lush countryside of East Bohemia). Gore was warmly taken into this cosmopolitan and aristocratic circle. As Howard wryly noted: "He liked being around royalty. Whenever we were in England and somebody played 'God Save the Queen,' Gore would stand up and wave."

He proceeded to Venice, where he stayed at the sixteenth-century Gritti Palace, his favorite hotel on the Grand Canal, attending a masked ball where he renewed his acquaintance with Clare Boothe Luce, the wife of the owner of *Time* and herself an accomplished diplomat and playwright (*The Women* had been a hit on Broadway in 1936). Under Eisenhower, she had served as the U.S. ambassador to Italy, which was only one of her many playgrounds. Gore joked about this high life in a letter to Dupee: "Sardinia, Venice, the life of the beautiful people, almost as tiring as Red Hook–Rhinebeck." But underneath the joke, one sees that "the life of the beautiful people" appealed to him, and he didn't regard Edgewater as a place where enough of them could now be found. "I may be away for some time," he told Dupee.

Money was not a problem. Little, Brown kept an account for him, with royalties rising there to more than $100,000, which Gore could withdraw at a pace that minimized tax liabilities. He had been dealing shrewdly with his publisher about what book would fulfill his three-book contract, and *Myra* did exactly that, allowing him to move elsewhere if he wished. At this time he found a new agent, too, an old friend from Los Angeles, Sue Mengers—a German immigrant who represented an impressive array of Hollywood stars, including Michael Caine, Candice Bergen, Gene Hackman, and Barbra Streisand. Mengers became a close confidante in years to come, someone whose phone calls Gore awaited eagerly. "Sue has the story on everything," he said, "and she's willing to tell me the stories."

With *Myra Breckinridge* high on lists of best-selling novels, several Hollywood producers fought for the right to make Gore's romp into a film. (Only in Britain did Gore meet resistance to the novel, as

Heinemann had rejected the book, fearing it would taint their reputation. But Anthony Blond, a smaller publisher, stepped into the breach, bringing out the U.K. edition in October 1968. The British censors refused to let Blond publish the book in its original form, and Gore agreed to allow a somewhat bowdlerized version to appear.)

Wondering what to write next, Gore pulled from a bottom drawer in his desk in Rome a sketch he had written "on a couple of transatlantic flights" in the previous year. He finished *Weekend* in the fall of 1967. By December, he had secured a producer, and the play previewed in February with some success in New Haven and D.C. before opening at the Broadhurst on West Forty-Fourth in New York in March. It would close after only twenty-three performances, a disappointing run, mostly because the critics hated it. "Gore Vidal's *Weekend* is a slick comedy," wrote Walter Kerr in *The New York Times*, "so urbane that its characters can sit on coffee tables without being rebuked, so up-to-the-minute politically that it knew in advance Rockefeller wouldn't run, so relentlessly civilized that you'd give absolutely anything if only one of its mannequins would interrupt another in mid-epigram. It sounds like the rattle of ice cubes in a long weak drink."

Gore recalled that review bitterly: "Kerr could close a play with the stroke of a pen, and he did." Adding to Gore's paranoia, Kerr had come to the play with Lynda Bird Johnson, the president's daughter, on his arm. She walked out in a fury when a nasty allusion to her father flashed from the stage. The audience generally seemed hostile to Gore's ultra-suave take on the current political scene. To many ears, the dialogue sounded sneering, even misanthropic. *Weekend* centers on a fictitious Republican senator about to announce his run for the White House. Just before he does, he learns of his son's engagement to a black woman. Other problems arise, making the timing of this announcement awkward if not impossible. It's not a bad idea for a play, but the cardboard characters and tiresome quips didn't endear it to anyone. It may also be that the audience who attended the early performances could not enjoy mere banter about politics when there was so much to trouble them in the real world. This light entertainment was a rare miscalculation by Gore.

Nor did he give the production his full attention, having other things on his mind as he rushed about the country appearing on talk shows, giving interviews to the press, visiting friends, working contacts as if about to run for the presidency himself. Exhausted, he flew back to Rome in April, hoping to settle into a quiet Italian summer and begin to think seriously about his next novel. He had any number of book reviews to finish—that never changed. But he was soon presented with an offer he couldn't refuse: to appear on ABC in a series of live prime-time debates with William F. Buckley during the presidential conventions scheduled for August. They would do seven or eight slots, each of them fifteen minutes long, moderated by Howard K. Smith, one of the most respected journalists in the country.

By now Buckley and Vidal were notorious as antagonists, and they seemed a perfect match, each being articulate, good-looking, suave, and telegenic. Their politics matched perfectly: right and left fitting like a jigsaw puzzle. Unlike Gore, however, Buckley had fully devoted himself to political propaganda, using the medium of television rather brilliantly, beginning in 1966 on *Firing Line*, where he interviewed (and often debated) a constellation of public figures, such as Ronald Reagan, Margaret Thatcher, B. F. Skinner, Noam Chomsky, Milton Friedman, Allen Ginsberg, Jesse Jackson, and Billy Graham. As Gore well knew, Buckley had crafted a style of debate marked by irony and combativeness. Being no slouch in either department, Gore seized the offer.

VI. The Vidal-Buckley Debates

"He was like a prizefighter getting ready for a big fight," recalled Howard, who accompanied Gore to New York in midsummer. There Gore made elaborate notes on a variety of hot topics, including the Vietnam War, housing for the poor, and the constitutional rights of assembly for protest. He knew Buckley would come well-armed with statistics and Jesuitical arguments. Following the Tet Offensive, the Johnson administration stepped up the draft, calling for forty-eight thousand new soldiers: a move that inflamed the college-age generation, creating resistance on a scale nobody in Washington could have foretold.

Events piled on events with a kind of furious malevolency. Martin Luther King Jr. had been assassinated in Memphis in April, Bobby Kennedy in Los Angeles in June. "We had always been a violent country," Gore said, "but these deaths confirmed what we knew already." Students protested the war in swelling numbers, beginning at Berkeley and Columbia, soon spreading everywhere. The United States became a divided country, largely along generational lines, and the debates between Gore and Buckley would articulate the lines of battle.

A number of writers, including Mailer, flocked to Miami and Chicago for the conventions, where the war in Vietnam would be argued in public view. In the wake of his loss of the New Hampshire primary to Senator Eugene McCarthy—a mild-mannered liberal who opposed the war—Johnson announced one night on evening television that he wouldn't run for reelection. Cheers broke out across the country in college dorms, and the nomination for the top of the Democratic ticket seemed wide open, though Hubert Humphrey, who had supported Johnson's war uncritically, appeared destined for the nod. (McCarthy had not proved a forceful strategist, much to the disappointment of many in the antiwar movement.) On the Republican side, Richard Nixon looked ready to triumph over Nelson Rockefeller, who occupied the liberal wing of the party, with Ronald Reagan on the right.

The eight Buckley-Vidal debates became major television events, with as many as ten million viewers tuning in for each session. There were only three networks at the time, so they could count on big audiences. And the kind of saturation publicity that Vidal and Buckley got during August 1968 turned them both into genuine celebrities. They confronted each other like vipers, coiled and ready to strike. By contrast with the Chicago debates that followed, the Miami debates at the Republican National Convention seemed almost tame, though viewers sensed the tension between them. Buckley's manner was feline, a slithering presence, with his tongue flicking, his eyes leering. Gore was only slightly less pompous, with affectations and mannerisms that seemed out of character. Buckley was snidely self-righteous, Gore snickering and self-consciously aristocratic.

The antagonism between them was evident from the start, as

Buckley attacked Gore for spending much of the year in Europe, implying that he was a traitor because he lived abroad. By the third debate, Buckley couldn't resist jibing at Gore for being the author of *Myra Breckinridge*, which he referred to as pornography. Gore hit back hard, in blatantly ad hominem terms: "If there were a contest for Mr. Breckinridge, you would unquestionably win it. I based her style polemically on you—passionate but irrelevant." Gore referred to Buckley as "the Marie Antoinette of the right wing" imposing his own "bloodthirsty neurosis" on American politics. Allusions to homosexuality were abundant, with Buckley implying that Gore was somehow "other." For his part, Gore quietly insinuated that Buckley was a closeted queen. Generally, however, each man put forward his positions with clarity and poise, summoning well-shaped sentences—even whole paragraphs—with facility. Both trotted out facts and figures with machinelike efficiency, hardly glancing at the notes on their laps. Gore had eloquent moments, as when he referred to the Republican agenda as a mixture of "socialism for the rich and free enterprise for the poor." What remains shocking is the degree to which most of the issues under debate on that occasion have remained ones that still roil our political discourse.

The real fight began in Chicago. More than ten thousand demonstrators belonging to various student movements converged, despite the refusal of Mayor Richard Daley to allow permits. As Gore saw it, this abrogated the "right to assembly" as put forward in the U.S. Constitution. On August 28, the day of the seventh Vidal-Buckley debate, there had been a "police riot," as it was described in the subsequent Walker Report. A young protestor had lowered the American flag in Grant Park, and the police swarmed. Tear gas filled the air and clubs swung. The entire nation watched in horror as the United States appeared to slip into anarchy.

A few blocks from the Democratic National Convention site, angry students with a smattering of antiwar intellectuals, including Mailer and Ginsberg, gathered in the parks, marched in the streets, danced, and chanted provocative slogans: "Ho Ho Ho Chi Minh!" and "Hell No, We Won't Go!" Among the groups represented were the SDS (Students for a Democratic Society), the Black Panthers, and the Yippies (Youth International Party). Many were filmed burning their draft cards.

That night was the fifth day of the Chicago convention, and the nation watched anxiously as a so-called "peace plank" was put forward and voted down. This provoked anger and some hysteria among the protestors, who streamed toward the convention center with placards, chanting slogans. They were confronted by thousands of policemen augmented by the National Guard, among others. Fred Turner, an engineer with CBS, watched from the fifth-floor window of the Hilton, describing the events below: "Now they're moving in, the cops are moving and they are really belting these characters. They're grabbing them, sticks are flailing. People are laying on the ground. I can see them, colored people. Cops are just belting them; cops are just laying it in. There's piles of bodies on the street. There's no question about it. You can hear the screams, and there's a guy they're just dragging along the street and they don't care. I don't think . . . I don't know if he's alive or dead. Holy Jesus, look at him. Five of them are belting him, really, oh, this man will never get up."

Inside the convention hall, Senator Abraham Ribicoff of Connecticut referred to the "Gestapo tactics on the streets of Chicago." Mayor Daley failed to respond in a reasonable way, shouting to Ribicoff: "Fuck you, you Jew son of a bitch! You lousy motherfucker! Go home!" As tempers flared and violence reigned, viewers tuned in for the Vidal-Buckley debate that evening with keen expectations of a showdown.

It was a withering encounter, with no real winner. Buckley spoke for the older generation when he decried the lawlessness in the streets, the lack of respect for laws and tradition. He exuded patriotism. Smith wondered aloud if raising a Vietcong flag in the midst of the Vietnam War wasn't unduly provocative. Buckley nodded sharply, saying it was like raising a Nazi flag in America during the Second World War. Gore shook his head, referring again and again to the "right to assembly." "What are we doing in Vietnam if you can't freely express yourself in the streets of Chicago?" he asked.

It was, from the outset, an exhausting exchange for both debaters. A heated moment occurred when Buckley once again referred to Gore as a pornographer, though Gore didn't take the bait. As Gore talked about the repressive treatment of protestors in Lincoln Park, alluding to the riots on the streets nearby, Buckley interrupted rudely. He remembered the time George Lincoln Rockwell, a leader of the American Nazi Party, had marched with his followers into a small town in Illinois. They had been turned away, and Buckley thought this had been justified by the circumstances. Taking the cue, Gore interrupted Buckley: "As far as I'm concerned, the only pro- or crypto-Nazi I can think of is yourself." It was a deadly assertion, and Buckley curled his lip and sneered: "Now listen, you queer! Stop calling me a crypto-Nazi or I'll sock you in your goddamn face and you'll stay plastered." Buckley added with a wicked glare: "Go back to your pornography."

These debates became legendary, and decades later people still recall them, if hazily. "They really sealed the deal on Gore's fame," says Matt Tyrnauer. Indeed, Gore proved he could handle himself at a very high level, staying cool under the hot lights, smiling at insults, dropping witticisms, remembering his facts and figures. Buckley had actually called Gore a queer on television, breaking a gentlemanly code. This wasn't done in 1968, not in prime time. Yet Gore had not behaved perfectly himself, calling Buckley a crypto-Nazi when, as he said, "I meant to call him a crypto-fascist." Hardly two decades after the war, Nazi was a dreadful word to attach to Buckley or anyone else. But ABC had scored a coup of sorts, even though the seventh debate had exceeded the usual bounds of polite discourse. (The network actually canceled the rebroadcast of this debate on the West Coast that night, considering it indecent.)

Responding to an interviewer in Chicago the next day, Gore said, "I've always tried to treat Buckley like the great lady that he is." This only fed the strong undercurrent of sexual innuendo and further infuriated Buckley, who wanted revenge. In fact, only a few months later, sitting in Rome, Gore learned that Buckley had asked Harold Hayes, the editor of *Esquire*, to let him write his own account of the debates. Hayes agreed, with the proviso that Gore should have an opportunity to respond in his own way. An incredible few months followed, with lawyers for Gore and Buckley reading their dueling pieces; *Esquire* also had lawyers scrutinizing their pages.

Meanwhile, Gore received a gentle letter from his relatively conservative father, who showed concern as well as support for his famous son: "Regularly I think of your convention debates, wondering whether or not with all its confusing angles you did or did not fare well. For instance, I find that I am quite alone in my reactions to the cop clubbing; at least, in these parts. Yet the TV viewers couldn't fail to see what I saw. I wonder if anyone really understands our average American. The current ones may be a lot simpler than we realize. At any rate, let me know whether or not you gained, if you can figure it out. I quite naturally feel that Buckley had a serious setback."

Buckley remained in a state of fury, perhaps angry with himself for losing his cool on television before so many people and using language that, at the time, was considered improper. Gore's written response, which Buckley read before publication, was inflammatory, with references to Buckley's family and their supposed anti-Semitism. Gore needled Buckley about his sexuality, too, with insinuating language. Lawyers scrutinized every phrase, making sure that each statement qualified in legal terms as reasonably substantiated. But it was difficult, if not impossible, to keep such rhetoric under control.

When the articles finally appeared, in August and September, Buckley sued *Esquire*, asking for $1 million in recompense for "emotional and financial damages." He claimed that Gore had willfully, without proof, implied that he was a Nazi, an anti-Semite, a homosexual, and a warmonger. It's interesting that Buckley's friends, including Hugh Kenner (an important literary critic) and John Kenneth Galbraith (with whom Buckley often went skiing in Switzerland), had urged him to refrain from a lawsuit. Kenner wrote to Buckley with a wise perspective on his situation:

> A celebrity is simply one who accepts pay for having no privacy. ABC is now playing the role of Jack Paar, i.e. putting on a show. With part of your mind you assume you will be giving political

> comment. With another part, you accept Gore Vidal as opposite number despite prior experience. What you have in fact done is accept a role as a Celebrity. You will be playing William F. Buckley, Old Antagonist of Gore Vidal. And you will be conceding the right to have your privacy violated, which means in the first instance being taxed with past statements you never made and leads right up to such imputations—bisexuality, anti-Semitism, etc.—as make up the texture of Gore Vidal's *Esquire* piece.

Kenner's analysis is shrewd. As an experienced publisher and polemicist, Buckley should have known better. Gore, characteristically, countersued, and three years of wrangling followed, resulting in a compromise in which *Esquire* settled, giving free advertising space to Buckley's *National Review* and paying his legal fees ($115,000). Buckley and Vidal each believed that he had won the skirmish, though bad feelings continued until the end of their lives. Shortly after Buckley's death Gore commented: "He sued me and got nowhere. He sued *Esquire*, in which our words appeared. By then the coming right-wing surge was in view. And so *Esquire* cravenly agreed to settle with him for a few paragraphs worth of free advertising for his weird little magazine *The National Review*, hardly the great victory he claimed."

VII. Furious Visions

"I had never seen Gore like this before," remarked Armstrong, who welcomed Gore back to his warm circle of Roman friends. "He was so tired, worn-out. I think the publicity around *Myra*, the failure of *Weekend* in New York, the debates with Buckley, the chaos on the American streets, everything—it all got to him. He was strangely silent at dinners, getting very drunk at night. Howard was worried about him. I don't think Gore knew what to do next, what form was best. He kept getting offers to write films, to polish scripts or adapt this or that. Mostly he wasn't interested. He was writing essays and reviews, but more slowly than before. He thought about writing his memoirs. Rome had become a place of retreat, and he didn't want to go back to the States, not to live. He wanted to sell Edgewater, as a way of cleansing himself from the past."

Howard was anxious about selling Edgewater, but he would never go against Gore on such a matter. It was Gore's house, after all. In the early winter of 1969, the house was sold to a businessman from New York for $125,000. Later, Gore remembered those years by the Hudson fondly, even sadly: "In some ways they were the best of times. I had such good friends." He especially missed Dupee, whose erudite conversation inspired him. But it was impossible to maintain such a house from a distance. Perhaps to make up to Howard for the loss of Edgewater, Gore agreed to lease an apartment in the Casa Willi, a large chalet in Klosters, Switzerland. "Howard loved it there," Gore said. "I didn't care that much for Switzerland, but we had friends there. Greta Garbo came by. Irwin Shaw was always there, and we liked him." Shaw was famous for *The Young Lions* (1948), a popular novel of World War II, and for a fierce antiwar play from the mid-thirties, *Bury the Dead*. Gore recalled: "I don't think people realize what an impact that play had. It was a cultural event." Like Gore, Shaw moved across genres, writing acclaimed novels, short stories, plays, and screenplays, including a poetic 1958 film adaptation of Eugene O'Neill's *Desire Under the Elms*.

In the meantime, Gore grew so annoyed, even repulsed, by the American scene that he thought briefly about renouncing his citizenship and applying for a Swiss or Irish passport. The latter made some sense, as Gore could claim Irish descent on both sides and had friends in Ireland, such as John Huston, the film director. He considered renting a house in Dublin or, perhaps, a country house in County Cork—they were ridiculously cheap at this time. Moreover, the Irish didn't tax writers on royalties at anything like the rate in the United States or Italy. "He had this fantasy of being some kind of Irish gentleman," Howard recalled, resisting Gore's impulse for once. "I think he was reading Trollope at the time. I said, No way! I wouldn't set a foot in Ireland!"

A sad turn came when Gore's father died on February 20, 1969. Gore had only recently visited Gene in Los Angeles and had found him surprisingly weak. This upset Gore. At seventy-three, the elder

Vidal had become a benign presence in his son's life, nothing like his strident alcoholic mother, who had been fiercely banished from Gore's world. "We had a very easy time, the two of us," Gore said of Gene. "I could rely on him. He stood behind me on most things." To Bob Bookman, a film agent and friend, he wrote: "It's odd but the older one is the worse it is when a father dies. It should be the other way around." In truth, the death of his father was a hard blow, loosening another key tie with the United States. (Strangely, he seems never to have commented on his stepsiblings, Vance and Valerie, who more or less disappeared from his life.)

As usual, Gore buried himself in work: for him, the only way to achieve any mental balance in times of stress. He had been asked to do a film adaptation of another play by Tennessee Williams, and agreed with reluctance, calling it "another of the Bird's awful late moments." This was *The Seven Descents of Myrtle*, a tragicomedy about a young man whose mother's death has been especially difficult for him. He returns to his ancestral home in the South, accompanied by a new bride named Myrtle. She had been a showgirl, a key member of the Five Memphis Hot Shots, a topless girl band of local fame. In the film of the play, retitled *The Last of the Mobile Hot Shots*, Myrtle and her husband return to his ancestral home, as in the play, where they meet his half brother, Chicken. Myrtle skips back and forth between the brothers, while their past lives flicker on the screen in a series of flashbacks.

Gore often liked to get away to a hotel to write, and he returned to the Luna in Amalfi for a couple of weeks to focus on the script. "I had stayed there with the Bird after the war. Wagner had liked working there. It was a good place to remember our friendship, and to write. I sat in the damp and dark courtyard, in an uncomfortable wrought-iron chair, drinking bad wine—the local motor oil." The script helped Gore's bank account, but it got little attention from critics or moviegoers. "It was truly terrible," Gore said, "with Lynn Redgrave as Myrtle. James Coburn had the male lead. It was implausible."

Back in Rome, Gore returned to his latest novel, at this point entitled *Two Sisters of Ephesus*. Although hardly in a league with *Myra Breckinridge*, it was a fairly ambitious and experimental effort that shifted among narratives as novel, diary, and screenplay. It's an odd, ill-formed performance, and one of Gore's least-read novels.

In March 1969, while writing it, he published *Reflections Upon a Sinking Ship*, a further volume of essays and reviews. The pieces surveyed a broad range of topics from the French *nouveau roman* to the work of John O'Hara and Henry Miller. Two of his essays on Kennedy are here: "The Holy Family" and "The Manchester Book," the latter a meditation on *The Death of a President*, William Manchester's popular 1967 account of the JFK assassination. There is a fine travel piece, "Passage to Egypt," and various political manifestoes, including a report on the Republican National Convention in Miami that had appeared in *The New York Review of Books*. Although not unlike Mailer's coverage of the same event in *Harper's*, Gore's writing is grittier and more reportorial, relying on his usual wry portraiture: "Ronald Reagan is a well-preserved not young man. Close-to, the painted face is webbed with delicate lines while the dyed hair, eyebrows, and eyelashes contrast oddly with the sagging muscle beneath the as yet unlifted chin, soft earnest of wattle-to-be."

Typically, Gore begins his essays off-center, with a personal reflection or some historical aside. In "John O'Hara's Old Novels," for instance, he starts with a comment by George Santayana (always a touchstone) on Somerset Maugham (yet another touchstone). He comes to a firm judgment quickly: O'Hara's novels are "graphic and plausible, impertinent and untrue." Then he moves, block by block, through the crowded neighborhoods of O'Hara's fiction. At last, he concludes that O'Hara's fiction "cannot be taken seriously as literature," although it offers an "unconscious record of the superstitions and assumptions of his own time."

Gore writes with iconoclastic glee on sex and pornography in two of the essays, beginning what would become a major line of argument in later work by insisting that an effort must be made to "bring what we think about sex and what we say about sex and what we do about sex into some kind of realistic relationship." He observes that "packaging pornography has become big business," anticipating the avalanche created by the intervention of the Internet.

In a poignant passage in "Writers and the World," he reflects: "The obvious danger for the writer is the matter of time. 'A talent is formed in stillness,' wrote Goethe, 'a character in the stream of the world.' Goethe, as usual, managed to achieve both. But it is not easy, and many writers who choose to be active in the world lose not virtue but time, and that stillness without which literature cannot be made." Gore felt the personal weight of this observation. He had lived in the stream of the world, especially of late, deprived of the stillness usually required to nurture talent. "Gore told me what he most needed was time, time to think, to read, to write," recalled Armstrong. "As the sixties drew to its clamorous end, this stillness seemed difficult to find."

In Rome, Gore was rarely free of distractions. "He lived a pretty high life," Armstrong said, "with visitors from Hollywood and New York, writers, critics, producers, actors. Gore knew everybody, and they all thought of him as a destination. Rome was a good place to visit." For many years he had thought about adapting his old novel *The City and the Pillar* for the screen. In 1965, he had revisited the novel in a major way, streamlining the narrative and rewriting the ending in which Jim rapes Bob instead of strangling him. "This just made more sense," Gore said. "It's what might have really happened, less sensational." He tried writing a screenplay based on the revised version, with promises of financial backing from friends and acquaintances in Rome. "Rossellini was interested," he said, referring to the producer (and sometime director) Franco Rossellini, "then he wasn't. Not a reliable man."

As the decade drew to a close, Gore focused in Rome on *Two Sisters*, as it was now called. Much of the book is unvarnished autobiography, a venting of personal gripes. The main character is V.—Gore himself, slightly fictionalized. The novel begins in Rome with V. in conversation with a version of Anaïs Nin called Marietta Donegal. Donegal has, like Nin, written several volumes of a diary that discloses more than it reveals, dropping the names of numerous ex-lovers. Donegal tells V. breezily: "Of course it was a very young book but—oh, what a good time we had in New York that winter!" It's all a bit confusing, self-referential in ways certain to irritate critics, who would sniff at its literary pretensions. Who did Gore Vidal think he was, James Joyce or Vladimir Nabokov?

Donegal lets V. read the diary of someone else, Erik Van Damm, knowing that V. lusted after him once upon a time, although he accepted Erik's twin sister, Erika, as a less than satisfactory substitute. Van Damm tells a revealing story of two decades before the novel opens. There is also an unproduced screenplay called "The Two Sisters of Ephesus," a kind of sand-and-sex romp through the fourth century BCE. The would-be film includes an incestuous scene between Herostratus and his sister, Helena—a deviation from the real-life original, wherein Erik writes covertly about his own incestuous relationship with Erika.

One can't help but notice that in 1969 Nabokov published *Ada, or Ardor: A Family Chronicle*, a vast novel that attracted lavish praise from many critics. Nabokov's adoring fan Alfred Appel Jr. declared in *The New York Times* that *Ada* was "an erotic masterpiece." Nabokov gives us the fictional memoir of Dr. Ivan "Van" Veen, and parts of this narrative recount an incestuous relationship with Van's sister, Ada. Two cousins, "Demon" and Dan Veen, marry twin sisters, Aqua and Marina. In obvious ways, Gore has raided the Nabokovian treasure house. Obsessions with twins, with incest, and with genre-crossing occupy the authors of both novels. In fact, Gore wrote long parts of *Two Sisters* in Switzerland, not far from Nabokov himself, whom he wryly called "the Black Swan of Lac Leman" in a piece in *The Observer* not long after writing his Nabokovian novel. There was obvious competitiveness here. But in many ways Gore's novel could be regarded as a kind of homage to a grand master, though Gore claimed that he had "resisted reading Nabokov's recent entertainment on the subject."

The autobiography in *Two Sisters* includes gossipy passages about Williams, Galbraith, André Gide, Jack Kerouac, Dwight Macdonald, and others well known to Gore. He vents at length about the decline of the American republic and rambles knowingly on subjects dear to his heart, such as power: "People who obtain power do so because it delights them for its own sake and for no other reason." Other obsessions course freely through the text, including Gore's aversion to academe: "It's a pity that what pleasure literature might still give to the not so happy few who like to read is undone by the explicators. Even the most devoted young reader is not apt ever to want to look at another novel after 'studying' the subject in any American university." Yet Gore's novel remains a bit of a mess, despite some glorious witticisms and rueful passages about the fleeting nature of life. "So ends that summer of twenty-one years ago," he writes, near the end of the novel. "Erik vanished, with Doris. Marietta about to take up with Derek or Guido or Benjamin. I to return to the States, life devoted to achieving some balance between furious vision and a talent still unformed."

Two Sisters was published in the summer, and widely panned. D. J. Enright, the English poet and critic, spoke for the majority view when he called the book a "skimpy leftover from *Myra Breckinridge.*" In fact, it represents yet another attempt by Gore to find a form suitable to his gifts. He doesn't find it here, but the novel remains tantalizing, a fictive space where Gore almost acknowledges that, at forty-five, his talent was still unformed. But the book displays the furious vision that was Gore's strength.

One of the more memorable remarks about this novel was made by Tynan in his diary: "I read Gore's *Two Sisters,*" he wrote on June 10, 1973. "What superb and seamless armour he wears, as befits one to whom life is a permanent battle for (social and intellectual) supremacy. It is of course a battle that cannot be won by anyone who is incapable of surrender. And Gore could never surrender (i.e. expose) himself freely to anyone. All the same, the necessity to stay on top keeps him writing." As it would.

Miss Sontag Writes a Novel

At dinner with Gore at a small Italian restaurant on the Upper East Side, we huddle in a dark booth at the back, with Norman Mailer and Susan Sontag crowding around. They're performing at Carnegie Hall tomorrow night in Don Juan in Hell.

"Shaw does the best dialogue," says Mailer.

"Better than you, Norman?" asks Gore. It's one of several remarks that brings nervous laughter followed by silences that take a while to break.

"Why do you always get to make the jokes?" Mailer asks.

I wait for a smart-ass reply from Gore, but he ignores Mailer and sips his Scotch, the second of the evening before he starts on the wine. Gore seems distracted tonight, a little angry. He's become fat, and his shirt is partly unbuttoned near the waist. He hasn't shaved in a couple of days, with a hoary stubble on his chin.

Sontag looks sharp in black pants, a maroon jacket. She has this streak of white hair mixed in with darker hair—a defining look, probably cultivated. She is formidable but pretentious, dropping names. Gore eyes her warily, half smiling. We talk about Shaw and his plays, and she says she really must read more of him. Gore recommends Mrs. Warren's Profession. *"It could be your profession, too," he tells her. Mailer seems to think this is hilarious and toasts Gore.*

During dinner, Gore drinks much of a bottle of wine by himself, and Mailer is annoyed, ordering another bottle for the rest of us. He is paying the bill, and doesn't like doing so. He orders light: a salad with chicken. The rest of us go for larger items. As ever, Gore orders a lot but eats very little, preferring to absorb his calories from booze.

At the end of the dinner, Sontag sips her coffee with a thoughtful look. Suddenly she asks Gore if he has read The Volcano Lover, *her most recent novel, set in eighteenth-century Naples (with Sir William Hamilton; his wife, Emma; and her lover, Lord Nelson, among the cast). She says it's her one and only venture into historical romance. It has been widely (and often well) reviewed.*

A pained expression crosses Gore's face as he reaches across the table and takes Sontag's hands into his own, then says, "I've read it, Susan. But you must make a promise to me. That you will never, ever try your hand again at fiction."

Chapter Seven

American writers want not to be good but to be great, and so are neither.

—Gore Vidal

1. A Bad Year

The hostile reception of *Two Sisters* by critics was accompanied by the premiere of the film adaptation of *Myra Breckinridge*, directed by Michael Sarne—a British actor and novice director, who had only one other credit to his name at the time. *Time* magazine called it "an insult to intelligence, an affront to sensibility and an abomination to the eye." And that was the kindest of the reviews. It had been, as Gore knew, a hopeless project from the start. "I had nothing to do with it, didn't even watch it. All I know is that critics and audiences hated it, and it killed the sales of my book. Never before had a film done so much damage to a novel." In the film, Myron was played by the film critic Rex Reed, who—after an operation—metamorphosed into Raquel Welch. Mae West and John Huston also had roles, but they were odd ones. That Twentieth Century Fox would gamble on such a project defeats conventional wisdom about Hollywood motives, though this was the era of unlikely successes, such as *Easy Rider*, which appealed to a countercultural audience in unexpected ways. Needless to say, the novel *Myra* had been a major commercial success, and that fueled the film adaptation.

In the meantime, Gore received a telegram from Anaïs Nin, asking for permission to include her comments on him in the fourth volume of her diaries. She wrote, for example, about his interest in boys—a passage that Gore asked her to remove:

> We aren't lovers anyway, and what he wants is impossible to me, to live with me, to be close to me, possessively, emotionally, but to sleep with boys. When he takes me out he does not conceal his interest in boys. He wants me to share this. I get hurt, though I try to act cynically. He discusses them with me, undresses them, tells me how it will be: "This one will be too white, and he will want all sorts of things I don't want. He will be complicated and make a scene. They do terrible things which I don't do. My approach is entirely non-phallic."

Gore met Nin in Paris, at a hotel bar, and told her to go ahead, with a few deletions, which he considered perfunctory. When she asked about the supposed caricature of her in his new novel, Gore explained that Marietta Donegal in *Two Sisters* had nothing to do with her. Fortunately for him, she had not read the book.

Meanwhile, Gore avoided the United States more than ever, preferring to "watch the disaster from afar," as he put it. While passing through London in the spring of 1970, he stayed as usual in a suite at the Connaught, where Christopher Isherwood came to lunch on March 4. Isherwood reflected on their encounter in his diaries: "He looks thinner, hollow-cheeked in a boyish way; terrifically attractive. He says he feels attractive, and he charmingly recalled that I was his present age when we first met and how attractive I was then. Indeed, we were very pleased with each other. I love his consciously aggressive careerism." He suggested that Gore was now "casting off the U.S."

Isherwood understood his friend's careerism. Gore was writing essays and articles at a furious pace, taking on numerous assignments from *The New York Review of Books* and growing closer to Barbara Epstein. He was also writing for *Esquire* and *Commentary*, for the London *Times* and even (of all places) *The New York Times*, where on September 26, 1970, he published a brilliant piece on America's obsession with fighting drugs: "It is possible to stop most drug addiction in the United States within a very short time," he wrote. "Simply make all drugs available and sell them at cost." In the coming decades Gore would tirelessly argue for treating drug addiction as a medical, not a criminal, problem.

In late spring, he accepted an assignment from Epstein to review a parcel of books on what in those days was known as women's liberation. This was the real beginning of the modern feminist movement, with groundbreaking work appearing by Kate Millett, Germaine Greer, and Eva Figes, among others. Gore decided to write about Norman Mailer, as Mailer had recently published an article in *Harper's* that would soon become a short book, *The Prisoner of Sex* (1971), an awkward stab at defending himself against an attack by Millett, who had skewered him in *Sexual Politics* (1970), which laid the groundwork for feminist criticism in the coming decades. For his part, Gore was less interested in "the girls," as he called them, and more attracted by the objects of their hatred, the macho males from Henry Miller through Mailer and the homicidal cult leader Charles Manson. Gore snidely referred to this trio as M3. "Women are not going to make it until M3 is reformed, and that is going to take a long time." The arch tone of Gore's essay still grates on the ear:

> M3 is on the defensive, shouting names; he thinks that to scream "dyke" is enough to make the girls burst into tears, but so far they have played it cool. Some have even admitted to a bit of dyking now and then along with warm mature heterosexual relationships of the deeply meaningful fruitful kind that bring much-need babies into the world ("Good fucks make good babies"—N. Mailer).

This gets exhausting. And it also infuriated Mailer, who didn't like reading lines like this: "Mailer's attitude toward woman is pretty much that of any VFW commander in heartland America." This was perhaps a step too far.

Gore's relations with Mailer had deteriorated since the day in 1968 when he saw him huddling with William F. Buckley at the Democratic National Convention in Chicago. Buckley and Mailer already knew each other well, so it was not such an unlikely thing for them to chat. They had debated each other publicly in 1962 and become reasonably good friends, with Mailer visiting Buckley in Connecticut a few years later, even sailing with him on his thirty-six-foot boat. After Mailer's death, Buckley wrote warmly of him in *National Review*, saying that "he created the most beautiful metaphors in the language." Their differences were intellectual and ideological, not personal. But for Gore, everything was personal.

He knew that Mailer was, like Buckley, homophobic, as suggested by his machismo in public (although contradicted by his long residence in Provincetown on Cape Cod, which has always been a magnet for gay men). Others shared Gore's suspicions. As Millett noted in *Sexual Politics*, Mailer was "a prisoner of the virility cult," a man whose "powerful intellectual comprehension of what is most dangerous in the masculine sensibility is exceeded only by his attachment to the malaise." Millett's reading appealed to Gore, as it chimed with his own growing dislike of Mailer, whom he began to regard as a reactionary—hardly the forward-thinking radical he liked to play.

Never one to lose an opportunity to have sex or be on television, Gore accepted an offer from Dick Cavett to appear on his talk show on December 15, 1971, along with Mailer. Cavett asked Janet Flanner, a staff writer at *The New Yorker*, to appear with them as well. "I knew it would make for some good television, and I had some business in New York," Gore said. "I thought it would be a pleasant evening." But in the greenroom, according to Mailer, Gore put a warm hand on the back of his neck, a gesture that he interpreted as one of veiled aggression. Mailer answered back with a not so playful swipe on the cheek. Much to Mailer's surprise, Gore slapped him back. Then Mailer leaned forward like a boxer and winked before butting his head into Gore's cheek, a move that suggested, to Gore, that Mailer had been drinking, which indeed he had.

It was time for Gore to go on, some minutes before Mailer, and he collected himself before walking out, smiling as if nothing had happened backstage. He bantered with Cavett in his usual breezy way and dropped a number of names, recalling a long-ago visit with Eleanor Roosevelt. Soon Flanner came on, with her own name-dropping anecdote about how once, in Paris, she had found Ernest Hemingway in her bathtub. When Mailer was announced, he came on like a prizefighter, bobbing and weaving, his fists balled. He bowed to Flanner but refused to shake Gore's hand, causing a mild stir in the audience.

Cavett seized an opportunity, drawing attention to the bad feeling between Mailer and Gore. Taking the bait, Mailer expressed his disapproval of his rival, saying he was intellectually shameless. He described Gore's writing as "no more interesting than the stomach of an intellectual cow." It wasn't eloquent, and Gore tried to ignore him. But Mailer attacked again, asking Gore why he didn't, for once, speak to him directly instead of talking to the camera and the audience. Gore moved in for the kill: "Well, we have not found ourselves in a friendly neighborhood bar, but both, by election, are sitting here with an audience, so it would be dishonest of us to pretend otherwise." As was intended, this further provoked Mailer, who attacked Gore for alluding to the fact that he had stabbed his wife in 1960, calling him "a liar and a hypocrite." Gore had learned from his debates with Buckley and stayed eerily calm when Mailer asked him to apologize for comparing Mailer to Manson in his essay on *The Prisoner of Sex*. "I would apologize if—if it hurts your feelings, of course I would," said Gore. Mailer replied, "No, it hurts my sense of intellectual pollution." Gore smiled serenely. "Well," he said, "I must say that as an expert, you should know about such things." The conversation grew ever more hostile, and—as anyone who watches a clip of this broadcast will notice—Gore never lost control of himself. On the other hand, Mailer came off as a bully.

This was reality television of a very watchable kind, and it set the stage for a full-blown confrontation at a party in New York in 1979, when hostility erupted into a fight between the two writers that has lodged itself in the annals of literary gossip. Throughout the seventies, they remained verbal sparring partners, dropping as many unpleasant remarks as they could about each other, frequently in the embarrassed company of friends who admired them both.

II. Writing Richard Nixon

Nothing seemed to go well for Gore as the seventies began. In a diary entry for February 20, 1971, Isherwood notes: "Gore was on the *Merv Griffin Show*, almost unbelievably fatter than when we saw him, less than three weeks ago." He also notes that Gore was being cagey about his homosexuality, "perhaps because he is now halfway into politics again, getting together this third party with Dr. Spock and Ralph Nader for their presidential candidate." Gore had, in fact, forged an alliance with the People's Party, which lasted for close to a year. The movement was organized by Jim McClellan, a young radical in his twenties, and Marcus Raskin, a prominent antiwar activist and writer on social issues. They hoped to recruit Eugene McCarthy, not Spock or Nader, to lead their party in 1972 against Nixon, but this effort failed.

The dream of a viable third party had long been part of American politics, as in Teddy Roosevelt's ill-fated Bull Moose Party in 1912 or the segregationist Dixiecrats in 1948. It made sense for Gore to move in this direction, as he had argued many times that there was just a single party in the United States, the party of business ("The Property Party"), which had two wings, Republicans and Democrats. He considered the People's Party an intriguing notion, and in November 1971 he attended their convention in Dallas, hoping to run at the top of its ticket in the next election. However quixotic such a run might be, it would have offered a broad platform for Gore's ideas.

Gore agreed to co-chair the party with Spock, though it annoyed him when he was not picked to run in the top position and instead was made a kind of shadow secretary of state, so he dropped away. "Gore wanted to run on his ego," says McClellan, while Spock intended to "run on his ideals." Gore simply "stopped being involved after we nominated Ben."

Meanwhile, the presidency of Richard Nixon unsettled Gore, who began to mull over a play about the man who would almost certainly win the presidency next time around. Who could beat him? Even in the wake of the Kent State shootings (on May 4, 1970) and widespread demonstrations against the Vietnam War in most states, there was a sense that Nixon had managed to fend off an uprising. The sixties had come to an end in every sense, and a Republican era would almost certainly follow. "I thought I could do a play with presidential voices, not just Nixon, though Nixon was irresistible," Gore said. It proved hard to make up more bizarre lines than what Nixon, and other American presidents, actually said, so he began to bring together a kind of surreal vaudeville composed of actual lines by Nixon and other presidents reaching back to George Washington.

Gore worked at this play through the spring of 1971, and was lucky to find a producer in Hillard Elkins, who had recently been involved with *Oh! Calcutta!*—a huge hit on Broadway and elsewhere. "Hilly had moved in with Claire Bloom," Gore recalled. Apparently she once sent a telegram to Elkins, who was visiting Gore, that Howard by chance intercepted and relayed on the telephone to Claire's husband, Rod Steiger, thus bringing that unhappy marriage to an end. "Let's say it was not one of Howard's finer moments," Gore said.

Elkins read the play in June and decided to produce it, securing funds from investors who disliked Nixon. The timing was good, with the upcoming election, and these theatrical angels probably imagined another hit like *The Best Man*. Thinking big, Elkins hired the cavernous Shubert Theatre. Ed Sherin, a seasoned director, would take the helm. Rehearsals began in early spring of 1972, and—unwisely—Elkins decided to forgo the usual trial runs in Boston, New Haven, or Washington. "He was confident of the script," said Gore, who attended most of the rehearsals. Hoping to draw attention to the play, he appeared on a variety of talk shows, including Cavett and Susskind. But it was an uphill fight in the political climate of the times. Susan Sarandon, who acted in the play, said that "there were actual bomb threats, terrifying." She recalls that "Hilly Elkins said he stood behind us, and we could count on him; but he was away in Bermuda. No sign of him. There was also the audience, many of whom thought they were really going to hear Richard Nixon talking."

An Evening with Richard Nixon was cleverly written and beautifully staged, but it closed after only two weeks, a total disaster, with an extra splash of cold water thrown in Gore's face from *The New York Times* by Walter Kerr, a critic with unusual power in the theatrical world. "Kerr could sink a play, and he was bound to hate mine," Gore said. "He hated anything that cut against the grain in any way." Howard remembered that "the play really bombed," and that Gore "was very upset. He was used to things running smoothly. This was a shitty time."

However clever, the play is a bit of a mess, with quotations (real and occasionally fabricated) from Nixon himself; from his wife, Pat, and daughter Tricia; from Spiro Agnew, Gloria Steinem, and an array of other public figures, major and minor. It was a neat confection, but—not unlike *Weekend*—it failed to engage a Broadway audience. The problem was that the sort of patrons who frequented plays in New York were either already against Nixon and would therefore find Gore's anthology of quotations familiar, or admired Nixon and didn't wish to hear him denigrated. On the other hand, Sarandon (in her Broadway debut as Tricia Nixon) struck up an immediate friendship with Gore, and she became a trusted member of his inner circle for the rest of his life.

III. Italian Hours

The urge to move rarely left Gore, not until his very last months. This seemed especially true in difficult times, when he and Howard took off for parts unknown. Now they traveled to the Far East, visiting India and Thailand—their first visit to Bangkok, which had a kind of legendary glow in their minds. "It's a perfect little country," Gore said, "with lots of trade, good food, lots to do." By "trade," of course, he referred to street trade or prostitutes: Then, as today, Bangkok teemed with brothels. And he would become fond of the legendary Oriental Hotel, which named a suite in his honor in later years. Gore liked India, too, and he and Howard met various old friends there, including Rosalind Rust, his first girlfriend. In New Delhi, he dined with Kenneth Keating, the U.S. ambassador—a moderate Republican and the former U.S. senator from New York. Keating rolled out the red carpet, hosting a cocktail party for Gore, introducing him to a number of Indian writers and journalists. He and Howard also traveled to Katmandu, a capital city that Gore found "delightfully medieval. Forget about horse-and-buggy. It was donkey-and-cart in those days." A stopover in Tehran set in motion thoughts about "the connected nature of all world religions," a moment of insight that would lead, after a few years, to his novel *Kalki*—a prophetic extravaganza full of cynicism and apocalyptic rage that would both delight and appall readers.

Back in Rome, Gore seemed determined to return to his preferred profession, that of novelist. The theatrical world had rejected his talents. It was "so difficult to gain traction there," he said, though he considered writing a play about Aaron Burr, Thomas Jefferson's controversial vice president, whom he regarded as a kind of distant relation through a remote connection with Hugh Auchincloss, his stepfather. Burr had always fascinated him, as one of the most sophisticated of the Founding Fathers. Burr of course ran afoul of Alexander Hamilton (whom he mortally wounded in a famous duel) and many others in power, often with dire consequences. Having soared to improbable heights, tying with Jefferson for the presidency in 1800, he found himself increasingly on the margins with those in power and was arrested by Jefferson for treason in 1807, accused of trying to foster a revolution of the western states against those in the east. A well-publicized trial led to Burr's acquittal, at which point he exiled himself for a period in London before settling into a relatively obscure legal career in New York City, where he continued to seek his fortune without much luck.

With the help of booksellers such as Andreas Brown at the Gotham Book Mart in New York, Gore acquired a considerable trove of books about Burr and spent several hours each day at his research. This work proved absorbing, and he found himself working harder on this project than anything since *Julian*. The material was, perhaps, even more congenial, because Gore had a kind of proprietary sense of American history. For decades he had watched how political animals feuded among themselves, and had even entered the cage himself. Though a cynical man by nature, he revered the essential principles of the republic, as embodied in the U.S. Constitution. Yet he delighted in the foibles of the Founding Fathers—not one of them was without major flaws—and became a dedicated student of their self-engineered reputations. He was, indeed, creating his own empire of self, so he understood what this work entailed.

He often retired to a café near the Pantheon to read and make notes on Burr, letting the details of American life in the post–Revolutionary War era sink in while he sipped coffee in the morning. "I was beginning to feel the weight of the book, and worked easily," he said, "drawing on biographies of Burr and letters and reading historians on the period. I had in mind only the glimmer of a sequence." Of course he already had a considerable store of knowledge about the early republic, so this was often a case of reminding himself of what he already knew, or clarifying events and time lines. He was also in the process of redefining the biographical novel, shaping its texture and direction. "I didn't have a lot of models for the kind of book I wanted to write," he said. "There was a best-selling bad novel about Saint Paul by Taylor Caldwell—that sort of thing was always around, had been since the time of Walter Scott. But serious writing about major figures in history was rare." Indeed, at a time when the postmodern novel by such figures as John Barth and Thomas Pynchon was in ascendance, the so-called historical novel was regarded by most critics as a déclassé genre.

Increasingly Italy seemed like the ideal place for Gore to live, with regular excursions to the United States, mostly for book tours and public appearances. His circle of friends in Rome grew wider, including Americans such as the journalist Donald Stewart; Gianfranco Corsini, a left-wing political analyst who wrote for *Paese Sera*; the novelist Italo Calvino, whom Gore would later write about at length, introducing him to an American audience in *The New York Review*; and Alberto Moravia, a novelist as well as film critic. Moravia recalled: "Everyone liked Gore very much. His Italian wasn't good, but he tried. His friend, Howard, could speak fluently, even in dialects. Gore had wonderful parties at his apartment, with the terrace overflowing. He knew film people, like Fellini. He was friendly with American and English and Italian film stars, but he also knew agents and script supervisors and cameramen. He liked to meet new people. I would sit with him in a bar, talking about films. He was very excited to play a small part in Fellini's *Roma*." In *Point to Point Navigation* Gore recalls the last time he saw Saul Bellow, when he took him to dinner in Rome with Moravia at "a restaurant run by a lay order of beautiful third-world nuns. I fear the two lecherous old masters ogled these psalm-singing nubilities. All in all, a cheery evening."

Gore had met Federico Fellini, whom he teasingly called "Fred," during the filming of *Ben-Hur*, when Fellini was working on *La Dolce Vita*. For his part, Fellini called his new American friend "Gorino." They met occasionally over drinks, often at Gore's apartment, and usually when Fellini was trying to understand Hollywood and its peculiar ways. In 1971, he approached Gore about playing a bit role in *Roma*, a film he hoped to shoot in the coming months. He wanted Gore, among other foreigners, to talk amiably about why they chose to live in Rome when they could live wherever they wanted. Never one to miss such an opportunity, Gore agreed, arriving one night in winter at a small piazza near the Via dei Coronari. Everyone was dressed in summer clothes, pretending it was warm, though the temperature had dipped low that night. He sat at a long table with a few American friends as waiters produced huge plates of food and the wine flowed. Gore improvised. "What better place to observe the end of the world than in a city that calls itself eternal," he said. He later said, "Modern Rome has only three industries: the government, the Church, and the movies; each a dream-dispenser." He liked being at the center of the dream factory and playing his favorite role: Gore Vidal.

A few weeks later Gore joined Fellini at a sound studio to dub his voice on the film, as was usual in those days in Italy (when sound equipment was fairly primitive). No transcript existed, so he had to improvise, in French and Italian as well as English. It was, for Gore, an effort, since his Italian had never been fluent. But it's amusing to review clips of this scene, to see Gore in full flourish, in a gold turtleneck sweater and navy jacket, talking fluently and smiling for the camera, his hair perfectly coifed.

What startles in this improvised conversation is the degree to which he already felt out of place in Rome. He had not, as Fellini supposed, gone native. He spent most of his time in libraries, alone in a café, or with the English-speaking residents of Rome (usually at restaurants). "He counted only a handful of Romans as close friends," Armstrong recalled. In truth, the quality of life in Rome had begun to rub him the wrong way, and he missed the calm of Edgewater and the ease of country life. From about 1970, he and Howard had discussed finding a retreat outside of Rome. "He envied the pope," said Howard, "who could get away to a country villa near a big lake in Lazio. He wanted something like that, somewhere to play the pontiff."

"The air in Rome wasn't any good," Gore said. "I found it difficult to breathe. The pollution was awful." Howard recalled: "One morning I was leafing through *Il Messaggero* after breakfast. I came across this ad for a villa on the Amalfi coast. It was bigger than anything we wanted. It would be me who would have to look after it. But Gore liked grand houses, and the price seemed very low for such a place." Gore recalled his visit to Amalfi with Tennessee Williams in 1948, when he had fallen in love with the rocky coastline along the Tyrrhenian Sea, with its deep blue inlets, expansive views, and flowery hillsides. He had visited Ravello, and then the ancient piazza, with a massive cathedral at its center, strongly appealed to him. The town had several famous palaces, such as the thirteenth-century Villa Rufolo, which overlooks the cathedral square. There were fine hotels like the Palumbo, and good restaurants, and the town commanded an unparalleled view of the coast.

Gore rounded up Howard and Armstrong, and they set off in a rickety Jaguar for Ravello. Armstrong recalled a sense of adventure as they climbed over the hills to the coast: "The town was lost in time, with winding streets and hidden gardens. We had lunch at the Palumbo, a lovely hotel. A woman showed us the villa, La Rondinaia. It was like a haunted house that Lord Byron might have owned, crumbling, seedy, moldy, overgrown. Access was difficult. It hung on the edge of a cliff, and you thought it would tumble down, a thousand feet, to the Gulf of Salerno below. But Gore saw the potential, with its sweeping public rooms and really high ceilings. There were balconies with stunning views, and many terraces. Endless rooms, and long corridors that Gore saw could be fitted with bookshelves. It had apparently been a convalescent home during the war, used by English soldiers."

An English aristocrat had bought the land during the Victorian period—he owned Villa Cimbrone above—and his daughter finished building the villa in the early twenties. Gore and Howard tried to flush the toilets, but they wouldn't work. Electrical wires hung dangerously from walls in the kitchen, attached to nothing. Lizards had made the living room their favorite place in Ravello. Scorpions crawled in the bathtubs. The lush gardens were a nest of stray cats, and this appealed to Gore, who said it reminded him of Guatemala. As you could only get to the house by climbing hundreds of stairs, this had made it difficult to sell. It had been on the market for almost a decade. Gore understood what he had found here, and he decided he must have it.

The villa featured a Roman floor plan, with rooms unfolding in a series with sea views along the outer wall. It had barrel-vaulted ceilings and bright tiles on the floor. The room just off the entrance foyer, to the left, had a terrace with superb views and a large fireplace; it would become Gore's study, the room where many of his finest books were written. The total price was about $270,000. It was exactly what Gore wanted, so he paid cash (mortgages were out of the question for most foreigners at this time in Italy).

"Howard was always desperate for a pool, as at Edgewater," Gore said, "but we didn't dig until 1984. It was then that I really settled into the house. We painted the bottom a dark blue, imitating the grotto in Capri. The surrounding deck of travertine was perfect, always gleaming, even when it clouded over. I could sit there for hours, reading or writing on a pad. Every night, before dinner, I would sit with a drink and watch the swallows drop from the sky, take a sip, and lift off. An agreeable spectacle."

Gore moved in quickly, sending boxes of books and memorabilia from Rome, bringing mementos out of storage from Dutchess County. He was able to buy adjacent land, too, making it possible to walk from the piazza to the villa along a cypress allée that followed from the imposing front gates. "It was called La Rondinaia," said Gore, "because, like a swallow's nest, it hangs from a cliff." It seems, perilously, to hover in place. "Guests are always sure they'll fall off the cliff," said Howard. "But they collapse before they reach the balcony," added Gore.

The surrounding gardens were appealing in their variety, laid out on several levels. Lord Grimthorpe, the original owner, had been an amateur botanist and planted a variety of odd specimens. Gore and Howard continued with the project, bringing in gaillardia, fuchsia, iris, and dozens of other flowers and shrubs. In season, there was always a profusion of wisteria and bougainvillea. An arbor below the house produced delicious grapes, which Howard got local boys to harvest and turn into wine. "We had our own figs, olives, and lemons as well," Gore said.

Now Gore and Howard spent long stretches in Ravello, and gradually—by the mid-eighties—their Roman life dwindled to short visits. Edgewater passed totally from the picture, although friends in the States continued to miss their presence beside the Hudson. Paul Newman wrote, for instance: "Coming back from skiing we stopped by Edgewater just to do homage. It was so quiet and peaceful and lovely, it just made me puke to think of you in that magnificent villa." Richard Poirier, too, missed them: "I would visit at Edgewater, then Rome. I couldn't imagine what kind of life they would have in southern Italy, in a remote place like that."

"I wished they had stayed in Rome," said Armstrong. "It was more fun when they were in town, at the center of things." But Gore wasn't in a party mood as his work on *Burr* intensified. He realized that he had something very special in this novel, and by the late winter of 1972 the book was more or less finished. Now Gore had a new publisher, too. "I wanted to publish him," said Jason Epstein, then the editor in chief of Random House. "We had been working together at *The New York Review*. Barbara, my wife, loved his writing. I loved his writing. The essays were so incredibly intelligent. And these historical novels seemed to me the best thing yet. *Burr*—and the novels that would follow in the American sequence—are his best work in fiction."

IV. Patriotic Gore

It's worth recalling that while Gore was in the midst of writing *Burr*, the Watergate scandal hovered in the background, as yet undisclosed. Nixon's thugs broke into the offices of the Democratic National Committee at the Watergate office complex on June 17, 1972, looking for something that might help reelect Nixon that fall. The public first learned that something of consequence had happened only in the summer of 1973, but this was perfect timing for Gore's novel about political subterfuge on a grand scale by one of the Founding Fathers, which arrived in American bookstores that fall.

As one might expect, the Watergate scandal enthralled Gore, who never tired of news about it. On December 6, 1973, while dining with Kenneth Tynan, Gore bet him $1,000 that "Nixon will be out of office by 1 April, next year," writes Tynan in his diary. (Gore was close; Nixon resigned on August 8, 1974.) Tynan added: "Gore is fascinating on the subject of E. Howard Hunt, the novelist, CIA man and Watergate conspirator who just may have had a hand in the killing of J.F.K. and the assassination attempt on [George] Wallace." It seemed that, once Pandora's Box of Scandal had opened, there was—in Gore's mind—no closing the lid.

In *Burr*, Gore stuck close to the historical facts. His chief narrator, a young law clerk and journalist named Charles Schuyler, was an invention, but a good one: Schuyler's alert eye provides a useful viewpoint on events. Most of the characters who dance across the pages of *Burr* are "real," if one can say that of characters in a novel. In the story's fictive present, Aaron Burr, a disgraced former vice president who nearly made it to the presidency, is in his late seventies. It's the 1830s (during the rowdy administration of Andrew Jackson), and Burr recalls (dictating to Charlie) his life during the earliest years of the republic. We see a wide-bottomed George Washington strut his stuff, an incompetent general who nevertheless had lavish political gifts. We meet a treacherously pompous Thomas Jefferson, who would eventually arrest Burr and charge him with treason. We hear about the conflict between Burr and Alexander Hamilton, and their famous duel at Weehawken Heights. (According to Burr, Hamilton took the first shot and missed.)

Vidal's revisionist history applies his cynical perspective to the mix of events in ways that would surprise and shock readers who idealized the Founding Fathers. Jefferson comes across as a manipulative fellow, charming yet deceitful, a politician who wants votes more than anything else. His democratic impulses do not extend to those on the margins, including slaves, Native American tribes, or women. He is a lousy inventor, not the universal genius of lore. He has dreams of empire, as when he more than doubled the size of the American landscape with the Louisiana Purchase. But he also, according to Burr, hopes to seize Cuba. A sardonic tone permeates Burr's memoirs. "I confess to not having listened to a word of the Declaration of Independence," he says. "At the time I barely knew the name of the author of this sublime document. I do remember hearing someone comment that since Mr. Jefferson had seen fit to pledge so eloquently our lives to the cause of independence, he might at least join us in the army. But wise Tom preferred the safety of Virginia and the excitement of local politics to the discomfort and dangers of war." With his usual fastidiousness, Gore would have combed the records to know that Jefferson had "spent a comfortable winter" at Monticello while the revolutionary army languished at Valley Forge. When British troops marched on Richmond, he remained at his estate in Virginia, where he "thought only of how to transport his books to safety."

Needless to say, Burr relished the irony that the great Jefferson fathered children with Sally Hemings, one of his slaves. At every turn in Gore's imagination, Jefferson strides across the American stage as a hypocrite with a huge appetite for power, as do Washington and Hamilton, among others. Was Burr's (and Gore's) view of these historical giants remotely accurate? No historian would approach these figures with such cynicism, yet Burr certainly rubbed shoulders with these men and, perhaps, suffered from their anger, their talent for revenge. Gore uses *Burr* to expose an obvious fact: the Founding Fathers were men with feet of clay, with flaws and foibles in proportion to their greatness. And these men, like all politicians in Gore's universe, served mainly their own interests.

Gore projected the ironic, even cynical, insights of his own political self onto a large historical screen, and the effect was bracing. As the tapes of Nixon at work in the Oval Office demonstrated to the world, politicians do indeed present one face to the public, another to their associates; their motives are rarely idealistic. Gore had heard politicians talking in his childhood home on Rock Creek Park; he had been a candidate for Congress and, indeed, sat in a sauna with JFK at Hyannis Port. The way Kennedy, for instance, had used his self-mythologized wartime experiences as captain of a PT boat to buff his credentials both fascinated and appalled Gore, as we saw in his portrait of Clay Overbury in *Washington, D.C.* Gore had few illusions about politics, and his cynicism partly derived from his own failure to succeed in that realm; yet he was able to lift his discourse above the petty, providing more than simply a pageant of American politics in what he would call his Narratives of Empire. Power compelled his attention, and he studied its dynamics with a cool eye.

Yet he retained sympathy for those in high office. In *An Evening with Richard Nixon*, he imagines a colloquium of former presidents in which Eisenhower replies to an accusation from Washington that he and Kennedy had wished to turn the American republic into an empire: "General, we deal with such a small space of history at a time—things are in motion when we arrive—so, like it or not we have to move with events." Even Kennedy gets a good speech in this play, responding to the same accusation: "I wanted a just society but I thought it could not be done if we gave up our empire." In many ways, *Burr* too has an undercurrent of idealism, moving toward a fairly benign assessment of its hero. One night Charlie visits the White House and has a quiet chat over dinner with Edward Livingston, a former congressman who had been present during the ballot that brought Jefferson to the presidency over Burr. Livingston recalls: "Colonel Burr was a very poor adventurer, and I told him as much when he came to see me in New Orleans. But he would have made a better president than Mr. Jefferson because he was in every way the nobler man."

A wan nobility courses through the memories of old Aaron Burr, a man of interesting ideas and ambition. "He was ambitious for the republic," Gore wrote, "not so much for himself, at least not at certain crucial points." At least in Gore's portrayal, Burr expresses shock, for instance, at Jefferson's blithe willingness to suspend habeas corpus and "set aside the Constitution" in the effort to arrest his enemies and to condemn Burr as a traitor. As Gore later noted, Jefferson had "misused the Alien and Sedition Acts, which John Adams had signed into law."

Burr was the ideal stand-in for Gore, opening a way for him to frame his developing notion of the origins of imperial designs in the American ruling class. More than ever, Gore's command of history seems impressive, replete with unlikely details (as in the width of General Washington's bottom). That Gore should take an iconoclastic position on the Founding Fathers surprised no one, of course. Some readers regarded Burr as, like his creator, a purveyor of gossip and innuendo. In many respects, his bitterness matched Gore's own, but the bitterness wasn't just personal—in either man. Gore, like Burr, was disappointed by the failure of the American republic to live up to its ideals. The U.S. Constitution had provided an elegant blueprint. But it had been subverted, repeatedly, from Washington and Adams to Nixon. In cutting the Founding Fathers down to size, Gore continued his work of revision, assembling a novel of history that shows him at the peak of his art: inventive, learned, sassy, and dispassionate.

Jason Epstein was delighted by this novel, which felt to him like a coup for himself as well as Random House. "I had been trying for some time to lure Gore to Random House," Epstein recalls, "and first asked him if I might include *Julian* in the Modern Library." He understood that this would appeal to Gore's ego, and it certainly did. But it's also true that Gore felt dissatisfied with Little, Brown, blaming them for the fact that *Two Sisters* had not sold well. On many levels, the move made sense to Gore, as Random House had become a hugely influential publishing house, with vast resources. There was also the Edgewater circle, of which Epstein had been a part, being friends with Fred Dupee and Richard Rovere. Epstein also offered to publish *An Evening with Richard Nixon.* (This was, for Epstein, a no-brainer: a small edition that would please the author with little risk to the house.)

The play appeared in April, followed in December by *Homage to Daniel Shays: Collected Essays, 1952–1972*. It was, indeed, the latter that cemented Gore's reputation as an essayist. Gore plucked the best essays from his two previous collections and added a baker's dozen from the past four years, including several of his best: "Meredith," a brief reflection on the Victorian novelist; "Doc Reuben," a funny (if dated) reflection on a popular best seller about sex; "Drugs," a pro-legalization manifesto of sorts; the title essay, which considers the legacy of an eighteenth-century American dissident, Daniel Shays; as well as astute reflections on Yukio Mishima and Eleanor Roosevelt. The latter is stunning, as in the final paragraph, in which Gore recalls Mrs. Roosevelt's funeral at Hyde Park in 1962. "Whether or not one thought of Eleanor Roosevelt as a world ombudsman or as a chronic explainer or as a scourge of the selfish, she was like no one else in her usefulness. As the box containing her went past me, I thought, well, that's that. We're really on our own now."

It's breathtaking to watch Gore stretch his wings in these essays. He had come a good distance from his earliest forays into this genre twenty years earlier. Of course one can still read the early work with interest, especially the essays on George Bernard Shaw and Suetonius, Mailer and John O'Hara. In some of his political writing, as in "The Holy Family," he combined memoir and political reflection in ways that anticipated his later manner. But the lofty intimacy of his mature style blooms fully in the last hundred and fifty pages of *Homage to Daniel Shays*. In the title essay, that style is brought to fruition. "Although the equality of each citizen before the law is the rock upon which the American Constitution rests, economic equality has never been an American ideal," he writes, utterly confident as he makes highly controversial points. "A dislike of economic equality is something deep-grained in the American Protestant character. After all, given a rich empty continent for vigorous Europeans to exploit (the Indians were simply a disagreeable part of the emptiness, like chiggers), any man of gumption could make himself a good living. With extra hard work, any man could make himself a fortune, proving that he was a better man than the rest. Long before Darwin the American ethos was Darwinian."

In *The New York Times Book Review*, Roger Sale suggested that Gore's essays outflanked his fiction by far. "His essays are almost always good and his novels are not so good," Sale wrote, striking a note that would swell in later years, much to Gore's annoyance. "It's what they say when they want to erase you," Gore said firmly. Sale went further, however, saying "Vidal is a writer without a center" and faulted him for his "timeliness." He says in the second paragraph of his review, with an odd disgruntlement that seems to betray a feeling of envy: "The trouble is Vidal is always timely."

It was true that Gore invariably had a finger on the pulse of the cultural moment. He had been a man of his time from the outset, whether writing one of the first openly gay novels in 1948, writing for television during its golden age, or opening *The Best Man* during the 1960 presidential campaign. He had been front and center at the Chicago Democratic National Convention, debating the issues of the moment with Buckley. He had confronted Mailer on Cavett's television show when the debate over the sexes had moved to the cultural front burner. Even with the historical novels, there was an urge to comment on the moment indirectly, to find a usable past, as in *Washington, D.C.* or *Julian* or *Burr*. In such books, he found in the past a mirror of the present. So in going backward, he could move forward.

Overall, he had made himself a citizen of the world, not unlike Mark Twain or Henry James before him. And this gave him a perch, a place from which he could speak with confidence. He felt at home (or equally homeless) in New York, Hollywood, Washington, London, and Rome. Moravia recalled, "Vidal was cosmopolitan in a fresh, unnerving way. He knew how they spoke in the U.S. Congress, in a Hollywood studio, in the back streets of Rome—even ancient Rome or America in the early days of the republic. At least, he made you believe this about him, and that was something."

V. The Swirl

Gore often talked about "the Swirl," meaning the crush of people who passed through his life, all whirling about him. He would regularly fly to the States to promote a new book, usually for a month at a time, giving interviews, with customary stopovers in New York, Boston, Chicago, San Francisco, and Los Angeles. He would stay at good hotels but visit with friends, such as Paul Newman and Joanne Woodward, who by now had started a family. (Gore played the role of affectionate uncle with the children.) Friends visited from England, including Tom Driberg, Diana Phipps, and John Bowen (an English playwright and novelist). Before Judy Montagu's untimely death from a stroke at the age of forty-nine in 1972, Gore frequently dined with her and her wealthy American husband, Milton Gendel. They lived in "jaw-dropping splendor on the Isola Tiberna, a tiny island," Gore recalled. "Milton was awkward, but Judy and I were very close. Her death left a huge hole." Princess Margaret came through now and then, and Gore looked forward to these visits (though her visits to Italy were less frequent after Montagu's death, much to Gore's dismay).

The Swirl, of course, included George Armstrong (a steady presence), Judith Harris, as well as the gifted sculptor Beverly Pepper (with whom Howard would later write a cookbook) and her journalist husband, Bill. Ned Rorem, the American composer, would stop by, though he bridled at Gore's cynical attitudes toward American life and his coy refusal to acknowledge romantic affiliations, even with Howard. Armstrong said, "It really annoyed some people, the way Gore refused to say that he loved Howard, and would hardly acknowledge him at times. But he loved Howard! Maybe it wasn't romantic or sexual love. It was something deeper, in Gore's view. And Gore took pains not to 'fall in love' with anyone else. Certainly none of the boys he picked up in the streets were romantic fodder." He was clinical about sex. It was a needs-based activity, hardly worth talking about.

Friends continued to play a large part in his life. Claire Bloom remained close to Gore, an important part of the Swirl. Gore had stood by through her difficult marriages to Rod Steiger and Hillard Elkins, neither of which had lasted. The marriage to Elkins fell apart in 1972, and Bloom sought Gore out eagerly for comfort. Paul Bowles paused in Rome occasionally, on his way back to Morocco from London or New York. Elaine Dundy turned up, though she and Gore mostly communicated by letter. Susan Sarandon would sometimes appear, a good friend since her performance in *An Evening with Richard Nixon*. Another regular visitor was Boaty Boatwright—"Botina," as he often called her. She kept him abreast of life in New York, where she lived in a grand apartment in the Apthorp, on upper Broadway. Boatwright recalls: "We often talked on the phone, and I would visit him whenever I could. Sometimes we took little excursions, as when we went to the Greek islands for a week. Gore liked to rent a sailboat, and we would swim off the boat and eat dinners in little harbors. He had an eye for the Greek boys, whom he thought quite beautiful."

Ravello was hardly a quick getaway from Rome. It took several hours to reach the Amalfi coast by car, with narrow winding roads over steep mountains. "The train was worse," said Howard, "because you had to go through Naples or to Salerno, then take a taxi." But they could easily afford to hire a driver. Indeed, with *Burr* having climbed high on best-seller lists in the States, money worries vanished completely, although Gore always retained a keen interest in his finances. He flew to Australia, for the first time, to promote *Burr*, and the landscape and people interested him. The prime minister invited him to dinner, and Gore made a splash on television. The Australian critic Dennis Altman recalls: "When Vidal visited Australia in 1974 he advocated licensing women to have children, with the possibility of them selling their license to others who wanted more than one child, an ironic foreshadowing of suggestions for trading the right to pollute, which has now become common."

Gore's consistent worry about overpopulation and its consequences broadened into a theme he would pursue in various books and essays. In his extemporized speech in Fellini's *Roma*, he had fretted about overcrowding and pollution. Going back to *Messiah*, he had brooded on dwindling resources, sensing an end to the world as we know it. Perhaps living in Rome, with its horrendous traffic and tumultuously crowded squares, he could not help but grow more pessimistic. "I found myself coughing up blood at night," he said, "the air was so bad, and it didn't help to live at the top of a building. Smoke rises. You couldn't escape it. The fumes were everywhere, in your hair and clothes."

The world, in his view, had fallen away from a beautiful moment at the inception of the American republic, when—briefly—the ideals of life and liberty seemed to prevail. It was a long slide, and Gore's own gloomy vision only grew more intense as he aged. His usual escape was in work, the one place where he felt truly at ease, and he settled back into a disciplined routine, getting to his desk by nine, working for at least four hours. As before, he wrote his novels in longhand, usually on legal pads, taking notes as he read books related to whatever subject opened before him. He would have a brief lunch with Howard, then return to his desk to answer letters, writing on sheets of specially designed lightweight blue stationery. "I thought of that," said Howard, "the little blue pages. It meant he didn't have to write much and it looked like a lot. A few sentences could seem like a full letter." He would usually write by hand, though he might type important responses on a portable Olivetti. He could type, in the hunt-and-peck style—a skill acquired during his period of writing television scripts.

Before the manuscript of *Burr* was even finished, he had *Myron* under way. He recalled reading somewhere that Thomas Mann always had the first page of his next novel before he put down the last words of his previous one, and this had been a kind of ideal. "You don't stop," he said. "It's a flow. One book leads to another."

VI. Myron Unmanned

"He couldn't let go of *Myra*. That voice rang in his head. It wouldn't let go of him," said Armstrong of Gore's most arresting character to date. Gore wrote to Poirier that he disliked sequels but found himself "again at [Myra's] mercy." As with *Myra Breckinridge*, its sequel came in a kind of rush. Howard said, "The historical novels, they came slowly. Gore needed lots of downtime, reading and making notes, walking by himself in the streets. But *Myra* and *Myron*, these came fast. He worked more hours than usual, day and night. They were written in a couple of months."

"I didn't like those strange novels, his satires," says Epstein, "and I couldn't encourage him to work in that direction. I didn't think they worked very well. Of course this put a distance between us. But Gore would do what he would do. He was so good at the historical books, I didn't like to see him wasting his time on other books." It wasn't possible to reject *Myron* outright. Gore was a diamond in the coronet of Random House, and *Burr* had sold briskly. It had been a critical success as well, and there was talk of a film. Gore's name was everywhere, and—even though he lived in Italy—he had become a fixture on American talk shows. *The New York Review of Books* featured his name on its front page in the boldest of letters, making Gore a major public intellectual who could be expected to weigh in on key political and literary topics with impressive regularity.

"Myra Breckinridge lives!" proclaims Myra as Myron at the start of the second chapter of *Myron*. She has bided her time for six years, lying in wait, creating her agenda for 1974, which is simply that she wants to return to her former glory and restore the golden age of cinema: "1935–1945, when no irrelevant film was made in Hollywood, and our boys—properly nurtured on Andy Hardy and the values of Carverville as interpreted by Mickey Rooney, Lewis Stone, Fay Holden and given the world by Dream Merchant Louis B. Mayer—were able to defeat the forces of Hitler, Mussolini, and Tojo." As ever, Myra has an exact and exacting knowledge of film and television history, and her megalomania rises to fresh and spectacular levels as she confronts her alter ego and former self, Myron: the eponymous hero of this novel. (Myron, his "manhood" restored by another operation, lives with his wife, Mary Ann, and twelve terriers in the San Fernando Valley, but Myra will not remain repressed, not forever. Myra, pre-Myra, was a film critic, and she believes that bad TV has been suffocating good movies; her mission is to save Hollywood before it's too late. Her first obstacle, of course, is Myron—her antithetical self—and she will be ruthless in executing her plans.)

The plot is simple in outline though too complicated for comfort in detail. Myron finds himself in an awkward situation, as he explains in the third chapter: "One minute I was fiddling with the volume knob of the TV and then suddenly there was this awful pushing and sucking and then suddenly there I was on my fanny about a yard away from Bruce Cabot, who is commander of the Babylonian royal guard as well as the rightful king of Babylon though he does not know yet that his rightful place was taken from him in childhood by Luis Calhern, who plays Nebuchadnezzar on whose dining-room wall God is going to write a pretty tough message in a later reel just before destroying Babylon." *Myron*, like its precursor, is a satire on Hollywood; but it's more than that. It's a time-traveling romp. Myron has been pushed by Myra through the looking glass of his TV screen while he was watching a film. Suddenly he's in an MGM studio in 1948, during a two-month shoot of *Siren of Babylon*, a fictitious film that nonetheless stars the very real Maria Montez, the sexy Dominican star of dozens of films in the forties. Everybody wants to get into the movies, of course, but not like this.

Gore plays with his conceit, not only satirizing the French *nouveau roman* again but dancing with Italo Calvino and Jorge Luis Borges as well. Gore mocks a nation glued to the TV, unable to capture the "reality" of the old films in this rectangular fizz of blue-gray dots, which offers a paltry version of the big screens of his youth. And, as usual, he's making a political and social point as well: Reality has become "reality." Life imitates art, but it makes a poor job of it.

Myron has some interesting company on the set, as many others have tumbled through their screens over the course of two decades, even Nixon. In a fine twist, Myron is a Nixon supporter, and from the outset praises him: "Like the president says, the American dream has been won for most of us who work hard and support our country," despite the fact that hardworking Americans have been forced to carry on their shoulders "the people on welfare." Unfortunately, this satire feels heavy-handed. Gore couldn't really hear the voice of Middle America, which he had never encountered in any extended fashion.

Taking up the problem of overpopulation, Gore allows Myra to run her mouth: "It is plain that nature and I are on a collision course. Happily, nature is at a disadvantage, for nature is mindless and I am pure mind. Wanting to preserve our species, nature idiotically made us able to breed at much too early an age and in too vast quantities. As a result of nature's mismanagement, any male in his lifetime can personally produce 43,800 children, using a different woman of course for each child." Her solution to overpopulation is fanciful, as expected: to turn every red-blooded boy into a "fun-loving, sterile Amazon." She notes wryly that these red-blooded boys used "to conduct those wars that in the past were so necessary to population control through the playful use of antipersonnel weaponry."

Myron "wins" in this novel, at least notionally. "Thank God, Myra was not able to change anything at all," he concludes with satisfaction, going on to say that "despite her meddling, this country is just like it was which is just about perfect no matter what the Com-symp senator from Massachusetts John F. Kennedy says as he starts his race for the President by unfairly and maliciously taking advantage of Mr. Nixon's current misfortunes." Myron appears stuck back in 1960, when that Communist sympathizer from Massachusetts whittled away at poor Nixon. It's very difficult for him to be in 1973.

This novel is mainly about the gender wars, now conducted within a single body. But the satire doesn't work, becoming a crude parody of an unconvincing Middle American male voice. In *Myra Breckinridge*, Gore had reached boldly into areas where writers in the American mainstream had never gone before. The sequel, however, wasn't as good, being hastily written, crippled by silly gags, flat lines, and scenes that never quite come off. It was no wonder Epstein recoiled at the thought of publishing it. "I just couldn't read *Myron*," he said.

Dutifully Epstein flew to Rome to spend time with Gore, reassuring him that Random House would get behind the book. Gore and Epstein had gone on "gastronomic tours" before, and now they traveled to France for a binge of eating and drinking at select restaurants in the countryside of Bordeaux. "We hired a driver, and lurched from meal to meal," Epstein recalls. "Gore liked the wine more than the food. It was a lot of fun, the two of us, laughing and eating and drinking. We made this a regular thing, taking off in a car, with a driver, trying different kinds of French food. He was the best company in the world, so cheerful, energetic. And he drank. I'd never seen anybody put away so much alcohol." Howard didn't approve of these gluttonous tours and was not invited. "I let him enjoy himself. But it was too much. They ate like pigs," he said.

The reviews of *Myron* in the fall of 1974 were, with a few exceptions, terrible. R. Z. Sheppard's notice in *Time* was decent: "Once again, Gore Vidal proves that in a market crowded with literary hookers, he is a true courtesan." More typical was Martin Amis, the young English novelist, who said this was Vidal's "worst novel yet: it reveals a marooned talent in all its vulgar radiance." Gore's home base, *The New York Review of Books*, struggled to find a sympathetic reviewer, and Robert Mazzocco did his best, describing Gore as "a master farceur," though he seemed uneasy, saying "the novel shuttles back and forth" between 1948 and 1973 "to no particular purpose." Howard recalled: "Gore found the whole thing depressing." That the book didn't sell was no matter, as far as Random House was concerned. *Burr* still flourished in paperback and many translations around the world, and Epstein expected a sequel to *Burr.*

Gore took to the road to promote his personal empire, lecturing at libraries and universities—not his usual environment. "In one four-week period," as he noted, "I gave fifteen lectures, starting with the Political Union at Yale and then on to various colleges and town forums in New York, New Jersey, West Virginia, Nebraska, Missouri, Michigan, Washington, Oregon, California . . ." He engaged in something like a perpetual campaign for a nonexistent office.

As he approached fifty, a gloom overwhelmed him, and no amount of public activity cheered him for long. The recent death of Montagu continued to upset him. Then he learned about the passing, in Guatemala, of his old lover and companion Pat Crocker, from whom he had not heard in many years. Feeling bad about Crocker, Gore wrote a note of condolence to Crocker's mother, Penny, who told him that her son lay in a graveyard in Antigua. Suddenly awkward memories rushed in from the wings. When Gore looked in the mirror, he saw that his youthful self had begun to recede, however slightly. A puffiness had emerged, and this would remain with him. His hair began to thin and turn gray. He found it more difficult to walk, as the old arthritis flared again in his knees. "I would see him struggle with the steps in Ravello," recalled Michael Tyler-Whittle, his neighbor in the nearby town of Scala. "He drank far too much. It used to be only wine, and he disliked spirits. But it was gin and whiskey now. I tried to warn him about the deleterious effects, but he waved me off. He kept saying the world was coming to an end. I told him that if he didn't take better care of himself, his world would surely end."

In Rome, Gore clung to his small circle, passing time in restaurants with Howard, Armstrong, Harris, Mickey Knox, and a few others. In 1974, Knox—a sometime actor who worked in various roles in the Italian film industry—was going through hard times with a divorce, and he turned to Gore for financial help. Ever generous with his friends, Gore gave him money. But Knox was also Mailer's close friend, and he mentioned the awkwardness of this situation to Mailer, who responded with a word of warning: "Stay close to Vidal on this one if it isn't too late." He warned Knox that Gore was "the one guy in the whole world" that you would never wish to count on. In sum, he said, "Watch yourself around him. Don't ever trust in his good will. It may be there and if it is, I'll be pleased for you. I really believe that, and I will admit that for once I was wrong about Vidal."

It's disconcerting to read some of Mailer's Iago-like comments about Gore. Yet Gore would grow fond of him at the end, though he was never deluded and understood that Mailer's old sense of rivalry would never burn out, that it would continue to smolder. They could not exist happily in the same room for long, and each wished the other would just go away—once and for all.

For the most part, Roman times were good times for Gore, full of delicious food, lively conversation, and lots of wine. "I remember Gore in the 1970s," says Edmund White. "He was extremely good-looking, self-possessed. He liked to go out to dinners at night, and he and his friends would sit at long tables in the Piazza Navona, and the street boys would waltz by and jingle their keys. But Gore always had sex in the afternoons, he said, so he could focus on his friends at night." Judith Harris recalls an evening in late September 1975. "We were eating pasta at Il Buco, an outdoor restaurant," one of Gore's favorite haunts. "I was almost seven months pregnant," she says. "My tummy extended perhaps unduly over Gore's table. Suddenly I felt a hand on it. It was Gore's. 'They say that rubbing it brings luck,' he explained brightly as my husband Aldo's Sicilian muscles tensed. It seemed to me that Gore, the ferocious, was warding off a kind of basic fear of pregnant women common to the Anglo-Saxon male. Face down fear with an aggressive gesture, render it innocuous by well-worn charm."

The Man Who Wouldn't Fall to Earth

A week with Gore and Howard at La Rondinaia. A quiet time, mostly reading. Rudolf Nureyev comes for one night, skeletal, with rank breath, and obviously dying from AIDS. He is bright-eyed, though, and full of gossip.

He and Gore huddle by the pool for a long time. "He has known everyone," Gore says to me afterward, "in the biblical sense."

It's sad to see this wasted body occupied by someone who had leaped so high in his prime. He is only ten years older than me but seems ancient and ageless, a creature of myth and history in strange ballooning pants, with a paisley shawl that hides bones that otherwise poke through. He seems cold much of the time and drinks two large glasses of white wine, Lacryma Christi. "It comes from Naples," he says, in a low voice. "The slopes of Vesuvio."

"He was only twenty-four when he defected," Gore says, after helping him to his bedroom for an early night. "I saw him dance many times. A marvel, especially with Margot Fonteyn. Together they become a single creature, not human. Les Sylphides *was his best."*

As ever, Gore is encyclopedic when it comes to ballet. Howard recalls that, when they first came to La Rondinaia, Gore still worked on his dance moves in the garden. He took ballet lessons in the late forties and knew everyone in the dance world of New York. "He fucked any man in tights," says Howard.

After breakfast on the terrace, Nureyev is ready to go. He has made it down the stairs with great difficulty. His legs seem like something a stork might balance on. His eyes glitter in a peculiar way, staring past death. The shawl wraps around his shoulders, and a purple scarf winds around his head. His lips seem painted, almost blood-bright. He has a knapsack on his shoulders and walks with an ebony cane with a silver knob.

I watch as Gore escorts him to the gate, so slowly it doesn't seem they are moving.

When Gore comes back, we stand together for several minutes as he leafs through some mail on the table by the door. I say, "It's a tragedy to see a man who could leap in the air in such a state."

Gore shakes his head, unhappy with my truism, offered as a way to fill an awkward silence. "No," he says. "It's not a tragedy. It may be sad, yes, to see him in this state. The tragedy would have been had he never danced, had he never taken to the air."

Chapter Eight

After a certain age, lawsuits take the place of sex.

—Gore Vidal

I. Half a Century

In late September 1975, Truman Capote was interviewed by *Playgirl* and observed in passing that Bobby Kennedy had once kicked Gore out of the White House during the Camelot years. Capote and Gore had been rivals for decades, and each bad-mouthed the other at every opportunity. But this latest taunt got under Gore's skin. "Distortions and lies had to be stopped, if they could be," he said. At nearly fifty, he imagined he should have relief from the barrage of rumors about him that swirled in the media, and anything about his relations with the Kennedy White House felt especially wounding. He had, to be sure, been pushed away from Camelot, although not literally. From that fateful night at the White House onward, Jackie Kennedy showed no interest in continuing their friendship, and certainly Gore's 1967 essay, "The Holy Family," warmed few hearts at the Kennedy compound in Hyannis Port. Now Capote's malicious lie poured kerosene on the flames of Gore's continuing hurt feelings about his relationship to the Kennedys.

Gore decided to sue Capote for a million dollars, assuming he would at least get back his legal fees. He didn't really care about the money. Capote had stepped over a line, and he must—so Gore believed—be punished. Gore also assumed that Capote had been told this nasty story by Lee Radziwill, Jackie's sister, whom Capote considered a friend. (Radziwill later denied relating this tale.) The legal wrangling would continue for several years, with Gore being deposed by a lawyer in New York over a two-day period in 1976.

"I get so monstrously bored with myself," Gore admitted to Judith Harris as he approached the half-century mark. "Once I pretended to be this famous orchestra conductor. For weeks I went around being him. Later I met him. I didn't like him." He seemed at a loss to understand himself, still searching for a true identity, although he would easily have agreed with Pablo Neruda, who wrote of himself: "My selves are many."

At fifty, Gore had reached an enviable level of fame as well as some measure of critical esteem. If *Myron* had not succeeded—and it had not—there was certainly more to come. He had another historical novel, *1876*, under way and wrote at great speed, often retreating to Ravello for weeks on end without emerging from the house except for an afternoon walk or evening drink in the piazza. In his usual way, he had begun writing that novel while *Myron* was being typed by George Armstrong. The shape of a trilogy had begun to emerge, if vaguely. "I realized, with *Burr*, that I liked writing about American figures. The idea of a sequence was still vague, but I liked my character, Charlie Schuyler, and wondered what had happened to him since the death of Burr. Writing this novel was a way to discover it."

He had an uncanny facility for composition schooled by long practice, and was writing "upwards of two or three thousand words in a single morning." *1876* came together rapidly, but writing at this pace required discipline, and Rome proved a distraction. So he stayed away from his penthouse at the Largo Argentina and worked through a cold spring on the Amalfi coast, knowing that he had a sharp publicity hook dangling before him: the American Bicentennial in 1976. What could be better than to have a novel about the first centennial in bookstores at the same time? "There wasn't much temptation to go outside that winter," he recalled. "I had a box of books on the period sent from a bookseller in L.A. And I liked this period, the final days of Grant's administration, the clash of Tilden and Hayes, a close election. The Democrats let the Republicans win in exchange for pulling all federal troops out of the South, ending Reconstruction—if, indeed, anything was ever Reconstructed." The novel followed nicely from *Burr*, reintroducing Schuyler as a famous historian with an eligible daughter, Emma, who had been briefly married to a minor Napoleonic aristocrat who died and left her penniless. As Charlie rediscovers the American scene, so would Gore's readers. In the United States of Amnesia (his phrase), Gore supplied its memory, again and again.

He didn't limit his teaching to novels and essays. On July 27, 1975, *60 Minutes*—the most popular television program in the United States—aired a profile of Gore that had, for much of the year, been under way, with segments shot in Rome and on the road as Gore toured in America. Mike Wallace, the interviewer, worked to distance himself (and the audience) from this libertine anti-American expatriate. The program began with shots of Gore in his Roman penthouse surrounded by elegant friends, all drinking wine as cigarette smoke swirls. As the microphone lowered, Gore dissed Norman Mailer, once again comparing him to "a VFW commander from Schenectady." He noted that Capote "spent most of his life trying to get into the world I'd been trying to get out of." Asked about Jackie Kennedy, he responded, "She has no interest in anyone but herself." Wallace chided Gore for his sour take on the fate of the republic, suggesting that perhaps he had not spent enough time among his countrymen to make the grand pronouncements he so relished. Gore's eyes narrowed in self-defense, but he didn't give an inch: "Mike, I am so in touch with reality and you are so far off base that I cannot begin to save your soul in the remaining seconds that are left to us." He explained that "cheap labor and cheap energy" were gone, and the results would be dire. "We're never going to have that again. We're going to have to have less gross national product, not more." He also took exception to the notion that he was an expatriate. This was a term used to denigrate him by his enemies, as he saw it. Gore's brow furrowed, and he said, "Now, as the times get bad, and I see darkness all around me, and I see disintegrating cities, and I watch these frightened people, I would be very inclined to return because if there is a disaster, then you have a part to play."

One is struck by Gore's composure in the face of harsh questions, especially on the subject of sex. Wallace wondered, for instance, why Gore disparaged love, asking him bluntly about the fact that he had lived with a man for decades. Homosexuality was rarely discussed openly in 1975, not on mainstream television during prime time; but Gore—the author of *Myra Breckinridge*—was the poster child for a libertarian life that both repelled and intrigued his audience. "I don't like the word love," he told Wallace. "Romantic love, as Americans conceive it, does not exist." He added: "I'm devoted to promiscuity." Of course he liked to startle television viewers, but it took a certain bravura to speak so frankly on *60 Minutes*. Gore took chances, letting the chips fall where they may. Risk was in his DNA.

With Gore's fiftieth birthday (October 3) approaching, Howard wanted an appropriate celebration. "He was the birthday boy," said Howard, "so I booked a large dining room at the Ritz in London. Fifty people, that's what I wanted. Fifty for fifty." Diana Phipps offered to help by figuring out who was in London, and she suggested that invitations be returned to her. The list was necessarily Anglo-centric, and the usual suspects came, including his old publisher John Lehmann, Kenneth Tynan, Ryan O'Neal, Peter Bogdanovich, Clive James, Tom Driberg, Lady Diana Cooper, John Bowen, and Princess Margaret. Claire Bloom was, of course, front and center. Lee Remick happened to be in town, so she got a last-minute invitation. Gore had known Antonia Fraser a little, and wanted her to come; she agreed, bringing her new boyfriend, Harold Pinter, whom Gore found sympathetic as well as amusing. Perhaps the most important guest was Tennessee Williams, who had seen much less of Gore in recent years. "Tennessee was like the cherry on the top of the sundae," said Howard.

"Gore was happy with the dinner," Howard recalled. "He didn't like turning fifty. Who does? But he and Tennessee got to talk, and he really liked Pinter. That Princess Margaret came mattered to him a lot." (So much for Jackie and her sister, Lee: this was *real* royalty.) Gore felt properly celebrated, although he also realized that a huge amount of time had passed since his twenty-fifth birthday party at

Café Nicholson in Manhattan in 1950. Only Howard and Tennessee were left from the original group of friends and family. Gene Vidal had died, and Gore wanted nothing to do with his mother.

As bad luck would have it, Jackie was staying at the Ritz, and she and Gore met in the elevator on the way to the lobby one morning. Gore had heard from friends that she had downplayed their connection, saying unflattering things about him. There was, indeed, a tenuous link, with Jackie now more of an acquaintance than a friend. Her life had changed dramatically since the death of her second husband, Aristotle Onassis, the previous March, and she had pursued a new life as a book editor, mostly in New York. Instead of greeting her as an old friend, Gore turned his back, watching her in the mirror of the elevator. When she stepped out, she said, in a voice recalling that of Marilyn Monroe (as Gore remembered it): "Bye-bye." It was almost like a dream.

No matter what heights Gore reached in his career, he felt dejected after a brief glimpse from the summit. An invitation to join the National Institute of Arts and Letters came, but he refused this honor, saying "I already belong to the Diners Club." He had no interest in rubbing shoulders with many of the same writers and critics he had traveled to Italy to avoid.

As the New Year approached, Gore entered discussions with Franco Rossellini (the film producer and a nephew of the director Roberto Rossellini) about adapting his own unproduced television script based on the life of the emperor Caligula. Gore loved the concept, but it was meant as a realistic drama, not an erotic dream sequence à la Fellini—which is what it became. He was offered $250,000, which seemed a good price for scripts at the time. "Bob Guccione agreed to finance this project," said Gore. "I should have known it would turn out badly, and it did." But he felt optimistic at first, telling an interviewer in London about the portrayal of Caligula: "We show him as a nice, happy boy. Perfectly normal. Not especially intelligent—though intelligent enough to know that some day he is bound to be murdered—and meanwhile having a good time with all the world to play with. The ideal casting would be Mickey Rooney, thirty years back. Andy Hardy in a toga." Gore saw Caligula, the third of the twelve Caesars, as an ordinary man corrupted by his power. "Megalomania took over." As he said to another interviewer: "We are on the dawn of an age of Caligula—think of the Pentagon, the CIA, the current national rulers. They, too, have the absolute power to treat other people as things. And just look at what happened to the Roman Empire."

Gore insisted that the film be called *Gore Vidal's Caligula*, a sign of his own megalomania. He didn't want to be cut out of the film credits, as with *Ben-Hur.* As it happened, the director, Tinto Brass (whom Gore now called "Tinto Zinc"), had his own ego issues, and wanted to have his name in the title. By the spring of 1976, it was apparent that Guccione hoped to steer the film in directions that appalled Gore. "It was pure porn," he said. Even Brass was appalled by what was happening and ultimately disavowed the film. It appeared simply as *Caligula* in 1980, with Helen Mirren and Peter O'Toole in prominent roles. Typical of the responses was that of Roger Ebert, who called it "sickening, utterly worthless, shameful trash."

Never one to linger over something that didn't work out, Gore busied himself with another project—a television miniseries based on the life of Abraham Lincoln. He had mentioned this idea to Norman Lear, who called Fred Silverman, a producer at NBC, who loved the idea. Gore quickly began to dig into the life of Lincoln, reading biographies and histories of the Civil War, taking voluminous notes, producing a script that, in the end, never got produced. Silverman left NBC and his replacement had no interest in American history, assuming it would bore American television viewers. Gore filed the teleplay in a drawer, where it sat beside any number of other unproduced works.

As the publication of *1876* approached, all signs were positive. Jason Epstein liked it very much, and believed it would sell. The Book-of-the-Month Club bid preemptively to publish its own edition, guaranteeing a large audience. Random House printed seventy-five thousand copies—a hefty first printing for a novel that wasn't a spy thriller, mystery, or romance. It was dedicated to Claire Bloom.

II. *1876* AND ALL THAT

"I liked being in the voice of Charlie," Gore recalled of his lead character. "I knew him well." In this book, after many decades in Europe Charlie has returned at last to his native land to cover the 1876 election as a journalist and reestablish his professional connections in New York. If he can marry off Emma, his widowed daughter, to a wealthy man, so much the better, as his finances have crumbled in recent years. Unlike *Burr* and, later, *Lincoln*, *1876* represents a throwback to the historical novel of an earlier era, when the lives of fictional characters took center stage against "real" history, which played out in the background. Schuyler is a Rip Van Winkle figure, waking up after more than three decades to an even newer New World. He rubs his eyes in disbelief, trying to make sense of what he sees, mostly because he hopes to sell his reports on the election to newspapers for badly needed sums.

Samuel J. Tilden, the governor of New York and a presidential candidate, is only a minor player in the novel, yet Gore endows him with energy, assessing him in fresh ways, allowing him a respect he was surely due, given his refusal to play along with the dishonest system. (In coming novels, Gore would also reassess apparently minor figures, such as Warren Harding and Herbert Hoover, in interesting ways.) Tilden comes off as a man of virtue who, because of his integrity, allows the ruthless Rutherford B. Hayes to win the White House, much to Charlie's chagrin (as he had hoped to win a diplomatic post in France in exchange for writing the campaign biography). Gore loved the intrigue of such battles, and would adoringly discuss the details of the Tilden-Hayes contest in later years, especially after *Bush v. Gore* in 2000: another case where a candidate won the popular vote but lost the election. It's too bad that Charlie so often appears befuddled, and the major politicians in this narrative—Ulysses S. Grant, Tilden, and Hayes—hardly seem as riveting as Thomas Jefferson and Aaron Burr, or even the waddling George Washington.

The business of marrying Emma to a wealthy and interesting man occupies a good deal of the narrative. Gore imagined her as a heroine in the manner of Henry James, though she lacks the moral complexity of Isabel Archer or the fizzy charm of Daisy Miller. Emma's story nevertheless provides intrigue and establishes bloodlines for characters who had already appeared in *Washington, D.C.* After much fuss, she weds William Sanford, "a married man without glory or charm, only money," as Charlie regards him before the mysterious death of Sanford's wife. He is left with an infant son—Blaise Sanford—who sets in motion a family saga. The Sanford clan will figure prominently in future novels in Gore's Narratives of Empire.

As the novel opens, Charlie describes New York in attractive prose: "Ships, barges, ferry boats, four-masted schooners were shoved like child's toys against a confused jumble of buildings quite unfamiliar to me, a mingling of red brick and brownstone, of painted wood and dull granite, of church towers that I had never seen before and old bulbous-domed creations of—cement?" Gore was at his best when evoking a scene like this, with the imagery at his fingertips as he wrote—a product of close reading and firsthand experience. Gore recalled: "I liked to walk around in New York and try to imagine what would be there in earlier decades, even centuries. The flesh of the city had added fat, but the bones remained. I knew that Charlie would have been shocked to see how, in the years he was gone, the city had spread. The civilized parts now reached up to the fairly new Central Park, which had only been completed a few years before Charlie returned."

Despite the centennial, this was a dark time in American history, not unlike the mid-seventies when Gore wrote *1876*. Trust in the federal government had eroded, with scandals breaking upon scandals. The Grant administration churned in a stink of nepotism, bribery, and cronyism, and the country awaited a shift of government as the hundred-year mark approached. The so-called Gilded Age had begun, a period when the wealthy paid no income tax whatsoever, and unseemly fortunes were made in heavy industry and railroads, shipping and manufacturing. Newly minted plutocrats lived in expansive mansions with small armies of servants, often dining at expensive restaurants such as Delmonico's, where (as Charlie says) "the lobster salad is a specialty of the house and it is as good as any dish I've ever had at Paris (paprika somehow makes the difference). Canvasback duck followed, enclosed in a savory aspic."

Perhaps stimulated by his "gastronomic tours" of France with Epstein, Gore's interest in food permeates *1876*. His fascination with the tiny details of everyday life brings the era into focus, as when Charlie and his daughter take a train to Washington: "I was not prepared for the amount of commerce that goes on. First, one is tempted by a doughnut salesman. Then a small boy appears with a large pile of magazines and cheap novels as well as bags of peanuts. Without a word, the boy shoved a ladies' magazine onto Emma's lap and a novel about the Wild West onto mine." Likewise, he describes the interior of the railway car, "with curtains of green plush, stuffed chairs that turn this way and that, gas lamps in good cut glass, mahogany wood fittings, and, all-pervading, the smell of burning fuel mixed with that of fried oysters."

The American world of *1876*, especially in the high-altitude political and social circles that fascinated Gore, makes a rich stew, full of gossip and corruption. Gore draws memorable portraits of real and imagined characters. Tilden himself comes to life, if sporadically; one even gets a glimpse of President Hayes in his glory, "an impressive-looking, rather stout man with a naturally fierce expression." In chapter ten, Mark Twain struts across the novel's somewhat overcrowded stage, drinking heavily and dropping aphorisms. Charlie reflects on Twain afterward: "Had he the character to be unpopular, he might have been greater than Swift, another Voltaire, a new Rabelais." If the plot of *1876* fails to cohere, there is nonetheless a good deal of entertainment in its pages, as one gets a strong whiff of the American republic at its centenary mark.

The novel arrived as the nation began to celebrate its bicentennial, another of Gore's deftly timed strokes. It flew its flag on most bestseller lists, and on March 1, Gore appeared on the cover of *Time*, as his grandfather and father had done before him. Reviewers largely bowed in appreciation, although some found the writing less vivid than in *Burr*, the plot without much focus or narrative tension. In a review in *The Times Literary Supplement*, Peter Conrad noted that *1876* and Gore's other historical novels were "the result of a precarious, dazzling partnership between Gore the researcher and Vidal the frivolous meddler with history."

III. Memories, Dreams, Self-Reflections

Michael Mewshaw is an American writer whom Gore teasingly referred to in conversation as Youngblood Hawke, the title character in a 1962 novel by Herman Wouk about a young novelist from Kentucky who achieves literary success but works himself to death in pursuit of a fortune. Soft-spoken and warm, Mewshaw lived in Rome throughout the mid-seventies, eighties, and nineties with his wife, Linda, and their sons. He and Linda saw a good deal of Gore and Howard in those decades, often joining them for dinner in local restaurants, occasionally visiting in Ravello. "Ravello was really Gore's workplace," says Mewshaw, "and it was never as glamorous as it seemed, despite the large-scale architecture and the great views of the coast. It was run-down, a place for research and writing. He didn't really have a social life on the coast, not unless there were visitors."

Mewshaw was with Gore one evening in 1975 when Pier Paolo Pasolini, the poet and innovative filmmaker, was murdered by a young man he had picked up on a beach outside of Rome. Gore knew and liked Pasolini. "He was a fellow degenerate," said Gore. "He cruised for trade in the same places. I knew that world." In fact, Gore knew the seventeen-year-old boy who had killed Pasolini and who had claimed that he acted in self-defense, that the fifty-three-year-old Pasolini had threatened to sodomize him with a stick. This murder both terrified and depressed Gore. "I think it was a shock to him," says Mewshaw.

The following summer, another "fellow degenerate," Tom Driberg, died in London, though not in such a dire fashion. Driberg was a longtime member of Parliament, a leader of the Labour Party insurgency after the war. He had been elevated to a peerage only a year before his death. He often spent time with Gore and Howard in Italy, especially in Ravello, which became a favorite writing retreat. Gore called him "a kind of stout Dracula," but he invariably opened his doors to Driberg. The sudden death of his good friend further depressed Gore, who had turned unusually introspective at fifty.

It was a time for memories, some nostalgic. And Gore eagerly accepted from Barbara Epstein the offer to review the memoirs of Williams. This served as the occasion for "Some Memories of the Glorious Bird and an Earlier Self," a recollection of his friendship with Williams, "the Bird." It is, as James Wolcott nicely observed, "a masterpiece of tender malice." "At that first meeting I thought Tennessee every bit as ancient as Gide and Santayana," Gore writes. "After all, I was twenty-two. He was thirty-seven; but claimed to be thirty-three on the sensible grounds that the four years he had spent working for a shoe company did not count. Now he was the most celebrated American playwright. *A Streetcar Named Desire* was still running in New York when we met that evening in a flat overlooking Rome: in those days a quiet city where hardly anyone was superfluous unless it was us, the first group of American writers and artists to arrive in Europe after the war."

Sumptuous images related to their early friendship give way to a warm (if cautious) reading of the memoirs themselves, noting errors and mistaken impressions, but mostly veering into recollections. This "review" is an autobiographical sideshow, as much about Gore as about Williams. "I think that the marked difference between my attitude toward sex and that of Tennessee made each of us somewhat startling to the other," Gore writes. "I never had the slightest guilt or anxiety about what I always took to be a normal human appetite. He was—and is—guilt-ridden, and although he tells us that he believes in no afterlife, he is still too much the puritan not to believe in sin." Unlike most others on this planet, Gore failed to connect sex and love. This was certainly a personality deformation, amplifying the usual loneliness that is part of being human.

Taking on the plays of Williams, Gore speaks candidly, with useful insights: "Tennessee is the sort of writer who does not develop; he simply continues. By the time he was an adolescent he had his themes. Constantly he plays and replays the same small but brilliant set of cards." He adds: "I am not aware that any new information (or feeling?) has got through to him in the twenty-eight years since our Roman spring," he says, no doubt playing off *The Roman Spring of Mrs. Stone*, a 1950 novel in which an American actress approaching fifty encounters a young gigolo, with predictable unhappiness all around. "In consequence," writes Gore, "we have drifted apart." This is breathtaking in its sweeping judgment and self-referential bent. Can there be any connection between the quality of Williams's work and the nature of his friendship with Gore? Williams had certainly not been attentive enough to his younger friend's feelings, and Gore felt this acutely. The mere fact that Williams continued to admire Capote didn't warm Gore's heart. In any case, these hurt feelings course boldly through this essay, and yet an indelible image of the dramatist emerges.

Gore's views of the Bird remained ambivalent to the end, a mixture of admiration and ill-concealed jealousy, especially as it became clear that Williams had logged a few plays in the permanent canon of classic American theater—a feat that eluded Gore. "He [Williams] is bitter but not a liar, a rare trait for an American writer," Gore wrote in 1976 to Bill Gray, his professorial friend, with notable candor. "I've done quite enough by the Bird—of Paradise, as he must now be known, pecking away at the golden grapes of eternal fame (if he went the other way, he will find not heat but an eternal panel of [Robert] Brustein, [John] Simon, Moses and Freud, shitting, like Dante, on his doomed feathers)." With some regret, he noted: "I can't say that the Bird and I had much connection during the last twenty years. Friendship with him was always a one way street; and I lived rapidly. Also, he was not the same person I first knew—to the extent I knew him at all!"

It annoyed Gore that Williams read so little and dwelled compulsively on the same few themes, refusing to "develop." Williams had, in fact, been on a downhill slide as a playwright for many years, with few late successes, and this made Gore's pronouncements sound accurate, if oddly biased in ways the reader might not quite understand. Of course Williams was badly addicted to alcohol and prescription drugs, which Gore did his best to ignore, being himself addicted to alcohol—not unlike his mother in this regard.

Gore's relationship with his mother had been limited for some time, reaching a fairly civil, if painful, standoff between them, but the situation took a dramatic turn for the worse in 1976, after Gore appeared on the cover of *Time*. Nina sent a letter to the editor, claiming that she was owed more credit for his success than her son ever allowed. She had helped him to get a soft berth in the war, had introduced him to important Hollywood people, and so forth. It was a sad, bitter letter, full of half-truths, accusations, and self-promotion. The editors chose to print it, with a nasty title above it: "A Mother's Love." "This was the last straw," said Howard. "Gore wanted nothing ever to do with her again—ever."

His connections to Hollywood had diminished since the move to Italy, although Gore flew into Los Angeles regularly to appear on talk shows or discuss film projects, most of which came to nothing. "I had a gift for getting involved with the wrong people," Gore said, and—often sounding petulant like his mother—felt that his work never had been fully realized on the screen, not even when he wrote the script himself. On March 29, 1976, he appeared as a presenter at the Academy Awards for Best Adapted Screenplay. "Those of us who write books are seldom happy with what the moviemakers do to our creations," he said, making a joke about the hideous version of *Myra Breckinridge*, which had quickly acquired almost iconic status as one of the worst Hollywood films ever produced.

Gore knew and liked Norman Lear, the producer of *All in the Family*—among other television hits—and in the late summer of 1976 he proposed that he might put in several brief appearances as himself on Lear's popular *Mary Hartman, Mary Hartman.* Gore adored the show, a subversive parody of American soap operas, full of heartfelt banalities, shallow values, and manufactured crises. The series acquired a kind of cult following, with Louise Lasser in the lead role as a dewy-eyed, neurotic dummy. Everything was tongue in cheek, and celebrities often walked onto the show as themselves. Gore shot seven brief scenes in a few weeks, playing himself and pretending on screen that he wished that Mary Hartman would co-author a book with him. "I had a little fun," said Gore, "and a great acting career was born."

He had, in fact, already appeared as himself on *Rowan & Martin's Laugh-In*, where he dealt with Lily Tomlin as a telephone operator trying to pronounce his name. In October of the same year, he appeared on *Dinah!*, a CBS talk show hosted by Dinah Shore, a popular singer, sandwiched on this particular program between the country singer Loretta Lynn and the Culinary Olympics Chefs. As ever, he never missed any opportunity to be on television, and this compulsion meant that whenever a book of his appeared he could bank on name recognition. When Johnny Carson, Merv Griffin, David Susskind, or anyone associated with the BBC called, he leaped to his feet, put on the mask of Celebrity Author, and stepped out smiling and waving to the audience. To make sure he looked thin enough for these appearances, he retreated regularly to La Costa, a "fat farm" (his words) in San Diego, where for weeks at a time he would drink no alcohol, eat very little food, and exercise.

IV. Apocalypse Not Quite Yet

As he traveled, Gore wrote every morning wherever he landed: in a rented house in Beverly Hills, in hotel suites in New York, London, and elsewhere, in Rome or Ravello. Now he began to work on *Kalki*, a fierce novel about world apocalypse. Begun early in 1976, the manuscript was finished by mid-summer. It had not taken long to write, which Gore often took as a good sign. Epstein responded favorably to Gore's draft, but he disliked the first-person narrator, who seemed cold and detached. Like Myra/Myron, this character was a transsexual male, and Epstein (wisely) urged him to make Teddy Ottinger into a woman. "So I set to work, rewriting. It didn't take long. And I think the changes actually made it a better book," said Gore. In later years he would, in fact, be far less generous about Epstein's talents as an editor of fiction, often harping on the subject and blaming Epstein for his failure to appreciate his satirical novels in particular.

While Gore chipped away at the revisions of *Kalki*, Epstein ushered *Matters of Fact and of Fiction (Essays 1973–1976)* into print in April 1977. It represents Gore at his peak in the genre, containing half a dozen of his finest essays. In only a few years, Gore had accumulated a quantity of first-rate work. In "The Top Ten Best Sellers," a piece of inspired hilarity, he celebrates (tongue in cheek) the virtues of popular fiction. The Wise Hack at the writers' table in Hollywood doesn't denigrate popular writing, and knows that "the sort of exuberant badness which so often achieves perfect popularity cannot be faked." Gore takes up some admirable writing as well. There are strong essays, for instance, on Louis Auchincloss, Vladimir Nabokov, and Italo Calvino. He begins the Calvino meditation in his usual way, recalling his own arrival in Rome after the war: "Acid-yellow forsythia on the Janiculum. Purple wisteria in the Forum. Chunks of goat on a plate in a trattoria." As ever, Gore remains the consummate autobiographer and knowing observer.

As a critic, he liked to hug the shore when he wrote about authors, circling the islands of their texts, chatting gaily as he sailed with a broad reach. He moves through Calvino's books, for instance, with admiration for what he sees, noting that "Calvino has now developed two ways of writing. One is literally fabulous. The other makes use of a dry, rather didactic style in which the detail is as precisely observed as if the author were writing a manual for the construction of a solar heating unit. Yet the premises of the 'dry' stories are often quite as fantastic as those of the fairy tales." He suggests that Calvino, relatively unknown in English at the time, has "advanced far beyond his American and English contemporaries, weaving fantastic webs of prose to which all things adhere." Not surprisingly, Calvino would influence Gore's own writing as he would try to write in "literally fabulous" ways on occasion.

In other essays, such as "French Letter: Theories of the New Novel" and "The Hacks of Academe," he takes apart academic critics, slicing the meat from their bones, boiling the leftover carcasses to make a delicious soup that will never go down well over lunches at the faculty club. He wonders why the academics contributing to a particular anthology of essays on the novel even bothered to get out of bed. Wickedly, he ventures a possible answer: "Because the ambitious teacher can only rise in the academic bureaucracy by writing at complicated length about writing that has already been much written about." He levels his gun sights at one critic in particular: Leslie Fiedler, who had not looked favorably upon him in his influential study, *Love and Death in the American Novel* (1960). Fiedler is described as a "redskin most at home in white clown makeup." Now Gore blasts away: "From a secure heterosexual base, he [Fiedler] has turned a bright amused eye on the classic American goyim and finds them not only homoerotic to a man (or person as they say nowadays) but given to guilty pleasures with injuns like Queequeg, with niggers like Jim."

A lively essay on West Point becomes a recollection of his father and the dark ethos of the academy, with its parochial loyalties and hardened traditions. As he often did in talks and interviews, Gore attacks the outsize budget of the Department of Defense. "Today the first order of business in the United States is the dismantling of the military machine," he writes. "Obviously, we must continue to make it disagreeable for anyone who might decide to attack us (this could be done by not provoking other nations but that is too much to ask). Nevertheless the military budget must be cut by two thirds; and the service academies phased out." A sweeping "State of the Union" concludes this volume, rehearsing many of the arguments (even phrases) used on the lecture circuit. He riffed, as ever, on the swollen military budget, the prejudices of the public, the idiocy of various political leaders, and foolish efforts by the state to regulate sexuality. "Therefore let us remove from the statute books all laws that have to do with private morals—what are called victimless crimes. If a man or woman wants to be a prostitute that is his or her affair. It is no business of the state what we do with our bodies sexually. Obviously laws will remain on the books for the prevention of rape and the abuse of children." Gore calls, in effect, for a revolution of American ways and means.

He shines in these essays, which display his formidable gift of assimilating information and setting forth arguments combined with a cool and lustrous style: the syntax neatly balanced, the intelligence palpable on every page. Yet voices of criticism still arose, as in Christopher Lehmann-Haupt's review in *The New York Times*, where he subjects Gore to a kind of lazy Freudianism: "So we are left to speculate over the psychological implications here, and to conclude that Mr. Vidal's animus toward everything from West Point to the American Establishment—not to speak of academicians, who are, after all, instructors—boils down to an unresolved hostility toward his father, further evidence of which, some would argue, is Mr. Vidal's cheerfully admitted homosexuality." This review only added to Gore's longstanding hatred of *The New York Times*.

Never one to let an unjust accusation go unanswered, Gore responded with a letter, but the paper refused to publish it. *The New York Review of Books*, however, happily displayed it. "There is no evidence of an 'unresolved hostility' toward my father in the pages under review or elsewhere in my work. Quite the contrary. I quote from *Two Sisters: A Novel in the Form of a Memoir*: 'My father was the only man I ever entirely liked. . . . ' Nowhere in my writing have I 'admitted' ('cheerfully' or dolefully) to homosexuality, or to heterosexuality. Even the dullest of mental therapists no longer accepts the proposition that cold-father-plus-clinging-mother-equals-fag-offspring." Howard recalled: "He was in a rage about that, and a lot of anger came into everything he said." His obsessions converged, indeed, in *Kalki*, where he could blow up the whole world in his mind's eye.

The novel imagines a misanthrope's dream scenario: The world ends with a bang, and only a chosen few remain. The narrator is quite appealing in Gore's makeover of Teddy as a female: frank, clear-eyed, strong. She seems like a refraction of Amelia Earhart, the iron-willed aviatrix whom Gore knew well as a boy. Teddy is also famous as the author of *Beyond Motherhood*—a best-selling piece of nonfiction about population control. As the novel begins, she lags in her alimony payments, forcing her to take on a journalism gig. Her assignment is to investigate the ex–army officer James J. Kelly, who resides in Katmandu, where he imagines he is Kalki, the last incarnation of Vishnu, the Hindu god. Gore describes the Nepalese capital and its environs: "The outskirts of Katmandu are like the outskirts of any city in the world. That is to say, ugly, raw, disorganized; cement-block metastasized. But the countryside was green and rolling, and on a good day (which this particular one was not) you could see the Himalayas, sparkling like masses of quartz and crystal." He had visited Katmandu some years before, and his astonishing memory for details served him well as he offers a guided tour of the city, recalling that "the Nepalese houses have small latticed windows, peaked roofs of yellow tile supported by carved beams that overhang the narrow streets."

As it happens, Kalki has read Teddy's book, and he asks her bluntly: "What is there beyond motherhood?" "Freedom," she answers, adding: "You can be both a woman and a man." As a character, Kalki is fetching as well as far-fetched, a true megalomaniac. "I am the avatar," he says without a trace of embarrassment, noting that before him came Zoroaster, Rama, Krishna, the Buddha, Jesus, and Mohammed. "Now I have come."

Teddy is overwhelmed by Kalki's vitality. He radiates charm, and his soft Southern baritone appeals to her (as it would have to Gore). He claims to be searching for the five Perfect Masters and hopes that Teddy might be among them. She understands perfectly well that Kalki is auditioning her for a part, though she doesn't (at first) know he wants to destroy the world in order to start over, with himself and his wife, Lakshmi, as Adam and Eve, and with the Perfect Masters as teachers and companions. In due course, she learns the details of his diabolical plan for a nuclear holocaust, but she dismisses the notion as fanciful: "At the most, I thought that there would be some sort of television spectacular. Then a number of explanations about a special reprieve for mankind. Or perhaps, cleverest of all, the announcement that the end had already taken place and that we were now all of us, miraculously, purified and living at the start of a new Golden Age."

Gore's revulsion for the world as he found it, with its hungry billions, its turbid rivers and oceans, its littered metropolitan streets, permeates this bleak, haunted, many-sided novel, which has been underestimated (or mostly ignored) by critics. Most reviewers regarded the book as an unhappy mixture of jeremiad and satire, calculated to amuse and chide. Angela Carter, herself a gifted novelist, took the book apart in *The Guardian*: "Vidal's apocalypse is as cozily flabby as yesterday's salad, the plotting looks like kittens got at the knitting wool and a bouquet of invincible boredom rises from the ill-conceived pages." But she missed the intensity of imagination that Gore displays in *Kalki*, which combines the sexual playfulness of *Myra Breckinridge* with the visionary social critique of *Messiah*. The essayist in Gore meets the novelist here: a mixture that unsettled many readers, though R. Z. Sheppard, at *Time*, understood its value, calling it "an apocalyptic extravaganza."

In the final pages of *Kalki*, Teddy sits on a log under a weeping willow in Washington, D.C., watching as monkeys released from the zoo cavort, a reversion to origins. "Small things give great pleasure now," she says. "Let me list today's delights. Apple-scented air. Bright red birds on the wing. Silver fish that briefly arc above the surface of a river which glitters in the sun like a silver fish's scales." This is superb writing. Gore seems wholly in command of his material, delighting in its black humor, his words an elegy to a world that has passed but might reemerge. As usual, however, a mix of loose ends and caricature undermined the project, a result of Gore's usual hasty composition. Epstein could not, it seems, rein him in.

In July, Harris came down from Rome for a visit of two weeks at La Rondinaia, where she found her friend eager to assert himself, full of anger, trying to regain control. In her diary, she writes: "Gore said, 'I'm a local icon, and am pointed out to tourists just like the thousand-year-old castle. Everybody comes to say hello to the Maestro. I talk to the Monsignore in the piazza.' Proud old priest-baiter. He says that he and Howard are still known to the locals, after all these years here, as 'the two English sculptors.' Later I wrote him a thank you note that I addressed, *Dear Icon*. But he's not an icon—he's in his own eyes only a partial success. Unable personally to exert power he must at least write about power. 'Everybody in America is writing about victims,' he said to me. 'Well, I've no interest in victims. I'm interested in those who exercise power.'" Harris noted that Howard mostly concerned himself with the garden, obsessed by the variety of its flowers. Gore tried to put into practice what he had come to Ravello to achieve: "creative boredom." Harris, while looking from Gore's balcony at the glorious stretch of coast, asked him what on earth he could want apart from this view. Tellingly, he said, "I want to make 200 million people change their minds." In this sincere and immodest ambition Gore resembled Mailer, his frequent antagonist and fellow provocateur.

In late October 1977, Gore and Howard spent a few days in New York en route to California from Rome. They checked in to a suite at the Plaza, and there was no shortage of invitations to lunches or dinner parties. The city had been home for many years. "Howard adored New York," said Gore. "I never did. It had all of the filth and confusion of Calcutta without the cultural amenities." They attended a party for Princess Margaret one night, moving afterward to an expansive apartment owned by Lally Weymouth, a journalist and the daughter of Katharine Graham, the publisher of *The Washington Post*. Guests crammed together, at a party ostensibly in honor of George Weidenfeld, the British publisher. "You could hardly breathe," Howard recalled, "everyone standing shoulder to shoulder." It was a gleaming party, with Jackie Onassis, John Kenneth Galbraith, Gay Talese, William Styron, and Jerry Brown—Gore's future rival for a Senate seat in California—among the guests.

Mailer was talking with Jackie in the kitchen as Gore entered the living room, and the image struck him: "Mailer leaning into her face, listening too hard," Gore recalled. What happened next varies according to the teller, but Howard's version accords with others: "Norman came into the big room from the kitchen loaded for bear. He saw Gore surrounded by friends, everyone talking and laughing. Gore was in a good mood as Mailer moved right up to him, got in his face, and everybody around them fell pretty silent. It looked like trouble. Norman told Gore that he looked like an old Jew, and Gore shook his head. He didn't want to get into anything with Norman. Then Mailer threw his drink in Gore's face, right in his eyes, then hit him in the mouth with a punch, a kind of glancing uppercut. Gore was stunned, and he stepped back. He wiped a dribble of blood from his mouth with a handkerchief. Then Gore said, 'Norman, once again words have failed you.' "

Mailer was wild that night, drunk, and came at Gore again. Howard and Morton Janklow, the literary agent, rushed to separate them. Now Mailer stumbled into Max Palevsky, the computer wiz and venture capitalist, who spilled his champagne on Weymouth's dress. Jackie watched from the kitchen doorway. "She was mortified," said Howard. Unable to restrain himself, Howard threatened to punch Mailer, who laughed harshly and told Howard that his fourteen-year-old son could take him out with a single punch. Gathering his wits, Mailer said to Weymouth, "Either Gore goes or I do." She properly refused to toss either guest from the party, so Mailer wisely left.

The confrontation at Weymouth's apartment became not only mythic in Gore's circle but emblematic of an age when literary lions roared at each other, even struck blows. Certainly the next day, on *The Dick Cavett Show*, Gore commented ruefully on Mailer's aggressiveness, causing Mailer to threaten a lawsuit. This was dropped in exchange for another appearance by Mailer on Cavett's show, a kind of "equal time" deal. "It was all very tedious," said Gore, referring to this encounter with Mailer as "the night of the small fists."

For his part, Mailer had a version he would write to his friend and future biographer, J. Michael Lennon: "I butted him, threw the gin and tonic in his face, and bounced the glass off his head. It was just enough to prime you or me for a half hour war but Vidal must have thought it was the second battle of Stalingrad for he never made a move when I invited him downstairs. 24 hours later he was telling everybody he had pushed me across the room. Mike, I'm beginning to think I'm innocent. I simply don't understand whole-hearted liars who gain strength by the distance they put between themselves and the truth." This seems wonderfully rich, as Gore himself deplored "liars."

v. Hollywood Redux

Meanwhile, life in Italy in the late seventies had acquired fresh difficulties. Violent demonstrations and kidnappings (the former prime minister Aldo Moro was kidnapped in March 1978 and murdered by the Red Brigade, a militant leftist group) added to the usual political turmoil. On the right were paramilitary groups such as the Ordine Nuovo and the Nuclei Armati Rivoluzionari, and their militant homophobia terrified Gore, who thought he might become a high-profile target. Making matters worse, the Italian government—now in a dark financial hole—decided to tax American residents as if they were citizens. "Nobody in Italy paid taxes," Howard said, "not like they were asked to pay. They all knew how to cheat the government, but it wasn't so easy for us, as foreigners."

Gore and Howard had rented a house in Los Angeles the previous winter, testing the waters, and Gore briefly contemplated a permanent move. Still preferring real estate over less tangible investments, like stocks and bonds, he bought a house on Outpost Drive in the Hollywood Hills, taking possession on March 24, 1977. It was a large

Mediterranean-style mansion on an impossibly steep road, only a few minutes' drive from Sunset Boulevard. It featured high ceilings and a grand wooden staircase, a massive sunken living room with an impressive fireplace and French doors that opened onto a patio, and a lovely pool. Not unlike La Rondinaia, the house itself seemed to hang in the air, a garden as much as a house, with a stucco façade and red-tiled roof reminiscent of Italy.

Gore and Howard moved in that spring, bringing Phipps from London to be their decorator. She imagined the place "like some sort of tent in the Arabian desert," with draping fabrics, Howard said. Gore felt mildly uncomfortable in these new surroundings at first, but gradually he came to like the decor. He spent much of the day in a silk dressing gown, writing at a vast desk in the study off his bedroom on the second floor, while at local cafés and bars Howard met with friends, including Carole Mallory (a writer, actress, and onetime lover of Mailer's) and Lester Persky, the producer of the movie *Hair*, who continued a friendship with Gore for many years. "Howard liked movie people," Gore said, although he himself often felt ill at ease in Los Angeles and soon longed for Italy. "Hollywood Hills was an option we liked to have, but I didn't want to live there, not forever."

As he often did, in December Gore retreated to La Costa, the "fat farm" near San Diego. Tynan stopped by one day and marveled that Gore would spend "$1000 a week to lose thirty pounds." He noted that "the place has four restaurants, all with lengthy menus and wine lists for visitors. In five weeks there Gore has forged ahead with a new novel working nine–ten hours a day, and his talk at lunch, on Perrier, is quite as vivacious as mine, on two vodka martinis and white wine." Gore explained to Tynan that, much as he loved Italy, the tax laws there made him feel squeezed in ways that he found uncomfortable despite having plenty of money.

Relief came when Italy loosened its grip on the earnings of foreign residents, and Gore felt safe to return after roughly six months in California. He eagerly resumed his life in Rome and Ravello. "We were a little desperate not to lose Gore, either to Ravello or Los Angeles," said Armstrong, who had come to depend on Gore. "He was like a brother," he said. "Perhaps a difficult brother, but one loved him anyway." One gets a glimpse of Gore's demeanor at this time from an entry in Thomas Powers's diary. The scene was a dinner at Armstrong's apartment:

> It was cool on George's terrace, four stories up, looking out over Trastevere. He was quick to refill our drinks. I smoked a cigar. [My wife] Candace was pretty in her yellow dress. Gore talked, imitated, made sexual allusions, mimicked accents, occasionally asked a question, and in general worked hard to be a good, entertaining guest. He'd been just the same way back in 1965 and 1966, gracious, friendly, but perhaps not quite so hungry. I mean that literally. He ate all the hors d'oeuvres, all the bread at dinner, finished his drinks at machine-gun rate, poured himself wine faster than Johnston [Armstrong's Indian boyfriend] could keep the carafe filled.

Gore worked hard in the mornings, frequently hungover but determined to write *Creation*, a novel set in the fifth century BCE. "Such a key period, the fifth century," he said. "West and East converged." It had occurred to him that Zoroaster, Socrates, Aristotle, Sophocles, Aeschylus, Thucydides, Confucius, and the Buddha—just to skim the cream off the barrel—were alive in the same century, and he imagined a novel that would somehow link them. But his knowledge of these figures remained patchy, so he found himself once again deep in research. This novel would, in fact, complete a $1.2 million contract for two novels that Gore had signed with Epstein, *Kalki* being the first. "I saw the novel in my head clearly, and I knew that—if I just did the research—it would write itself."

The death of Gore's mother in April 1978 seemed like a turning point of sorts. She had been undergoing treatment for cancer at the Sloan Kettering Hospital in New York, looked after by her son Tommy (another of Gore's Auchincloss half brothers). Gore had by now banished Nina from his life. He would go further, in letters, and say he "detested her" and that his feelings were not "thwarted incestuous love but hatred of evil." The very idea of an Oedipus complex made him wish to run from the room screaming. "I agree with Nabokov," Gore said. "Freud was a Viennese quack."

A final development in the old lawsuit with Capote came at nearly the same moment. The story Capote had told about Gore being tossed onto the streets in front of the White House by Bobby Kennedy was untrue, at least in a literal sense, and many friends, including Arthur Schlesinger, George Plimpton, and Galbraith, stood behind Gore's version of events in depositions. For her part, Radziwill told an interviewer flatly that she had never said anything about this episode to Capote, thoroughly squashing his hopes for success. *People* recapped the feud, quoting Capote: "I'm very sad about Gore—very sad that he has to breathe every day." They quoted Gore in response: "Truman has made lying an art form—a minor art form." Radziwill is once again quoted, in all her royal eloquence: "They are just two fags."

The publishers at *Playgirl* knew that Gore had a watertight case, and they printed a retraction of Capote's statement. More or less satisfied, Gore told his lawyers to drop the case and send Capote a bill for his legal fees, totaling $50,000. By now deeply soaked in alcohol and addled by drugs, with few savings, Capote could hardly afford this and paid nothing to Gore. After another three years of mild wrangling, the affair subsided. When Capote died, in the summer of 1984, Gore remarked to Epstein: "It was a wise career move." There was the added insult that Capote had died in the Los Angeles home of Johnny Carson's ex-wife, Joanne. Gore wrote to her: "I shall have to die in your house now, just to even things out."

VI. GRACE AND HOPE

The ultimate value of his work as a novelist now began to worry Gore. Was he a serious writer of fiction or, as some critics said, a mere entertainer? In a review of Doris Lessing's sci-fi novel *Shikasta*, he began to think aloud about the possibilities for fiction. "Currently, there are two kinds of serious-novel," he wrote. "The first deals with the Human Condition (often confused, in Manhattan, with marriage), while the second is a word-structure that deals only with itself." He disliked the makers of word-structures, who wrote (as he later said) novels that "could not be read, only taught." He wanted, in digging into the ancient world, to go beyond what seemed to him like the contemporary options for a serious writer. He hoped that *Creation* would be viewed as a serious book, a work of art as well as of historical evocation. He needed, and hoped to create, a kind of masterpiece.

While not quite that, *Creation* is nevertheless an impressive book, summoning the Persian world of its narrator, the blind old Cyrus, a grandson of Zoroaster (who seems a good deal like Senator Thomas P. Gore in a toga). In recent decades, scholars have questioned the received wisdom of decades ago, when historians placed Zoroaster in the sixth century BC. But that isn't important, as this is fiction anyway. Imagine that Zoroaster lived then, and that he grandfathered old Cyrus who, in the span of a long public life, met Master Li and the Buddha in India, sat with Confucius in China, and encountered Anaxagoras and Socrates in Greece, while missing Plato by mere decades. If the scenario tests credulity, remember that Gore himself had personally met a dizzying range of figures from Amelia Earhart, Eleanor Roosevelt, and André Gide to Jack Kennedy, Tennessee Williams, Mikhail Gorbachev, and Hillary Clinton. In a sense, he imagined history as he lived it.

The elderly Cyrus dictates his memoirs to a younger man (his handsome great-nephew)—a typical Vidalian mode of narration. The voice shades into irony from the start: "I am blind, but I am not deaf." Because no recent visual impressions have caught his mind's eye, he sees the past with uncanny clarity and, at seventy-five, recalls his long diplomatic career in detail. It's heady stuff: "My grandfather in his seventy-fifth year used to talk for hours without ever linking one subject to another. He was absolutely incoherent. But then, he was Zoroaster, the prophet of Truth; and just as the One God that he served is obliged to entertain, simultaneously, every aspect of all creation, so did His prophet Zoroaster. The result was inspiring if you could ever make sense of what he was saying."

This witty narrator leads us through an array of religious visions, including that of the Jain prophet, Lord Mahavira—an intriguing figure who, like the Buddha, abandoned a life of luxury (as a prince) to become an ascetic, seeking spiritual awakening while rejecting the material world. After his enlightenment, Mahavira traveled for decades in India, spreading his ideas and attracting converts. Time, he explains to Cyrus, is an illusion one must overcome. Cyrus is a nonbeliever to the core, although he does seem to believe in the Wise Lord, a kind of mystical God above all gods. "Personally," he says, "I am all for nirvana—a word hard to translate. Nirvana is something like the blowing out of a flame, but there are other aspects to the word that are not only impossible to translate but difficult for a nonbeliever like myself to understand." When he meets the aged Buddha, he listens keenly to the voice, which he describes as "mild." The Buddha tells him a little of what he has learned during his years of contemplation and religious practice: "I know how perception begins and ends. How consciousness starts, only to stop. Since I know these things, I have been able to free myself from all attachment. The self is gone, given up, relinquished."

It's difficult for a novelist to put forward a flesh-and-blood Buddha or Mahavira. Such figures are, perhaps, best left to mythos, the realm of legend. Yet Gore valiantly puts words into the mouths of spiritual masters, often inventing the kinds of things they might well have said. Cyrus (like Gore, perhaps) admires the Buddha's wish to remove himself from the world of illusion; but he cannot understand the desire to renounce individual responsibility. "The absence of purpose," Cyrus declares, "makes the Buddha's truths too strange for me to accept." In due course, Cyrus comes to realize that "there is never a true account of anything." A monotheist like his grandfather at the outset, his experience of many religious visions at last undermines his certainty.

The middle section of this long (and quite literally meandering) novel has Cyrus back in Persia, where he spends his time with the powerful prince Xerxes, a son of Darius, the king. The bulk of this material comes from Herodotus, the Greek historian, although Gore chooses to tell the story from the Persian viewpoint. After succeeding his father as king, Xerxes ships his friend off to Cathay, hoping to open a trade route. There are episodes of considerable excitement, although Gore keeps the narrative at a level of fantasy that owes much to Calvino in places. At one point, Cyrus meets Master Li, who teaches Taoist restraint, saying things like "Wise is chaos." And this might well be the motto of this long novel.

Confucius is more to Gore's liking than any of the other spiritual masters in *Creation*, and Cyrus responds warmly to his teachings. "You know, when I was fifteen I set my heart upon learning. At thirty, I had my feet planted firmly in the ground. At forty, I no longer suffered from . . . perplexities. At fifty, I knew what were the biddings of heaven. At sixty, I submitted to them. Now I am in my seventieth year," recalls Confucius. "I can follow the dictates of my own heart because what I desire no longer oversteps the boundaries of what is right." What Gore has Cyrus say of Confucius is, perhaps, what one might say of Gore himself: "He made himself an expert on the past so that he might be useful in the present." As Gore later recalled: "I think I felt closest to the figure of Confucius in *Creation*. He was a this-worldly person."

When he returns from Cathay to Persia, Cyrus discovers that Xerxes has been drawn into another unproductive war with Greece. Yet after a while, things settle down and, according to Cyrus, a period of relative calm arrived. "The next dozen years were the happiest of my life," he tells his scribe. "There were no wars of any consequence, and the life of the court was more than ever delightful." The peace ends when Xerxes is murdered; but the drama seems weakly dramatized, and the novel ends abruptly with a period in Athens, where Cyrus converses with Pericles, the great general and statesman, among other notables. We learn that Sophocles has become a thorn in the general's side. "Sophocles has been able to hold office and seduce youthful citizens," says Cyrus, who with his Persian background disapproves of the Greek penchant for homosexual and pedophilic relations. Of course Pericles has no same-sex tendencies: "Never touch one of your own soldiers," he supposedly told his officers. Cyrus notes with approval: "Pericles has never shown the slightest interest in boys."

Apart from such slight nods by Cyrus in the direction of vaguely lost erotic opportunities, *Creation* is a sexless novel—very odd from the author of *Myra Breckinridge*. For the most part, the grand figures in this panorama of the ancient world speak in orotund voices, coming off like cardboard cutouts. Cyrus is especially orotund, which is perhaps appropriate for the testimony of a blind old man who recalls so many decades. Yet Gore's tour of the ancient world is comprehensive, with no great tombstone left unturned. The knowledge on display in these pages is dazzling if also dizzying.

Gore put the unwieldy manuscript into the lap of his new agent, Owen Laster, who came to Ravello to get better acquainted with his illustrious client. "Owen wasn't sure it was going to work," said Gore. "He told me it might need severe editing. I'm afraid I was not easy with that suggestion." Indeed, he terrified Laster, who backed off immediately. They took a taxi into Amalfi, where Gore insisted on celebrating the novel with a large meal at Da Zaccaria, a small restaurant overhanging the bay. It was always Gore's favorite place to dine, with its dime-size clams in fresh linguine, with langoustine cooked on a wood fire. He could easily drink a carafe of the zingy white wine by himself, preferring a table on the terrace, where you could hear waves crash on the black rocks below and see the winking lights of Amalfi. Zaccaria himself, a wiry black-eyed young man, treated Gore like a king, and would bow before him, uttering in a gravel voice: "*Maestro. Quello che vuoi.*" (Master, whatever you want.)

Back in New York, Epstein proved less easy to placate. "It was going to be a hard sell," he said. "I wanted another book on American history, not this." He and Gore jousted for several months, with Gore contemplating a return to Little, Brown, where he had never felt any ripples of dissent. Epstein had hoped for a more "realistic" novel of history, but Gore had been reading Calvino, and he liked the idea of a novel of ideas that backed away from realism. "*Creation,*" Gore said, "was a dream of sorts. I was Cyrus. I wandered in the corridors of history, at night, in my blindness. But I was all ears." Of course Epstein didn't want to lose Gore, so he urged him to revise the novel to foreground the realistic elements, such as they were. He also got him to cut large portions (which Gore defiantly added back in a 2002 edition that he called *Creation: The Restored Edition*). In the end, Gore would always feel that Random House failed to get behind the novel, which found an appreciative audience nonetheless. Published in 1981, it rose quickly up the lists of best sellers, defying gravity. Even the reviews were surprisingly positive. In *The New Republic*, for instance, Stefan Kanfer wrote: "Vidal writes with extraordinary concentration and little of the predictable reversals that mar much of his work." Further, he called it "a novel of grace and hope."

Gore and Isaiah Berlin in Oxford

After a long dinner at high table at Christ Church—roast beef, Yorkshire pudding, and string beans followed by lemon tart—Gore and I sit with Isaiah Berlin in the hushed Senior Common Room under a portrait of John Locke, one of the most illustrious former students of the college.

In the tradition of Oxford, I get a bottle of port from the drinks table, although Gore wonders if there is any Scotch.

There is, of course. I pour Gore a stiff one, since he seems anxious tonight—the academic world always makes him nervous.

Berlin looks at him sternly, as if the exam is about to begin.

"That's John Locke," I say, feeling a need to step in quickly. I nod to the picture on the wall. "He was a student here in the middle of the seventeenth century. They pray to him every night after dinner."

Berlin has intimidated Gore throughout the evening: I've never seen that before. He wore a look of sheepish amazement on his face throughout the meal, listening more than talking. Of course everyone in Oxford considers Berlin the best talker in the university, possibly in Britain, and Gore knows this. Berlin's lectures are flawless performances, without notes, full of quotations that he has memorized verbatim. He seems to have read everything, exuding a wisdom and calm that Gore has rarely encountered.

"I'm sure you know, Gore, that Locke influenced Jefferson," says Berlin. "Called him the most important man in history, with Bacon and Newton his closest rivals."

Gore shuffles through his memory, looking for the correct note card. "I think he quoted Locke in the Declaration of Independence," he says.

"Indeed," says Berlin. "He was among the first to see that the separation of church and state was essential in a sane republic."

"I would get rid of the church altogether," Gore says.

"No! We need the church. I'm a Jew, but I like the fact that people pray. It opens them to an experience beyond the self."

"Do you believe in God?" Gore asks.

"That depends, as always, on one's definition. We'd be very small in this universe without the idea of God."

"Locke argued for tolerance," I say. "He's the father of tolerance, when it comes to religious belief."

Berlin nods eagerly. "We're all liberals, aren't we? We owe that to our man here."

"Me?" Gore teases.

"Of course we mean you," says Berlin. "You're our guest tonight."

Gore seems out of witticisms, and he slouches into the deep cushions of the chair and holds out his glass for another Scotch.

Chapter Nine

> We should stop going around babbling we're the greatest democracy on earth, when we're not even a democracy. We're a sort of militarized republic.
>
> —Gore Vidal

1. Acting President

Gore appeared on *The Merv Griffin Show*—at the time one of the most popular talk shows on television—soon after the election of Ronald Reagan, whom Gore invariably called "our acting president." It was a deft performance, with the best-selling author in a dark business suit looking presidential himself, a kind of senatorial girth making it difficult to button the jacket. He had begun to weather, and not well, with a ripple of age darkening on his right cheek. His hair had grown gray at the edges, thinning slightly. Griffin teased him about the election, eager to provoke a good line: "Mr. Reagan has received a mandate from the people." "Well," said Gore, sniffing as if a bad odor had suddenly emerged, "he has received something. It was certainly better than the Old Actors' Home."

Approaching sixty, Gore seemed at ease in public situations, himself a kind of acting literary president. But he wanted badly to return to Rome, and with the unexpected easing of the tax situation in Italy, he and Howard flew home. The old circle of friends greeted them warmly, and they moved back and forth between the Largo Argentina and Ravello often, chauffeured by Mario, a driver from Ravello, whom Howard only had to call and he would appear in a black Mercedes. "Rat always traveled with us," Howard recalled, referring to their beloved dog, who had become a part of their lives—Gore and Howard frequently had dogs as well as cats, and they were often the subject of good-humored conversation. Now Gore hoped for a long peaceful stretch, when he would return to another of his satirical novels, which were more fun to write than the hefty historical ones (although he enjoyed the research).

The accidental death of Tennessee Williams on February 25, 1983, upset Gore more than he guessed it would, and it broke the calm he was hoping for. Williams died in a suite at the Hotel Elysée in New York from suffocation, when a bottle cap stuck in his throat. He had apparently been trying to ingest a barbiturate when it happened. "The Bird had been drinking and taking drugs, God knows what, for such a long time. It didn't surprise me when he died, but it was not a good end. We hadn't been on good terms for a bit. He pitied himself, and that was the worst part of it." Gore had watched anxiously as Williams began to lose his touch in theaters, and thought his later plays were simply bad. He did not, himself, wish to exit in such a sad way.

With *Creation* barely finished, he began *Duluth*, a dark, satirical novel that would appear in 1983. He was also doing research for a novel about Abraham Lincoln, and this put fresh demands on his reading. It was a time to withdraw, to read and write without hectic travel or undue interference. In Rome, he and Howard mainly saw George Armstrong and Luigi Corsini. They also spent time in Ravello with Corsini, who had a teaching post at the university in Salerno, which Gore could see from the balcony of his study in the middle distance. There were dinners with Judith Harris and Mickey Knox, as well as Donald and Luisa Stewart, who had an apartment in Rome on Via Margutta. Michael and Linda Mewshaw were available for meals, too, and Mewshaw put Gore in touch with a number of American visitors as they came through Rome, including the novelist Pat Conroy, whose writing Gore admired. In Ravello, Michael Tyler-Whittle was a frequent companion. "I liked our padre, don Michael," said Gore. "He combined the best of English traits: real learning, a love of language, and a chaotic sense of everyday life. His life was a shambles, but he didn't worry. Good cheer got him through anything."

Gore and Howard continued their periodic excursions to Bangkok, usually in the winter, staying for a week or two at the Oriental Hotel. Gore loved the food and would visit the male brothels, often wandering along the back streets of the sweaty city. In later years he referred to these wanderings ruefully as part of his "relentless pursuit of AIDS," though he genuinely believed that being a "top" with no interest in being anally penetrated meant he was safe. But he worried about this, and had begun to think hard about what it meant to be gay, though he normally rejected that term. It was during this period that he wrote "Some Jews and the Gays," a searing essay—one of his finest—that Barbara Epstein didn't want to publish in *The New York Review of Books* unless Gore toned it down considerably. But he wouldn't change a word, sending it to Victor Navasky, his friend and the editor at *The Nation*, where it appeared on October 14, 1981. *The Nation* would, indeed, become a repository for some of his best work—pieces that larger publications deemed too hot to handle.

This essay was given a fresh title, "Pink Triangle and Yellow Star," in Gore's next book of essays, *The Second American Revolution and Other Essays (1976–1982)*, which came out in 1982. It was a controversial piece that was bound to create discomfort. Yet it's a sharply drawn, daring essay in which Gore's cool intelligence and unsparing logic shine out as he attempts to come to terms, yet again, with the complicated matter of sexual identity. "The American passion for categorizing has now managed to create two nonexistent categories—gay and straight," he writes. "Either you are one or you are the other. But since everyone is a mixture of inclinations, the categories keep breaking down; and when they break down, the irrational takes over."

Appealing quickly to authority, Gore quotes George Orwell: "It is impossible to mention Jews in print, either favorably or unfavorably, without getting into trouble." This allows him to mention Jews. "Like it or not, Jews and homosexualists are in the same fragile boat," he writes. That is, both were subject to prejudice and marginalization. The pretext for his essay was "The Boys on the Beach," a homophobic article by Midge Decter that appeared in *Commentary*, which was edited by her husband, Norman Podhoretz (Gore called them "the Pod people"). Gore tosses a bit of gasoline on the fire now—given that Decter was Jewish: "For sheer vim and vigor, 'The Boys on the Beach' outdoes its implicit model, *The Protocols of the Elders of Zion*."

Decter's piece is bizarre. She muses on life on Fire Island, a gay enclave, and comments on how the gays have ruined everything by their freshly discovered militancy, post-Stonewall. She asks: "What indeed has happened to the homosexual community I used to know—they who only a few short years ago were characterized by nothing so much as a sweet, vain, pouting, girlish attention to the youth and beauty of their bodies?" She recalled the "slender, seamless, elegant and utterly chic" clothes that gay men wore in earlier times. There is an undertone: Why can't they just be normal—or amusingly abnormal, like in the old days? Why get so . . . political?

Decter attacks Susan Sontag's well-known essay on camp, arguing (inaccurately) in a footnote that Sontag fails to realize that "camp is of the essence of homosexual style, invented by homosexuals, and serving the purpose of domination by ridicule." Gore fires back: "Decter seems unaware that all despised minorities are quick to make rather good jokes about themselves before the hostile majority does." Without pause, he dismantles her shallow Freudian take on homosexuality, as when she writes: "The desire to escape from the sexual reminder of birth and death, with its threat of paternity—that is, the displacement of oneself by others—was the main underlying desire that sent those Fire Island homosexuals into the arms of other men." Gore says with arch irony: "But Freud has spoken. Fags are fags because they adored their mothers and hated their poor, hard-working daddies." He wonders about the fact that Decter's twaddle, her "unproven, unprovable thesis" could still be found within the pages of a supposedly respectable magazine.

Gore continues in full attack mode, striking at the neocon critic Joseph Epstein (no relation to Jason), who in *Harper's* a few years earlier had written: "If I had the power to do so, I would wish homosexuality off the face of the earth." Needless to say, Gore could hear in such a remark the undertones of fascists who, in the twenties and thirties, wished the same for Jews. He finds it inconceivable that Jews could speak against "fags," as Gore calls them, and suggests that this new kind of Jewish intellectual, those identified with the ruling classes, were like "so many Max Naumanns," referring to a German self-hating Jew who was out to save his neck by identifying with the oppressor and joining the Nazis. In a conclusion that lowers the temperature of the discourse by several degrees, Gore calls for "a cease-fire" in the war between Jews and homosexuals, "and a common front against the common enemy, whose kindly voice is that of Ronald Reagan and whose less than kindly mind is elsewhere in the boardrooms of the Republic."

This essay was a spectacular performance by Gore, who summoned every ounce of wit and good sense. It's rude, of course: He can barely conceal his scorn for Decter. And some would find his isolation of a class of neoliberal Jews as anti-Semitic in itself. Yet Gore did not, at least in this piece, sound an anti-Semitic note, though he was hardly beyond such a thing in conversation. (When he was drunk, he could seem terribly racist and anti-Semitic. It was the least attractive side of Gore, although neither of these prejudices ran deep, and he could be just as fierce in attacking racists and anti-Semites when sober.) In this essay, he makes sense—unless, of course, you take exception to hyperbolic characterization of Reagan and those in power in American boardrooms as the "common enemy."

Sitting in Rome or Ravello, he assembled a consistent and detailed worldview, putting the random witty remarks he had offered on ephemeral talk shows into permanent form, creating art from cultural politics. The essay as genre became an ideal vehicle for his waspish voice. Wit leavened the work, whether he wrote about a literary icon (Scott Fitzgerald, Edmund Wilson, Christopher Isherwood, L. Frank Baum) or deconstructed an American political figure, as in "Theodore Roosevelt: An American Sissy." In "The Second American Revolution," the title essay of the collection, he calls for what in his view has been long overdue: a fresh look at the U.S. Constitution, suggesting that the American republic had long ago given way to an empire run by oligarchs, and "the oligarchs are a good deal more dangerous to the polity than the people at large." He calls for reining in the imperial presidency and getting rid of the executive order, which allows the president to bypass Congress and, therefore, the wishes of the people. As for the House of Representatives, he argues for a parliamentary system where "whoever can control a majority will be the actual chief of government, governing through a cabinet chosen from the House . . . Since the parliamentary system works reasonably well in the other industrially developed democracies, there is no reason why it should not work for us." As for the Supreme Court, he suggests—a shocking idea!—that it should be "entirely subservient to the law of the land." He envisions a reformed Senate that would vaguely resemble the lifetime lords of Britain, "a home for wise men" who would look at the laws made by the House and consider whether or not they are constitutional as well as rational.

Gore was willing to take things back to basics, and to regard the U.S. Constitution not as the stone tablets of Moses but as a living document in need of regular visitation and revision (as Thomas Jefferson, in fact, had argued, suggesting that each generation should take a hard look at the document and make appropriate changes). As Gore observed, the original document drafted in Philadelphia would soon—in 1987—reach its second century. "I had seen how much trouble it caused," Gore later said, "and my proposals were fairly modest."

The reviews were mostly respectful, and no reviewer—however hostile to Gore's political views—could doubt that this collection of essays "was written by a man of taste and seriousness," as *The New York Times* suggested. A number of reviewers pointed out, fairly enough, that Gore liked to harp on old themes. In one of the few sweeping notes of dismissal, Julian Symons in *The Times Literary Supplement* called Gore "a lightweight" who was nevertheless "a sparky little fellow prepared to shadow-box twice his own size in the ring." More typically, Thomas Mallon in the *National Review* (William F. Buckley's magazine, of all places) wrote: "No one else [in America] . . . can combine better sentences into more elegantly sustained demolition derbies." (This review endeared Mallon to Gore, and they became friends. Indeed, when Mallon became the literary editor of *GQ*, he would commission pieces by Gore.)

By the early eighties, Gore had become a landmark on the cultural scene—on television, in print, on public stages, where he held forth before assorted audiences with grave authority and mercurial wit. In his own measure and style, he combined the role of public intellectual with that of writer and public scold, and it remains a testament to his work ethic. "He just wouldn't stop," said Howard. "I wanted him to slow down, take it easy. He was getting old. But Gore did what Gore did. He had things to say. He is a genius."

II. Running in Place

Now Gore was famous around the world, and the demands on his time began to weigh on him. It proved difficult to write for extended periods without interruption, and he could not resist traveling to New York, Los Angeles, Paris, or London to give talks or television interviews when reasonable offers came. He was by nature a social animal, and when friends called—on the phone and in person—he never turned them away. London played a huge part in his life, and he relished encounters with Princess Margaret, as in July 1983 when he went to a lunch at Kensington Palace: "We drove to the Royal Lodge at Windsor," he wrote to Judith Halfpenny, an enthusiastic fan from Canada with whom he corresponded, "in a sort of station wagon with a Scotland Yard man next to the driver, making it impossible to see anything except through the side windows. 'One sees a great many backs, traveling,' said herself. The Queen Mother had just vacated the RL, which is pretty much her house and gone to Sandringham and the household wanted to shut it up because no one was there but, ever forceful, she said, 'I know there are three stewards, and the maid.' 'But no cook, your royal highness!' We lunched beneath a great oak tree in the lawn. We dined on the terrace in front of the one great room of the lodge, built by the Regent whose mad peevish little face not yet as porcine as it would become stares down at one from above the fire place."

The Hollywood connection meant even more to him than his associations with British royalty. And keeping these fires going required meetings, parties, phone calls, and letters. Visitors came and went, usually staying for a day or two, including Norman Lear, Claire

Bloom, Walter Matthau, Lee Remick, Susan Sarandon, and, as ever, Paul Newman and Joanne Woodward. Movie agents Sue Mengers and Boaty Boatwright remained close friends, and they stopped by whenever they came to Italy.

Any number of English or American writers sought and received invitations to dinner. Among them was William Styron, who came to Ravello in 1981, though he disliked Gore and had trouble disguising his contempt. "Styron had a thing against fags," said Gore, "and thought we were all rich because we didn't have to support armies of children and grandchildren. He, of course, married an heiress. I never read his novels." American visitors wanted to meet Gore, and he was happy enough to see most of them. He was himself often a guest at the residence of Maxwell Rabb, the U.S. ambassador. Rabb, despite being a Reagan appointee, found Gore delightful and lured him to his house on Sunday afternoons to watch the latest Hollywood films, which weren't easily available in Rome, not in English. "They dubbed American actors into Italian," Anthony Quinn recalled. "I always came out sounding like Bugs Bunny." Rabb liked to meet Hollywood stars. He once pulled out of a major international conference in Naples in order to meet Woodward at one of Gore's parties. (Only once, when Nancy Reagan came to Rome, was Rabb compelled—by the White House—to scratch Gore's name from the guest list.)

Piqued by the popularity of Reagan, Gore began to take seriously the idea of running in the Democratic primary for U.S. Senate in California in 1982. "That was all Max Palevsky," Gore recalled, referring to the wealthy liberal entrepreneur who had become a good friend. Palevsky disliked Jerry Brown, the two-term governor and Democratic favorite for a Senate seat, and had been pushing Gore to run for a while, offering to act as campaign treasurer and helping to raise money. Paul Ziffren, an influential lawyer who rose to prominence as a backroom operator in Democratic politics in the fifties, encouraged Gore as well, offering to help raise money and introduce Gore to the right people. As word about this potential primary bid leaked out, the *Los Angeles Times* printed a small story that fueled interest in his candidacy, and Gore found he enjoyed being in the political limelight again.

By the winter of 1982, he had firmly decided to run, so he moved from Italy back to Los Angeles, where he would base himself during this adventure. His house in the Hollywood Hills doubled as campaign headquarters, and he accepted speaking engagements throughout the state in January and February. On March 9, 1982, he filed for the nomination, and from that moment on it was a whirl, with too much to do. He lived "on rubber chicken now, and plastic carrots," he said. Though a few friends put up money, he decided it was best to rely mainly on his own funds, as it would give him the kind of flexibility he preferred. It was, however, expensive to print posters and to manufacture lapel buttons, brochures, bumper stickers, and the usual paraphernalia of American elections.

As a cultural icon and iconoclast, he attracted large crowds at places such as Berkeley and UCLA, but the press never quite caught up to him, as three years later he told one interviewer: "Thousands of people came to hear me, but the press insisted on saying that I was very unpopular. On TV they showed two sleepy students and the voice-over of the announcer said, 'Of course, Vidal couldn't attract a crowd.' What they don't want you to know, they don't tell you. Take, for example, the corruption in the aerospace industry in California. It's astounding. Poor Jerry Brown, for all his liberal credentials couldn't quite explain why he liked the B-1 bomber, which is totally impractical militarily but totally necessary for him to endorse for his campaign coffers."

Palevsky asked Gore to hire a publicist to help with daily appointments and setting up interviews, and he took on Robert Chandler, a young man who thought of himself then (as now) as a conservative. "The prospect of having Gore Vidal as a client couldn't have been more delicious," Chandler says. "Not just for the irony, but because I'd always gotten a kick out of Vidal as a public personality." He entertained some skepticism about Gore's sincerity in running, but soon discovered Gore meant what he said. "Vidal was, as I'd hoped, a kick, although quite serious and earnest about the race. And not the least haughty or intimidating or acerbic, but helpful, constructive, and conscientious. And though we were nominally running against Jerry Brown, he wanted really to be running against Ronald Reagan. Or, more precisely, he wanted not a partisan run against Reagan or the Republicans. Way beyond that, Gore Vidal was running against the way America was turning out."

One can watch Gore run—the documentary filmmaker Gary Conklin followed him with a camera crew as he appeared at dinners, town hall events, and small gatherings. (*Gore Vidal: The Man Who Said No* appeared in 1984). He catches the candidate in candid scenes with bystanders or, less spontaneously, as he gives his stump speech. Gore seems fully engaged, running with all his might. He kept hammering away at several key ideas, such as when he argued that taxing corporations was preferable to loading the weight of running an empire on the backs of the poor. He proposed cutting the Pentagon budget by a quarter—not so terribly radical, as he said: a matter of closing a few anachronistic bases and suspending the production of irrelevant weapons systems. He shifted from venue to venue, traveling light, with no entourage except for Howard and one or two friends—plus the camera crew. For three months, he ran as hard as he could, with a focus on college campuses and liberal-minded areas around Los Angeles and San Francisco. "I could see little point in visiting Orange County, but I went there anyway," he said. As expenses ballooned, a few Hollywood friends put extra cash into the kitty. "I think he was quite worried," said Gavin Lambert, an expat English novelist, screenwriter, and close Hollywood friend. "We sat by his pool on Outpost Drive one night drinking Scotch. He looked very tired, and I wondered aloud if the whole thing was worth the effort. Gore rounded on me, furious. He had no choice, he said. Jerry Brown was beginning to move toward his positions, and this was a good thing."

Brown assumed he would defeat whatever candidate the Republicans put up, especially if the mayor of San Diego, Pete Wilson, won the primary. In fact, he never considered Gore a serious rival, but one sees a look of annoyance crossing his face as Gore teases him at one political banquet filmed by Conklin. "I think Gore actually might have done better, even won," said Lambert, "but he wasn't used to the pace of a modern campaign. It had been some years since he ran, in upstate New York. This wasn't a book tour, and he wasn't getting any younger." Not surprisingly, exhaustion set in, and at times one can almost see Gore yawning in Conklin's film. He came in far behind Brown, with 15 percent to Brown's 45 percent. Quite sensibly, Brown appropriated many of Gore's ideas, emphasizing in his campaign the need to cut military budgets and focus on those in society who were most in need of government assistance.

Gore knew, at least on a subconscious level, that he wouldn't win the nomination. "I spoke with Vidal during his Senate primary campaign," says William Bradley, a political reporter, "and he acknowledged the obvious, that he had no realistic sense that he might win, but that he *did* hope to provoke debate with Brown about the nature of democracy in America, something for which Vidal had a notably jaundiced view." Lambert found the whole effort on Gore's part "Quixotic," but tilting at windmills was in character for Gore.

Another view comes from Conklin: "I do think he wanted very much to win, but unfortunately he didn't spend his own money on good political ads, which seems to be the only way you can be elected to office in this country. Yet the audiences were large and responsive." Conklin noticed that Gore's political ambitions, though largely extinguished by this primary run, would sometimes flare briefly: "From one telephone call I received from Ravello after the campaign, I believe that Gore dreamed when he had drunk a bit more than usual that he might still run for president." The fantasy would never quite die, though Gore knew perfectly well it was a fantasy.

He returned to Italy, eager to get back to writing: his only true refuge. The run for Senate had forced him to put his writing aside, and he saw how much he really hated that. Owen Laster came for a visit, having in hand a proposal from Jason Epstein for another political novel. Lincoln was the obvious subject, and Gore had planned on writing this book in any case. Soon Gore signed a deal with Random House and, in a gesture of peace with Epstein, offered to pay back all unearned money from a previous contract—an unheard-of suggestion, which Epstein dismissed. He knew, of course, that a novel by Gore on Lincoln that focused squarely on the tumultuous years of his presidency would sell in large numbers.

Gore dug into his bottom drawer for the teleplay about Lincoln he had written, without luck, for Norman Lear in 1979. It would not be easy for him to transform this sketchy material—more a treatment than a finished script—into a full-length novel about the sixteenth president, but he accepted the challenge. For his part, Epstein, who had been unhappy about *Duluth* from the outset, relaxed. He would soon have a big political novel from Gore, and this would make up for any losses that Random House might still have on its books. Epstein would even hold his nose and publish *Duluth.*

III. *DULUTH*: LOVE IT OR LOATHE IT

Epstein's bright assistant, Gary Fisketjon, took over editorial duties on the novel. "I was of course thrilled," says Fisketjon, who would later become the editor of many celebrated novelists, including Richard Ford, Jay McInerney, and Cormac McCarthy. "Gore was a challenge—a very difficult man at times to edit, as he didn't like anyone to change anything he wrote, but I was game. We seemed to get along well." So Epstein stood back and watched. In May 1983, the novel appeared, less than robustly supported by its publisher, or so Gore claimed. It failed to attract many readers and received tepid reviews, at best. Peter Conrad, a sympathetic commentator on almost anything by Gore, wrote in *The Observer* that Gore "laughingly debauches the novel with an anthology of skits, mimicking Regency romance, soap opera and science fiction." More typically, Jonathan Yardley wrote in *The Washington Post Book World* that Gore "relishes retailing a brand of witless, slapstick humor that would cause a sophomore to blush."

Reviewers missed the anarchic energy of *Duluth*, which has many virtues, though its lack of narrative coherence makes them less visible. The novel is ruthless, silly, and shrewd at the same time, a riff on the American language itself and how it shapes American realities. Making fun of soaps and popular novels, it centers largely on Rosemary Klein Kantor, a past winner of the Wurlitzer Prize, who works doggedly "at the console of her word-processor, which is connected with a memory bank containing ten thousand popular novels." But it's also the portrait of a city, one with no purchase on space or time. Gore writes: "If, as it has been so often said, every society gets the

Duluth that it deserves, the United States of America in the last but one decade of the twentieth century has come up with a knockout."

At times, the novel veers toward a kind of poetry, reminiscent of John Ashbery, who has made a career out of reformulating, riffing on, luxuriating in the detritus of American speech as it passes into or around thought. Consider a couple of representative paragraphs from *Duluth*:

> August is the month of Duluth's Coming Home parties, of which the most important, socially, is the lovely reception that is being held at The Eucalyptus Club for the Bellamy Craig IIs.
>
> All things considered, both Bellamy and Chloris enjoyed the kidnapping, while their marriage, though by no means altogether shut, is a lot less open than it used to be as a result of the happiness each experienced during a week in Rome—preceded by a single uncomfortable night in Bonn—where they were able to attend the showing of Valentino's new line of evening wear.

The language mocks the rituals of middle-class life in nondescript cities, as when Gore sends up "Duluth's Coming Home parties." That "lovely reception" (with a clichéd adjective so typical of the way experience gets homogenized by language) happens at a club with a perfect name for it, one that mocks all such clubs, as in city streets called Happy Valley Road or Sunny Avenue. Heterosexual marriages, as ever, come under a barrage of linguistic meddling, with a play on "open marriages," a maneuver that literalizes the metaphor and makes it seem ridiculous. This builds to the ultimate happiness for this couple, who were "able to attend the showing of Valentino's new line of evening wear." As ever, Gore sends up the mania for brand names, deconstructs the reliance on certain linguistic turns that provide (for some) a kind of comfort, a sense of reality.

Of course a political rivalry occupies the city of Duluth. Captain Eddie Thurow, head of the Duluth Police Department, wants badly to be mayor; he's running against the incumbent, Mayor Herridge, who had the misfortune to be named Mayor by his parents, thus confusing his achievement. Herridge thinks that he must win over the teeming barrios of Duluth, which exist in slums "just off ethnic Kennedy

Avenue." In a related turn, Captain Eddie has a lieutenant, Darlene Ecks, who has been strip-searching illegal aliens and stepping on their corns—which they produce in abundance because their shoes are too tight. (Political correctness annoyed Gore, who never lost a chance to debunk it.)

Duluth is a mad, campy novel that relocates the city of the future in the present, even as it draws on a disenchanting past. It's a place of corrupt politics, fierce local prejudices, race hatred, and an insatiable love of kitsch. The narrative builds to the usual Vidalian climax, with alien insects planning to destroy the world even as Rosemary Klein Kantor, the prizewinning author, presses the Erase button on her machine, dissolving at a keystroke the neighborhood of Garfield Heights (named for a presidential nonentity), where the elite of the city live in luxury, a part of Duluth known for "its mansions and houses, its bitter homes and gardens." In an instant, there is "now nothing at all where the Heights once were." Soon all is lost, though it's no loss in Gore's wan view, as he gives a final withering glance at the American scene from an enormous height.

Needless to say, it upset Gore that critics failed to realize his intentions or accomplishment in *Duluth*, though a small band of admirers would emerge, including Italo Calvino, who wrote about it as a brave experiment in narrative method. "To be sure, Vidal's explicit intention is to parody the current university vogue for 'Narratology,'" says Calvino, "but his mythology seems to me to be no less rigorous and his execution no less perfect. For that reason, I consider Vidal to be a master of that new form which is taking shape in world literature and which we may call the hyper-novel or the novel elevated to the square or to the cube." Perhaps having one appreciative reader at this level was enough.

IV. HONORARY CITIZEN

Calvino's remarks were delivered at a celebration of Gore in Ravello, where he was made an honorary citizen on September 24, 1983. Howard knew how much this distinction meant to Gore, and organized a party after the ceremony at La Rondinaia. In her diaries, Harris recalls the occasion in some detail:

> Gore received honorary citizenship from the town of Ravello in a touching ceremony: the coming out party organized by Howard. The evening before, a Friday, we sat out in the piazza at a table: Gore, Howard, the Italian writer Alberto Arbasino, AP's chief Dennis Redmont and his wife Manuela, Italo Calvino and his wife Esther, Luigi Barzini, the journalist, Peter Nichols (the English playwright) and his actress wife and their very young son, all at tables with beer and wine before us. Calvino said he's loved the book *Duluth*, its synthesis of America, "the density of its comic effects." Said Calvino: "Gore is an ubiquitous enfant terrible who doesn't respect anyone or anything except for the Preamble to the Declaration of Independence. He has been away from the U.S. and in Italy for long periods, but it's as if he never left. He is a harsh and happy critic and polemicist such as only a fully mature nation could produce, unlike our fragile Italy.

Luigi Barzini said, "What makes Gore a good writer? Not because his books are all best sellers (though they are); not because they are performed upon the stage of the United States of America; but because he found the emotive streak inside of the Americans, the anguish of modern life." For Gore "Ravello is an oasis, here there is ancient life all around, not just for the viewing of it; man has left his mark here everywhere the eye rests."

By now, Gore and Howard felt entirely at home on the Amalfi coast, and could be found most nights of the week before dinner at the San Domingo, a bar in the piazza where you could sit at tables overlooking the cathedral. They had a sizable number of reliable local friends, including Tyler-Whittle, who recalled: "Howard liked everyone in the village. Everybody knew him, and he paid for their beer and wine. Gore enjoyed watching Howard enjoying them. Gore's Italian wasn't terribly good, but Howard knew the local dialect, and used always to light up when he'd see one of his friends, Andrea or Pepe or Giovanni.

Sometimes the boys came back to the pool for a swim in the evenings. It was all good fun, nothing sexual. Gore would sip Scotch and look on with amusement."

Gore occasionally looked for "trade" on the streets of Rome, but this had become less urgent in later years—alcoholism played a role in this—and his life in Ravello rarely included sex. "I was largely celibate there," Gore said, "as it was where I did my research, kept long hours at my desk." He wrote for three or four hours in the morning and, in the afternoon, corresponded with countless friends and strangers, some of whom he found interesting, such as Jonathan Ned Katz, who published the *Gay/Lesbian Almanac* in 1983, which Gore found entertaining. As he would with admiring fans, he wrote to Katz about the almanac's insights concerning himself and novelist James Baldwin, whom Gore had known a little: "I thought the Baldwin '49 piece brilliant; I never knew it existed, which explains Jimmy's nervousness with me at the time—'his panic' is an excellent description of a state of mind which my characters in *The City and the Pillar*, perhaps, shared—though the author not. But I was a realist back then—if you succeed in driving a stake through those false nouns 'homosexual' and 'heterosexual,' statues will be built in your honor—or perhaps just a large stake to burn you at." (In private, less than magnanimously, Gore often referred to Baldwin as "Martin Luther Queen," claiming that he had heard Jack Kennedy make the same joke at the White House.)

A couple of intense months in 1983 were devoted to Gore's magisterial essay on William Dean Howells for *The New York Review of Books*. The occasion was a new Library of America volume of the Gilded Age novelist, critic, and editor, which reprinted a decade's worth of Howells's longer fiction. Thinking about this neglected author—the model of the traditional man of letters—Gore thought about himself, and his survey of Howells's career reads like autobiographical stock-taking. Howells, alone among such peers as Mark Twain and Henry James (who were close friends), took a principled stand on the Chicago Haymarket Riot of 1886, which saw seven men convicted of capital murder even though nothing could really connect them to the crime except hearsay. Gore reflects:

> Of the Republic's major literary and intellectual figures (the division was not so clearly drawn then between town, as it were, and gown), only one took a public stand. At forty-nine, William Dean Howells was the author of that year's charming "realistic" novel, *Indian Summer*; he was also easily the busiest and smoothest of America's men of letters. Years before, he had come out of Ohio to conquer the world of literature; and had succeeded. He had been the first outlander to be editor of the *Atlantic Monthly*. In the year of the Haymarket Square riot, he had shifted the literary capital of the country from Boston to New York when he took over *Harper's Monthly*, for which he wrote a column called "The Editor's Study"; and a thousand other things as well.

Some years later, Gore reflected on his time with Howells: "I lived in Howells for weeks, reading him through a damp winter in Ravello, sitting by the fire in my study, wrapped in a blanket. Pussy cat wondered what had happened to his master, why he didn't move. That piece was probably the best one I did." Criticism is often covert autobiography; almost certainly, Gore looked into the mirror of Howells and found himself. "Howells, a master of irony, would no doubt have found ironic in the extreme his subsequent reputation as a synonym for middlebrow pusillanimity," he wrote in the essay. "After all, it was he who was the spiritual father of Dreiser (whom he did nothing for, curiously enough) and of Stephen Crane and Harold Frederic and Frank Norris, for whom he did a very great deal."

The piece has a strangely prophetic aura, as when Gore writes: "Howells lived far too long." It was something Gore feared: becoming a rumor in his own time. And he wondered to what degree one could outwit the forces that invariably conspire to push away a writer, especially one as prolific, diverse, controversial, and successful as Gore had been. In the act of creating his imperial self, he sent out emissaries to far-flung posts, distant colonies of readers in at least thirty-five languages. A mortal fear of erasure dogged him to the end: "One feels the Great Eraser always at work," he wrote to Elaine Dundy—a line repeated endlessly in letters and conversations over the years. As he sat at his desk in Ravello, beneath a dozen framed magazine covers of himself, he wondered how and where to get the continuing reflection he required in order to sustain a sense of reality. He could only see himself in print, in photos, on television. The mirror in his bathroom didn't suffice, especially as the light grew dimmer by the decade.

"My thoughts turned to Lincoln in the mild wake of *Duluth*," he said, "a president at the height of his power as the war drew to a close." As he wrote *Lincoln*, he had in mind what he said at the end of his Howells essay. "The fact that a novelist like Howells—or even Bellow—is probably no longer accessible" weighed on him. It was a fate he must somehow avoid, if possible. "How could I make a man like Abraham Lincoln accessible, real?" he wondered. "In a way I think I worried him into being."

V. Land of Lincoln

The year spent writing *Lincoln* was calmer than usual, and intentionally so. Gore traveled less, spoke in public a bit less often, avoided camera crews whenever he could. He needed to sift through a trove of material, taking notes, drafting scenes. He read the writings of John Hay, Lincoln's devoted young secretary, who later became the secretary of state under William McKinley and Theodore Roosevelt (presidents who would figure prominently in *Empire*, the next novel in the Narratives of Empire series). He also swept through all the major biographies of Lincoln, including an early biography-cum-memoir by Lincoln's former law partner from Illinois, William H. Herndon. With some dismay he read what he referred to as "the sweet, insufferable" life of Lincoln by the poet Carl Sandburg. Lincoln's private correspondence and public writings, and the memoirs of men associated with Lincoln, both friends and enemies, helped Gore to fill in the details of Lincoln's life, especially during the period of his presidency.

Among the great men of American politics and history, only Aaron Burr and Lincoln attracted Gore's complete admiration, although he looked at Old Abe without rose-tinted glasses, aware that every generation needs its own Lincoln, one that speaks to its current needs. Gore's Lincoln is a man who understands politics in a visceral way, willing and able to manipulate those around him to achieve ends he regards as worthy. As Gore saw it, Lincoln wished to maintain the Union above all else. As he struggled to achieve this end, he became a tragic hero who sacrificed everything, including himself, for a greater cause.

Gore centers *Lincoln* during the Civil War years, when the president's character—like a photograph—developed in the harsh solution of repeated bloodbaths. Historians and biographers had extensively studied and chronicled the man and his political life, going back to Josiah Gilbert Holland's 1866 biography. From Holland and Herndon to Sandburg and beyond, the life of the greatest American president had been fully excavated and described. Most recently, there had been a range of books by historians such as David Herbert Donald, Peyton McCrary, and Stephen B. Oates. Novelists had also written about Lincoln before Gore, as in (the American, not the English) Winston Churchill's forgotten *The Crisis*, a best seller in 1901; or Thomas Dixon's infamous pro-slavery novel, *The Clansman* (where Lincoln wants all African Americans expelled); or *Love Is Eternal*, a piece of schlock by Irving Stone about Abe and his beloved Mary. Gore, however, steps closer to history than his predecessors, creating political history in fiction that advances the genre of biographical fiction itself by placing a major figure at the center of the narrative in a way that allows us to regard Lincoln in all his alienated grandeur, the man whom Walt Whitman in his elegy called "the sweetest, wisest soul of all my days and lands."

With Gore's natural grasp of political banter and his love of cabinet-level machinations, he fleshed out the cast around Lincoln, a swirl of politicos, generals, journalists, conspirators, corrupt bankers, and social climbers. Among the major figures in this crowd are John Hay, of course, and William Seward, Lincoln's monomaniacal secretary of state and chief rival for the Republican nomination in 1860—a rival whose ambition ultimately gives way to a recognition that Lincoln is the greater man. One also meets Salmon P. Chase, Lincoln's self-important head of the Treasury Department, who also thirsts for Lincoln's job. Chase had been a devout abolitionist well before Lincoln, who was a latecomer to the cause. Chase seems mildly foolish in Gore's portrayal, as he collects the autographs of famous people, in one scene hunting down Whitman in an attempt to wrest a letter by Ralph Waldo Emerson from the vagabond poet. (He succeeds.) Another nicely drawn character in Gore's novel is Kate Chase, Salmon's daughter—a society hostess who holds the capital in her thrall. Young Hay calls her "the most attractive girl in the town." Indeed, she was a type Gore recognized and admired from his youth, and his affection for her shows.

Gore never enters the thoughts of Lincoln directly but circles around him, as when the president and Seward discuss a politician from Pennsylvania who had recently joined the Republicans as a fierce abolitionist and "the sworn enemy of all moderates beginning with the President." Being a canny fellow, Seward has an idea about how to deal with this man. "Good," says Lincoln. "But don't tell it to me. I'm not made for secrets." Gore writes (from Seward's point of view): "Actually, he had never known a man so secretive as Lincoln when it came to keeping to himself the direction that he planned to take in some great enterprise. On the other hand, Lincoln tended to be quite free with the secrets of others."

The novel begins as Lincoln slips into Washington unnoticed under heavy guard on the cold morning of February 23, 1861. Assassination anxiety is already in the air. As it must, the novel ends shortly after his assassination in Ford's Theatre by John Wilkes Booth: The scene is swiftly, brilliantly conjured as "from a distance of five feet, Booth fired a single shot into the back of the President's head." The emotional conclusion of the novel, however, occurs earlier, as the Confederacy crumbles and Lincoln enters the Southern White House of Jefferson Davis in Richmond. An elderly black man shows Lincoln into the office that once belonged to Davis. "That was Mr. Davis's chair," he says. An emotionally overwhelmed Lincoln sits in the chair. Gore writes: "Suddenly, Lincoln looked about the room, as if aware for the first time of the magnitude of what had happened. 'It is so much like a dream,' he said at last, 'but then I dream so much these days that it is hard for me to tell sometimes what is real and what is not.' "

As he runs his hand across the smooth tabletop before him, he declares that the war will soon end: "And the Union be so restored that no one will ever be able to see the slightest scar from all this great trouble, that will pass now the way a dream does when you wake at last, from a long night's sleep." Gore chose to relay this great story in the third person, giving it an old-fashioned, almost Tolstoyan, aura. "I liked the natural authority of the third person, the knowing eye, a feeling of measured distance," Gore recalled. "I was measuring that distance, line by line."

Apart from Lincoln himself, Hay—the wide-eyed young man who understands the luck of his vantage—often takes center stage and becomes one of the keenest observers of the president. The narrative muscles seem to grow stronger whenever he comes onstage, as when the war begins with volleys of cannon fire across the river that have already awakened Mary Todd, seeming to her like "the sound of doors slamming." But Hay knows the significance of what he hears, unlike the often confused First Lady. "At the first sound of artillery, Hay tumbled out of bed . . . After all, this was history."

Lincoln commands Gore's respect; but Gore punctures the myth repeatedly, giving us a plainspoken and practical man of politics (not so terribly dissimilar from the Great Emancipator of legend) but one who will do whatever he needs to do, never losing sight of his larger purpose, to maintain the Union. Controversially Gore suggests that Lincoln had picked up a venereal infection in his youth and transmitted it, unawares, to his wife and, perhaps through her, to his sons. Gore tracks the gradually darkening mind of Mary Todd throughout *Lincoln*, her illness accounting for her famous headaches and tantrums. The tensions in the marriage contribute to the president's evident melancholy, although he rises to heights of good humor in the company of friends and associates.

As Harold Bloom argued in *The New York Review of Books*, *Lincoln* is a visionary achievement, the keystone in the arch of Gore's novels about the American past. Bloom writes: "Vidal's imagination of American politics, then and now, is so powerful as to compel awe." In *The New Republic* a few years later (in a review of *Empire*), Andrew Delbanco says: "The writing in *Lincoln* reaches for sublimity, as in the moving account of the president's visit to the Confederate wounded, or the telling of Willie's death and Mary Todd's encroaching madness.

There are passages that make one weep. This novel will, I suspect, maintain a permanent place in American letters. There has been no better prose in the last 50 years than that with which Vidal narrates the streaming of the panicked people down Pennsylvania Avenue to the 'soft thud of cannons' from the debacle of the first Bull Run."

A few passages in *Lincoln* rise to a level rarely seen in Gore's writing, before or after; yet for long stretches the novel feels ponderous, with perhaps more detail about the politics of the Civil War in the capital than any reader needs or wants. Another drawback is that only Lincoln has any real depth in a populous crowd of figures, with the possible exception of Hay. Those in the president's entourage have a kind of Dickensian flatness, identified largely by a handful of metonymic traits, such as Seward's imperial obsessions or Chase's physiognomy: "a large man with a small nose." We hear perhaps once too often about Chase's bad eyesight—a blindness as much symbolic as literal.

Yet it could not have been easy to write about a major historical figure who lived during complex times. Gore's habit of rapid composition made it especially difficult for him to avoid errors, and he turned for help, as often before, to others, among them David Herbert Donald, a kindly and brilliant Harvard historian, who was generous with his time. He also got assistance from Heidi Landecker, who had been a fact-checker at *The Atlantic Monthly* in the early eighties. The magazine planned to run an excerpt from the novel, and asked Landecker to check for errors and inconsistencies. "I found so many mistakes," she said, "serious ones, like Civil War battles Vidal said were won by the Union that were in fact won by the Confederacy." Gore appreciated her gifts, and asked her to fact-check the entire manuscript, saving himself a good deal of embarrassment later.

Academic historians attacked him anyway, as Gore expected, ferreting out small errors wherever they could. The controversy over the presentation of Lincoln himself would unfold slowly, as unfriendly experts and history buffs in due course read and dismissed the novel. Richard N. Current, a Lincoln biographer, and C. Vann Woodward, a well-known historian at Yale, found the book full of mistakes that, however small, undermined the whole project. Roy P. Basler, the editor of *The Collected Works of Abraham Lincoln*, suggested that "more than half of the book could never have happened as told by Vidal." In a letter to *The New York Review of Books*, Gore outlined the charges against him by these "scholar-squirrels," as he called them. It was an awkward piece of self-justification that nonetheless contains jewels of wisdom, as when he explains that he tends, in these historical fictions, "more to history than to the invented." He adds, by way of explanation: "I am still obliged to dramatize my story through someone's consciousness. But when it comes to a great mysterious figure like Lincoln, I do not enter his mind. I only show him as those around him saw him at specific times. This rules out hindsight, which is all that a historian, by definition, has; and which people in real life, or in its imitation the novel, can never have."

To Gore, Abraham Lincoln was a mountain that could only be glimpsed from different sides, and part of him would always remain invisible to the naked eye. In his portrait, he looked—as he usually did—for foibles, and took an important cue from Herndon, an early biographer who set afloat the syphilis rumor. Gore couldn't resist the dramatic potential of such a story line. He also understood the long tradition of anti-Lincoln sentiment, which had grown virulent during the president's lifetime, coming from abolitionists in his own party and from antiwar Democrats or pro-slavery Southerners. Lincoln was neither the hero of Whitman's great elegy nor Sandburg's sentimental portrait; he was hardly the face on Mount Rushmore, nor was he the rabid warmonger who assumed dictatorial powers, as many at the time (even the critic Edmund Wilson) believed. Nevertheless, the assassination made sainthood immediately accessible, and there can be no doubt of his greatness in so many respects.

Gore put forward a very human Lincoln, a man not quite in control of his own destiny, though driven by the usual ambitions of political leaders, especially those capable of winning the White House. His portrait of Lincoln, however flawed, will remain a major take on this iconic figure, and this novel added mightily to Gore's unfolding chronicle of the American republic, which—in the post-Jackson era—

becomes a tale of expanding imperial interests, the picture of a nation driving westward, expanding beyond its borders in Mexico, the Philippines, and beyond.

VI. AH, VENICE!

The popular success of *Lincoln* pleased Gore, who watched as it rose to the top of most national best-seller lists. He could sit back, draw a long breath, and resume his life in Italy. It was time for a quiet, smaller project, and one caught his imagination: a chance to write and present a film about Venice. The invitation to do this made-for-TV documentary had come from Mischa Scorer, a British director and producer. It would feature both Vidal and Venice, a two-part series sponsored by ITV in Britain in collaboration with the Italian network RAI-TV. PBS in the United States was another possible sponsor, although they refused to commit at first. Armstrong urged him to go forward. "I loved Venice," he said, "and I volunteered to write the coffee-table book for him, *Vidal in Venice*. It was a little money for me, and I knew we'd have a good time."

Gore had never spent much time in Venice. He had attended a ball there with Clare Boothe Luce in the sixties, and fondly remembered dancing at the Ca' Rezzonico, arriving at the palazzo's steps by gondola, with torches burning. The rooms in the palace were full of mirrors, and the candles flickered. Gore thought about Elizabeth and Robert Browning, Henry James, and other writers who had passed through those rooms over the years. With Lincoln in the rearview mirror, he needed a holiday, and what better holiday than a working holiday?

The first part of the series focused on the history of Venice, its rise in the fifth century from a nasty backwater to the center of an empire. "How was it even possible," Gore wondered on camera, "that a piece of real estate roughly the size of Central Park could extend its reach so far?" The second part concerned its art and architecture, those features that still make Venice one of the glories of the world. Gore said, "I loved the color and movement in a Tintoretto, the stately balance of a Veronese. But the palaces, the apartments all seemed beyond magical, a dream. The architecture of Palladio was a gift to the world, who kept doing what he did. It's where Jefferson got the idea for Monticello."

He also suspected that he had familial connections to Venice, although this wasn't the attraction. "Ah, Venice," he sighs on camera. "I couldn't quite understand it." As one watches him climb a grand stairway of the Doge's Palace, it seems clear that this setting appealed to his grander self. He lost no chance to link the Venetian and American imperial dreams. "In an odd way, the founders of the American republic were fascinated by the Venetian republic," he says. What links these two empires? "Just human greed." As per usual, he leaps at the opportunity to chide Reagan and his hatred of "the evil empire," which in the president's mind was the Soviet Union. For the Venetians, the "evil empire" was Turkey, the enemy as framed by Venetian imperial politics. Gore imagines a Venetian public-relations push to demonize Turkey and establish "strategic defense systems to protect the free world." One suspects that his ironies were lost on many television viewers.

But no matter. This was mainly a holiday in Venice with a camera crew and Armstrong. Gore loved performing in the role of Gore Vidal, and the documentary was called *Vidal in Venice*. On these terms he couldn't lose, as Venice never failed to do its part as backdrop, with splendid churches and palaces, dark canals, a sumptuously realized history. In his introduction to the coffee-table book (which Armstrong wrote, working from notes by Gore), he says: "There is nothing quite like writing and appearing in a two-hour television documentary on Venice to stumble on a truth: as, talking and talking, I slowly sank into a mud flat near Torcello, I realized that not only did I have nothing to say but there is nothing to say." That is, Venice is always itself, beyond criticism, probably beyond comprehension.

After Venice, Gore resumed the life he had made for himself in Rome over two decades. Anthony Quinn (who had married an Italian woman) often met Gore at parties, in restaurants, or at the apartment of Mickey Knox, a mutual friend. Quinn recalled: "I don't know what it was, but he looked so Roman. It was the nose, the profile, the way he stood. He looked like somebody who had once been the emperor. When he went out in public, he was a performer. 'You're the actor,' he would say to me, when we'd meet over dinner. 'No,' I'd say. 'I think you're the actor, but you've only got one part, Gore Vidal. But it's a good part, and you get to write the script yourself.' "

Knox was also Mailer's friend, and he and Gore often talked about the feud that had lasted so long. Knox had done his best to soften them toward each other, and on November 20, 1984, Mailer wrote to invite Gore to participate in a PEN fund-raising event. "Our feud, whatever its roots for each of us," he wrote, "has become a luxury. It's possible in years to come that we'll both have to be manning the same sinking boat at the same time. Apart from that, I'd still like to make up. An element in me, absolutely immune to weather and tides, runs independently fond of you."

Gore said, "I never actually disliked Norman, not really. So now the feud—for what it was worth—was officially over. This was fine with me, as long as I didn't have to read another of his books."

The Lesson of the Master

All afternoon I've been sitting by Gore's pool working on a piece of fiction about Walter Benjamin and his flight across the Pyrenees in 1940—an ill-fated journey that led to his death by suicide in Portbou, Spain. The manuscript began as a short story but is rapidly expanding into a novel.

It's about six o'clock, and the sun has begun to slope toward the west, but only just. It's sweltering in August, and I pour myself a glass of sparkling water, watching as swallows dip and drink from the dark blue pool.

"Frustrated?" asks Gore, as he suddenly appears beside me, stepping from the shadows into brilliant sunshine on the travertine deck, giving me a start. He wears a white terry-cloth robe and pulls up a chair beside me.

"Do I look frustrated?"

"I've been watching you," he says.

"The fact is, I'm not sure about something," I say. "Do you think it's possible for two people in a piece of fiction to talk about the theology of Kierkegaard for about twenty or thirty pages?"

He winces, as if I've asked him if mules can fly. "Of course you can do that," he says, after a long pause. "Even forty pages. But only if your characters are sitting in a railway car, and the reader knows there's a bomb under the seat."

Chapter Ten

> I am at heart a propagandist, a tremendous hater, a tiresome nag, complacently positive that there is no human problem which could not be solved if people would simply do as I advise.
>
> —Gore Vidal

I. "It's a Trade"

Ravello had replaced Rome as the center of life for Gore and Howard by 1985, although they continued to spend weeks at a time at their apartment on the Largo Argentina. Gore's contacts with the American embassy afforded interesting encounters, as when Clare Boothe Luce came through Rome on her last visit to Italy. The ambassador "gave a dinner for her, which Imelda Marcos excitingly crashed. A ten-year-old godchild of mine was put next to Clare. She spent most of her time at table amusing the wide-eyed girl, who could not believe that an interesting and witty grown-up would want to talk to her when there were so many fascinating folk at hand to dazzle." Susan Sarandon recalls that when she was filming the HBO series *Mussolini and I* in the spring of 1985, she spent a good deal of time in Rome "and Gore was so welcoming. Our friendship deepened, and he invited me down to Ravello. I loved his company, and Howard's, too. They had such a loving relationship, in their own way. Howard would keep Gore on track. I remember bringing my little baby, Eva, to his apartment, and he was enthralled. He lit up. I think he loved children, and he was a wonderful godfather to another child of mine, Miles." Rather famously, when asked to take on the role of godfather to Miles, Gore replied: "Always a godfather, never a god."

Ravello was a place for research and writing, as Sarandon noticed. "Work was always so important to him. No matter how much he drank or talked or partied the night before," she recalls, "he got up early and went to his study, where he read and wrote. He said to me the writing was a muscle he had to flex." His study in La Rondinaia, with its long trestle table, its ornate globe and leather couch and fireplace, its shelves of books and memorabilia, felt exactly right to him.

The house itself was comfortable if less than perfectly maintained, with endless unfinished projects. Howard had insisted on having a pool, and a large one had been dug—a five-minute walk from the house, through a pergola. It had a wonderful cabana, and travertine decks with views of the coast over the tips of cypresses. In summer Gore would often spend the morning there, in a terry-cloth robe, writing on his lap. Whenever the heat overwhelmed him, he would cool himself with a quick dip, even doing some laps.

In the eighties, Gore worked out regularly in the gym on the lowest floor of the villa, trying to keep his waistline in temporary check. It was just down the hall from his bedroom, with its dark Empire furniture, including an oak bedstead that had come from Edgewater. The long hallways were book-lined, with more than eight thousand volumes—many of them valuable first editions that Gore liked to collect. Howard had his own bedroom at the end of the corridor, but he and Gore could easily talk to each other on a phone that doubled as an intercom system. (Howard invariably answered the phone when anyone called, saying in a deep baritone as Italians do: *Pronto!*) Almost every floor in the five-story villa had balconies with astonishing views of the sea, and Gore could occasionally be found on any one of them, reading or just savoring the view.

In the spring, there were lemons. In the summer, a profusion of fruits and vegetables, flowers, flowering bushes. Gore recalled that the villa and its grounds had drawn a wide range of notable guests before he moved there. In the thirties, Virginia Woolf had come with her husband, Leonard, or accompanied by Vita Sackville-West, her lover. "In the late thirties," Gore recalled, "Leopold Stokowski came with Greta Garbo. Humphrey Bogart, Peter Lorre, Orson Welles, they all came." Needless to say, the list of distinguished visitors swelled when Gore took possession of the villa, with friends such as Princess Margaret, Paul Newman and Joanne Woodward, Susan Sarandon and Tim Robbins, Andy Warhol, Mick and Bianca Jagger, Johnny Carson, Norman Lear, George McGovern, Sting, James Taylor, Dick Cavett, and Hillary Clinton making appearances. Of course one often saw George Armstrong, Michael Mewshaw, Judith Harris, and others from Rome, as well as Gore's American agents and editors.

Gore spent occasional weekends on the nearby island of Capri, sometimes dining in Anacapri with Graham Greene or Shirley Hazzard and her husband, the Flaubert scholar Francis Steegmuller. Gore's friend Mona von Bismarck died in 1983, but until then he might stay with her at her villa, Palazzo Fortino. "Capri always has this wistful quality," he said, "with ghosts of long-dead friends and figures from Old Times. I often see Willie Maugham sitting at a table in the piazza. Or Compton Mackenzie. Or Norman Douglas." He and Howard usually stayed at the Grand Hotel Quisisana after Palazzo Fortino was sold, and they would frequently take guests there for an outing, stopping in Positano for lunch along the way.

In good weather, for exercise, Gore descended the nearly vertical stairs through a lemon grove to Amalfi, where he would buy the *International Herald Tribune* and one or two Italian newspapers from the tobacconist overlooking the beach and harbor, next to the bar Sirena, where he would sit over a glass of beer to catch up on the news. Teresa, the daughter of the owner, would serve him, shaking her head. "He is called *lo scrittore*, the writer. But look at him: His shoes are terrible, his trousers old and filthy. He wears sweaters with holes in them. They say in Ravello that he has fallen on hard times."

In fact, the opposite was true. Gore had reached the peak of his literary life and now took his legacy seriously. He wanted someone to write a full-length biography while he was still alive, and Walter Clemons, who had done a cover story on him for *Newsweek*, accepted the commission. As Gore later complained: "I supplied Walter with endless details, interviews with all of my close friends, documents. I had high hopes for this book, but he was a magazine writer after all, and didn't understand that a biography is a long and demanding piece of work. He began to trudge through my papers, which I had given to Wisconsin. I watched him work with a feeling of dread. He got a small fortune from Little, Brown for a project that would never materialize."

Offers to adapt novels for the movies kept coming, and once in a while Gore took on a project, as with *Dress Gray* by Lucian Truscott. It was just his sort of story, dealing with the murder of a closeted gay cadet at a military academy much like West Point during the height of the Vietnam War. A major plotline involves the struggle of the scheming Commandant of Cadets to suppress the real story. It's the sad tale of a young man who, wrongfully accused of the murder, seeks justice and truth. "It was written by the grandson of a great general from the Second World War," said Gore, who would notice that sort of thing. More important, it was a novel about a gay man in love with a straight man: a consistent theme in Gore's life as well as his art.

The project fell apart but Gore persisted, and in 1986, *Dress Gray* appeared as a TV miniseries on NBC, directed by Glenn Jordan, who had a fine grasp of the material. The cast was strong, with Alec Baldwin as the cadet and Hal Holbrook as the commandant; Eddie Albert and Lloyd Bridges also had important parts. After the program aired in March, it received three Emmy nominations, including a nomination for Gore for Outstanding Writing in a Miniseries or a Special. Gore recalled: "It wasn't the Nobel Prize, but *Dress Gray* wasn't *War and Peace*. The critics considered it 'workmanlike,' which is what they say when they really hate something." It was in fact a wooden script, lacking in cinematic interest. As it happened, Norman Mailer had privately warned Truscott about the dangers of allowing Gore to adapt his novel: "Let's break a cup when you get to New York and watch out for Vidal. He'll pretend to like you, and he'll pretend to like *Dress Gray*, but neither will be true. He'll fuck the script. He's not a bad novel writer but between us he can't write a script to save his ass. That's just one of the ten thousand secrets kept by Hollywood." Needless to say, this seems rather scheming on Mailer's part, given that he had recently extended an olive branch to Gore.

In April, the American film director Michael Cimino called Gore from Rome. He had in hand another project, a Mafia movie. Gore sighed. "It's a trade, so I took on the work. The fee was $250,000, and I didn't have a novel to write. It gave me a way to pass my time through a damp spring in Ravello." The existing script was an adaptation of a third-rate Mario Puzo novel, *The Sicilian*. Throughout the spring of 1986, Gore wrote and rewrote the script. He would ship portions of the manuscript by car to Rome, where Cimino would make suggestions for revisions, and Gore would rewrite what he had done. Recalling his problems with *Ben-Hur*, he suspected that he would never get credit for the work he had done on this project. "I had to sue the original writer, Steve Shagan, as well as the Writers Guild," Gore said. "It was such a mess. But the film was, in fact, so bad that I didn't much care in the end."

The lawsuit gave him no satisfaction, nor did he get credit for the screenplay, even though a court in California upheld his claims. "As usual, things went badly for me when it came to scripts and Hollywood." He recalled that, at one point, he completed a script for a film based on the life of Justinian, the late Roman emperor, and his wife, Theodora. "I wrote it for Martin Scorsese, and he liked what I did, but nothing came of it. Film projects always hang, perilously, on momentum, and when a project stalls, the energy goes." Gore had been involved in dozens of film projects in the past three decades or more, but only *Suddenly, Last Summer* and *The Best Man* had any real success (unless you counted *Ben-Hur*).

Sometimes Gore refused to let a project die, as with *Dress Gray* or his early project on Billy the Kid. *The Left Handed Gun* (1958) had been hijacked from his 1955 teleplay, much to his annoyance. Now the prolific producer Frank von Zerneck, who had brought *Dress Gray* to NBC the year before, listened to Gore's pitch for a film about Billy the Kid with a new script by himself. Von Zerneck loved the idea, and the production went into fast-forward. Val Kilmer would play Billy, and Gore would have a cameo. As before, Gore conceived of Billy as a decent (if somewhat boisterous, even unruly) young man who fell in with the wrong crowd. It would premiere on TNT, a second-tier cable channel that seemed about right for this unsatisfactory product. Gore could not escape the sentimental idea that Billy was a sweet young man who couldn't control his urge to murder people. (Fans of Billy will be better served by Sam Peckinpah's sardonic and gruesome *Pat Garrett and Billy the Kid* from 1973, with a score by Bob Dylan.)

11. "One Disaster After Another"

When Gore turned sixty in 1985, Howard threw a fairly small party in New York—not quite like the fiftieth in London. It was here that Gore met Harold Bloom for the first time, and they treated each other with respect, even admiration. "Harold Bloom is the only critic in the academic world I can read with pleasure," Gore said. He had begun to soften in his attitude toward the academy, and increasingly he saw Harvard and Yale as enviable bastions of intellect. Harvard, in particular, often cropped up in his conversations as an interesting and admirable place, somewhere he might have attended had the stars aligned in different ways.

But the world to Gore seemed a place of disaffection, full of pitfalls and disappointments. "April was the cruelest month, for sure," he said, in 1986, as Ronald Reagan initiated a bombing of Libya in response to the bombing of a nightclub in Berlin—an attack traced to Libyan agents in East Germany. The raid on April 14 proved intensely worrying, as nobody knew if Mu'ammar Gaddhafi had the means or will to return fire. Southern Italy was not far from Libya, and Gore felt quite sure that darkness would soon fall. A few days later, he began coughing blood and convinced himself that the end was nigh. His sinuses had become inflamed, and he got terrible headaches. "He's just hungover," Howard said, but Gore insisted it was a radioactive isotope that had drifted to southern Italy from the Chernobyl nuclear power plant in Ukraine, which had imploded. "The food, the water, is all bad," he said.

He and Howard needed to get away, and soon took off for their annual visit to Bangkok, where the air could not have been much cleaner. After a week in the Oriental Hotel, and visits to their favorite brothels, they returned to Rome by way of Laos, Tahiti, Australia, Hong Kong, and Los Angeles. In the States, Gore was present when

Vidal in Venice appeared on PBS, and it got pleasantly warm reviews. John Corry in *The New York Times* said: "Mr. Vidal, who wrote the film, has interesting, often witty, things to say." Yet he faulted Gore's portrait of the famed Venetian intelligence service. On screen, Gore says, "It is one of the eternal laws of government that the more money that you spend on intelligence and counterintelligence, the less you know about what's going on in the world." Corry sniped: "Actually that's not an eternal law; it's a law Mr. Vidal just invented in the Doge's Palace. It allows him to then say that the Central Intelligence Agency spends billions without learning very much. Mr. Vidal will have his parallels, but he's got to bend history to do so."

III. Fear of Flying

Gore had been upset by the response to his provocative essay on Jews and gays, later published as "Pink Triangle and Yellow Star." An alliance of conservative commentators, including Norman Podhoretz, Midge Decter, Joseph Epstein, and Hilton Kramer, had been poking at Gore for months, and his irritation at their attacks came through in "Requiem for the American Empire," an essay written for the 125th anniversary issue of *The Nation*. There Gore noted that he had recently been at a PEN conference in New York, onstage with Mailer, where they had agreed that military spending under Reagan had spun out of control. Podhoretz, whom Gore called Poddy, attacked their position, as Gore recalled:

> Poddy denounced Mailer and me in the pages of the *New York Post*. According to him, we belong to that mindless majority of pinko intellectuals who actually think that the nation spends too much on the Pentagon and not enough on, say, education. Since sustained argument is not really his bag, he must fall back on the ad hominem attack, a right-wing specialty—and, of course, on our flag, which he wears like a designer kaftan because "the blessings of freedom and prosperity are greater and more widely shared [here] than in any country known to human history." Poddy should

> visit those Western European countries whose per capita income is higher than ours. All in all, Poddy is a silly billy.

The essay was harsh, and to many ears it tilted in the direction of anti-Semitism. Gore pulled no punches, implying that American Jews who supported Israel in a fanatical way formed a kind of fifth column. Going way too far, he suggests that these Jews were not fully assimilated Americans. He singles out Decter for her refusal to understand American imperial dreams: "Oh, Midge, resist. Resist! Don't you get the point? We stole other people's land. We murdered many of the inhabitants. We imposed our religion—and rule—on the survivors. General Grant was ashamed of what we did to Mexico, and so am I. Mark Twain was ashamed of what we did in the Philippines, and so am I."

The controversy provoked by this essay persisted long past its publication. Soon after Gore's death in 2012, for example, Paul Berman remembered this essay, describing it in *The New Republic* as "the most cunning, odious, and successful of Gore Vidal's provocations." Berman correctly heard Gore's racist overtones in writing about the danger posed to the West by "one billion grimly efficient Asiatics." The response at the time to Gore's provocation was, as Berman said, exactly as he expected: near hysteria broke out. Podhoretz struck again, in *Commentary*. Further responses followed in *Dissent* and elsewhere. It was, according to Berman, "quite as if Vidal and *The Nation* had staged a pogrom."

Gore grew terribly shrill, especially when drunk. Even when sober, he sometimes attacked without care, with a whiny rasp in his voice that didn't add to his stature as a reasonable commentator on public affairs. Yet he did important work, pointing out repeatedly that the American imperial dream continued unabated, and—with Reagan in the White House—he had a useful foil. Reagan's cheerful anti-Communism and defiant anti-intellectualism offended Gore, who had lived through the McCarthy era. "America always required a great enemy," said Gore, "and if not Communism, something else would have to take its place. Otherwise, how could the government justify a defense budget on such a massive scale. We had created a monster." His view that a dangerous national security state had evolved after the war grew more intense than ever.

Invitations to speak his mind in public poured in, but he proceeded with caution. "I didn't want to spend the rest of my life touring American campuses. I could have been a teacher, but I chose another life." The life he found himself inhabiting, willy-nilly, was that of elder statesman. "I went overnight from being a promising young writer to an old man of letters," he said. "With gray hair came requests to sit on more and more panels. I hated panels. But I liked giving talks now and then. I preferred the television interview as a way to get across my ideas in public. Radio was good, too. Even better, as they can't see your sagging features."

In December 1986, an invitation to visit Moscow came from the Soviet premier Mikhail S. Gorbachev, who had decided to hold a peace conference at the Kremlin. It was a three-day affair that brought together the likes of Gore, Graham Greene, Mailer, John Kenneth Galbraith, Yoko Ono, Armand Hammer, and several entertainers, including Gregory Peck and Kris Kristofferson (who was coincidentally starring in a TV miniseries about a Soviet takeover of the United States called *Amerika*). Greene recalled: "It was a very odd assortment. I gave a short talk at one point. We met in a grand ballroom, with a good deal of vodka, and mostly listened to speeches. Gorbachev was delighted with himself, and he had done many good things, as he told us. I liked talking to Gore, who looked the part of a Roman senator. Orotund, cheerful, authoritative."

Gore and Mailer got along well in Moscow, meeting over drinks in their hotel bar. "We'd never been enemies," said Mailer. "Antagonists, sometimes, in small ways. That was theater. We agreed on most things." They had dinner at the home of their Soviet publisher, and Gore listened to Mailer trying "to convince the poor man to publish *Ancient Evenings*," Mailer's seven-hundred-page novel about Egypt in the time of the great pharaohs. Gore later referred to this as "possibly the worst historical novel in the language, which is a distinction." He sat through several working sessions with Greene and Mailer, mingling with Russian writers, including the poet Andrei Voznesensky, who had—or was having—an affair with Jackie Onassis, or so Gore believed. Greene felt that the French novelists hogged all the air time. He and Gore slipped away for drinks before the sessions officially closed. "Gore was full of energy," said Greene, "chipper, gossipy. He admired Gorbachev, who was making huge changes in the Soviet system."

Gore flew from Moscow to Brazil, where he had won a large following. "I was told that, in Brazilian prisons, I was the most popular American writer after Zane Grey," he said. His essays had just appeared in Spanish and Portuguese editions, and he found reporters eager to interview him in São Paolo, Brasília, Rio, Buenos Aires, and—a few weeks later—Madrid and Toledo, in Spain. "I think my name helped. Vidal fell easily on Hispanic ears. Everyone had a relative called Vidal." He realized that his work had, more than most American authors, a worldwide following.

IV. Imperium

Gore rarely lost a step when it came to putting his work before the public. In this sense, he converted the same will to power that had pushed him to run for political office in New York and California into a drive to seize control of the national narrative in his writing, whether whimsically in his "inventions," as he called his satirical romps along the lines of *Myra Breckinridge* or *Duluth*, or more seriously in his "reflections"—novels like *Julian* or *Lincoln* (a distinction he liked to make between the two strains of his writing). With the California race behind him, he trained his eyes on the possibilities before him at the writing table. Never liking to waste an already published word, he convinced Random House to bring out a joint edition of *Myra Breckinridge* and *Myron* early in 1986, hoping that a fresh wave of interest for these novels would follow.

He had already begun work on another installment of his Narratives of Empire—a massive project that would extend to *Empire* (1987), *Hollywood* (1990), and *The Golden Age* (2000), mixing the life and times of invented characters, such as Caroline, Blaise, and

Peter Sanford, with "real" figures from history, including John Hay, Theodore Roosevelt, Henry Adams, Henry James, Woodrow Wilson, and FDR. "It was rather like knitting," Gore said, "and the scarf got longer and longer. I could wrap it around my neck several times."

The writing of *Empire* coincided with Gore's growing realization that the United States under Reagan had become an aggressive force in Central America and elsewhere, bolstered by the right-wing president's unwavering faith in the capitalist system coupled with his fear of the Soviet Union. In his mind, at the writing table, Gore "thought about the shift from republic to imperial dragon." It all begin, he decided, in 1847, "when we drew Mexico into a war that would gain us a great deal of real estate, with California thrown into the bargain." It was one thing, however, to overflow the American continent, a process begun with Jefferson's Louisiana Purchase. But now, in 1898, "we pushed beyond our natural borders, annexing the Philippines." A sleeping giant woke and flexed its gigantic muscles.

Gore turned to his favorite historian, William Appleman Williams, to understand the nature of American expansionism, reading *Empire as a Way of Life* (1980), a seminal work by this progressive historian, with particular interest. Williams had become something of a pariah in polite foreign policy circles because he regarded the Cold War as yet another means by which the United States sought to widen its footprint (economic, cultural, and military) in the larger world. Examining the process of economic and cultural imperialism, Williams questioned whether America could possibly maintain its affluence without gaining territory (and resources) wherever it could. He noted that in the late nineteenth and early twentieth centuries, the great European empires invariably sought raw materials abroad, being desperate to fuel their economies. The British, of course, flew their flag over large parts of the world by the end of Victoria's reign in 1901. Teddy Roosevelt and William McKinley, among others, felt a similar need for American power to extend its reach. Tellingly, Gore's *Empire* begins on August 13, 1898, just when the so-called "little war" with Spain had ended and the American empire went on cruise control.

Gore tracked the movement toward empire, singling out Alfred Thayer Mahan, Brooks Adams, Theodore Roosevelt, and Henry

Cabot Lodge as key architects of American expansion. Roosevelt, who had greatly admired Mahan's *The Influence of Sea Power upon History, 1660–1783*, seized the reins of government at a critical juncture. *Empire*, which Gore at first planned to call *Manifest Destiny*, explored the dimensions of this argument from different viewpoints. His real and invented characters participate in a discourse that evolved during these years, with results that would reverberate throughout the twentieth century. "With *Empire*," said Gore, "I began to see the broad outline of a dream, an imperial dream, and how it could be realized."

The novel opens at a house party in England, where John Hay and his wife, with their friend Henry Adams, gather. Henry James is present as well—a writer who had long appealed to Gore's imagination. "In what they call 'real life,' James was actually there. I wasn't name-dropping," Gore said. He had recently reread *The Golden Bowl* when he began *Empire*, and the influence is apparent; the language has a self-consciously Jamesian quality, with complex sentences that pulse like waves to the shore. (There are sly allusions to *The Golden Bowl* throughout, as when we learn that James Burden Day, one of Gore's chief protagonists, is from an invented town called American City, which in *The Golden Bowl* is seen as one of the last places in the United States one might wish to visit.)

Gore weaves his fictional characters into a Jamesian tapestry, where personal and national identities merge. Caroline Sanford and her half brother, Blaise, who just happen to be at war over the family money, move among historical figures with ease, their voices all mingling. The novel dwells on the empires of Teddy Roosevelt and William Randolph Hearst, titans of history who deployed their energies over separate but converging political and media fiefdoms. As Gore notes, the newspapers controlled by Hearst had helped to instigate the war with Spain, which has just ended as the story begins.

We last saw John Hay in *Lincoln*, a young man on the make. Gore had continued to find him interesting, and studied his career as a diplomat and statesman, as a biographer of Lincoln and journalist. In the opening scene of *Empire*, Hay at fifty-nine serves as the American ambassador to Britain, although he will soon move to Washington as secretary of state. After the assassination of McKinley, he remains in this post, where he exerts considerable influence on foreign policy. He would, in this role, become a cheerleader for extending American power abroad, although—as Gore says in *Empire* with a wry disdain—"he felt that the Administration ought never to associate itself with such un-American concepts as empire."

Hay's reluctance is shared by Caroline Sanford, one of Gore's most engaging female characters. "Why drive poor weak old Spain out of the Caribbean and the Pacific?" she asks. "Why take on far-off colonies? Why boast so much?" Caroline plays the part of grande dame without hesitation, acquiring a newspaper and dipping into "yellow journalism" to make sure it succeeds. She is therefore able to influence her times in unprecedented ways for a woman, holding a good deal of power in her delicate hands. She is a prime example of what was then called the New Woman—an early feminist. "Caroline is a woman in every sense aware of her sex but unwilling to allow that biological fact to dampen her ambitions," Gore says.

As in *Burr* or *Lincoln*, Gore liked to poke fun at the great and good, drawing close to observe all foibles—their flabby double chins or popped buttons or twitching eyeballs; he also wanted to expose their self-mythologies. Teddy Roosevelt is a case in point. Toward the end of *Empire*, Caroline attends a dinner at the White House, where she converses with Alice Roosevelt, the president's feisty daughter, and her new husband, Nicholas Longworth, who have recently come home from a honeymoon in Cuba, perhaps in tribute to Teddy's charge up San Juan Hill on July 1, 1898, with his Rough Riders. "Well, I've been to the top of San Juan Hill, and it's absolutely nothing," Alice says, pricking her father's balloon. "I looked for the jungle—remember the famous jungle? Where Father stood among the flying bullets, ricocheting off trees, and parrots and flamingoes—he always added them to every description—sailed about? Well, the place couldn't be duller. The hill's a bump, and there is no jungle."

Gore's characters often announce their intentions too directly, a narrative flaw that makes *Empire* seem contrived at times, too eagerly seeking to persuade us, as when Hearst comes to the White House—"the house which he would never, short of an armed revolution, occupy"—to visit Roosevelt for a personal chat in the final chapter. Roosevelt scowls, noting wryly that Hearst has raised the Fourth Estate "to a level quite unheard of in any time." "I know I have. And for once you've got it right. I have placed the press above everything," Hearst declares baldly, giving away the game. "When I made—invented, I should say—the war with Spain, all of it fiction to begin with, I saw to it that the war would be a real one at the end, and it was. For better or worse, we took over a real empire from the Caribbean to the shores of China. Now, in the process, a lot of small fry like you and Dewey benefitted. I'm afraid I couldn't control the thing once I set it in motion."

Even if such a conversation actually took place, the job of the artist is to make it sound real. Instead, this kind of dialogue (which is everywhere in *Empire*) sounds like the author's own underlying thesis brought to the surface. The novel lacks subtleties of expression at just those junctures where it most requires them. The novelist tacks too close to the essayist.

If Hearst, as a bloated press lord who creates "fictions" that become reality, is a caricature, the cartoon serves Gore's wish to gain control of the American narrative, as an author, in ways he could never do as a politician. He would never know what it meant to hold the levers of real political power in his hands, much as he would have liked that experience. But he could write the history of his country as he saw it, mastering and owning the story, and this was power of a kind.

Empire ends with Roosevelt sitting alone in the Cabinet Room, "with its great table, leather armchairs, and the full-length painting of Abraham Lincoln, eyes fixed on some far distance beyond the viewer's range, a prospect unknown and unknowable to the mere observer, at sea in present time." The implication is, of course, that neither Roosevelt nor anyone after Lincoln could begin to fathom that depth of character or hope to emulate the grandeur, the balance, the humanity of the man who saved the Union. "There was a falling off from that peak," Gore said, "and nobody quite matched him, not ever." *Lincoln* was, consequently, a peak in Gore's Narratives of Empire, although *Empire*—despite its clumsy explicitness at times—remains a readable, even absorbing novel.

v. Sailing the Coast

In June 1987, Gore set to work on *Hollywood*, a further installment in his Narratives of Empire, focusing on the period of 1917 to 1923, when the United States entered the Great War and dealt with its complex aftermath. "The story came easily," said Gore, "as I had begun to enter the realm of memory. My grandparents talked about the war, and so did my father. They spoke of Wilson and Harding, even the Roosevelt family, as neighbors. I didn't need to do a lot of research. It wasn't like *Burr* or *1876*, or even *Empire*. These were everyday dreams."

As usual, he and Howard entertained friends from abroad, and this time Leonard Bernstein was among them. Gore and Bernstein (who was called Lenny by his friends) had been acquaintances for many decades, going back to New York after the war, when Gore's onetime lover Harold Lang—a dancer in Bernstein's musical *Fancy Free*—introduced them. They would often meet at parties in New York and Los Angeles over the years, though they treated each other warily until, at a dinner in Rome with the U.S. ambassador, Max Rabb, they found themselves in sympathy over their dislike of Reagan. "Lenny tried to outdo me in mimicking the great man," Gore said. "But he didn't get the head-wag, the aura of perpetual frustration. He didn't see how dumb our president really was."

As Reagan's appointee, Rabb tried to calm the discussion, but he apparently enjoyed the fireworks. "Max knew exactly who had hired him," said Gore. "He even knew who had hired Ronnie."

Bernstein would turn seventy in 1988, and gaudy celebrations would occur in multiple cities. The composer hoped that *1600 Pennsylvania Avenue*—a musical of his that had failed spectacularly on Broadway in 1976, running for only seven performances—would be among them. "It was Lenny's only major catastrophe," said Gore. "And he asked me to rewrite the libretto. I tried to explain to him that I could not make Lazarus walk out of the tomb. But Lenny insisted, and came to Ravello to work with me." Bernstein was en route to Amsterdam, where he would soon conduct the Royal Concertgebouw Orchestra in symphonies by Mahler and Schumann. But he settled into the villa happily, working late into the night, with musical scores spread before him, half-drunk cups of coffee around him. "He talked all day, all night, and seemed to work at the same time," Howard recalled.

Gore had other guests that summer, including Diana Phipps, Princess Margaret, and the actress Maria Britneva (also known as Maria St. Just, having married the English aristocrat Lord St. Just). Britneva had appeared in Gore's adaptation of *Suddenly, Last Summer*, and was a co-executor of the estate of Tennessee Williams (with whom she had fallen in love). "Maria made it difficult for everyone who wanted to stage one of the Bird's plays," Gore recalled. "She asked me to revise something of his. I can't remember what. But this was not work I needed or wanted." Barbara Epstein had, by now, become one of Gore's closest friends, and she stopped by for a few days, as did Elaine Dundy, who came down from London for a week. Michael Tyler-Whittle said, "Visitors came and went, especially in summer. These were good years for Gore. He had found a kind of serenity, though he might have fits—fits of passion, even jealousy. He could feel an unspoken insult from a thousand miles away, though it probably helped that he lived in a part of the world where he didn't have to listen to American television or see the papers. He preferred the Italian papers. And went less and less to Rome. As you might suspect, the apartment there had begun to look tired. That's a kind description."

Late in October, Gore traveled to Brown University in Providence, Rhode Island, for a three-day symposium on John Hay. After the ceremony, I had dinner with Gore and John Hay, the grandson of Lincoln's secretary, who at seventy-three was himself a fine writer and naturalist. "Gore seemed to know everything about the Hay family," said Hay, "more than I did. The university gave him an honorary degree, and he liked that. He had trouble with the academy, and said this was one of the rare times he felt comfortable on a campus." This was one of the few academic honors Gore would receive in his lifetime, and it meant a good deal to him.

In November, in Britain, André Deutsch published a new collection of Gore's recent essays, *Armageddon? Essays 1983–1987*. Comprised of work published after *The Second American Revolution*, the collection embodies Gore's then-current thinking about politics and the history of empire, as in "The Day the American Empire Ran Out of Gas." Originally published in *The Nation* on January 11, 1986, as "Requiem for the American Empire," this piece was written in Ravello the previous spring. It was a chance for Gore to distinguish between American and Soviet imperial dreams, a meditation prompted by his recent visit to Moscow. He saw Reagan as a man driven by strange fantasies, many of them shared by his compatriots. "As the curtain falls on the ancient Acting President and his 'Administration,'" he writes, "it is time to analyze just what this bizarre episode in American history was all about." In his view Reagan was a politician hired by the wealthy "to prepare us for the coming war between the Christ and the Antichrist. A war, to be specific, between the United States and Russia, to take place in Israel." He quotes James Watt, Reagan's secretary of the interior, who in 1981 actually said, "I do not know how many future generations we can count on before the Lord returns." That is, the Judgment Day was coming.

Beginning with *Messiah*, Gore had taken sardonic delight in the kookiness of America's apocalyptic religious visionaries. Indeed, he relished a dinner in Amalfi in the early 1980s with none other than Oral Roberts, the empire-building televangelist and healer from his grandfather's state of Oklahoma. "A local American heiress who lives nearby asked if I would like to meet him," Gore recalled. "I could not have been happier to meet anyone. He was a fake shaman of a type we seem to specialize in creating. Glorious." Gore dismissed with a flourish the feverish dreams of fundamentalists who imagined a final battle between Good and Evil, as embodied in the United States versus the Soviets. He quotes Reagan as saying, "You know, I turn back to your ancient prophets in the Old Testament, and I find myself wondering if we're the generation that's going to see that come about." The tragicomedy of American politics provided endless fodder for witty essays.

The political essays in *Armageddon?* seem more improvisational than his solid and acutely sensitive readings of Henry James, William Dean Howells, Dawn Powell, and Paul Bowles: each of them exemplary, full of sustained reflections that display Gore's wide knowledge of American and European literature. It was, at times, difficult to take some of his campy and often malicious essays on politics as seriously as his criticism, but he certainly had a kind of shrill perceptiveness about American politics, and many of these ideas needed expression. If, like Noam Chomsky (with whom he was often compared), Gore stood outside the normal range of American discourse, the problem was more with the culture than with Gore and Chomsky, each of whom in his own way offered a radical view of American foreign policy that could rarely be found in the mainstream press, where it must be taken for granted that the United States is always a benign force in the world.

The response to his essays always provoked a lot of correspondence, and Gore spent his afternoons answering mail from admirers, some of them well-known writers such as James Dickey, the author of *Deliverance* and of many volumes of poems. On December 14, 1988, Dickey wrote to thank Gore for paying such close attention to Frederic Prokosch in one essay. "Like you," wrote Dickey, "I have been strongly influenced by him, and since there has been no attention to his work in all the years I can remember, I was especially pleased with what you had to say." He added: "I am sorry we have never met, for I admire your mind very much, in whatever form it chooses to exhibit itself. I make no real distinction between fact, fiction, history, reminiscence and fantasy, for the imagination inhabits them all. This is the place that Frederic Prokosch occupies: a kind of all-place. You yourself do the same, from Tarzan on up. As Whitman said, it all tastes good to me."

Gore responded warmly, telling Dickey he should write personally to "Fritz," as he called Prokosch, and gave him an address. "He's in his eighties," said Gore, "but looks to be a lively athletic sixty, and he keeps on writing novels, which the French publish and we don't. It's curious that with the rise of his literary descendants in South America, some bright school teacher hasn't discovered him and his importance and his legacy. But our poor teachers are as dumb as those they teach." Needless to say, Professor Dickey—then teaching at the University of South Carolina—didn't feel compelled to continue this conversation.

VI. ADDING WINGS TO THE MANSION

In the fall of 1988 Gore saw into print an expanded American version of the British *Armageddon?*—with a fresh title: *At Home: Essays 1982–1988*. Meanwhile, an adaptation of *Lincoln* appeared as a two-part series on NBC, starring Sam Waterston as Lincoln and Mary Tyler Moore as his wife. Some critics sniffed at the casting and used the occasion to criticize the novel it was based on. "Mr. Vidal's novel was an unqualified commercial success with more than a million copies sold," said a reviewer in *The New York Times*. "Yet, many Lincoln scholars have criticized it, and scholarly symposia these days invariably boast a session devoted exclusively to the Vidal novel." This comment prompted Gore to wonder why this newspaper, "the Typhoid Mary of American journalism, should have wanted to discredit me, one week before airing the television dramatization of my book." (His relations with the *Times*, rarely peaceful, only seemed to get worse.)

The series aired in early spring, and found many sympathetic reviewers and a broad national audience. Despite an abundance of minor inconsistencies and factual errors, it presents a Lincoln close to the one portrayed in Gore's novel, and the audience gets a sense of what it might have been like to preside over a divided nation during the Civil War. There are smart touches, too: We don't see Lincoln actually delivering the Gettysburg Address, but we watch him working on it and trying out portions of the speech on his secretaries. The intelligent direction of Lamont Johnson, who won an Emmy for his efforts, enhances the production, although Mary Tyler Moore as Mary Todd Lincoln didn't remotely seem right for the part: her already familiar TV persona intruded.

Only a week before the series debuted, Gore addressed the National Press Club in Washington, playing the role of elder statesman. The first of four addresses to that body of journalists, it was given a generic title: "Proposals to Improve U.S. Government." Gore was treated like a former president, and he looked the part in a dark suit. He opened in a droll fashion: "It's nice to be back in my native city. I was horrified, however, to see that Ronald Reagan's library has burned down, and

The likeness of Myra Breckinridge on a parade float.
Inset: The first-edition jacket of *Myra Breckinridge*, 1968.

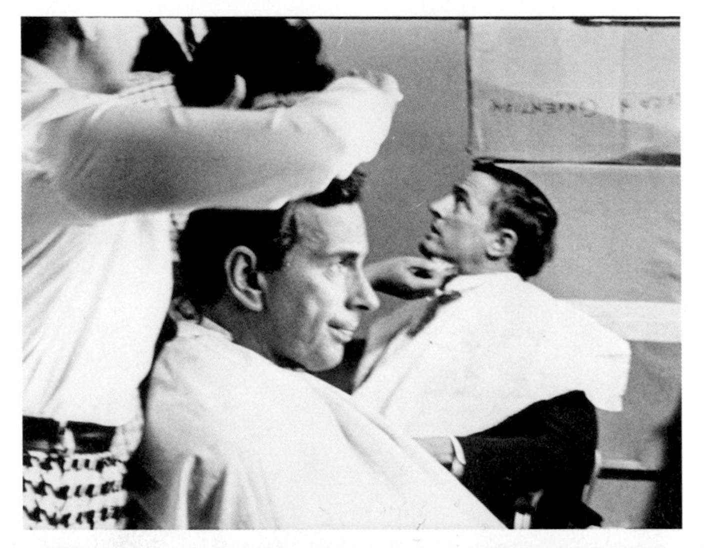

In makeup with Buckley before their epic confrontation in Chicago in 1968.

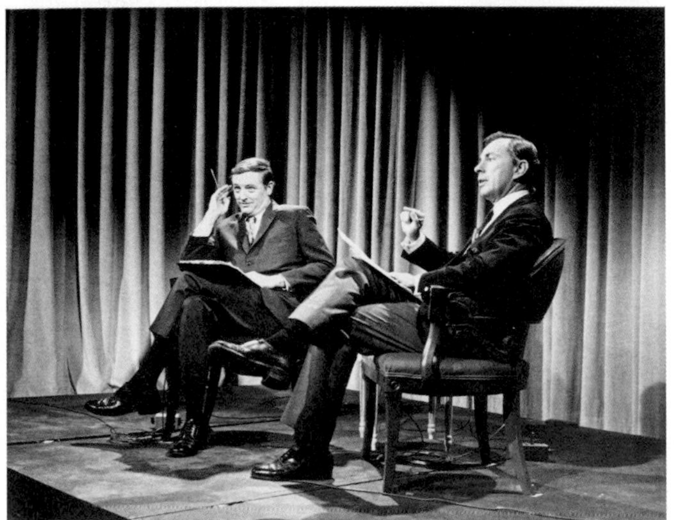

Buckley versus Vidal on set, a vicious verbal duel that would rivet the nation.

Dick Cavett welcomes Gore to his show, during which Gore and Norman Mailer had at one another.

Gore with his close friends Paul Newman and Joanne Woodward in Italy.

La Rondinaia: Gore's paradise in Ravello.

Climbing the steps in Ravello.

With his editor, Jason Epstein, in Venice, 1975.

Gore and "Fred" (Federico Fellini) in Rome.

Johnny Carson and his wife, Joanne, pay a visit to Gore.

The Tonight Show: "And here's Johnny," with Gore during one of numerous appearances.

Time puts Gore and his novel on the cover, 1976.

Running for the U.S. Senate against Jerry Brown, 1982.

With the Italian literary master Italo Calvino in 1982. Each admired and wrote eloquently about the other's work.

Walking the beach in Amalfi, 1987.

Leonard Bernstein pays a visit of state to Ravello 1988.

Gore and Howard in Ravello in 1988.

Gore in 1989 in costume during the filming of *Billy the Kid*—a subject that preoccupied him for his whole writing life.

Gay Talese, Susan Sontag, Norman Mailer, and Gore before a benefit reading by all four of *Don Juan in Hell,* 2002.

Gore (alongside Tom Wolfe) voices an episode of *The Simpsons* in 2006—true fame.

Gore in conversation with Jay Parini in Key West, 2010, one of the many such events they staged.

Gore at eighty-five, contemplating his exit.

A collage of the many figures in Gore's life, assembled by Diana Phipps for his fiftieth birthday.

that both books have been destroyed. The real tragedy was, of course, that he hadn't finished coloring the second one." He noted that he had been alive for nearly a third of the American republic: "The American empire came to a peak in 1945, when I was still part of that army that had won mastery of two hemispheres." He shook his head, saying it had all been lost: "Our ending was implicit in our beginning." In his view, the decision to keep the American economy on a full military basis was bound to bankrupt the nation.

With eloquence and force, Gore ran through postwar American history, describing the national security state in sobering detail. The Soviet Union, he argued, must be seen as threatening in order for the United States to maintain a constant (and very expensive) war footing. He spoke frankly about what he frequently called the Israeli lobby—a verbal hand grenade he liked to toss into the room, if only to listen to the glass that shattered around him. Among other proposals, he called for the abolition of the war on drugs, as prohibitions never worked and only guaranteed the success of the Mafia and the cartels. As a kind of liberal shadow president, he put forth idea after idea, drawing on his usual storehouse of political and economic statistics. Not incidentally, he was adding to his stature as a serious political commentator, "adding wings to the mansion," as he put it.

He talked at length about the fact that the American public had been so poorly taught that the knowledge base of the voting population was insufficient for the proper exercise of democracy. Asked about the apparent homophobia of the Reagan administration, which had done nothing to combat the spread of AIDS, Gore seemed less than forthright, refusing to acknowledge that this was a major crisis, saying it was actually quite difficult to catch this disease. As ever, his relationship to homosexuality was vexed, and he didn't—in this personal state of the union address, which went out on C-SPAN and NPR—wish to come across as the first gay head of state. The truly devastating nature of the AIDS crisis would not hit home in a visceral way until 1995, when his beloved nephew Hugh Steers died of complications of the disease.

In a tribute to Hugh, which his brother, Burr Steers, read at the funeral, Gore tried to make amends:

> I'm not an art critic and can pass no judgment on my half-nephew Hugh Steers's work other than to say that it very much moved me thematically, in the same way those 17th century *memento mori* can set off, even today, great resonances. But I *am* a professional judge of character: I think that my admiration for the way he conducted his life and death is well-grounded. Now that he has done with both, we should try and recall that the victims of this plague have often had splendid lives. And, certainly, they did a lot else other than die. This should never be forgotten in Hugh's case, or that of anyone else.

He noted the "real triumph" of Hugh's persistence in the face of a mortal disease. It was a moving tribute, frank as well as fond, and Gore allowed for its publication in *POZ*, a gay magazine. Steven Abbott, Gore's bibliographer and friend, says "Gore and Howard were amazingly uneducated as late as 2001 about the transmission of HIV. Gore told me that Nureyev, who lived on Li Galli (near Positano), came several times to visit and swam naked in their pool. He expressed concern that he and Howard might be exposed to AIDS. I told him not to worry unless they had sex or shared a needle with him." Abbott considered it "astounding" that Gore could be so "totally uninformed" about the disease at this late date.

Gore's work as a screenwriter was over by now, though he would dabble in the genre on occasion. For instance, he helped to revise a third-rate Italian thriller (in English) about a man who is elected mayor of New York City with a mandate to legalize drugs. It was a favorite theme, so he agreed to help the producers. "It was a total mess," Gore recalled, "and the film, with James Belushi in the lead, was terrible." His rewrite of the Billy the Kid teleplay also appeared now, without getting much attention. "It was a lot better than the first version, which had been ruined, back in the fifties," he said. "But it wasn't high art."

Hollywood, his novel in progress, came together quickly—a natural extension of *Empire*, the penultimate installment of his Narratives of Empire. The novel is set in the twenties, and it features Caroline Sanford again, as well as some of Gore's other fictional characters, including Blaise Sanford and James Burden Day. His characters move easily among people from real life, most of them seen in the previous volume, including Hearst, Teddy Roosevelt, and Alice Roosevelt Longworth. Fresh faces include Woodrow Wilson, Warren G. Harding, Franklin and Eleanor Roosevelt. A number of Hollywood stars also enter the mix: the irrepressible Charlie Chaplin, Marion Davies (the actress and producer, and William Randolph Hearst's lover), and Mabel Normand, who often acted with Chaplin and Fatty Arbuckle. William Desmond Taylor, the Irish director and actor who was murdered on February 1, 1922, also figures in the story.

It's Caroline and Blaise, however, who carry this novel. Caroline had "bought and revived the moribund *Tribune*; then, and only then, had she allowed her half-brother to buy in. Now, jointly, amiably, they co-published." The capital shines in Gore's evocation of his hometown, whose backroom maneuverings always fascinated him. Early in the novel we meet such characters as the Duchess, the wife of the Ohio senator Warren G. Harding, as she consults Madame Marcia, a clairvoyant popular among the upper classes, who foresees all, or nearly all. There is a lot going on in this prodigious, somewhat diffuse narrative, which in various stages brings us to the table of several presidents or near-presidents, any number of influential senators and newspaper magnates, and the crème de la crème of Hollywood, who themselves long for power—making Reagan their natural heir.

Gore couldn't help adding a bit of bisexuality into the novel: Blaise, it seems, has had the occasional fling with men. And we meet the young Eleanor Roosevelt here, the astonishingly ugly but radiant wife of Franklin, the future president, who hires the gorgeous Lucy Mercer to be her husband's secretary because she, as much as her husband, finds Lucy attractive. (Gore always came to life when talking about Eleanor's lesbian leanings.) He writes about her from Caroline's viewpoint with a confident flourish: "Although Eleanor blushed easily, Caroline suspected that this was not the result of shyness, as everyone thought, but the weapon of a marvelous social tactician for whom the blush was an evasionary tactic like that of the sea-squid which could spread a cloud of ink all round itself and thus vanish in order to chart a new course."

The plot turns on Caroline's awakening to the potential of Hollywood as a center of power. She has been sent there to convince the studios "to make pro-American, pro-Allies photo-plays." Soon hooked on the movies, Caroline bites the apple in Eden, and turns into a whole orchard herself. Soon enough, she "found herself daydreaming about movies," much as her creator had done for nearly six decades. "There was a power here but she was not sure what it was." Soon Gore leads her toward an understanding of this mysterious power. "Reality could now be entirely invented and history revised," she says—an insight that provides the link between the two power centers of the novel. "Suddenly, she knew what God must have felt when he gazed upon chaos, with nothing but himself on his mind."

Gore's insights are worthy, even if his characters often speak in stilted ways. He understood the strong and lethal mix of politics and propaganda, and quite rightly saw a dangerous confluence as Hollywood became a center of the American imagination. Ingeniously tapped—as during Reagan's presidency—there were few limits to its potential for political propaganda. "The audience for the movies is the largest there is for anything in the world. So if we can influence what Hollywood produces, we can control world opinion. Hollywood is the key to just about everything," says an influential politician, providing Gore with his thesis, worked out in luxurious detail in the course of *Hollywood*.

Gore's novel spent a month on the best-seller list at *The New York Times* and received largely appreciative reviews, although Michael Wood noted in *The Times Literary Supplement* that "a good deal of Vidal's prose is curiously, uncharacteristically wooden." Too often, when presidents and senators gather, the conversation is pompous and forced; even when Gore's grandfather Senator Thomas P. Gore steps onto the great stage at the end of *Hollywood*, his dialogue seems unreal. Indeed, Senator Gore speaks with a misanthropic glee more characteristic of his grandson: "I tell you, if there was any other race than the human race, I'd go join it."

In 1990, Gore turned sixty-five, "the age when much of the world retires, but I didn't see myself taking up golf. I left that to John

Updike." Indeed, he now thought a good deal about Updike, who had recently published the fourth volume of his Rabbit tetralogy, *Rabbit at Rest*—a hugely lauded novel that won the Pulitzer Prize that year. "Updike was doing the lower middle classes," said Gore. "That was safer, for the critics, and easier for them to understand. That wasn't my world." In due course, he would take on Updike in a full-length (and harshly dismissive) essay.

Gore had his grandfather's family on his mind when, in May 1990, he traveled to Mississippi with a television crew from the BBC, who was making a documentary about his life—one of many that would appear in these later decades. He had only come to this state once before, and it proved a revelation now. "Everyone at this family reunion I attended had my nose," he recalled. He found it moving to visit the house where his grandfather was born, to walk around the courthouse where the young lawyer had first practiced. "I don't think they quite knew what to make of me," he said, "nor did I know what to make of them." With the camera crew in tow, he called on Eudora Welty in Jackson. The eighty-one-year-old writer greeted him warmly, and Gore complained to her about how much time his relatives spent in church. "There really isn't anything else to do up in the north of Mississippi," she explained to him patiently. She reminded Gore of his grandmother, and he behaved deferentially in her presence, obviously enjoying her sharp tongue.

In September he returned to Venice to chair the annual Venice Film Festival. There he swayed the jury in favor of Tom Stoppard's debut as a director, an adaptation of *Rosencrantz and Guildenstern Are Dead*, Stoppard's first major play. "It was simply the most literate film I'd seen in years," said Gore. But the audience booed loudly at Gore's announcement of the Gold Lion Award for Stoppard. The committee had bypassed Martin Scorsese's masterpiece, *Goodfellas*, and overlooked Jane Campion's *An Angel at My Table*. A local favorite was Marco Risi's *Boys on the Outside*. Of course Gore didn't care what they thought, grumbling into the microphone: "The prize I am about to give is a tribute to the force of the mind, of wit, and of logic in human affairs."

The negative response in Venice didn't faze Gore. Back in Ravello, he busied himself assembling a fresh volume of essays for his British publisher, having recently added a number of pieces, including thoughtful reconsiderations of the lives and careers of Orson Welles, Somerset Maugham, and Ford Madox Ford. In *The Observer* in late August 1989, he published his first essay on the demonization of the Islamic world, which he correctly foretold would now take the place of the collapsed Soviet Union as enemy number one, since the national security state required a fresh enemy. "One billion Muslims and the Arabs in particular," he said, would make a fine new evil empire to oppose. More than ever, he assumed the role of beleaguered elder statesman, wearily observing the way his country had lost its freedom over the past two centuries.

In early July, Gore delivered the keynote address at the 125th anniversary of *The Nation*, a magazine that had often been the receptacle of his most radical essays. It was a "State of the Union" speech, and he addressed the large audience in Berkeley, California, in a presidential voice: "I speak for the nation, as always, but specifically for the mag as well. My subject is the state of the union, and I can only say of that no matter how bad things are, I always think of those immortal words of Spiro Agnew: 'For all its faults, the United States is still the greatest nation in this country.'" He touched on a number of "highlights in our past and darkness in our present." This wide-ranging history of American "freedom" was both trenchant and relentlessly funny, the sort of State of the Union address no president could ever make and keep his job. He effectively dismantled the idea of democracy in America, noting how the system was rigged to keep the people out of it. "To have a third party," he said, "one must have two other parties," and he noted that in an oligarchy such as the United States, this was impossible. "The Property Party," he said, rehashing a familiar line, "has two right wings: Republican and Democratic." Like most politicians, he had a stump speech, but it had evolved, grown more complex, taking into account current events. "A garrison state, forever at war, hot or cold, is easily controlled by the few, unlike the relatively free society the Founding Fathers had in mind," he declaimed. But he did see hope: People had begun to notice their poverty, and they were looking around for answers. He ended his speech with Thomas Jefferson's injunction that should all else fail, "the Tree of Liberty must still be nourished with the blood of tyrants and patriots."

After this rousing stump speech, Victor Navasky—the editor of *The Nation*—asked, "And you didn't elect him senator?"

Lenny and Gore

A hot June day in Amalfi. My wife and I join Gore, Howard, and Lenny Bernstein for a day on the water on a wooden motor launch that has seen better days. We meet in the harbor and, with a laconic captain who ignores us completely, head north along the rocky coast toward Positano.

Howard and Lenny look oddly alike: short, potbellied, smoking, talkative. Both wear gold necklaces, like Mafia dons. Gore seems distracted, probably hungover. But he comes to life when we pass a villa where Sophia Loren used to live with Carlo Ponti. Lenny is dismissive: "You're such a star-fucker, Gore."

We stop for lunch at a cliff-side restaurant that hangs over the water. I'm the last off the boat, with Lenny, who will leave tomorrow to conduct a concert in Amsterdam. I ask a stupid question: "Do you get to practice with the orchestra?" He grins. "It's called rehearsal!" When he sees I'm embarrassed, he kisses me on the forehead. "Nobody takes what I say personally, so don't you!"

We climb a slippery limestone stairwell to a terrace, where lunch is served under a grape arbor. Lemon trees are everywhere, and flowering bougainvillea, dahlias, roses. For three hours we sit over lunch, with successive courses, many bottles of wine, listening to Lenny as he describes the wonders of Brahms, whom he calls "the least appreciated of the major composers." He is about to embark, he tells us, on a major revival of Brahms. "I'm one of the few conductors in the world who can do this. In fact, there are only two star conductors in the world. There's me, and there's Herbert." Herbert, I assume, is Herbert von Karajan.

Gore has been silent until now, when he suddenly pounds his fist on the table, sending a plate crashing to the tile floor. "And there are only two star novelists in the world. There's me, of course. And there is Bellow."

Without a pause, Lenny pounds his side of the table, sending another plate to the floor. "I'm the fucking guest here!" he shouts. "And I can't get a word in edgewise!"

Becalmed by wine, we sail into the Amalfi harbor in time for drinks along the broad street that fronts the beach. Gore orders Campari and soda for everyone. Now in a great mood, Lenny crosses the street where a string of cheeses hangs in the open window of a butcher shop. He hands over a thick stack of bills to pay for them. In an antic mood, he strings them like a necklace around my wife's neck. He and she waltz in the street as Lenny sings into her ear a famous tune from West Side Story. *"Parini! I've just met a girl named Parini!"*

Howard leans to my ear, and says, "I wish I had his ASCAP. It's insane, the money he makes."

Gore is not amused. "Don't I make enough for the two of us, Howard?" he asks.

Chapter Eleven

The United States was founded by the brightest people in the country—and we haven't seen them since.

—Gore Vidal

1. "Our Country's Biographer"

The last decades of Gore's life were contradictory, with a few peaks and many valleys. He had become an international figure, a star. His name attracted attention on book covers in dozens of languages around the world. He was popular in far-flung places: Bulgaria, Brazil, Australia, Chile. He was in demand as a speaker, and could ask for large fees. Mostly he spoke for free at public forums of one kind or another and sought out television appearances eagerly, convinced that this medium remained the best way for him to maintain his profile. As ever, he wrote in the morning, even when hungover or jet-lagged. But the urgency of the fifties, sixties, and seventies had somehow vanished. Gore realized he could no longer hold center stage in the culture as when he debated William F. Buckley in prime time in 1968. The dynamics of the media had shifted in ways alien to him. Johnny Carson and Dick Cavett were gone, and the talk shows no longer wanted intellectuals as guests; they wanted celebrities, and while Gore could certainly pass as one, the younger generation no longer quite knew why anyone should pay attention to somebody who seemed old, pompous, and self-centered.

Yet Gore still found himself summoned to give talks, and sizable numbers of readers bought his books, especially the historical novels. He could draw large audiences whenever he appeared in public. Paradoxically, the man who detested academics and "school teachers," as he referred to all professors, became professorial himself, delivering well-written lectures at a range of American colleges from Berkeley to Harvard. And he often seemed to court academics, prizing their friendship and approval. Increasingly, he saw himself as a radical historian on a mission: He would explain to the United States of Amnesia what had happened, how the promise of the early republic had turned into oligarchy, and how empire had begun in earnest with the acquisition of the Philippines. He would often, in lectures, focus on the postwar development of what he called the national security state, and derided the pretense of democracy in America, repeating his line that the Property Party had two wings, Republican and Democrat. As ever, the American passion for religion—going back to the Puritans and running through a variety of evangelical and mystical strains—concerned him, and he would address the subject in essays and novels. He would also campaign for the legalization of drugs whenever he could, arguing that "drug addiction is epidemic, particularly among the poor, while those who make and sell drugs are very rich indeed—and beyond the law."

His views on sexuality also continued to evolve, although he never would allow for himself to be pigeonholed as gay, despite his obvious predilection for men. "I don't care about sex anymore," he often said. There was alcohol to blame for this, of course, but depression also played a role; Gore often seemed incredibly bleak as he moved into his sixties and seventies. His paranoia, always present, deepened as well—no doubt exacerbated by drink. "He just had a very very thin skin," Jason Epstein noted. "He saw, and found, enemies everywhere." This led him to make statements that could, in the later years, seem embarrassing. Increasingly he relied on friends for support and for confirmation of his views. (If you disagreed with him on anything, this would cause trouble, which meant that people tended to agree with him.)

Until his death in 2003, Howard remained the key person in his life, but Gore also talked on the phone with Barbara Epstein, Boaty Boatwright, Sue Mengers, Paul Newman, and others. He saw Roman friends less frequently, preferring Ravello as a base, but he stayed in close touch by phone with George Armstrong, Judith Harris, Donald Stewart, and others. His agent, Owen Laster, was a steady support. In personal dealings with friends, Gore was usually kind, open, and concerned about their welfare. His prodigious memory came in handy, and he never forgot the details of a friend's life: family issues, work problems, plans. His gift for friendship is often neglected in discussions of his personality, and this overlooks a major aspect of the man, as his cousin Miles Gore points out: "I think one can't emphasize enough how kind he was. My wife, Michelle, and I would visit him in later years, and he was unfailingly generous with his time, and he really listened and asked questions. That side of him is too often overlooked." This aspect of his personality sits uncomfortably, perhaps, with his narcissism, although one could argue that he used his friends as reflectors. (I certainly felt this strongly whenever he would call. After a quick few questions about my life, we would turn to his, and he was desperate to get "news" of his reputation, to find out through someone else how "Gore Vidal" fared in the world.) His empire of self grew, but at considerable cost to him.

The mask of Gore Vidal, the one he wore in public, did him a disservice in many ways, as it occluded the shy man hidden beneath its rubbery texture. But what would Gore be without his mask? Not the dazzling public figure who could, with pluck and skill, debate Buckley or Norman Mailer or any number of opponents. The mask helped when he stood in front of a political rally, sat on a panel, spoke from a podium—often treating serious issues, bringing a perspective to the national discourse of the United States that is sadly missing without him. "We've become a culture of screaming ninnies," he said, late in life. "I don't see reasoned argument. The illusion of debate happens on cable channels. Try stepping outside of the allowed parameters of opinion and see what happens. Nothing happens. A voice is not heard."

He took his work as historian seriously, becoming a man with a mission. "I had become our country's biographer, retelling the story of a nation very close to me and my family," said Gore. His public talks—becoming more frequent in the eighties and nineties—sounded more and more like witty lectures that detailed the history of the republic and a gradual loss of freedom for ordinary citizens. Moving about frequently, he was on CNN one night in the summer of 1990, the next day sitting on a panel sponsored by Fairness and Accuracy in the Media in Los Angeles, where he addressed the subject of censorship. He frequently used the same lines to warm up the crowd, who rarely needed much prompting: "I'm going to look up once in a while to give an air of spontaneity to my remarks. My mentor has always been Dwight D. Eisenhower, who always read his speeches with a great sense of discovery." This line never failed him, although he might use it for Ronald Reagan as well, depending on the audience.

He deployed his lines with an impish glee, and once he had an audience in his hands, he transmogrified before their very eyes into Professor Vidal, hitting the high points of American history from the Founding Fathers through the dark years of Reagan and George H. W. Bush. His career as an essayist had by now blossomed, with a new range of publications open to his work, including *The Observer* in London, where many of his most ferocious pieces appeared. Another volume of essays came out from André Deutsch: *A View from the Diners Club: Essays 1987–1991*. This British-only collection found enthusiastic critics, from Hilary Mantel writing in *The Spectator* to James Wood in *The Guardian*. "The Brits," said Gore, "were a reliable audience for my essays, but not so much for my novels. American history, in particular, bored them." It helped, of course, that he often traveled to London to appear on television and radio programs.

II. "The Other Side of the Camera"

Gore's passion for film never waned, and when Alan Heimert, a professor at Harvard, invited him to give the William E. Massey Senior Lectures in the History of American Civilization, Gore decided to talk about the movies. It was a prestigious series that had previously featured Eudora Welty, Irving Howe, Conor Cruise O'Brien, and Toni

Morrison, among others. (David Herbert Donald, the Lincoln scholar and longtime Harvard historian, had urged the committee to choose Gore for these lectures, and they happily agreed, knowing he would draw an enthusiastic crowd.) After the war, Gore had given a reading at Harvard, and this stayed in his memory as a glorious early triumph. He told Steven Abbott that "lecturing his former Exeter classmates was one of the greatest moments in his life." Now he felt ready for another visit to Cambridge, and these lectures became *Screening History* (1992), a wonderfully unorthodox blend of gossip, personal history, film criticism, and reflection on what he considered the primary art of our time. "Today the public seldom mentions a book," he told the standing-room-only audience in Memorial Hall on the first night, "though people will chatter about screened versions of unread novels."

As so often before, he circled back to his grandfather. Thomas P. Gore's time in the upper chamber was Gore's platinum credit card, and he pulled it from his wallet repeatedly, recalling his grandfather's first archenemy, Woodrow Wilson:

> It had been hard enough for Wilson to maneuver us into the First World War, as my grandfather believed that he had meant to do as early as 1916. We got nothing much out of that war except an all-out assault on the Bill of Rights in 1919 and, of course, the prohibition of alcohol. The world was not even made safe for democracy, a form of government quite alien to the residents of our alabaster cities, much less to those occupants of our fruited plains.

Gore meandered, but his crowd roared, clapped, and nodded. His evident delight in lecturing on hallowed ground was apparent. "The only thing I ever really liked to do was go to the movies," he said, with considerable hyperbole, recalling his life as a boy in Washington, enthralled by Mickey Rooney's prepubescent Puck in *A Midsummer Night's Dream* or *The Prince and the Pauper*, that marvelous Mark Twain story of two boys born on the same day but separated by circumstances. This was Gore's first awakening to the harshness of the class system, and it stimulated in him a longing for a twin brother, for his lost half, later discovered in the highly eroticized vision of Jimmie Trimble.

A central thesis of the Harvard lectures is Gore's perception that "in the end, he who screens the history makes the history." As suggested in *Hollywood*, he embraced a conspiracy theory in which the film industry colluded with Washington to shape our sense of reality, creating fictions that took the place of experience itself, or distorting experience in ways that it was difficult to separate fantasy from reality. He discusses at length the British films of the thirties, which he regarded as nothing less than a media offensive: "The English kept up a propaganda barrage that was to permeate our entire culture, with all sorts of unexpected results. Since the movies were by now the principal means of getting swiftly to the masses, Hollywood was subtly and not so subtly influenced by British propagandists." As in the period before the United States sided with Britain in World War I, in the thirties one had to choose: "On both sides of the Atlantic the movies were preparing us for a wartime marriage with our English and French cousins, against our Italian and German cousins." He points to *Fire Over England*, a 1937 film about the reign of Elizabeth I, whose navy defeated the Spanish Armada in 1588. This was useful propaganda for the British, of course, and Hollywood tilted in that direction.

The last of the three lectures dealt with versions of American history as played out on (and often distorted by) the silver screen. He lingers over *Young Mr. Lincoln*, a sentimental film by John Ford, which starred Henry Fonda as Honest Abe. Needless to say, Gore found this treatment of Lincoln far removed from reality, observing that depictions of Lincoln often avoided the treacherous war years (or observed those years from a Southern viewpoint). He himself had focused on these years, of course—on Lincoln's complex negotiation of a national crisis. Taking his usual revisionist approach to history, Gore says: "In life Lincoln wanted to colonize the ex-slaves in Central America. During the 1960s this was not god-like; so a number of Lincoln priests in the universities were able to prove to their satisfaction that he had been not only an Abolitionist but an integrationist. In the god-business, it is Proteus who prevails."

He concluded his lectures with a joke calculated to make his Harvard audience cheer: "Screen-writing has been my second career for close to forty years. By and large, my generation of writers did not become schoolteachers; if we needed money, we took a job at Columbia—the studio, not the university." Once again, Gore managed to prick the balloon of academic pomposity, which buzzed around the room and flew out the window. For him, the writing of scripts now faded as an activity: He didn't need the money and intensely disliked the tendency of young directors to consider themselves as auteurs. The quick cuts of contemporary films unsettled him. "I feel dizzy in the movies now," Gore would say. "The camera never lingers, except for close-ups. And they do close-ups instead of building drama. And I don't do car chases." On the other hand, he liked what he called "the other side of the camera," and looked for roles in films with surprising luck for someone who had never trained as an actor.

Susan Sarandon and Tim Robbins would visit Gore whenever they came to Italy, and this friendship intensified in the late eighties. In 1991, Robbins developed a mock documentary called *Bob Roberts*, based on a character that he had played briefly on *Saturday Night Live*. The film, backed by Paramount and written by Robbins, chronicles the rise of a right-wing Senate candidate and folksinger. His foil is the incumbent Democrat, Senator Brickley Paiste, and Robbins approached Gore about playing the part. Needless to say, he leaped at the chance. "I didn't have to act," Gore recalled. "I played myself, with my own opinions. There was no script for my part. Just a space where I could act as myself, though I was of course acting and it was a character."

The film is a brilliant piece of political satire that draws on earlier documentaries, such as D. A. Pennebaker's classic Bob Dylan film, *Don't Look Back*, or Rob Reiner's 1984 *This Is Spinal Tap*, another mock documentary. Seen through the eye of a British filmmaker, the film follows Roberts on his campaign across Pennsylvania. Shot for only $4 million, it appeared in 1992, at the beginning of the Clinton era, and proved remarkably prescient, paving the way for films such as *Wag the Dog* (1997) and *Bulworth* (1998). A key scene in *Bob Roberts* features a debate in Pittsburgh between Senator Paiste and Roberts. Standing stiffly behind a podium, Gore looks eerily plausible in his three-piece dark suit and fluffy bow tie. Roberts accuses him of inappropriate behavior with a young girl, which Paiste dismisses with a wave of the hand, saying: "This is America. Virtue always prevails." At the end, Gore parodies the summation moment in many political debates. "So let us be real together," he intones, shaking his head gravely. "Thank you for your vote." In another scene, Gore sits behind his desk and lectures in a weary fashion, playing himself as well as Paiste. "The film," he said, "understood that the media creates our politics, that image takes the place of reality. It was a theme I'd been writing about for a long time, going back to *Messiah*."

III. Attacking the Sky-God

Increasingly Gore inhabited the role of public intellectual as a wide-ranging commentator on politics and society, including sexual politics and religion. He read and admired Noam Chomsky, whose tightly argued and well-documented essays on American foreign policy gave Gore lots of ammunition. He had learned a great deal about the history of American interventions in Southeast Asia from books such as *American Power and the New Mandarins* (1969), often saying that the essay in that book called "The Responsibility of Intellectuals" was one of the great tracts of our time. Chomsky saw that intellectuals were in a position "to expose the lies of governments, to analyze actions according to their causes and motives and often hidden intentions." His work on the Middle East, especially with regard to Israel and American foreign policy, fascinated Gore and he wanted very much to meet Chomsky.

In September 1991, I brought them together for a television interview in Boston, asking about their motivations for the kind of political work they did. Chomsky responded that "looking in the mirror in the morning and not being appalled" was what drove him. Gore said, "For me, it's looking out of the window and not being appalled." And Gore asked, "Why is empathy in such short supply?" He worried about the inability of some to "picture what it's like to be other people. In my profession as a novelist I have to do that, but I've always had that tendency. I'm always startled when people start going on about the blacks or the Jews or gay people, and you suddenly see there is no ability to identify with anybody else except themselves. If I had a motivating thing it would be an overwrought empathy, an irritability with its absence in others."

In November, Gore spent a week in New Hampshire as the 1991 Montgomery Fellow at Dartmouth College, having been invited by Donald E. Pease, a cultural critic and professor of English. There he befriended James H. Tatum, a professor of classics. Tatum comments: "This was a prestigious fellowship program that the college established to invite public figures of all kinds, politicians, writers, poets, composers, scientists, anyone and everyone sufficiently distinguished to merit a visitor's spot in the academic calendar." With his partner Bill Noble, Tatum invited Gore and Howard to their home in Vermont for dinner during the week, and they were entertained by Howard's singing. It was after a grand dinner "with copious drinks" when Gore asked Howard to show off his skills. Tatum elaborates:

> Gore himself never seemed to me to be particularly musical, nor Howard. They lived in Italy but rarely if ever went to concerts or opera anywhere that I'd heard of. But Howard's voice was another matter. He didn't need accompaniment, and launched right into singing. And he was so good at it the effect was mesmerizing—like having Mel Tormé live in your living room. He sang for twenty minutes or so and, when he finished, Gore solemnly informed us that we had been present for a rare event. Howard might sing for him when they were alone, but rarely around other people and never in public. It was a touching moment, about as intimate as I ever witnessed Gore and Howard being. Many years later when I visited Gore in the Hollywood Hills, perhaps the last time I saw him before he died, I found him listening to recordings of Howard's singing.

Interviewed at Dartmouth before a large crowd, Gore dropped more names than a phone book and, as an avowed atheist, railed against "the sky-God," declaring that monotheism lay at the heart of "the American problem, the Western problem." He said it was "that tedious text from the Bronze Age known as the Old Testament" that had troubled the waters. "From its pages we get Judaism, Christianity, and Islam—the sky-god religions. They have not been bearers of peace." It was a theme he would develop at length in "Monotheism and Its Discontents" on April 20, 1992, when he gave the Lowell Lecture at Harvard.

The fact that the premier American university had invited him back made a deep and favorable impression, and it played some role in his final choice of Harvard as the repository of his papers and, indeed, his entire estate. His lecture was an incendiary bomb aimed at "them," the monotheistic religions:

> Let us dwell upon the evils they have wrought. The hatred of blacks comes straight from the Bad Book. As descendants of Ham (according to Redneck divines), blacks are forever accursed, while Saint Paul tells the slaves to obey their masters. Racism is in the marrow of the bone of the true believer. For him, black is forever inferior to white and deserves whatever ill fortune may come his way. The fact that some monotheists can behave charitably means, often, that their prejudice is at so deep a level that they are not aware it is there at all. In the end, this makes any radical change of attitude impossible.

Not one inclined to modesty or half measures, Gore called for a nation "not under God but under man—or should I say our common humanity?"

During this same period he wrote "in a few months" a short satirical novel called *Live from Golgotha*. "Jason Epstein hated it," recalls Gary Fisketjon, "and I think that his response to this book really ended their friendship. I would imagine Jason was stunned. He didn't mean to have it end. But it did." Gore's next editor at Random House was Sharon Delano, whom he liked a great deal. "Sharon listens," he said, probably meaning that she didn't try to change anything in his books.

The novel opens with a flourish: "In the beginning was the nightmare, and the knife was with Saint Paul, and the circumcision was a Jewish notion and definitely not mine." These words emerge from the lips of one Timothy, later an apostle and saint. The son of a Jewish mother and a Greek father who writes from his kitchen in Lystra, he speaks of his own good looks like a first-rate narcissist: "I have golden hyacinthine curls and cornflower-blue, forget-me-not eyes and the largest dick in our part of Asia Minor." Timothy refers to Paul (who of course is gay in Gore's vision) simply as Saint, and—as Bishop of Macedonia—he wants to get Paul's version of the gospel out there before it's destroyed by a computer hacker from the future, known simply as the Hacker, who has been feverishly erasing all versions of the gospel, hoping to seize control of the Christian narrative. Perhaps not unsurprisingly in this wacky book, a crew from NBC (Nuclear Broadcasting Company) slips into the past (computer software enables this reversion) with a plan to broadcast the Crucifixion live from Golgotha: a TV special to end all specials. Visitors from the twentieth century stream into the Holy Land to be present at the great event, including a couple of Gore's favorite fakes: Mary Baker Eddy and Oral Roberts. His old friend Shirley MacLaine also appears on the scene, as she has a strong interest in spiritualism.

The novel swirls around Gore's recent obsessions, including his hatred of monotheism. The real object of his scorn, however, is mainly Saint Paul, the author of two famous letters to Timothy. With the "greatest story ever told" being erased and refashioned by the Hacker, Timothy has to scramble. The plot thickens as Chet from NBC tries to persuade Timothy to act as the anchorman for the Crucifixion—rather a plum job. But interference occurs from a range of sources, many of them fantastic, futuristic, and perhaps unbelievable. "I got carried away," Gore said, "and probably outdid myself."

The Hacker (whose name is Marvin Wasserstein) is scary. "If he has found some way of entering my mind," says Timothy, "then I must find a way of keeping him out." The true nature of Wasserstein will be revealed in time, with plenty of anti-Zionist vitriol, which Gore can't keep a lid on: The wounds from the print battles with Midge Decter and Norman Podhoretz remained open, and they stung, and he unfortunately allowed himself to vent here. Gore's dislike of Zionism doesn't just obtrude; it overwhelms the narrative. Saint Paul says, "Render unto Caesar that which is Caesar's, and unto God that which is God's." That remains, as they say, biblical. But one gets a Vidalian twist here: "Saint's formula, which pleased the Roman administration, was never understood by the Romans. To the dedicated Zionist, Palestine was not Caesar's country but God's. So what sounded like a nice acknowledgment of the separation of Church and State was really a secret Zionist war cry. I don't think Saint actually thought it up, but he is always given credit for it in Bartlett's."

In all of this, Jesus seems the least of it: a hapless figure whose real message (at least in Gore's estimate) seems difficult to grasp. He has a terrible weight problem, which Timothy repeatedly refers to as a "glandular problem." Indeed, he "weighs more than a Japanese wrestler, more than Orson Welles even." He's not even Jesus, as it happens, but a substitute. Wasserstein is the "real" Jesus, and he winds up crucified in the end, thus allowing history to proceed as usual.

Unsurprisingly, the novel puzzled reviewers, many of whom thought Gore had gone over the top. "Readers were far and few between," Gore recalled. For the most part, *Live from Golgotha* slipped by without notice, attracting none of the attention that had greeted *Myra Breckinridge* or any of the novels in the Narratives of Empire. Its theme harks back to *Messiah*: the need for a religion to control the story in order to survive. In trying to control the message, of course, the media comes into play, and Gore understood these dynamics as well as anyone, having made himself a master of the airwaves (at least in the sixties and seventies). The sexual fluidity of Timothy fits nicely with another persistent theme in Gore's work. Its linguistic texture, too, is obviously Vidalian, with its mix of high and low, serious and inane. Sometimes these blend in attractive ways, as when Timothy visits Rome with Saint:

> Saint and I stared at everything like a pair of yokels. It was a hot summer day, and I was all for heading for the baths that are Rome's glory, but Saint wanted to see his lawyer, Zenas, first. So, we got lost in the Forum. If it weren't for the sight of the two hills, the Palatine, which is covered with the emperor's place—several acres of offices and porticoes and gardens—called the Capitoline Hill, where the temples of Jupiter and Juno brood over the Forum like—like two rundown temples—you would never find your way to any-

> where because something like a thousand statues and monuments have been jammed together in the Forum, which isn't that large to start with.

Such well-developed scenes are few and far between, and it's likely that the sloppy casualness that blurs the writing on too many pages arose from its hasty composition. Gore didn't trouble over the prose in this novel, and he allowed his pet peeves and obsessions to poke through the cracks in the narrative pavement. As a result, the novel failed to find many admirers, and it marks a low point of his work in this decade.

IV. Thinking About Sex

As the nineties began, Gore found himself sleepless at night and anxious during the day. He traveled too much, saw too many people, and did too many interviews. He often turned to whiskey for solace, drinking half a bottle without much trouble. "I sleep better when I've drunk a great deal," he said. "Scotch is mother's milk to me. Soothing." Needless to say, Howard worried about him and thought he should cut back on everything: travel, socializing, drinking.

Friends were also in decline, including Rudolf Nureyev—a good friend and luminous performer in the world of ballet and modern dance who spent a good deal of time on the Amalfi coast, in Positano, where he had bought a handful of small islands. He liked to visit Gore in Ravello, though by the early nineties he seemed desperately ill. "He was a ghost of himself," said Gore, "and he could barely walk on his last visit with legs like sticks. He had to lean on me to get up the stairs." HIV had turned into full-blown AIDS, and the extent to which Nureyev's once perfect body had withered upset Gore terribly. The wages of sex, as he saw, could be death.

Gore had been trying to come to terms with sexuality for decades, moving toward acceptance of his own "degeneracy," as he called it. In 1991, he wrote "The Birds and the Bees" and, seven years later, "The Birds and the Bees and Clinton." Both of these often silly yet occasionally brilliant essays appeared in *The Nation*, where Gore took cover when he wished to say something that could not fit easily in main-stream pages, such as *Vanity Fair, Esquire*, or *The New York Review of Books*. In the first, he comments on a recent book where Americans "tell the truth" about their sexual desires. "A majority of men and women like oral sex," Gore notes. This was their deepest desire, and next to that "was sex with a famous person." Gore observes: "Plainly being blown by George or Barbara Bush would be the ultimate trip for our huddled masses."

Wearing the mask of Professor Vidal, he gives readers a lesson in sex ed. "First, the bad news: men and women are not alike." Moreover, they are "dispensable carriers, respectively of seeds and eggs." The purpose of sex, as our wise teacher explains, is to procreate. He reduces this activity to its most clinical: "The male's function is to shoot semen," and the woman's job "is to be shot briefly by a male in order to fertilize an egg, which she will lay nine months later." It's simple arithmetic: Man plus Woman equals Baby. Gore strips away anything sentimental about relationships, rummaging in his own past: "In the prewar Southern town of Washington, D.C., it was common for boys to have sex with one another. It was called 'messing around,' and it was no big deal. If the boy became a man who kept on messing around, it was thought a bit queer—sexual exclusivity is odd and suggests obsession—but no big deal as long as he kept it quiet." He notes that Kinsey in his report said that 37 percent of men had "messed around."

Gore believed that he knew how things worked, not simply the way they worked for him. He could be funny in these pieces, and right, too: It's obvious that sexual activity has a profoundly biological meaning. When he harks back to what happened in the prewar South, he is doubtless recalling the time when he and Jimmie Trimble frolicked on the banks of the Potomac—if indeed they did. But the self-referential aspects of the piece reflect an author trying hard to work out his own sexual predilections, and Gore's were eccentric, with a desperate need *not* to allow such a thing as love to interfere with sex. Of course procreation had no place in the hydraulic work of homoerotic activity that once occupied him in the late afternoons after a day of writing.

In “The Birds and the Bees and Clinton,” written after Kenneth Starr had published his full report on the sexual peccadilloes of Clinton on September 11, 1998, Gore continues in his role of sex-ed professor: “It was not until Mr. Starr published his dirty book at public expense that I realized how far off-track I have allowed these sad dummies to get. Simple truths about the birds and the bees have been so distorted by partisanship that blow jobs and hand jobs are now confused with The Real Thing.” That Clinton and Monica Lewinsky did not actually “have sex” was his point; they had “messed around.” His rage mounts as he writes, until at last he explodes: “Christian fundamentalists and their corporate manipulators seem intent on overthrowing two presidential elections in a Senate trial. This is no longer comedy. This is usurpation.”

v. Retreats, Advances

When the owner of the apartment in the Largo Argentina suddenly raised the rent in 1993, Gore decided to pull the plug. Ravello had become his base of operations by now, and many friends had moved away from Rome. So he and Howard gave up the lease, moving out on St. Patrick’s Day. It was the end of a major phase in their lives. Yet they traveled as much as ever. In July 1993, for instance, they went to Austria for a week at the Salzburg Global Seminar, attending the educational conference held every summer at the Schloss Leopoldskron—the mansion made famous as the home of Captain von Trapp and his family in the film version of *The Sound of Music*. Gore lectured on literature as a political force, and the audience, Alastair Reid recalls, “found him riveting and irreverent. He was afraid of nothing, and said things nobody was saying except him and a few others. He understood that politics and literature aren’t terribly far apart, and that writers too often play into the dominant narratives. Gore stood apart, as he’d done throughout his life, and he ruffled feathers in the room, as he did in the world at large.” Gore discussed his ideas about the “national narrative” on a panel with André Brink from South Africa, Nawal El Saadawi from Egypt, Victor Erofeyev from Russia, and the American writer Erica Jong. I was there, and recall sitting at dinner one night with Gore and Jong. Gore politely asked her what she was working on, and she said, "I'm writing my memoirs." Not missing a beat, Gore responded: "At last, you're trying your hand at fiction." This was, in fact, an especially revealing moment, as Gore had begun to write his own memoirs, *Palimpsest*, which he would publish two years later.

He wrote to Judith Halfpenny about the manuscript that became *Palimpsest*: "I am doing my own memoir. I've just done a large chunk on a weekend with the Kennedys in Hyannis after the Berlin Wall went up and Jack is both scared shitless and longing for a war. I kept note of everything said, and as I transcribe them, he comes over as charming as ever but definitely creepy. Of course he was only alive thanks to drugs and so, perhaps, felt undead. Jackie comes out rather well, outraged at the men starting a war that would kill her children."

Gore continued to travel frequently to the States, on one occasion taking on a small role in *With Honors*, a 1994 film. He played the part of a Harvard professor, which now seemed to come naturally. He also worked with Delano at Random House to assemble a volume of collected essays. Published on June 1, 1993, *United States: Essays 1952–1992* marked Gore's coronation as one of the country's leading essayists of the century. It was an immense book that should have been published with a retractable handle and little wheels. Its thirteen hundred pages contained most of the work he had done in the essay form, though he had been so prolific that any number of pieces failed to make the cut. Its cover featured a 1958 painting of the American flag by Jasper Johns, with a handsome photograph of the author on the back by Jane Brown—Gore's favorite picture of himself.

There are three sections in the collection, each with its own table of contents: State of the Art, State of the Union, and State of Being. But Gore's essays didn't fall into such neat categories, as he usually mixed memoir with literary criticism or political or cultural commentary. "Vidal's essays go back to the nineteenth century of Bagehot, Carlyle, even Macaulay," wrote Anthony Burgess in *The Observer*, adding that Gore's essays "inform before they judge." Other reviewers agreed. "Vidal is the master-essayist of our age," declared Michael Dirda in *The Washington Post Book World*. John Lanchester, in the

London Review of Books, noted that the essays are "unmistakably a performance—more of a self-celebration than a self-interrogation, and none the worse for that." With few dissenting voices, this publication was a triumph, and Gore knew it when Harry Evans—then editorial director at Random House—informed him that he had won the National Book Award for criticism. "I had given a note for Harry to read at the dinner in the unlikely event that I should win." This wry note, read by Evans in the author's absence, said:

> Unaccustomed as I am to winning prizes in my native land, I have no set piece of the sort seasoned prize winners are wont to give. Who can forget Faulkner's famed "eternal truths and verities," that famed tautology, so unlike my own bleak relative truth. As you have already, I am sure, picked the wrong novelist and the wrong poet, I am not so vain as to think you've got it right this time, either!

He went on to recall the winners of the National Book Award event he had attended some fifty years earlier, noting that he had been at that dinner with Dylan Thomas, who retired with him afterward to a bar in the Village. He could not, it seems, restrain the urge to suggest that he was there, always, before anyone else. Literary history, if not history itself, started in his mother's womb.

VI. In the Widening Gyre

There were other milestones and turning points now. For a start, Gore began to repair his relationship with Norman Mailer in earnest. Gay Talese recalls: "They'd never been enemies, not in any real way. But they battled in public, and sometimes took different sides on issues. They insulted each other on television. They could be fierce, battling in private, too. But there was a grudging respect. Mailer and Gore had been rivals out of the gate, in the late forties. But they came together to perform *Don Juan in Hell* from George Bernard Shaw's *Man and Superman* at a benefit for the Actors Studio at Carnegie Hall." That was on February 15, 1993, when Gore joined Mailer, Talese, and Susan Sontag onstage for this benefit performance. It was a glittering occasion, with numerous movie stars and wealthy entrepreneurs in the audience (tickets ranged from $500 to $1,000), along with a few writers as well. Gore was in terrific form that night, in a dark blue suit with a blood-bright vest. When it ended, he crossed the stage, grasped both of Mailer's hands, and said in the loudest stage whisper he could manage, "You have always understood me, Norman." The audience loved it, giving a standing ovation to the foursome.

In June 1994, Gore accepted an honorary degree from the University of South Dakota, motivated by his father's connections to that state. When he returned to Ravello, he planned to write what he knew would be the final volume in his Narratives of Empire, *The Golden Age*—the title had lodged in his mind some years earlier. But life kept intervening. That summer, he welcomed an array of visitors, including Hillary Clinton and her daughter, Chelsea, who came down from Naples (where President Clinton was attending an international conference). The visit went well, and Gore would soon find himself invited for an evening at the Clinton White House, although he declined, preferring to dine privately with Hillary and Paul Newman at a nearby hotel. In October, he was back in England for the Cheltenham Literature Festival, where he appeared with Kurt Vonnegut, who had become (with his wife, the photographer Jill Krementz) a friend, although they were never close. Afterward, he came back to Oxford with me for a few days, where I took him to dinner at Christ Church College with Iris Murdoch and, the next day, Isaiah Berlin. One morning I found him staring into the mirror in his hotel room, noting the puffiness around the eyes, the double chin. "Who would have thought I'd become an Old Master in my own time?" he asked, talking to himself.

Gore hoped that Walter Clemons would have delivered his biography by now, but rumors floated in from various quarters. Clemons, who suffered from both diabetes and writer's block, would fail to complete the assignment, and Gore knew it. At sixty-four, Clemons collapsed at his house in Queens one morning. I was staying with Gore in Ravello at the time and recall his profound feeling that nothing in his life ever went according to plan. Over lunch he asked me if I would take over from Clemons, as I had recently edited *Gore Vidal: Writer Against the Grain*, a kind of Festschrift. Gore thought that, as a novelist myself, I could manage a long book of this kind. I knew, however, that the job would prove impossible, and that nothing I wrote would ever meet his expectations.

I told him, not untruthfully, that I had a contract for several books in hand and couldn't possibly get to his biography at the moment. One day, I told him, I would write about him at length. (He once introduced me in London as "his dear friend, Jay Boswell.") Meanwhile, I spoke to Fred Kaplan, whom I admired as a biographer. He had written thoughtfully on Henry James and Mark Twain, among others, so he could put Gore's life and work in its proper literary context. Kaplan soon took over the project, producing a sturdy and intelligent biography in 1999, one that did not please its subject. How could it? It remains, however, a considerable work, a skillful biography that puts forward the facts of Gore's life without pulling too many punches.

Gore had begun to find a new rhythm of travel, shifting regularly to California to get out of the worst of winter on the Amalfi coast, which can be horribly damp and gray, with a slicing wind. So January and February were times for a visit to Thailand or to La Costa, Gore's favorite health spa in Southern California. Howard liked returning to the Hollywood Hills, where he had a circle of friends. As before, Gore found himself in demand for talks at universities and colleges in the States, although he turned down most of these offers. Wherever he went now, a camera crew from BBC's *Omnibus* followed him, as a major documentary was under way. (It would run over two nights in 1995.)

That same year Paul Newman and Joanne Woodward threw a small but elegant party for Howard's sixty-fifth birthday in New York, at their penthouse apartment overlooking Central Park. Among the twenty or so guests that night were Mailer and his wife Norris Church, Joan Didion, and Susan Sarandon and Tim Robbins. After dinner, one of Newman's daughters sang, then Gore rose to toast his partner of more than four decades. "You all know him, which is why you're here," he said, "and I know him better than you do. He's a wonderful friend, and he makes life possible. He could have had a career in music—everyone has heard him sing—but he put that to one side. So, Howard—here's to you." Howard smiled and wiped tears from his eyes, then blew a kiss to Gore.

Gore's nephew Hugh Steers died in March 1995—an event that seemed to hit Gore especially hard. Hugh's death from AIDS brought the disease close to home. Until this moment, in fact, Gore had managed to push it away, saying that only foolish people got AIDS. Absurdly, as noted earlier, he believed that he could never get it himself, as he didn't go in for anal penetration.

Gore had also become fond of Hugh's younger brother, Burr—a tall, willowy, good-looking young man who had bumped around in the world of New England prep schools. Burr recalls: "I think he saw me as a kind of son he never had. I had been kicked out of my schools, and he liked that sort of thing. I was a rebel. I looked up to him, and he responded to this affectionately." Burr would please his uncle by taking up a career in film, as a director, and Gore played a small part in *Igby Goes Down*, a coming-of-age film about a young man who is trying to escape from his upper-crust family and the oppressive world of snobbish prep schools. "It was a marvelous script," said Gore, "and beautifully directed by Burr, and it showed a world that most people don't know about." This was a world that not only interested but obsessed Gore, who now recalled fondly his time at Exeter. "He actually hated Exeter," said Howard, "but he talked about it now like it was heaven."

Another obsession was Franklin Roosevelt and his world, so he readily agreed to a request from Barbara Epstein to review *Closest Companion: The Unknown Story of the Intimate Friendship Between Franklin Roosevelt and Margaret Suckley* by Geoffrey C. Ward. Gore had met Suckley, known as Daisy, and his tender review of this book allowed him, once again, to link himself with the old-money inhabitants of big houses along the Hudson. He writes in this piece: "Fear of class war is never far from the River mind." He knew, deep inside, that he didn't belong in this class, although he had lived among them, or beside them, for twenty years. He heard them talking and could mimic these voices that echoed in his head. But he understood that the grandson of a senator from Oklahoma could not really match a Roosevelt, an Astor, or any descendant of the great families who lived downriver from Edgewater in towns like Hyde Park, Rhinebeck, or Rhinecliff. "I was an outsider from nowhere," he confessed, in a rare moment of frankness on the subject of class.

Gore was a memoirist by nature, but *Palimpsest* (1995) was a more systematic treatment of his life than anything he had yet attempted. It's a fine-grained and evocative book, in a genre that Gore both understood and valued. He frequently noted in conversation that perhaps the major strain of American writing was autobiography, reaching back to Benjamin Franklin, moving through Henry David Thoreau, Henry Adams, and any number of others. He had resisted writing this book for decades, being aware that memory plays one false, and that it's impossible not to invent the past as much as recall it. He had endlessly retold the stories about his blind grandfather, his drunken mother, his Exeter days, his Edgewater and Hollywood capers, his troubles with *The New York Times*, adding and subtracting details, shaping each story like a piece of fiction. He had a cast of characters in his head who had become, in time, figures of monstrous proportion: Tennessee Williams, Truman Capote, Mailer, Buckley. Even Richard Nixon played a prominent role in his theater of the mind. And there were saints, too: Eleanor Roosevelt, Fred Dupee, "the most charming of men," Paul Newman. Oddly enough, in *Palimpsest* one heard no mention of Gore's usual circle of Roman friends, his real "family." The names he would mention were those that added to his imperial self: fellow senators in their togas, adjacent faces on the cultural Mount Rushmore of his dreams.

The erotic passages about Jimmie Trimble stood out, and they surprised many of Gore's friends, even Howard, who said with some bitterness: "I didn't hear much about Jimmie for decades. Hardly a word. Suddenly he's front and center in Gore's mind. Where did he come from all of a sudden? What was *that* about?" At least in its explicitness, this was a fairly recent obsession, and perhaps a necessary fiction for Gore. Jimmie became an idealized figure in his mind, the young heterosexual male who would "mess around." He was giving a local habitation and a name to something he had thought about, fantasized about, for much of his adult life.

Gore begins the memoir with the question in italics: *A Tissue of Lies?* He knew he would be accused of making everything up, but he had decided to put his stories together in the ways he remembered them. Serious readers were expected to understand that *Palimpsest* is a work of fiction, as in the Latin *fictio*, which means "to shape," narrative as an arrangement of facts. And Gore worked hard to get the facts right: the dates and names, the places. But what he made of them was his own business as he returns, in memory, to the Hudson River valley, wondering if he did the right thing: "I have recurring dreams about Edgewater," he says, "and sometimes I wonder if I should have given it up." He dreams about a visit there. After saying hello to the old postmaster and storekeeper nearby, he steps into the house. It's in disrepair. Looking out his bedroom window, he sees that the river "has eaten away most of the lawn. In fact, the water is alarmingly close to the house, while some sort of factory has been built on my nearby island." Relief comes as he walks through the house and sees "a long vista of splendid rooms, with painted ceilings, like a Roman palace." He has the same dream, over and over. What did it mean? Freud says that a dream of a house is usually a dream of the dreamer's soul.

At seventy, Gore remained uncertain about his true place in the world. And he tried to second-guess himself. Should he have pushed on, leaving Edgewater, which he adored? The move to Italy had been a bold one, of course. But what about the beloved country left behind, the one he had written about so often, becoming (in his view) its biographer? With a subtle fondness, Gore circles the first four decades of his life, avoiding linearity, dipping into scenes from the past, summoning images, erasing them, building a palimpsest—a script where earlier erasures bleed through the present writing, not unlike the past itself, which colors the present, distorts it, informs it. Toward the end, Gore writes with startling insight into his process of self-creation:

> While I've been here, I've also been reading through this memoir, adding, subtracting, writing over half-erased texts—"palimpsesting"—

> all the while looking for clues not so much to me, the subject, if indeed I am the subject, as to what those first thirty-nine years were all about as we grew more and more ingenious in finding new ways of killing off the human race and its support system, the small planet that each of us so briefly visits. No, I haven't found any pattern at all to life itself, but then there is probably none other than birth and growth, decay and death, something we all know from the start. As for who I was then as opposed to now . . .

The "I" gives way, halfway through this paragraph, to the collective "we" who destroy the world around the "I." The writer creates a palimpsest before our eyes, searching for a pattern, falling back on the usual human story—birth, growth, decay, death. In some ways, the memoir itself substitutes for life; the voice lives beyond the words, lofty and bemused, world-weary, all-knowing, tentative, curious, embracing. It's also very funny at times in ways that undermine the pomposity of the Self and celebrate and sing its accomplishments, as in the memory of a dinner for Gore in Washington where he sits next to Alice Longworth—the eldest child of Teddy Roosevelt—who says to him by way of compliment: "I loved *Justinian*."

Toward the end of *Palimpsest*, Gore confesses that he has written not a ghost story but a love story, referring to Jimmie Trimble. But Trimble simply stands in for everything Gore wanted but could never quite have. This is a tale of self-love, dedicated to a mask: the carefully wrought persona that Gore could summon in a moment, the face that glowed in the dark of his imagination, but which in the mirror often sagged or, more frighteningly, disappeared.

The reviews of *Palimpsest* were largely positive, acknowledging its "unflagging brilliance." Christopher Hitchens wrote at length in the *London Review of Books*, saying: "We come to understand how divided a self he is; not just as between love and death but as between literature and politics, America and the world, the ancient and the modern, the sacred and the profane." In *The New York Times*, Christopher Lehmann-Haupt, who reviewed many of Gore's later books, observed with some truth "that much cruelty is present . . . on the author's part, in varying degrees, toward most of the people he has ever known." He adds that "none of this is gratuitous." On the other hand, the name-dropping annoyed some reviewers, and one could argue—many actually did—that this memoir was an extended gossip column, with a litany of famous names in boldface. Certainly it delighted Gore that such luminous figures as Amelia Earhart, Eleanor Roosevelt, Paul Newman, Johnny Carson, John Kennedy, Tennessee Williams, and Hillary Clinton had paraded through his life. It was a very big parade, a Mardi Gras of celebrity. But it was a dream as well. Each of these characters played a part in his psychic reconstruction, reflecting some aspect of himself.

While Gore was promoting *Palimpsest* in London, Michael and Linda Mewshaw met him for dinner one night at the Connaught, where he was staying. It surprised Mewshaw that, at seventy, Gore looked so "thoroughly dissipated," with a bulging stomach and stiff knees that made it awkward for him to cross a room without wincing. Howard looked even worse, tired and pale, with a scarlet rash on the right side of his face. "We joined them in their suite, and Howard and Gore were already drunk before dinner," recalls Mewshaw. "Room service sent up a magnum of Veuve Clicquot and a pot of caviar, much of which dribbled down Gore's shirt front, along with hard-boiled egg yolk and toast crumbs. He razzed me that my hair was thinning." Howard chimed in: "Look who's fucking talking." At dinner, Gore insisted on ordering for everyone: quail's eggs, roast beef and Yorkshire pudding, a new wine with each course, and spotted dick, a dessert he favored for the name alone. But he didn't eat a bite of it, content to consume his sugar in liquid form."

Of course he got up the next morning and wrote for several hours. Work came first, even when traveling. He began a series of long personal essays and reviews for *The New York Review of Books*, *The New Yorker*, and other publications, each of which might be considered an outtake from *Palimpsest*. These included an evocation of the Greenwich Village–based novelist Dawn Powell, his friend from New York in the fifties (and whose neglected fiction Gore exhumed and praised in two of his best critical essays) and a shrewd recollection of Clare Boothe Luce, "the recent widow of the founder of *Time*, in whose giggly pages both my father and I had so often been fictionalized." He clearly adored her, saying: "After Eleanor Roosevelt, Clare was easily the most hated woman of her time—she was too beautiful, too successful in the theater, in politics, in marriage. Feminism as we now know it was a minor eccentricity in those days. Otherwise, she might have been admired as what she was, a very tough woman who had so perfectly made it in a man's world."

Gore had befriended a wide range of women in the course of his adult life. "I think people don't realize how much Gore liked to be with women, enjoyed their friendship, their company. He loved women, and they loved him," says Sarandon. In the late nineties, he began to understand fully that women were as marginalized as gay people. "To be a lesbian," he said, "was to be sidelined even further." He had warm friendships with Claire Bloom, Boaty Boatwright, Sue Mengers, and Barbara Epstein. And he liked Erica Jong, who first met him at the Salzburg Global Seminar in 1993. Jong recalls: "We had a friendship over the next decades. Once he sent me a note, very upset about something I'd written about Princess Margaret. He invited me to lunch at the apartment in the Largo Argentina—and I remember that he first said, 'How do you like these chairs? I bought them from the set of *Ben-Hur*.' He was very protective of Princess Margaret, and I apologized for saying something that, in his view, was slandering someone I'd never met. He was right about that. I found this protectiveness very touching." Jong was also struck by his relationship with Howard, which "was intense, and loving."

In the late nineties, he relied on Howard even more heavily than before, anxious about his whereabouts if his companion disappeared from the house for several hours without saying where he had gone. He also liked to complain to Howard about his health, as mortality had begun to knock loudly. Gore's arthritis returned—the old problem that dated from his wartime experiences in the Aleutian Islands; now he had considerable difficulty walking any real distance or climbing stairs. He slept badly, drinking quantities of whiskey to soothe his nerves most nights: a form of self-medication that would, in due course, only aggravate his health problems. In the spring of 1996, five rectal polyps were removed at a hospital in Los Angeles, after which he flew straight to Naples, getting so drunk on the plane that he fell in the airport in Rome. Back in Ravello the next day, with a bad hangover, he swallowed five or six aspirins to deal with the pain. That night, he felt queasy and went to bed before ten. "I woke up in a pool of blood in the middle of the night," he recalled, "and I thought it was over. Howard called the boys from the village, and they carried me into the piazza on a stretcher. An ambulance took me to a hospital in Salerno, where I nearly died." It was the aspirin, of course, that had provoked the bleeding, and the Italian doctors told him to rest.

He lay in bed for days at La Rondinaia, reading proofs of a long article on John Updike's career that he had written for *The Times Literary Supplement* before he fell ill. It had been commissioned by Ferdinand Mount, who got more than he expected. For a long time Gore had felt resentful of Updike, who had won every award that American authors can win—the darling of the establishment. But these accolades were, in Gore's estimate, undeserved. "Although I've never taken Updike seriously as a writer," he wrote, "I now find him the unexpectedly relevant laureate of the way we would like to live now, if we have the money, the credentials, and the sort of faith in our country and its big God that passes all understanding."

"I could not understand how anybody could rebel against a system so clearly benign," wrote Updike, in a line that was bound to set off Gore, who had never found the system "so clearly benign." Updike writes of the Vietnam War that he felt "uncomfortable" with what had happened in Southeast Asia, yet he wonders "how much of the discomfort has to do with its high cost, in lives and money, and how much with its moral legitimacy." Updike admits that he actually favored intervention in foreign countries with military power "if it does some good," expressing a legitimate concern about the need for "genuine elections" in South Vietnam. Furious with such talk, Gore is all over him with the facts of history. "But the American government had stopped the Vietnamese from holding such elections a decade earlier," he writes, "because, as President Eisenhower noted in his memoirs, North and South Vietnam would have voted for the Communist Ho Chi Minh and 'we could not allow that.' "

From here, Gore takes aim at Updike's famous Rabbit tetralogy:

"At times, reading Updike's political and cultural musings, one has the sense that there is no received opinion that our good rabbit does not hold with passion." Then Gore goes to work on Updike's style in his most recent novel, quoting from *In the Beauty of the Lilies*: "The hoarse receding note drew his consciousness . . . to a fine point, and while that point hung in his skull starlike he fell asleep upon the adamant bosom of the depleted universe." Gore asks: "Might Updike not have allowed one blind noun to slip free of its seeing-eye adjective?"

Was Gore fair to Updike? Probably not. He ignores the lyrical early stories, which subtly evoke small-town life, the author's countless insightful reviews in *The New Yorker*, the genuine allure of the Rabbit novels, and the deft portrait of the sexual politics of suburban America's "post-pill paradise" in *Couples*. Gore's piece was polemical, yet he performed a kind of cultural service, speaking his mind, drawing Updike's career—especially his political views—into fresh focus. And his take on Updike influenced a number of younger critics, such as James Wood, who would suggest in a review a few years later that Updike "is a writer for whom different subjects have the same sensuous textures, whether a vagina, an air-conditioner or a petal. All is 'more matter' for his prose, all can be given the same beautiful finish, the same equalizing enamel." Updike had been given a pass for too long, in Gore's view.

At the Harvard Faculty Club

Lunch at the Harvard Faculty Club with John Kenneth Galbraith and David Herbert Donald. "They're really the two most important professors in this school," Gore says. "I met Ken during the 1960 election, in Los Angeles. He was running the brain trust for Jack."

As we approach the stairs of the redbrick building, he grows somber. "My friends from Exeter came here right after graduation. I preferred the army, real life, war. They invited me to give a reading after the war. I wasn't yet twenty-four. I think I was the only person of my generation to speak at Harvard who had never gone to Harvard, never spent a day in any college."

"Do you wish you'd gone to college?"

"No, but you're like the rest of them. You think it's only possible to think if you've been properly trained. But I trained myself. I read everything. The classics, history, literature, politics. I didn't need professors like yourself telling me what to do."

"When did I ever tell you what to do?" It's a rhetorical question, and he ignores me.

"Gore!" says Galbraith, waiting for us, an absurdly tall man with thick white hair, a baritone voice. He exudes professorial gravitas. "You're lecturing tonight. I can't make it. But my emissaries will take notes. Break a leg."

Gore frowns. David Herbert Donald, the most genial man in the world, comes into view, smiling. He welcomes us warmly. Gore seems in heaven in the oak-paneled dining room.

"Gore is talking about the movies tonight," says Donald to Galbraith. "His own experience of the movies. Is that right, Gore?"

"It's the history of my times. And your times, Ken."

Galbraith says, "We miss you around here."

"Miss me? I'm here."

"You live in Italy. You ran away from home, lit out for the territory."

"So did you. Aren't you a Canadian?"

As ever, Gore has done his homework. And remembers it.

"Gore is our national historian—among novelists," says Donald.

"I've read one or two of your novels," says Galbraith. "It's the essays that interest me."

I wonder if Gore is going to like his time at Harvard. Somehow I don't think so.

Chapter Twelve

Every time a friend succeeds, something in me dies.

—Gore Vidal

1. Rethinking Washington

In 1996, Gore hosted a three-part series on British television called *Gore Vidal's American Presidency*, treating the fortunes and misfortunes of White House occupants from George Washington to Bill Clinton. "I saw very little to admire in most of them," he recalled, although he found James K. Polk "surprisingly intelligent if low-key." In the past century, he saw the modern Oval Office as a stage set, where the president broadcasts on behalf of corporate constituents. "Mostly, the president's backers get what they paid for," Gore said.

Yet Gore regarded Washington, D.C., as home, and he often drifted back to Rock Creek Park in memory. He now conceived a short novel set in the Smithsonian—a fantastic romp through history with T., a thirteen-year-old boy who encounters a group of nuclear scientists in the basement of this fabled museum. The recursive effects of time travel would allow him, as in *Live from Golgotha*, to go back into history, encountering figures such as Abraham Lincoln, Charles Lindbergh, Grover Cleveland, and Eleanor Roosevelt. He had made notes toward writing this novel in 1996, and went full bore on the project the following winter in Los Angeles, finishing a draft in the spring of 1997 in Ravello.

As usual, he took on review assignments that interested him. In the fall of 1997 he reflected at length in *The New Yorker* on *The Dark Side of Camelot* by Seymour M. Hersh—an explosive study of John Kennedy. Hersh saw JFK as a reckless man whose behavior nearly destroyed his presidency. Hersh was a relentless investigator and had done his homework. Gore writes:

> For some reason, Hersh's "revelations" are offensive to many journalists, most of whom are quick to assure us that although there is absolutely nothing new in the book (what a lot they've kept to themselves!), Hersh has "proved" nothing. Of course there is really no way for anyone ever to prove much of anything, short of having confessions from participants, like the four Secret Service men who told Hersh about getting girls in and out of Jack's bed. But when confronted by these smoking guns the monkeys clap their hands over their eyes and ears and chatter, "Foul allegations by soreheads."

He concludes: "In retrospect, it has always been incredible that someone as thoroughly disreputable as Joe Kennedy should have been allowed to buy his sons major political careers."

Gore never lost the itch for public office, and still dreamed, however unrealistically, of running again. He did make it into Congress in the movies, playing a tiny role as Congressman Page in *Shadow Conspiracy* (1997), a political thriller that starred Charlie Sheen, Donald Sutherland, and Sam Waterston (Gore's TV Lincoln). "It was among the worst films ever shot on celluloid, almost in a class with *Myra Breckinridge*," said Gore. Made for more than $40 million, it grossed just over $2 million. "For that money, I could have got into Congress." He also acted in *Gattaca* (1997), playing the head of a space program in this excellent sci-fi film written and directed by Andrew Niccol. This was Gore's best performance on film, but these tiny acting jobs were amusements, a way of coming up out of a different hole every time, keeping his enemies off guard and his brand in mass circulation.

His serious journalism attracted a literate audience, as before, as when he published "Shredding the Bill of Rights" in *Vanity Fair* in

November 1988. It opens with one of Gore's drollest lines: "Most Americans of a certain age can recall exactly where they were and what they were doing on October 20, 1964, when word came that Herbert Hoover had died." The piece runs through recent abridgments of American freedoms, ending with a note on Timothy McVeigh, the terrorist who bombed the Alfred P. Murrah Federal Building in Oklahoma City. Gore makes a genuine attempt to understand McVeigh's criminal madness, although he says pointedly: "Nothing could justify the murder of those 168 men, women, and children, none of whom had, as far as we know, anything at all to do with the federal slaughter at Waco, the ostensible reason for McVeigh's fury." McVeigh inevitably read Gore's piece and wrote seductively from prison. And Gore was intrigued. Although he condemned the murder of innocents, he regarded McVeigh as a kind of existential hero. (One recalls that Norman Mailer made the same mistake in 1981 with a murderer called Jack Henry Abbott, who, when extricated from prison with the help of Mailer and others, killed someone else almost immediately.)

In due course Gore somehow became convinced that McVeigh didn't actually participate in the bombing. Responding to Gore's sympathy, McVeigh invited him to witness his execution in Terre Haute. Still intrigued by this deluded young man, Gore agreed to do so, but the date of the execution shifted and he didn't go. "I wish I had been there," Gore said, "I don't know why. It was a curious thing." To him, McVeigh was another Billy the Kid, an outlaw who acted in violent and lawless ways yet wasn't, at heart, a bad fellow. Gore had certainly been seduced by the tone of McVeigh's letters, which were surprisingly intimate, as when he wrote to chide Gore about his preoccupation with getting old. "Not to worry," McVeigh wrote, "recent medical studies tell us that Italy's taste for canola oil, olive oil and wine helps extend the average lifespan and helps prevent heart disease in Italians—so you picked the right place to retire to."

In his post-execution piece on McVeigh in *Vanity Fair*, Gore quotes excerpts from these letters, explaining that McVeigh had been outraged by the siege of Waco, Texas, where federal authorities (responding to reports of child abuse) raided a religious community and killed more than eighty members of a cult known as the Branch Davidians. Members of this eccentric Christian group were burned to death with their leader, David Koresh. At this time, McVeigh denied knowing there were children in the Murrah Federal Building—as if this mitigated his crime. "Bombing the Murrah federal building," McVeigh told Gore, "was morally and strategically equivalent to the US hitting a government building in Serbia, Iraq, or other nations."

Gore's thinking about McVeigh anticipates later misjudgments that would cause many to dismiss him as some kind of crank. Even Howard found Gore's obsession with McVeigh a bit extreme and possibly dangerous for his reputation, but Gore dug in his heels. In mid-August 2001, for example, he gave a speech at the Edinburgh Festival where he called McVeigh "a Kipling hero, a boy with an overdeveloped sense of justice." The audience hissed loudly, but Gore overrode them, even comparing McVeigh to John Brown, the fiery abolitionist who was captured in a raid at Harpers Ferry, West Virginia, in 1859. The most embarrassing moment came when, onstage, Gore declared: "I am about to drop another shoe. I have been working with a researcher who knows at least five of the people involved in the making of the bomb and its detonation. It may well be that McVeigh did not do it. In fact, I am sure he didn't do it. But when he found out he was going to be the patsy, he did something psychologically very strange. He decided to grab all credit for it himself, because he had no fear of death."

II. Dreams of Wholeness

Gore was also upset by the impeachment proceedings against President Clinton. Charged with perjury and obstruction of justice, the president was officially impeached by the House of Representatives on December 19, 1998, although the Senate overturned both charges on February 12, 1999. During this period, Gore gave a blistering talk at the Woodrow Wilson International Center for Scholars in Washington. Michael Lind recalled that occasion, as Gore wandered off script in an obvious state of rage:

I found myself as uncomfortable as the other members of the auditorium audience, when, during his speech, Vidal launched into what sounded like a defense of Timothy McVeigh, the far-right would-be revolutionary whose bombing of the Murrah Federal Building in Oklahoma City in 1995 was the most devastating terrorist attack on American soil before the al-Qaida attacks on Sept. 11, 2001. While not exactly condoning McVeigh, Vidal told us that a violent reaction was inevitable, given the way that the federal government was oppressing American farmers.

I could sense that others in the audience shared my disquiet. The farmers? What the hell is he talking about? As his speech degenerated into a tirade, his accent changed from mid-Atlantic to a distinctive upcountry Southern twang. Before our eyes the polished, patrician public intellectual metamorphosed into a ranting backwoods populist politician.

The Smithsonian Institution appeared soon after. The book was, Gore noted, "a story that kept pulsing in my head, a novel about a boy lost in the fun house of a museum, who needs desperately to change the course of events." The central character in his twenty-third novel is T., a thirteen-year-old who resembles Jimmie Trimble as well as Gore at that age. T. (like Gore and Jimmie) is a student at St. Albans when the story opens on Good Friday in 1939. The plot thickens as T. discovers that World War II is coming, realizing with a shudder that either he or his clone at St. Albans will perish in that war, much as Jimmie Trimble did at Iwo Jima on March 1, 1945. This larky fiction is set at the venerable institution that lends its title to the book. Gore knew the Smithsonian Castle well, with its "dark dried-blood crenelated towers and wide moat." He had wandered among its waxwork exhibits as a boy, much like his hero, a young genius who heeds the call to adventure, immersing himself in the various worlds of these historical figures. T. encounters an Iroquois tribe; Lindbergh's airplane, *Spirit of St. Louis*; a number of well-known nuclear scientists; and, of course, assorted presidents of the United States, such as Grover Cleveland (whose young wife is captured by the Iroquois tribe here). Lincoln presides over the waxworks in the basement, and—in a superbly comic turn—happens to be reading Carl Sandburg's sentimental, six-volume biography. Alas, this Lincoln is not himself, or he would be reading *Lincoln* by Gore Vidal. (The bullet from the gun of John Wilkes Booth has turned Lincoln into a ghoulish halfwit.)

T. spins through time, covering many bases, as when he loses his virginity with an Iroquois squaw (who in the intersecting realities of this fictional simulacrum turns out to be Mrs. Cleveland). "Like most teenage mathematical geniuses," writes Gore, "T. had read the dirty part of a lot of forbidden books and now he understood the cataclysmic nature of what he had done with the white squaw." Needless to say, none of this is politically correct or especially tasteful. The novel blends veiled counter-autobiography with sci-fi fantasy, creating a fairly light but entertaining mélange of genres. Gore had been here before, of course, mixing time zones and realities, as in *Kalki* and *Live from Golgotha*. Yet the radical edge of satire is missing here. The impetus of the novel was Gore's longing for T., his lost "other half," and this endows the narrative with an almost tender feeling.

The novel's multilayered story unfolds over a bizarre weekend, moving from Good Friday to Easter Sunday, and it duly ends with a kind of resurrection. But it's not a happy Sunday as James Smithson (the British scientist who left his money to a nephew who founded the museum that bears his name) talks with T. near the end, fielding the boy's worried question about what comes next in history. "The human race will kill itself. That goes without saying. The virus—us—will kill our host the earth, or at least make it uninhabitable for us." These dire echoes of *Kalki* coincide with Gore's previous visions of destruction—a consistent motif in his work for many decades. But it's a game, at least in this tale, as Smithson reminds the suddenly not-so-innocent boy.

The Smithsonian Institution completes Gore's cycle of fantastic novels or "inventions," as he called them; it does so gently, without the savage quality that permeates his better novels in this vein, such as *Messiah*, *Myra Breckenridge*, or *Kalki*. On the whole, the reviewers were kind; they scratched their heads and nodded, seeing this as a form of light entertainment. "It didn't sell much," said Gore, "but nobody expected it to sell. It spun off from *Palimpsest*, I think: I thought about my early days in Washington, at St. Albans, and my lifelong run through history. I was bringing so many aspects of my life together here, wondering if I could rewrite the past, redo it, fix it. But you can't. I couldn't."

III. Elder Statesman

Enjoying the role of elder statesman, Gore offered regular "State of the Union" addresses to audiences from the National Press Club in Washington to college campuses—mostly in California. He was a frequent guest on talk shows, although it upset him that none had the broad reach of programs from earlier decades. He missed Johnny Carson, in particular. "I could never find the right venue," he recalled. "The television culture had changed, with a younger and even more ignorant audience, and my sort of commentary didn't play. You couldn't even trust the hosts anymore. Even the morning shows turned away from guests with serious opinions."

His preferred format for appearances in his last decades was that of the interview, where an interlocutor would ask him questions. I performed this role numerous times—at the 92nd Street Y or other venues in New York, at the Key West Literary Seminar, at the Writers Block in Los Angeles, on various stages in Salzburg, London, Rome, and Naples. Gore was a natural improviser, a ham with perfect timing. My job was to lob softballs for him to knock out of the park. He liked to riff on familiar topics, such as the metastatic growth of the American empire since Teddy Roosevelt, the spread of the national security state after World War II, the erosion of the Bill of Rights, the need to decriminalize drugs, or the various insults to good sense by such presidents as Reagan and—in later years—George W. Bush. He did his usual pitch-perfect impressions of Eisenhower, Nixon, and Reagan.

His command of history was obvious, but when challenged by someone in the audience, he could reply with deadly ferocity or sarcasm. Often, when asked about the future of the nation, he responded with a world-weary nod of the head, as at the Writers Guild Theater in Beverly Hills on March 19, 1998, when he declared: "The system has worn out. I don't know what's next. They keep trying to persuade us that if we get a nice man for president, all will be well. But we don't have nice corporations." When asked about the American political system, he said, in typical fashion: "Everyone knows it's a con game. We have only the one party." Someone asked him about attacks on American interests around the world and our need to defend ourselves. He waved a dismissive hand: "You can't go on treating people like dirt and not get kicked in the face with it sometimes."

As the millennium drew to a close, Gore wrote a major essay for *The New York Review of Books*, based on a 1995 lecture he had given in Oxford for Amnesty International. In that piece, he reflected on the ideas of Giambattista Vico, the eighteenth-century philosopher and political theorist who opposed all manner of reductionist thought, arguing famously that truth is something made, not found—a precursor of what is often referred to as constructivist epistemology. Vico predicted an age of chaos, to be followed by a new theocratic age. This gloomy forecast appealed to Gore, who argued that "as the curtain falls on our dismal century and ungraspable millennium," everywhere one could see "signs of religious revival." Once again, his thoughts proved oddly prescient.

IV. Reviewing the Life

At seventy-three, Gore had already lived a long life, moving from the passionate young man who stepped onto the national stage with a novel about the war, followed soon by one of the first mainstream novels on a gay theme. He dug into history and religion, struggling to define himself as he shifted into work for Hollywood and Broadway, often with eye-popping success. He turned overtly political as the sixties approached, running for office, writing *The Best Man*, becoming an essayist who fearlessly addressed political and social themes, a talking head on popular American and British talk shows, a gadfly at times, an American dissident. Then he returned to the novel, reaching back to the ancient world in *Julian* and *Creation*, extending his Narratives of Empire to six novels, with a seventh on the way. In the meantime, he wrote anarchic satires of American life, from *Myra*

Breckinridge to *The Smithsonian Institution*—half a dozen novels that challenged the French *nouveau roman* as well as the American postmodernists for inventiveness, drawing on a range of genres, from the sci-fi thriller to the dystopian novel, often with a comic edge that was purely and potently Vidal: arch, droll, and anarchic.

Yet he had evaded serious attention from critics, with only a few monographs focused on his work. He was more a creature of publicity than literature—much to his annoyance. "The academy turned away from him," said Richard Poirier, "probably because he was too popular. But he invited dismissal. His TV appearances didn't help much. Hollywood charmed him, and he charmed them. His subjects or narrative strategies didn't accord with the kinds of fiction that proved interesting to scholars or critics in the sixties and seventies, and so he never found a place on the syllabus."

Critics had an opportunity to weigh in about Gore when, in 1999, Fred Kaplan published *The Essential Gore Vidal*, collecting many of his major essays as well as examples of his fiction. The problem was, of course, that most of this work—the essays in particular—were easily available in *United States*. The compendium reprinted large sections from the Narratives of Empire, especially *Burr* and *Lincoln. The Best Man* and *Myra Breckinridge* appear in full. There is almost nothing from the early Vidal except for a passage from *The City and the Pillar. Messiah*—surely one of Gore's best early efforts—is missing entirely. It's a curious publication altogether, and—as reviewers noticed—readers could easily acquire most of Vidal's best work elsewhere.

Kaplan's life of Vidal appeared at more or less the same time, allowing for a reconsideration of Gore's career. As it were, Gore had pushed hard for this book, hoping to control his legacy in whatever ways he could. He had labored mightily to imprint the story of his life in the public mind, writing countless autobiographical asides in essays over five decades. He had recently published *Palimpsest*, his own lengthy record of the first thirty-nine years. And he had probably given more interviews to date than any author in the history of literature. A question arose on the lips of reviewers now: How did one compete with Gore himself in describing his life?

As it inevitably would, the biography infuriated Gore. Kaplan had delicately peeked through the veil of his sexuality. (Tim Teeman—an American-based British journalist—would rent the veil completely in 2013 with *In Bed with Gore Vidal*, a lively account of Gore's sex life, where even the size and shape of the Vidalian penis gets some attention.) Kaplan avoided probing deeply into Gore's sexual habits, but he revealed with patient genealogical research that this writer was not, as the public imagined, a blue-blood aristocrat but the son of a young man from South Dakota who had, by his athletic prowess, managed to get into West Point. Eugene Vidal had moved into the great world of Washington society by marrying the daughter of a U.S. senator. Yet this politician wasn't a Roosevelt but a country lawyer from Webster County in Mississippi, a man who by grit and determination had found a perch in the Senate. Kaplan also revealed that Gore was not—as he often implied in conversation—a Kennedy insider but merely an onlooker. Nevertheless, Kaplan marveled at Gore's energy, his brilliance and composure, his capacity for self-invention.

"Gore hated the book," said Howard, "and threw it across the room. I never saw him like this before. He didn't like mirrors." Gore disputed nearly every fact about his family that Kaplan had unearthed, and loathed all references to his prodigious eating and drinking, his bloating waistline, the sense that his career had somehow faded. In repeated interviews he referred to "this dread biography which I've never read." Yet Kaplan was a well-disposed and intelligent critic, and his book has a candidness that annoyed Gore but spoke well for Kaplan, who had plunged through the thicket of Gore's unruly handwriting in the archives in Wisconsin (now at Harvard) and interviewed many figures of importance in Gore's life. Nevertheless, reviewers found the biography lacking in narrative momentum and without an overarching theme; the caustic reviews by Richard Davenport-Hines in *The Times Literary Supplement* and James Wolcott in the *London Review of Books* confirmed Gore's sense that he had chosen the wrong biographer.

v. *The Golden Age*

Throughout 1999, Gore worked steadily on *The Golden Age*, the concluding novel in his Narratives of Empire. He kept to his usual routine, moving back and forth between Ravello and Los Angeles, with trips to New York and, for diet and relaxation, to La Costa. When he wasn't writing or socializing or flying over vast territories, he was reading. "I rarely went to bed without a good book," Gore said, and now he was rereading *Doctor Faustus*, Thomas Mann's retelling of the Faust legend in Germany in the decades before World War II, and *The Golden Spur* by Dawn Powell, a novel set in bohemian New York during the period when Gore and Powell moved in similar circles there.

Appearing at the Writers Bloc in Los Angeles on November 14, 1999, he spoke at length about the upcoming presidential election and, with unerring salesmanship, set the stage for his new novel. Insisting that FDR badly wanted to involve America in the war against Germany and Japan, he claimed that eight out of ten Americans in 1940 opposed intervention, forcing Roosevelt to manufacture their consent by whatever means he could. He noted that his novel would "deal with this subject at length." Asked by a member of the audience where he got his inspiration, he replied, "I have an exaggerated sense of injustice."

In mid-August 2000, the Democratic Party held its convention at the Staples Center in Los Angeles, and Gore liked being near the fun, especially since Al Gore would probably win the nomination. Although the two were not closely related, Gore enjoyed claiming kinship and often referred to him as "cousin Al." The irrepressible Arianna Huffington, among others, organized a shadow convention at Patriot Hall, not far from the main affair. She invited Gore and Christopher Hitchens to respond to President Clinton's convention address. "But a funny thing happened on the way to the fair," recalled William Bradley, who also helped to organize the event. "We got shut down by the Los Angeles Police Department on a bomb threat." Gore calmed nerves by recalling the Chicago riots in 1968, where he had debated Buckley on national television while chaos erupted on the streets. These very mild protests (and fake bomb threats) in Los Angeles were, by contrast, laughable.

The Golden Age appeared the following month. It was a palimpsest itself, a novel with another novel, *Washington, D.C.*, lying beneath it, barely legible, its plot occasionally poking through the new narrative surfaces. The novel covers roughly the same period, beginning in 1939, when Americans wondered if the country would soon join the fight against Hitler. Of course Roosevelt, with his "amoral mastery of world politics and his ability to get what he wanted," would use this crisis to guarantee an unprecedented third term for himself. Caroline Sanford—by now well-developed in both *Empire* and *Hollywood*—pushes to the forefront of the story, working the levers of power. Her nephew, Peter Sanford (who often looks and speaks like Gore), shares the influence wielded by Aunt Caroline as he works both coasts with skill, even founding a magazine, *The American Idea*—meant as an antidote to the corrupt press. Blaise Sanford, James Burden Day, and Clay Overbury reappear—figures from the earlier novel, and we meet a number of new people, such as Harry Hopkins, FDR's right-hand man. But overlaps and echoes from *Washington, D.C.* confuse the narrative, and coherence evaporates in episodes where the author himself, Gore Vidal, appears in Ravello in conversation with Peter Sanford. It's as if Gore simply had to meet his stand-in personally, in fictional time and space (with a touch of metafictional riffing). In *Washington, D.C.*, Clay was obviously meant as a JFK figure; now, in *The Golden Age*, we get both of them, creating a tug-of-war between fact and fiction.

The novel has very little in the way of story. The fictional superstructure mainly opens a space where Gore can debate the pros and cons of America entering the war. In its last chapter, Aaron Burr Decker stands in for the reader, wondering why both Sanford and his double, Vidal, feel so passionate about the attack on Pearl Harbor. He refers to *Day of Deceit* by the historian Robert B. Stinnett, a book that had fired Gore's imagination. Indeed, Gore adopted Stinnett's view wholesale, believing that FDR had known in advance about Pearl Harbor but chose to do nothing to stop it because he wanted to push the United States into the war. Peter says testily about Roosevelt: "He did what no president has ever done. Set us up. To be attacked."

Decker says, "But didn't it all end well? We won the war. We got the world. We saved as many of Hitler's victims as we could. So some old ships got sunk." "Some three thousand men got sunk, too," replies Sanford. "And died."

The novel ends, as do most historical novels by Gore, with a moment of wan rhapsody, a cynical withdrawal from mere human history:

> As for the human case, the generations of men come and go and are in eternity no more than bacteria upon a luminous slide, and the fall of a republic or the rise of an empire—so significant to those involved—is not detectable upon the slide even were there an interested eye to behold the steadily proliferating species which would either end in time or, with luck, become something else, since change is the nature of life, and its hope.

Few readers or critics considered *The Golden Age* one of Gore's better efforts in fiction. Gore liked to compare himself with Aldous Huxley as a novelist of ideas, but this is a novel of lectures whose title gives away the game. As noted, "the golden age" as a phrase became Gore's mantra for various things, most of them joyful: the golden age of television or Hollywood, for instance. But in this novel irony gives way to cynicism, and all gold seems more like tarnished silver as Gore reflects on American imperial overreaching in the aftermath of World War II. The transmogrification from republic to empire, traced in the course of the Narratives of Empire, needed a final statement, and Gore provided one. And despite an exceptionally thin plot, the novel has moments of high comedy and serious reflection. Peter Kemp, a shrewd English critic, called Gore a "modern-day Suetonius" who observed the wickedness and pettiness of those in power with a cool eye. In a vast, intelligent, persuasive review of the entire sequence of American historical novels, Zachary Leader in the *London Review of Books* offered a judicious assessment, recognizing the "enormous task" that Gore had set for himself in these books, though he often missed the mark.

The reviews of *The Golden Age* were generally negative, and this upset Gore, who had expected plaudits for this capstone of his career—as he saw it. He wrote to Thomas Mallon: "I have a hunch that my books must look to be written in some strange code for reviewers who have no notion that there is a USA with an interesting history that never ceases to bear down on us and so, in order to explain the increasing lumbago, we blame it on Mrs. Portnoy." (He refers, of course, to Philip Roth's novel *Portnoy's Complaint*.) "I don't mind that our literary people know nothing, but I do mind that they don't want to know anything."

So how should one judge the Narratives of Empire? The series is focused almost exclusively on life at the top, on those who rule the United States from Washington, New York, or Hollywood. The limitations of such an approach are obvious, and Gore offers a narrow lens through which the reader must view American history. Yet his easy knowledge of the periods at hand give them an authenticity and presence, and his familiarity with the governing classes is entertaining as well as revelatory in its way. "Gore liked, understood, and respected power," says Matt Tyrnauer. "He liked watching people with power, too." Gore also noticed the self-destructive tendencies of such people, grinning as they climbed the greasy pole and stepped on the heads of those beneath them. His disappointment in the loss of our early republic, with its lofty aspirations and Enlightenment values, is palpable throughout. Of course he tends to lecture readers rather than embody an argument, but this was the kind of fiction he himself enjoyed. In any case, he took pleasure in writing these novels, and—in *Burr* and *Lincoln*—hit his stride, working at the top of his form and re-creating the biographical novel as a genre. It's a pity the final installment was, indeed, a rather tepid performance.

VI. Still the Best Man

As the presidential campaigns kicked into high gear in 1999, Gore was approached by Jeffrey Richards, a young American producer, who came to Ravello to talk about reviving *The Best Man*. Gore liked it that Richards understood how political conventions had lost their unpredictability, becoming stage-managed coronations. No attempt was made to update the script. Apart from a few voice-over recordings by Walter Cronkite, the play went on as before, now a period piece with a sturdy cast that included Chris Noth, Charles Durning, Elizabeth Ashley, and Spalding Gray. It was retitled *Gore Vidal's The Best Man*, in case anyone walking along Broadway might wonder about the name of the playwright.

In the early summer of 1999, Howard began feeling sick, coughing more than usual and complaining of headaches and back pain. An extensive rash spread from his neck to his right cheek, and he seemed confused at times. Gore decided that Howard was drinking too much, insisting that he stick to beer, which he believed was less toxic than whiskey or gin. "I knew things were going downhill," said Gore, "but how quickly, I couldn't guess."

In years past Gore had declined invitations to join the American Academy of Arts and Letters. Joining such an establishment group had seemed ridiculous to him, even though he paradoxically sought academic and cultural affirmation. "I don't want to prance about with professors and academic writers," he would often say, disingenuously. But his much-admired friend Louis Auchincloss urged him to relent, and in 1999 he did, flying to New York for the installation.

On this visit to New York, Gore met Gerald Howard, his new editor at Doubleday, the baton having been passed once again. (And Doubleday was still part of the Random House family.) A new agent, Lynn Nesbit, had taken over from Owen Laster, but she soon passed her fractious client along to Richard Morris, who lavished professional and personal attention on Gore in his later years in comforting ways. "The last of my U.S. chronicles [*The Golden Age*] goes to Doubleday," he had written to Mallon, "with Gerald Howard as editor. He has actually read me over the years." He added a characteristically sour note about Laster, saying he "gave up agenting for social climbing long ago." He tells Mallon that he has begun to notice how "in this golden age of the historical novel—my re-invention in the twentieth century—I am never mentioned." It was, indeed, a constant refrain now that nobody understood his contribution to the genre of historical fiction.

Gore and Howard stayed at the Plaza, and Gore drank more than usual after the installation dinner at the American Academy. At a late breakfast the next day he told me that Howard had been poisoned by the food the night before: "I never thought they'd sink *that* low." Howard was indeed yellow the next day, and he complained about blurring vision and abdominal cramps while Gore kept insisting it had been the food the night before. "The salmon was a month old!" he shouted. In Los Angeles a few days later, Howard (having been properly examined by doctors) underwent an operation for appendicitis. As Gore later said, "Howard's abdominal cavity was awash with poison." Howard improved at once, much to Gore's relief, and they flew back to Italy for the start of the new millennium.

They had a few good months, with the spring of 2000 being their last happy time in Ravello. Gore assembled his latest crop of essays, which would appear in 2001 as *The Last Empire*. But in May it seemed that Howard's coughing had become more than simply a tiresome symptom of smoking since the age of twelve. On a visit to Los Angeles in late June, a lung X-ray revealed a significant tumor, and the surgeon explained to Gore that because Howard's lungs had been weakened by decades of smoking, an operation might be dangerous. But Gore, ever imperious, insisted on surgery and Howard acquiesced. Gore later wrote: "As the nurse opened the door to the operating room where I could not follow, Howard turned to me in his wheelchair and said, 'Well, it's been great.' Then the door closed behind him." He waited for more than three hours, or so he imagined, for news of Howard. It was, he eventually learned, a successful operation, and the doctors told Howard that his lungs were cancer free, at least for the time being.

Back in Ravello, life continued much as before, with Gore writing in the mornings. In the afternoons, he answered mail or read books for review or research. Interviewers would visit, and he didn't mind: It meant that the Great Eraser would have to work harder to catch up. He no longer walked into Amalfi—his arthritic knees hurt too much for that—but he still swam in the pool on sunny days. He and Howard went to the San Domingo in the evenings, where they met local friends, dining at one of the nearby restaurants. They rarely made it home sober, stumbling along the narrow path to the villa. Gore often leaned on Howard for support; somehow Howard, a square-built man with sturdy legs, held him up. Once, as Gore told me, they tumbled into a bed of flowers and woke up several hours later, covered in insect bites.

Unpleasant feelings about the response to *The Golden Age* continued to frazzle Gore. Critics had considered his ideas about FDR and Pearl Harbor conspiratorial, and he found this infuriating. He picked a fight on the subject with Ian Buruma—a well-known Dutch historian and fellow contributor to *The New York Review of Books*. In an exchange in the magazine, Gore pointed out that in 1948 Charles A. Beard had written *President Roosevelt and the Coming of the War*, arguing that Roosevelt had provoked Japan into the war. Buruma strenuously objected. But the facts do present a challenge for historians who think Roosevelt was genuinely surprised by the attack on Pearl Harbor. Gore noted some obvious points: Why had we anchored more than seventy ships in such an obviously vulnerable area, especially since American intelligence had broken the Japanese code? We knew about Japan's warlike intentions, even if we didn't know what the exact place and time of the first attack would be. Of course it's possible that intelligence mistakes and miscalculations about Japan's intentions led Roosevelt to assume—at the least—that any attack lay in the future, thus allowing time to make adjustments in U.S. defense positions.

Gore harped on the subject, arguing again in *The Times Literary Supplement* on December 1, 2000, this time in response to a provocation by Clive James, that Roosevelt knew the attack was coming. He noted that American intelligence had cracked not only the Japanese diplomatic but also the military codes, and that General George Marshall, the U.S. Army Chief of Staff, had called a meeting with journalists just three weeks prior to Pearl Harbor, informing them frankly that "war with Japan would start sometime during the first ten days of December." Only a few days later, Secretary of State Cordell Hull presented a ten-point proposal to the Japanese, demanding complete Japanese withdrawal from China and Indochina. They were also asked to support the Nationalist government in China and, indeed, cancel their agreement with the Axis powers. "FDR had dropped a shoe," says Gore. "Now he waited for the Japanese to drop the other. They did."

When *The Last Empire*—effectively Gore's last major collection of essays—appeared in the spring of 2001, the book was largely ignored by the mainstream press. "It was like the early days again," he said, "without a review in the daily *Times*, although the Sunday paper attacked." Paul Berman, a neoconservative critic, was perhaps not the ideal reviewer for this volume of provocative essays, many of which revealed an old man with many axes to grind. Berman writes:

> Having scrutinized all these essays—on literature, American history and politics, in nearly equal portions—I have come to know Vidal's manias, and to fear them. Apart from the horribleness of Lincoln (which is owing to Lincoln's dictatorial behavior in the Civil War, which ruined America forever), they are, in no particular order, the perfidy of Franklin Roosevelt in regard to Pearl Harbor, the income tax and Harry Truman's decision on Feb. 27, 1947, to put up a fight against the Soviet Union, thus replacing America's republican traditions with a sinister American empire.

This review caricatures the style and substance of Gore's writing. In fact Gore never touted the "horribleness of Lincoln." He did, to be sure, question Lincoln's obsession with holding the Union together and doubted the depths of his abolitionist feelings. In the opening essay of *The Last Empire*, a review of Edmund Wilson's journals, Gore approves of Wilson's reading of the pre–Civil War Lincoln: "Wilson questioned the central myth of the American republic, which is also, paradoxically, the cornerstone of our subsequent empire—*e pluribus unum*—the ever tightening control from the center to the periphery." Gore could easily envision a less perfect union, less centralized and centralizing. On this and other topics, he called received American opinion into question.

The Last Empire contains a few exemplary samples of Gore as literary critic, as in "Dawn Powell: Queen of the Golden Age," a revisiting of an earlier interest in this still-neglected writer. He writes: "It was Dawn Powell's fate to be a dinosaur shortly after the comet, or whatever it was, struck our culture, killing off the literary culture—a process still at work but no less inexorable." Even better is the lengthy reexamination of Sinclair Lewis, a novelist who put his mark on American culture with such popular novels as *Main Street*, *Babbitt*, *Dodsworth*, and *Arrowsmith*. Gore observes wryly that this once-celebrated author "seems to have dropped out of what remains of world literature." He puts the blame for this neglect on Lewis's biographer, Mark Schorer, whose 867-page biography displayed a "serene loathing of his subject and all his works" that was nonetheless "impressive in its purity." Gore reminds us that after a miraculous decade of productivity, the 1920s, Lewis won the Nobel Prize in 1930: "That was the period when the Swedes singled out worthy if not particularly good writers for celebration, much as they now select worthy if not particularly interesting countries or languages for consolation." Looking at *Main Street* and *Babbitt*, he says, "There is a Balzacian force to the descriptions of people and places, firmly set in the everyday."

His devastating essay on Updike is a piece of masterly deconstruction, a corrective to received opinion, which held that Updike was a great stylist and, possibly, one of the most important writers of the postwar era. Gore considered Updike's meticulous and often poetic prose as mere "fancy writing," and he dismissed Updike as a writer too narrowly focused on domestic life in the American suburbs, one far too wedded to a limited patriotic view of history and politics to create major fiction. He attacks Updike's "blandness and acceptance of authority in any form." Updike's Christian faith also rubs Gore the wrong way, striking him as a passive form of piety.

Then comes a lengthy review of A. Scott Berg's life of Charles Lindbergh—ever a subject of fascination to Gore, who had indeed sympathized with the America First movement (led partly by Lindbergh) as a schoolboy at Exeter. As ever, there is a loudly rung autobiographical bell: "Towards the end, he had come to dislike the world that he had done so much to create. First, he noticed the standardization of air bases everywhere. The sameness of food, even landscape. The boredom of air travel in jet liners. The fun was gone." Gore ambles down memory lane, with the usual evocations of his grandfather and father, concluding that Lindbergh was probably "the best that we are ever apt to produce." Now this lane has become crowded with figures such as Franklin and Eleanor Roosevelt, with JFK and Clare Boothe Luce, all ghosts of Gore's past who rise again and again.

The last half of the collection fast-forwards to the present, with essays on Bill Clinton, Al Gore, Tony Blair, and others. Reframing an old idea, Gore calls for a "People's Convention," suggesting it was time that the American people gathered to revise the U.S. Constitution, overhauling it to correct mistakes and update language that had become stale and, in some cases, misleading. This is late Gore at his most radical: "If we so choose, the entire Constitution could be rewritten. At this point I part company with the American Civil Liberties Union, who, for once, are more pessimistic about the people than I. The first thing they will get rid of is the Bill of Rights, the liberals moan. On which the answer is, first, I don't think the people are suicidal and, second, what is the difference between losing those rights at an open convention as opposed to a gradual loss of them behind the closed doors of the current Supreme Court?" Other essays target familiar themes, often with a touch of barely controlled mania. In "Mickey Mouse, Historian," he attacks Arthur M. Schlesinger Jr.—a former ally who had, of course, devoted himself to the blessed memory of JFK in ways that rubbed Gore the wrong way. Schlesinger had recently criticized Gore's three half-hour programs on the American presidency, and that was the last straw. No enemy could go unchallenged for long. "Shredding the Bill of Rights" is stronger than many of the political essays here, a survey of the loss of American civil liberties, with an emphasis on the rise of the surveillance state.

As the uncertain presidency of George W. Bush began, Gore was in an awkward position: less relevant, with a dwindling audience and, indeed, much of his writing career behind him. Ill health, his own and Howard's, put obstacles before him that would be difficult to overcome, and his alcohol addiction didn't help. Could he continue to work at the same level? Could he regain the spotlight? Did anyone really care about his critique of the American empire and its bulwark, the national security state? These questions would soon be answered, in fact. The coming wars in Iraq and Afghanistan would give him a lot to write about, and the excesses of the USA Patriot Act, enacted in the wake of 9/11, would present fresh opportunities for a man whose rhetorical skills had been blunted by age and alcohol but not destroyed.

Songs in the Hollywood Hills

"Maestro," I say, kissing Gore on each cheek as I come into the room. He's sitting in state, on an expansive couch in the alcove off the dining room: an Oriental feel to this chamber, with draping curtains that Diana Phipps rigged up decades ago. It's a room fit for a sultan, and Gore seems very like one: wrinkled skin, wispy hair, fat belly, bossy as hell.

"Norberto! Drinks!"

Norberto rushes in with a glass of whiskey for Gore, a glass of Sancerre for me. He knows what everyone wants. I've never seen anyone so loyal and professional in this role of servant.

"I'll be dead soon," Gore says.

I can see no point in responding. It's true enough.

"It's not the drink that will kill me," he says. "I'm eighty-five. I never thought I'd get to sixty, but we're tough. My grandfather used to say about the Gores that we're indestructible. You can't drown us."

He doesn't sip, he gulps. It's suicidal drinking, and I feel sorry for him. He has been trying to end his life since Howard died in 2003, but he can't manage. It's hard to watch a companion die, and harder to live alone like this.

"Listen to something," he says, and puts on a tape of Howard singing old Frank Sinatra and Tony Bennett hits. "You never believed me, did you? He could have been a star."

"Two stars in one house? This would have been a very bright spot, visible from outer space."

"I did what I could to help his career along, but he was lazy. I was never lazy."

I agree that they will never say that about Gore Vidal.

"Sinatra was the greatest voice of our time," says Gore. "When Tommy Dorsey played the trombone, he could hold the note. Let a little air in through the side of his mouth, he would say. Sinatra did that with his voice. Howard understood that, and he could hold a note so long! Of course the smoking ruined it. It ruined everything. You need lungs for singing, and Howard needed lungs for smoke. In his heyday, he could hit a high note—the A-flat. Sinatra could do that, did it again and again. But with Howard, it fell away too quickly. He didn't practice. He gave up."

"You loved Howard," I say, "and you miss him."

Gore looks into his drink. "Listen," he says, after a few minutes. He plays Howard singing "Hello Young Lovers." He almost swoons. His eyes are watery. I have never before seen him cry, but he's crying now.

Chapter Thirteen

The four most beautiful words in our common language: I TOLD YOU SO.

—Gore Vidal

I. The Pamphleteer

After the 9/11 attacks in New York and Washington, Gore seemed more relevant than ever, a critic of American foreign policy whose opinions were sought by interviewers from around the world. His contrarian thinking offered a point of view that was seldom heard in the mainstream media. Gore told a British television interviewer, for instance: "The truth on 9/11 was that we had many enemies around the world, everywhere, but specifically in the Islamic world: partly due to our support of Israel, partly due to collision over changing ways, in places like Saudi Arabia—we support the royal family, the royal family is unpopular. So, as far as we know, Osama bin Laden decided to hit us—if it was he, it might have been someone else. Most of the people I respect think a government of some kind was involved, such as Pakistan." He added: "What surprised me was the extraordinary technical brilliance of what they did. Not just coordinating the planes and all that—it was the timing: at the moment when our economy was beginning to go down." He believed that George W. Bush had used the attacks on New York and Washington as a pretext for striking Afghanistan and recalled that Bill Clinton had planned to go after bin Laden for some time. He asked, provocatively, if Bush knew in advance about the strike on the towers—a replay of his old obsession with FDR and Pearl Harbor. "Bush certainly had lots of evidence that something was afoot," he said.

Gore had often in the past referred to *Common Sense*, the pamphlet by Thomas Paine that had inspired the American Revolution. After 9/11, he began to write his own pamphlets, attracting a large audience. His pamphleteering began with a lengthy screed, "September 11, 2001," that was rejected by *Vanity Fair* as well as *The Nation*. The piece was too hot to handle in the immediate aftermath of a national tragedy. But an Italian publisher agreed to publish the essay as a pamphlet, in Italian. An immediate best seller there, it was soon translated into a dozen other languages. Soon Gore approached Thunder's Mouth Press/Nation Books about publishing a pamphlet in the United States, and in April 2002 they saw the opportunity, bringing out *Perpetual War for Perpetual Peace: How We Got to Be So Hated—Causes of Conflict in the Last Empire*.

Carl Bromley, the editor of Nation Books, recalls: "The supposedly liberal profession went into hiding after 9/11. But we saw an opportunity and rushed at the chance to do this. It included the original essay turned down here and there with a few older essays to highlight the themes. The response was immediate and enormous. We sold 120,000 copies in a short time. It was also very moving to see Gore addressing large crowds in New York and Washington, in Los Angeles: He would get a standing ovation when he came onstage. People cheered, screamed. He was filling a void, and doing so with such energy and style. This was before the Internet came into its own, and Gore's pamphlets in the couple of years after 9/11 played a role in the culture. This was the last gasp of the great tradition of the American political pamphlet. Gore was there in a crucial hour. It was very moving."

The key essay begins on a prophetic note: "According to the Koran, it was on a Tuesday that Allah created darkness. Last September 11 when suicide pilots were crashing commercial airliners into crowded American buildings, I did not have to look to the calendar to see what day it was; Dark Tuesday was casting its long shadow across Manhattan and along the Potomac River."

In full attack mode, Gore zeroes in: "The Bush administration, though eerily inept in all but its principal task, which is to exempt the rich from taxes, has casually torn up most of the treaties to which civilized nations subscribe—like the Kyoto Accords or the nuclear missile agreement with Russia." Now he raced through his arguments with lots of statistics. Much of the body of the essay concerns bin Laden and poses a reasonable question: Why would anyone with the background of bin Laden—a wealthy, devout Muslim—want to attack the American empire? Was it because of American connections to the Saudis? "War is the no-win all-lose option," Gore suggests, observing that Americans in particular were set to lose many of the liberties to which they have grown accustomed. He ended by quoting a great line from Charles A. Beard, the historian whom his grandfather had known: "Since V-J Day 1945 ('Victory over Japan' and the end of World War II), we have been engaged in what the historian Charles A. Beard called 'perpetual war for perpetual peace.' " He added: "I have occasionally referred to our 'enemy of the month club': each month we are confronted by a new horrendous enemy at whom we must strike before he destroys us."

Less than a year later, Gore published *Dreaming War: Blood for Oil and the Bush-Cheney Junta*, where he offered a shocking list of countries that America had struck over the years. Though it leaped onto the best-seller lists, it contains only two original pieces. The first is a retitled version of an article about 9/11 that appeared in *The Observer*, where he asks what really happened and why. "The unlovely Osama was chosen on aesthetic grounds to be the frightening logo for our long contemplated invasion and conquest of Afghanistan," he writes. He claims that we "still don't know by whom we were struck that Tuesday, or for what true purpose." Nevertheless, he notes that "9/11 put paid not only to our fragile Bill of Rights, but also to our once-envied republican system of government which had abruptly taken a mortal blow the previous year, when the Supreme Court did a little dance in 5-4 time and replaced an elected president with the oil-and-gas Cheney-Bush junta." This sounds paranoid to American ears, and yet Union Oil of California had actually proposed a pipeline from

Turkmenistan to Afghanistan to Pakistan that was scrapped because of Taliban resistance. As ever, Gore asks useful, if sometimes outlandish, questions. Like Noam Chomsky, who also produced a pamphlet on the meaning of 9/11, Gore was regarded as a conspiracy nut by many. Both men have been proven right over time, at least on Vietnam and Iraq. Yet there is a powerful urge in the American people to assume that their elected leaders have their best interests at heart: an idea that both Chomsky and Vidal have repeatedly mocked. "What Chomsky and I have in common," Gore writes, "is an interest in public matters and a fascination with the lies that power tells us, lies we deconstruct, lies which also fascinate—and affect—a number of our countrymen who do read seriously."

The establishment media struck at Gore as well as Chomsky. Louis Menand, at the time an English professor at City University of New York, reviewed both pamphlets in *The New Yorker*, noting a streak of anti-American sentiment in both. It seems clear that Gore's arch tone—that of a snobby know-it-all—didn't help his cause. And yet Gore had, as before, put his finger on something. The United States had been "hijacked" by a political group that would spend vast sums in Iraq alone, killing more than five thousand Americans and well over a hundred thousand Iraqis. They would create more than a million refugees, who would flood into and destabilize neighboring countries. Wounded veterans would in due course overwhelm Veterans Administration hospitals. Key American civil liberties would disappear, one by one, with mass surveillance becoming routine. Our reputation in the world would suffer. One could go on, and Gore did.

A third pamphlet, *Imperial America: Reflections on the United States of Amnesia*, appeared in 2004. As before, Gore would combine a couple of new pieces with older essays to fashion a marketable pamphlet. The first was a recent *Nation* piece: "State of the Union: 2004"—a rambling and unfocused lecture that nevertheless builds to a memorable conclusion: "We hate this system that we are trapped in, but we don't know who has trapped us or how. We don't even know what our cage looks like because we have never seen it from the outside." He wonders who will let us out of this cage, "with its socialism for the rich and free enterprise for the poor." As always, Gore excelled at the peroration, pulling together the strands of his narrative, revealing a pattern, striking an emotional chord that lingered.

He sought out live interviews when he could. One of the best of these occurred on June 4, 2004, on the nationally syndicated radio show *Democracy Now.* When the co-host, Amy Goodman, mentioned the name of the show, Gore jumped right in: "This is probably my first encounter in the United States with democracy, and I feel free." "Why use the word imperial?" she asked, alluding to the title of his new pamphlet. Gore smiled and said, "Because everyone hates it so much. And yet everyone uses it, so perhaps I'll have to think of something new." He was, as ever, scathing about the president. "Bush is like a kind of crazy kid in a dream," he said, "and he thinks he's invulnerable, and he's marching along through a dry forest, and he's lighting matches, setting fires. I always assumed he was a hypocrite, especially in religious matters. But it recently struck me that he may be another Reagan, and actually believe these things."

II. Finding Founding Fathers

Inventing a Nation: Washington, Adams, Jefferson had appeared in 2003, published by Yale University Press—a short study of three of the Founding Fathers. Its seven brief chapters are anecdotal, not quite professional history yet certainly not fiction. "The book had its genesis in a conversation I had with Jack Kennedy," Gore recalled. "I was sitting in Hyannis at the time of the Berlin Wall crisis, in 1961. Jack suddenly recalled what a miracle it was that this little backwater of a country produced three unqualified geniuses: Franklin, Hamilton, and Jefferson. 'Maybe it was something in the water,' he said. So there I was, fifty years later, writing a little book about my favorite Founders. I dropped Franklin and Hamilton for my own reasons." Whatever its genesis, the book displays a mastery of style, an impressive command of the material. It opens on a strong note: "In the fall of 1786 the fifty-four-year-old president of the Potomac Company, George Washington, late commander in chief of the American army (resigned December 23, 1783, after eight years of active duty) was seriously broke."

He has a wider target than Washington's personal finances, hoping to disrupt assumptions about the American republic and its origins. Among historians, the idea that the United States was created by a group of plutocrats to benefit people like themselves—landowners, people of property—has enjoyed a good deal of currency. Gore overturns this notion in subtle ways, finding a genuine idealism in those who met in Philadelphia in the hot summer of 1787 to construct a constitution from the gauzy tissue of Enlightenment values. As Gore says: "Washington knew that something would have to be done" about the Articles of Confederation, which seemed insufficient to a rapidly growing and independent nation. Gore sympathizes with the drive toward Federalism, toward a centralized government with considerable powers.

Yet the potential for despotism in this urge to consolidate power worried many of the Founding Fathers. This comes out in the informative second chapter, largely devoted to the convention, which neither John Adams nor Thomas Jefferson attended. Benjamin Franklin was there, the éminence grise who watched anxiously over the summer's proceedings in his hometown. His final remark on the U.S. Constitution struck Gore with the force of revelation: "I agree to this Constitution with all its faults, if they are such: because I think a General Government necessary for us, and there is no Form of Government but what may be a Blessing to the People if well-administered; and I believe farther that this is likely to be well administered for a Course of Years and can only end in Despotism as other Forms have done before it, when the People shall become so corrupted as to need Despotic Government, being incapable of any other." Two centuries later, Gore observes, "Franklin's blunt dark prophecy has come true." He alluded darkly to the Patriot Act and latter-day Federalists who had brought firm closure to the republic, in his view, saying that "not even Franklin could have foreseen today's never-ending corporate funded elections entirely devoid of actual politics, while we can only guess what Jefferson, during one of his periodic readjustments of the Constitution, would have done with the ultimate constitutional arbiter of our popular elections, the Electoral College, which consists not of the people but their rulers' surrogates." Indeed, Gore's warning was prophetic, as in 2010 when a sharply divided Supreme Court ruled in favor of nearly unlimited corporate political spending in its *Citizens United* decision.

Gore takes his readers on an entertaining tour of the Constitutional Convention of 1787, the two terms of the presidency of Washington, the anxious presidential leadership of Adams, and Jefferson's election, soon followed by the acquisition of vast western territories with the Louisiana Purchase. One gets a fine sense of what was at stake for the men in leadership positions: not only the three in the subtitle but also Franklin, Alexander Hamilton, James Madison, John Marshall, George Mason, John Jay, and others. Washington comes across as an admirable figure who balanced competing interests, never losing sight of the need to unify the fractious colonies. With his democratic (and high-minded intellectual) instincts, Jefferson appealed to Gore as well. Adams was seen as a man of rigorous morality, although he let Gore down by signing into law the Alien and Sedition Acts, a series of four bills created in the wake of the Quasi-War with France, which were passed on Bastille Day (July 14), declaring that citizens could be prosecuted for "printing, writing, or speaking in a scandalous or malicious way against the government of the United States." Needless to say, Gore associated the Alien and Sedition Acts with the USA Patriot Act of 2001.

He had always disliked Hamilton, whom he regarded as an upstart crow who "tended to go to the top of whatever tree confronted him." This ambitious and fawning young man stood up for business interests in the major northern cities, and as secretary of the Treasury under Washington had a hand in shaping policies (especially in the area of market economics) with large historical implications. "He was something of a professional orphan," Gore writes, a young man ever seeking father figures, even wishing for a king. Gore calls Hamilton "a born political theorist" who nevertheless "played little part in the great business at Philadelphia." In fact, Gore gets this wrong; Hamilton had pushed strongly for this convention, and his ideas were hugely influential on those present in Philadelphia. Moreover, he served on the committee that set forth convention rules and defended the proposed constitution mightily in *The Federalist Papers*, more than two-thirds of which were written by him.

As the historian Joseph J. Ellis says in a review that appeared in the *Los Angeles Times Book Review*, Gore's book contains a "boatload" of errors, as when he misidentifies the early "Republicans" as the forerunners of Lincoln's party, which didn't come into existence until the mid-1850s, or suggests that "the French fleet came to Washington's aid at Yorktown, and that was the end of that revolution." In fact, British forces had lost only a quarter of their strength at this time, and still outmanned the Continental Army. These errors, and others like them, might be considered simplifications. Gore refuses to qualify statements, as professional historians would feel compelled to do, and this creates problems. Yet one forgives Gore, as he gets so much right, making what actually did happen seem both interesting and useful as a backdrop to current American affairs in the wake of 9/11.

Overall, one gets a fine sense of the challenges facing the Founding Fathers as the American republic took shape. Gore admits that he "quarried much of the history" in this book from the nine volumes of Henry Adams's *History of the United States of America During the Administrations of Thomas Jefferson* and *History of the United States of America During the Administrations of James Madison*. But he drew on recent historians, too. His narrative generates the atmosphere of a genial conversation about history with a very knowledgeable person. Gore writes with the eye of a novelist for telling details, as when Washington arrives at home after having made a round of his farms: "When he got home, a servant noted that there were flecks of snow in his hair." Such moments enliven this story, which is indeed a story, and it's well told.

III. A Death Before Bedtime

In the early summer of 2001, Howard fell as he stepped from the pool in Ravello and hit his head on the travertine deck. Gore found him dazed and bleeding, and called for help. Four young men from the San Domingo rushed to the villa and carried Howard on a stretcher to a waiting car. With Gore at his side, Howard was driven to Salerno, an hour away, along a winding road overlooking the coast. At the hospital, Howard was moved into a ward with three others, all of them old men "without teeth, without resources other than some cousin with a plastic dish full of cold pasta." The godforsaken, run-down quality of the hospital belied the technical capabilities of the doctors, and within two days one of them pulled Gore aside to explain that a lesion had formed on Howard's brain. The lung tumor had obviously spread, and the diagnosis was grave.

Gore's first instinct was to get Howard back to Cedars-Sinai, the hospital in Los Angeles that he trusted. But the Italian doctor dismissed Gore's plan, explaining that the cabin pressure of an Atlantic crossing might exacerbate Howard's condition. "The doctor gestured madly, saying that Howard's brain would explode," Gore said. They hired a car to Rome, and there Howard was checked into the Villa Margherita, a respected private clinic, where further tests revealed the extent of the problem. Specialists recommended an immediate operation.

At one point Howard tried to get to the bathroom and slipped to the floor, bruising a knee. Gore dragged him to the bed, rupturing a disk in his own back. Howard looked at him searchingly. "Kiss me, Gore," he said. Gore kissed him on the lips, the first time that had happened in half a century. "I loved him," Gore said to me in 2010. "Of course I did."

The operation went forward, and Gore waited for hours in Howard's room above the operating theater, fearing the worst, yet he was startled when the naked body—only a light sheet covered him—was wheeled into the room. "Does he speak Italian?" the nurse asked. Gore assured her that Howard did, and she kept calling his name. At one point Howard opened his eyes, saw Gore, winked, then fell back into a deep sleep. In a few days he was up and walking in the hallway, asking for a cigarette—much to Gore's disgust, as he blamed the whole problem on Howard's chain-smoking. "I told him to stop," Gore said. "But he never listened to me."

Back home in Ravello, Howard seemed happy but confused, often rambling in conversation, not even quite sure what had happened to him. He could walk with a cane, and liked sitting in his bathrobe on the terrace off the main living room. Even with the splendid view below, he couldn't decide where he was, in Rome or Ravello. The Roman doctors had warned Gore about this, saying that Howard's situation was unpredictable; several lesions had not been removed from the brain and might create more problems of cognition. Soon Gore, with deep anxiety, decided he would take Howard back to Los Angeles, where better doctors could assess Howard's condition.

He hired a hospital plane at vast expanse, but cost didn't matter now. Gore had the money, and Howard's health was at stake. The small jet was cramped but outfitted for medical purposes. Howard lay like a corpse on a narrow bed, while Gore sat beside him and held his hand. Two nurses hovered, and a medic from Los Angeles kept checking the patient's vital signs. Howard seemed oblivious to the flight, although sometimes he smiled thinly at Gore, who patted him on the head like a child and called him Tinker, as in the old days. It was a zigzag journey, with a stop in the Azores, where Gore stretched his legs on the boiling tarmac. There were further stops in Iceland and Indianapolis for refueling—the flight took more than twenty hours.

At last Howard lay in the bedroom next to Gore's in the house on Outpost Drive in the Hollywood Hills. Within days, a series of radiation treatments had begun. The doctors, as Gore noted, exuded a kind of "euphoric good humor" that reminded him of American presidents, who radiate a "depersonalized charm." For relief, Gore turned to work, trying to restore *Creation* to its original form, before Random House had made the severe cuts that probably helped to sell the book to a wider audience. "I wanted everything back to where it was, twenty years ago," Gore said. (The obsession with revising earlier works suggests a need to present himself to history in a certain way. He cared deeply how future readers would react to his work. To whatever degree he could, he also wished to control their views.)

When Howard collapsed in the hallway one morning en route to the bathroom, Gore assumed that the brain cancer had returned, but this time it was a heart problem, made worse by the emphysema. Back at Cedars-Sinai, Howard was hooked up to an oxygen tank. When he detached from it now and then, he asked Gore for a cigarette, infuriating him. Soon a companion was hired to sit by Howard's bed, a gentle sixty-year-old man from Manila named Leto. Of course Gore visited Howard daily, but Howard seemed confused and these visits proved difficult. One day Howard imagined that he and Gore were being held prisoner in a government hospital but felt optimistic that both of them would soon be released. To amuse Howard, Gore brought in a tape player with recordings of Barbra Streisand. "He loved her music, more than anything else," Gore recalled, noting that Streisand had attended a birthday party for Paul Newman arranged by Gore and Howard many years ago. "How old am I?" Howard asked one day. "Seventy-four," Gore told him. Howard asked, "That's when people die, isn't it?" Gore explained that neither of them was dead, not quite yet. Howard's response spoke volumes: "Didn't it go by awfully fast?"

Norberto Nierras, a dignified Filipino cook, had become a crucial figure in Gore's life, acting as a kind of nurse as well as a butler. He would say, in a mild accent and without the slightest irony, "Yes, Mr. Vidal," no matter what Gore asked for: a double Scotch at breakfast, another cup of coffee for Howard, a change of sheets, an item from the supermarket. Gore praised Norberto's cooking to his face whenever visitors arrived: "He is the best cook in Hollywood," he would say, and Norberto would happily frown, embarrassed by the praise. This became a kind of ritual. "Nobody else in California knows how to make a soufflé," Gore would say. "They rise, and they float in midair—a miracle!"

Meanwhile, the house in Ravello was occupied by Muzius Gordon Dietzmann, a kindhearted, elegant young man with straw-colored hair pulled into a long ponytail. He was Gore's godson, the child of a German man who had been Gore's lover at one point. Speaking fluent German, French, and Italian, Muzius was "all boy," as Gore would say, and he adored him. He had often been employed to look after the villa when Gore and Howard traveled, as he was reliable and knew how to fix pretty much anything. He had close friends in Ravello and was, Gore said, "always the toast of the village." Gore could rest easily with Muzius looking after the villa.

Gore resumed life as best he could, working on essays, greeting the never-ending stream of television crews and journalists who asked the same questions repeatedly: Why did you not like Truman Capote? Was John Kennedy a good president? When did you realize you were gay? Did Norman Mailer really hit you? Gore had a tape in his head with ready-made answers, and he didn't have to think. He just talked, and out came the words: another interview with Gore Vidal. He also gave public talks, although they became less frequent during his last decade.

On March 18, 2003, Howard sat in the wings at Royce Hall on the campus of UCLA listening with pleasure as Gore spoke to nearly a thousand people. "That was the day before the invasion of Iraq," Gore recalled, "and I told the audience what would happen soon. I explained that Bush could not resist the opportunity. He was desperate to attack someone, anyone. He thought it wouldn't last very long, just a few days or weeks. That's what they always think when they invade. They never calculate the cost. I predicted that millions, even billions, would be spent over the course of many years. I didn't take into account the cost of taking care of wounded veterans for decades. This will cost taxpayers, according to most estimates, over a trillion dollars. As with all foreign wars, the negative effects continue for generations, and there is the fact of destabilization, which creates power vacuums. You begin to drop bombs and you can't tell where they will land. On your own head, eventually."

On the evening of September 22, 2003, Howard sat in a chair by his bed, attended by Leto. He had been suffering from a bout of pneumonia for two weeks, and a large intake of antibiotics had left him exhausted. Gore took Valium each night to sleep, washed down with three or four glasses of Scotch. As he stood in the kitchen, making a sandwich (it was Norberto's night off), Leto suddenly appeared at his side, and said, "Mr. Auster has stopped breathing." (Howard had, interestingly, switched back to Auster from Austen in recent months.)

Gore sprinted upstairs—as best he could with his arthritic knees. Howard sat upright, obviously dead. He had eaten most of his dinner when his breathing stopped. Gore waved a hand in front of his eyes, his nose and mouth, looking for signs of life. "The eyes were open and very clear," Gore recalled. "I'd forgotten what a beautiful gray they were—illness and medicine had regularly glazed them over; now they were bright and attentive and he was watching me, *consciously*, through long lashes. He had been sitting straight up when I came in the room but now, very slightly he slumped to the left in his chair." He had "a sort of wry wise-guy from the Bronx expression on his face."

When the EMTs arrived but couldn't revive Howard, the mortuary was called. Gore waited for them in a daze, swept by waves of grief. Leto cried. Gore wished he could join him, but—as he said—"the WASP glacier had closed over my head." That night Gore dreamed about Howard. They were in Rome again, in a side street near a greengrocer they often frequented. "Howard had grabbed a handful of fava beans and started to shell them. For what it is worth the fava bean itself resembles a miniature fetus and the Pythagorean cult believed that each bean contains the soul of someone dead, ready to be reborn. In the dream Howard was eating these forbidden fetuses—preparing for rebirth?" A few years later I asked Gore about this passage in *Point to Point Navigation*, and he said, "Rebirth? Who knows. All I know is how little I know, and I trust the poets more than the scientists. Nothing will surprise me after death, much as everything has surprised me during life."

Gore sank into a period of astonishing darkness. When Gerald Howard wrote to offer condolences, Gore wrote back with grim honesty: "Thanks for the sensitive words on the rawest of subjects. Stoicism is a useful mask and nothing more."

IV. Marching to the Sea

"The smell of greasepaint," Gore said, "drew me near the stage. I had always been an actor at heart. But not on stage, not often." He had performed in *Don Juan in Hell* with Mailer in 1993 at Carnegie Hall, and now Mailer asked him to reprise his role, playing the Devil again to Mailer's Don Juan. It was irresistible, and so Gore traveled to Provincetown during the second week of October 2002. It was, in fact, a memorable night at the Provincetown Town Hall, with the two old men facing each other in this benefit performance for a local theater that Mailer supported.

"This was the culmination of fifty years of friendship," says J. Michael Lennon, who performed with Gore and Mailer that night. "Norman had wired Gore in Ravello, asking him to join the company for this benefit. Howard was ill at the time, but Gore wanted very much to do this. He accepted at once, though he had difficulty walking and needed a cane. He stayed down the street at the White Horse Inn, close to Norman's house. Norman was the director, and Gore understood this, listening carefully. We rehearsed in the morning and afternoon, stopping only for lunch. But Gore knew the script by heart. He was the only one who did. And, of course, when he got on stage, he did as he pleased, flashing the red lining to his jacket to great applause. He was perfect as the Devil." Gerald Howard, who attended the event with his wife, confirms that "Vidal shone as the Devil." He also recalls that Mailer seemed "incapable of shedding his persona, as an actor must." At the reception after this event, at Mailer's Commercial Street house, Howard recalls that "Gore held court in an armchair while much of the gay population kneeled before him one by one. Mailer, standing with crutches, presided over the room in a patriarchal fashion. It felt like the twilight of the literary gods."

Lennon noted an intriguing point of conflict over Norris Church Mailer. He says that "Gore really liked Norris and told her she was beautiful, and that if Norman died, he would marry her. This enraged Norman. But in the course of the week Norman and Gore got along pretty well. It had been a long and rocky friendship, and it came to a kind of culmination here. We had wonderful dinners at the Red Inn in the evenings, and Gore would drink nearly a bottle of Scotch by himself. Once I delivered him to his room, left him with a glass in his hand. The next morning I went to get him, and he was still on the bed with the glass in his hand. He hadn't moved."

The parting of these old rivals was touching. "There was the sense of an ending," says Lennon. "They would never see each other again, and they knew that. They both had bad knees—Gore had recently had one of his knees replaced—and used canes. They waved them in the air, on the deck of Norman's house, while Norris took a picture."

After Howard's death, Gore needed to get out and about. Acting was always a good release, as he could play someone else. Another opportunity to act came when Gore was asked to perform in *Trumbo*, a play about Dalton Trumbo—the blacklisted Hollywood screenwriter and novelist. Gore took the part of Trumbo in this sold-out Off-Broadway production at the Westside Theatre. He agreed to play this role for a brief period because it allowed him to take his mind off himself and his problems: To be someone other than Gore Vidal for a little while came as a relief. As he notes in *Point to Point Navigation*, he was in manic flight from the death of Howard: "I could never memorize in youth but *Trumbo* is a series of letters that he wrote, often to his son." He would appear on a near-black stage, with screens showing film footage from the 1940s, when Trumbo "fell afoul of congressional Red hunters with his sharp responses to their deeply un-American catechisms." Gore had known Trumbo only slightly, when the screenwriter—twenty years Gore's senior—lived in Rome. "He wanted to talk to me about the Byzantine Empire," Gore remembered—the backdrop of a project he was writing for an Italian producer. "In the end," said Gore, "I had the impression that Trumbo was enjoying his well-paid martyrdom."

With Howard gone, Gore could no longer tolerate Ravello. "I couldn't bear it," he said. "Howard was everywhere in the house, his voice and shadow. I could hear him laughing in distant rooms. I thought he was sitting on the terrace." He now spent much of his time in a wheelchair, and the long trek to the house from the piazza proved an impossible journey. But he would miss the villa terribly. "It was a happy place for me when Howard was alive. I always had big houses because I collected books," he said, "and I had eight thousand volumes or so in Ravello. It was where I worked. I didn't know if I could work in California, with so much movie chatter around me."

With reluctance, he put La Rondinaia up for sale, for $17 million. That was a considerable jump in value from when he bought the villa in 1972; as usual, Gore landed in the right place at the right time. Nearly every house or apartment he bought over the years produced a sizable profit when sold, although he claimed it was dumb luck, not a gift for real estate. He left Muzius in Ravello, tasked with making the villa ready for sale. (It would, unfortunately, take several years to sell.) His favorite books and furnishings were shipped to his house in the Hollywood Hills, which increasingly began to mimic the house in Ravello in colors and tones, absorbing many of the same paintings and pieces of furniture; among these was a large eighteenth-century painting by the baroque artist Paolo de' Matteís, which Gore now attached to the ceiling of his sunken living room on Outpost Drive. By necessity, he left behind the bulk of his possessions, such as a first-century floor mosaic that he'd had mounted on the wall. (It was valuable enough that it could not, in any case, leave Italy.)

When he drove away from Ravello for the last time, a number of old friends from the San Domingo gathered to say goodbye. It was a melancholy occasion, and Gore seemed lost in thought, waving but not smiling. As his neighbor and friend Michael Tyler-Whittle said, "Gore meant as much to Ravello as it meant to him. He was the *grande uomo*, the great man. Italians love a great man. He brings dignity to the village."

After returning to the Hollywood Hills, Gore completed work on *Point to Point Navigation*, his final memoir, which he explained to Gerald Howard at Doubleday was modeled on Santayana's *Persons and Places*. He was also working on a play—a revision of *On the March to the Sea*, which he had written as *Honor*, a teleplay that aired on NBC in 1956, and which he then expanded as a stage play in the early sixties but never finished to the satisfaction of any Broadway producer. It involves John Hinks, a wealthy Southern merchant who sends his sons off to war with a feeling of dread, wondering if he and his neighbors shouldn't burn their large houses to keep Union soldiers from using them as a base of operations. He doesn't burn the house, and it's soon taken over by Union troops, as feared. They occupy the mansion for ten days during Sherman's infamous march through Georgia in 1864. The plot mainly turns on the relationship of the Yankee officer in charge, Colonel Thayer, and the Confederate mistress of the house, Minna Hinks, who eventually murders him.

It's a decent play about a painful era that Gore had treated in various genres. "The Civil War just didn't end," he said. "It made this country what it is, for better and worse. It defined us." A repertory theater in Hartford, Connecticut, asked him to develop the script for a staged reading, and he welcomed this opportunity to revisit a piece of work that he felt had potential. It had moved from Hartford to Duke University for further development, and Gore joined the rehearsals for a reading in Durham, North Carolina, stopping en route to deposit Howard's ashes at Rock Creek Cemetery, where Gore would eventually lie beside him. "Gore arrived in an understandably somber mood but quickly engaged in the project," recalls Zannie Voss, who was developing the project at Duke. She notes: "It was a fantastic cast—Chris Noth, Michael Learned, Charles Durning, Isabel Keating, Harris Yulin, Richard Easton, among others. The play, which is set during the Civil War and centers on honor, resonated with North Carolina audiences." The producers thought the play might actually go far. "The hope was that this play might one day get to Broadway. But this obviously didn't happen," says Jody McAuliffe, a member of the Duke theater department. Plans to continue developing the play in Seattle fell through, and Gore soon lost interest in the project.

Even less happily, Gore became embroiled in the controversy over a new dramatic work by his acquaintance Edmund White, who had written *Terre Haute*—a two-man play set at the federal prison in Indiana where Timothy McVeigh was executed in 1995. White invents a gay writer who seems much like Gore, with a dash of Henry James: a voluble patrician novelist named James Brevoort. Brevoort visits a young terrorist named Harrison only days before his execution—much as Gore would have done with McVeigh had the timing worked out. Brevoort is a credible version of Gore in high dudgeon, saying: "No one wants to admit that you, as a single outraged individual, were responding to a government that engineered the deaths of Allende and Lumumba, that has unsuccessfully tried to assassinate Castro and Qaddafi for years and years." "I hear you, brother," Harrison says. "Don't forget gun control. Don't forget Ruby Ridge, Idaho." Brevoort tries to respond in kind, mentioning that "Americans are now kept under electronic surveillance." He talks about the Fourth Amendment's protections against "unreasonable searches and seizures." Harrison listens intently; but the two seem to talk over each other, and their politics don't quite mesh.

The novelist probes the young man's past, intimating that he wants to write Harrison's biography as a way of getting him to talk about his personal life, especially his sex life. A seductive dance begins. In the last scene, Harrison allows Brevoort to see his chest, unzipping the top of his jumpsuit before he is led away to his death. "James scarcely looks, he's so overcome with emotion," the stage directions read. In a final soliloquy to the audience, Brevoort admits that Harrison was "cracked if not crazy." And yet he admires his lone-wolf rebel status, "his loneliness, his forlornness." It's a vivid ending to a moving play.

White recalls: "I based the writer on Gore, obviously, but it's also myself. It was close enough to Gore that I thought I should get his permission. I wrote to him, sent him the play, and he replied saying it was okay for me to go ahead with the project. Later he changed his mind. He took quite violently against it. I'd been friendly with Gore for a long time. We first met at Peggy Guggenheim's villa in Venice in the mid-seventies. He'd written a blurb for one of my novels, and we saw each other occasionally. But the play obviously upset him." After being workshopped at Sundance, the play opened in 2007 at the Edinburgh Festival (and later in New York City). The next day Gore gave an interview to *The Observer*, threatening a lawsuit: "Edmund White will yet be feeling the wrath of my lawyers. It's unethical and vicious to make it very clear that this old faggot writer is based on me, and that I'm madly in love with Timothy McVeigh, whom I never met." He didn't wish to be "lumped together with Mailer and Capote. They both went for murderers, and I don't go for murderers."

V. The Last Memoir

Palimpsest had been a clear success, an evocative stream-of-consciousness account of Gore's first four decades. Another four decades had passed now, and there was a lot to recall. For the title of his new memoir, and a governing concept, he drew on a maritime term: point-to-point navigation—a method of steering a ship through potentially dangerous waters without a compass, with an eye trained for landmarks, such as capes or outcroppings of rock. In the Bering

Sea, Gore had learned this navigational method. In his later years, he often felt reliant on his own reserves, on close observation of his environment, moving from one observable point to the next through heavy waters. Some of these well-known points were, of course, people, and Gore relied on his starry universe of friends and acquaintances for direction.

It would be too easy to blame Gore for name-dropping. He couldn't help himself, and without his personal associations, and the beloved anecdotes in which they appeared, he wouldn't have been Gore Vidal. It's true, however, that in this last memoir the references to famous people seem inadvertently comical at times, as when seeing a newsreel of Hitler marching on the Sudetenland brings forth the following: "I used to chat with Prince Philip of Hesse, the only person I ever knew who knew Hitler." As Gore listens to rain in the Hollywood Hills, he remembers a time in Bangkok: "The monsoon is early, I think, moving backward in time. I must get dressed for lunch with Crown Princess Chumbhot." Sympathetic readers simply enjoy these name-dropping digressions, letting Gore be Gore; others might cringe.

Point to Point Navigation appeared in November 2006, clearly a swan song. *Palimpsest* had been meandering, but its successor was more so, wandering from image to image, scene to scene, like a strangely vivid dream. It begins: "As I now move, graciously, I hope, toward the door marked Exit, it occurs to me that the only thing I ever really liked to do was go to the movies." And a good deal of these memory snippets involve the movies, ones that Gore saw or wrote or almost wrote. Television and movie stars shimmer through its pages, a Milky Way of acquaintances: Johnny Carson, Bette Davis, Clark Gable, Greta Garbo, Judy Garland, Val Kilmer, Charles Laughton, Paul Newman and Joanne Woodward, Laurence Olivier, Omar Sharif, Frank Sinatra, and Orson Welles. Typical of these cameo portraits is one of Welles, whom Gore hobnobbed with in the mid-sixties when he was working on the script of *Is Paris Burning?* with Francis Ford Coppola. Gore says of Welles: "Considering what he ate and drank, it is amazing that he lived to be seventy. When he laughed, which was often, his face, starting at the lower lip, would turn scarlet while sweat formed on his brow like a sudden spring rain." Without a thought,

Gore recycles a good deal of material from *Palimpsest*, *Screening History*, and his essays: He had very little concern for "self-plagiarism," convinced that if something was worth saying once, it was worth saying again, and then again.

His memories of writers include moments with Saul Bellow, Joan Didion, Graham Greene, Christopher Isherwood, and Tennessee Williams—the usual suspects, often recalled fondly here. He also includes a bemused portrait of the ancient romance novelist Barbara Cartland, "a monument draped in damp pastel colors." He dwells on his friendship with Paul Bowles, rummaging through their past in atypical detail, lighting on key incidents. He recalls, for instance, a time when Bowles narrowly avoided arrest for spending the night with "a youth at a hotel." Gore elaborates:

> The youth departed, to be replaced by two plainclothesmen. Since Paul did not have the cash they asked for, he made a date to see them the next day. By the time they returned, if they did, Paul was on the high seas. There are more details to the story but I have forgotten them. The essential point is that the criminalizing of drugs and sex is very much a sign of that malign primitivism which has always reigned in Freedom's Land. For Bowles, Morocco was freedom, particularly as he penetrated the high Atlas and the Sahara desert, recording music that he was certain could be traced back to Roman times, while noting down stories that go back to the early days of our race which gave us Puritan New England that also gave birth to that original mind, masked or not, of Paul Bowles whose imagination responded with civilized hatred to the sort of primitive laws the two New York plainclothesmen were eager to exploit.

It's worth quoting at length to show the strengths and weaknesses of *Point to Point Navigation*. It is full of rich memories of people and places, all colorfully drawn, with prose that occasionally aspires to the condition of poetry. But it's also rambling, disjunctive, and syntactically confusing. It seems that grief, alcohol, and age had begun to take their toll.

Certainly the best part of this memoir is chapter sixteen, which centers on Howard's death—a mere thirteen pages, but written with such severity and sublimity that it might have been published as a small pamphlet on its own. Gore restrains his emotions admirably, but the intensity of his feeling comes through, as when he's waiting for the ambulance to take the body to the mortuary: "I pulled back the sheet for one last look at those clear gray eyes—could they still see?—but the substance of the eyeballs had collapsed and two gelatinous streaks of the sort snails make had coursed down his cheeks. I would not see him in any corporal form again until the ashes at Rock Creek Cemetery." It's worth noting that Gore changed Howard's name back to Auster from Austen on the tombstone—as Howard had requested. (Of course Gore would never change his own name back to Eugene Luther Gore Vidal.)

While *Point to Point Navigation* is not a masterpiece, it adds a reasonably valuable piece of territory to Gore's empire of self. Reviewers would note that Gore recycles many of the same tales, but this was to be expected. In *The New York Times Book Review*, Christopher Hitchens—now having fallen out with Gore over the Iraq War—calls it "almost alarmingly laconic, as if offhandedly dictated." Adam Kirsch, ever an intelligent reviewer, described it as "a weary book, fragmentary and repetitive, stuffed with twice-told tales." But it was more than that: a kind of elegiac hallucination, a transcript of Gore's starry pinwheel of a mind, which now spun into the ether or, perhaps, off-stage.

VI. Mopping-Up Operations

Apart from new collections of previous work, *Point to Point Navigation* was Gore's final book, which he personally narrated in full as a seven-CD set, released in 2006. That same year, short stories from early in his career appeared as *Clouds and Eclipses: Collected Stories*—essentially a reprint of *A Thirsty Evil* with the addition of the title story, which turns on an awkward moment from the childhood of Tennessee Williams. Gore had suppressed it when the volume first appeared in 1956, for fear of offending the Bird, who had objected to the tale. But its rediscovery in his papers led him to allow for its publication in this largely autobiographical volume of stories that often deal with homoerotic themes. The short story was among the few genres that Gore didn't find suitable for his talents. "I preferred the longer form for fiction," he said. "I never had a style I could call my own, not in short fiction."

In 2008, I assembled a volume of selected essays for Gore, choosing what I considered his best essays, which was meant as an introduction for readers not familiar with his work in this genre. His publisher felt, quite sensibly, that the complete essays, as found in *United States*, appealed mainly to die-hard fans. This slimmer volume refocused the attention of reviewers on Gore's career at a time when he felt, accurately, that the spotlight had shifted elsewhere.

In his old age, it became difficult for him to find suitable venues for expressing himself in public, and he continued to love being onstage before a live audience. While I interviewed him several times in New York and elsewhere, with appreciative crowds in attendance, Gore missed the days of Johnny Carson and Dick Cavett. He didn't have much luck with the new crop of talk-show hosts, such as David Letterman or Jay Leno, and he often repeated his old line about the Great Eraser, believing that it had finally done its work, and that Gore Vidal was finished.

But it wasn't over, not quite yet. The election of 2008 brought fresh interviewers—especially from abroad—who wondered about his reaction to the election of an African American to the White House. Gore was among the few public intellectuals of a certain age who might put the rise of Barack Obama into perspective. On election night, he went live via satellite on British television. But he was visibly drunk and confused, and his performance created a minor scandal in Britain. The famous interviewer David Dimbleby was taken aback. "May I talk the facts of life to you?" Gore asked before explaining that the Republican Party in the U.S. wasn't like the Conservative Party in Britain. "It's a mind-set," he explained. "They love war, and they love money."

Gore was in London during the week of Obama's inauguration in mid-January. His latest assistant, Fabian Bouthillette, was a handsome twenty-eight-year-old ex–naval officer who helped with Gore's medications and correspondence, pushing him in his wheelchair from room to room. Gore had been invited to address a select committee at the Houses of Parliament. I will never forget sitting in the members-only bar of the House of Commons with Gore, Fabian, and crowds of MPs, watching Obama on television as he gave his inaugural address. Gore said, “Oh, dear. I think I’m almost happy. Is that possible?” He was joking, but there was a sense in which he believed, as did millions of Americans, that a page had been turned in the political book, with the end of George W. Bush and the election of an eloquent, progressive president.

When Gore was wheeled into the packed committee room, he suddenly realized that he didn’t have his speech. It had been carefully written for this occasion but left behind. Forced to speak extemporaneously, he tried his best to recall what he had written. It didn’t go well, however. He mumbled about his years as a politician, and his friendship with Jack Kennedy: “The beach was milky white in Hyannis, and I played a game of backgammon with Jack.” He recalled the Bay of Pigs, noting that both Jack and Bobby Kennedy wanted to see the end of Castro. He looked anxiously around the room, then said that he hoped Fidel Castro was still alive. Sensing that he was in trouble, Gore turned the floor over to Fabian, who had been an active member of a group called Iraq Veterans Against the War. Fabian gave a rousing antiwar speech, referring to his own service in the Middle East. “He’s a remarkable young man,” said Gore, who considered himself a kind of father figure to Fabian. And he took pleasure in his young assistant’s moving, improvised speech about American resistance to the Iraq War.

On his last night in London, a party was held in Gore’s honor at Chatham House in St. James’s Square—an elegant eighteenth-century building with one of the finest addresses in the city. In attendance was a crowd of British politicians, activists, journalists, and writers. Gore, looking frail in his wheelchair, already drunk, smiled and spoke warmly to people he didn’t really know. Tom Stoppard, the great British playwright, was present, and he gave an impromptu toast to the elderly author, saying, “I know how much Gore has meant to all of us. Certainly his essays in *The New York Review of Books* meant a great deal to me." He praised Gore's "clear and brave" thinking, and toasted him warmly. Gore was hugely pleased, as Stoppard, he said, "is perhaps the most intelligent writer alive."

What astonished me in the last years was Gore's wish to keep going. We spoke frequently on the telephone, and he delighted in telling me about guests who dropped by Outpost Drive. Patty Dryden was a faithful friend and neighbor, and she paid regular visits, as did Peter Bogdanovich whenever he was in town. Susan Sarandon would see him when she could, as did other friends of long standing. Gore often called to say that Stephen Fry or Shirley MacLaine or the Ohio congressman Dennis Kucinich had called. (MacLaine seemed to have forgiven Gore for her portrayal in *Live from Golgotha*—or perhaps she didn't really care, since Gore was just having fun.)

Gore's nephew Burr Steers became a fixture in his life, tending to his needs, inviting him to his house for holidays, checking in with whoever was Gore's "minder" at the time. One of the most reliable of these was Daren Simkin, a young Dartmouth graduate whom Gore found admirably competent and reassuring. (Daren published *The Traveler*, a book for children, soon after he left Gore's employ.) In the last years, a succession of assistants came and went, not all of them as reliable as Fabian or Daren or Gore's beloved godson Muzius, who came as often as he could manage. The most consistent presence in the house was Norberto, the faithful cook and butler who never wavered in his politeness or dedication to Gore. (He and I would confer about Gore's health and mood on a regular basis.)

Gore's agent, Richard Morris, kept a close eye on his welfare too, talking to Gore's lawyer and accountant, consulting with Burr and myself. We all had one thing in mind: keeping Gore as healthy and happy as was possible during these last years. Alcoholism had begun to make him quite unstable at times, full of delusions; yet Gore could be immensely lucid, even during his last months.

Despite age, alcoholism, and diabetes, Gore still got around a good deal in 2009 and 2010. I traveled with him to the Key West Literary Seminar in January 2009, for instance. He had called me some time beforehand, saying, "I want you to push my wheelchair and give me shots of insulin." I told him I could do neither of these: My back wouldn't survive pushing the wheelchair, and I would kill him with an overdose of insulin. "You can become the Claus von Bülow of the literary scene," he said. Wisely, he brought Fabian and a male nurse with a Slavic name. Gore referred to them as his "bunnies," and called them "my sailor boy and my Hungarian rhapsody." Arriving in Key West, I saw that Gore was in a self-destructive mood, on some kind of inner warpath. He looked uncommonly frail in his suite at the Marquesa, a boutique hotel on Fleming Street. He would sit in his wheelchair by the pool and drink tumblers of Scotch, entertaining any number of old friends who happened to be in the area, including the writer Ann Beattie and her husband, the painter Lincoln Perry, and old friends from Rome, such as Michael and Linda Mewshaw or Donald Stewart.

Given the severity of his alcoholism, it became increasingly hard to imagine that he would make it through the interview with me at the San Carlos Institute (which would be aired on C-SPAN). But benevolent friends drove Gore around the island for three hours before he was rolled onto the stage, where he responded to the warm applause from an audience that considered him a kind of folk hero or legend, as indeed he was. He talked in a leisurely fashion about his life in politics and literature, addressing the usual run of topics, including the presidency of George W. Bush and its assault on American freedoms. This was hardly the Gore Vidal of ten years earlier, but it still seemed remarkable that he could pull it together as well as he did for a large audience. "Nothing brightens my day like applause," he whispered to me at the end.

Later that night, we attended a party given by a wealthy heiress, who had invited a hundred people to meet Gore. He sat in state on a couch near the entrance hallway, with perhaps two dozen guests in line to shake his hand, bring greetings from so-and-so, or get a book signed. "I have fans, you see," Gore said to me as I handed over the requested glass of Scotch. He swallowed half of the glass, then signed a book for an elderly man in dark glasses who claimed to have known Gore in New York in the early fifties. "I don't remember you," Gore said. This went on for nearly an hour, until a prominent Key West version of the grande dame pushed others aside and loomed over Gore.

"Mr. Vidal," she said, "I consider you one of the great homosexuals of our time."

The blood drained from Gore's cheeks, and he turned to me with a grimace, saying loudly, "Will someone please get this cunt out of my sight?"

VII. Snapshots of the End

Gore's last year was especially unhappy, as he raged against his situation. There were a few distractions, such as when he assembled *Snapshots in History's Glare*, a volume of photographs from his life that was published by Abrams. It was a sumptuous coffee-table book with photographs that Howard had collected in a scrapbook over the years. "This is my homage to Howard," Gore said. "I know he loved these snaps, and I do, too." It was another trip down memory lane, with images of his family and famous friends.

He appeared on a few talk shows to promote this collection. On one of these, the host Joy Behar asked him what he considered his greatest achievement. He replied, "Despite intense provocations over the course of what is becoming rather a long life, I have never killed anybody. That is my greatest achievement." His intemperate remarks about President Bush on this program, combined with the remark about trying not to kill someone, prompted a visit from the Secret Service to his house on Outpost Drive. They needed to reassure themselves that this elderly author in a wheelchair was not planning to assassinate anyone.

Gore was losing himself, even though he could be cogent at times, even incisive. He stumbled through a small part in the 2009 film *Shrink*, playing a television host. "I had a larger part than the final cut suggests," Gore said. "I didn't like it. It's more like a snapshot than a role." He continued to entertain television and film crews, most of them traveling from abroad to visit this literary lion. A kind of surreal moment occurred when Sacha Baron Cohen arrived in the guise of Ali G, a hipster TV interviewer supposedly from a London ghetto.

Ali speaks in a comic patois that seems to parody Jamaican slang, although the persona is a countercultural mishmash. "I am here with my main man," says Ali, "none other than the boss man, Mr. Gore Vidal." He asks him about history. "Is history happening all the time?"

"We are history," says Gore, vaguely bemused as well as puzzled.

Then Ali asks Gore about the U.S. Constitution, and why it was written "on these two tablets."

Gore replies: "No, that's Moses. He had nothing to do with the Constitution."

"You is an amazing guy," remarks Ali, after Gore explains further about American history and the history of racism. "You ain't just a historian, and a writer, and a speaker, you is also a world-famous hair stylist."

Gore looks startled. "That's Vidal Sassoon, not me."

"But that's what you go under?"

"No, that's someone else. I know him, and he's a nice guy."

Ali persists: "If you could cut any First Lady's hair, which one would it be?"

Shortly after this interview, I got a call from Gore. "A madman was just here," he said. "British television, dear God, is over. It's over!" (He never caught on that this was actually a joke.)

In the spring of 2010, I spent a week with Gore when he seemed thoroughly engaged, even endearing. We sat up late most nights, often until three or four, listening to Frank Sinatra, Tony Bennett, and—indeed—Howard. Gore had rediscovered an old tape of Howard singing from the great American songbook, and he was teary-eyed as he leaned toward the music. Howard, he said, was the only person he had ever loved, and he didn't want to live without him. He wanted to die. (The Jimmie Trimble obsession had, at last, faded.) We also talked a good deal about Hitchens, who had published a nasty piece about Gore in *Vanity Fair* called "Vidal Loco." Hitchens had criticized Gore's three post-9/11 pamphlets, calling them "half-argued and half-written shock pieces." He attacked Gore for an intemperate interview with *The Independent* in London where Gore railed against Bush and Cheney, did his usual turn on FDR and Pearl Harbor, and suggested that "the whole American experiment can now be regarded as a failure." Gore said, "The country will now take its place between Brazil and Argentina, where it belongs." Hitchens was especially irritated when Gore said of Britain: "This isn't a country, it's an American aircraft carrier."

Gore denounced Hitchens himself, in conversation. "What has he ever done? Show me a novel, a play, anything that readers will look at in twenty years." (As it happened, Hitchens had been diagnosed with esophageal cancer, and on October 2, 2010, I debated him on the Iraq War and its aftermath at a book festival in Pennsylvania. He would die fifteen months later, but he was already fragile, with a shaved head—a consequence of the chemotherapy. After this event, we sat together in a hotel room and talked, and he asked me as I left if Gore had spoken about him recently. I could not tell him the unpleasant truth. "He wasn't happy with your piece about him in *Vanity Fair*," I said, "but he still thinks of you fondly." Hitchens smiled, saying, "I looked to him as a model. We all did.")

Soon the elderly Gore descended to lows not quite seen before. This was, perhaps, a result of "wet brain," a stage in alcoholism when the drinker begins to lose touch with reality. He lived his nightmares, unable to distinguish between his dreams and waking life. He rambled most nights, thoroughly drunk, and fantasized about moving to rural France with Muzius—he had bought a small house for his godson there, although when Gore saw it a few months later he changed his mind. "It's a poky little thing," he told me. "I could never live in a small house." He talked about moving back to New York, where he had any number of good friends, and thought that an apartment at the Plaza would be just the right thing for him. But, in truth, he didn't have the energy for another move.

I met him for a final trip to southern Italy in the hot summer of 2010. We stayed at the Vesuvio, his favorite hotel in Naples, and I did an interview with him one night in the ancient amphitheater at Pompeii. Some of Gore's old friends, such as Judith Harris, came down from Rome, and Gore clearly relished the occasion, which included a final visit to Ravello a few days later. He was attended throughout by Fabian and Muzius, who looked after his needs with great care, even love.

I left Gore in their hands, and they moved on to visit Diana Phipps at her castle near Prague before continuing as planned to France. I lost track of Gore for a couple of weeks, when he called in a state of near panic to say that Muzius and Fabian had "kidnapped" him. "They put me in the back of a refrigerated truck, and they drove me around for about three weeks, and they refused to take me back to California." His cousin Miles and his wife, Michelle, were with Gore at the time, in the Czech Republic. Miles recalled that Gore felt ill, and he wanted to go home: "He didn't like the idea of going with Muzius and Fabian to France. He needed to fly back at once to Los Angeles. He was extremely unwell, and when his caretakers wouldn't switch plans to accommodate him he probably felt 'kidnapped,' as he would say."

Whatever really happened on this trip, the results were visible. He had declined horribly in just a few weeks. I visited soon after his return, and we spent some evenings at the Polo Lounge of the Beverly Hills Hotel, his favorite hangout now. He would sit for hours by the piano, listening to the songs, drinking Scotch, sometimes singing along in a soft voice. But he had become incontinent, and life grew increasingly miserable for him. He was trying, without luck, to write fresh introductions to his Edgar Box novels, which Vintage planned to bring out in a uniform edition. (I wrote them for him, asking questions that would lead to appropriate introductory material. As ever, he had that astounding memory for the past, and recalled every editor he ever worked with and every bad review he ever got.)

Even in bad health, however, he longed to travel, and he did, heading off with a new "minder" to Istanbul in September 2011. This would be his final trip abroad. "Today I have walked [been pushed in a wheelchair, of course] around the greatest city on earth, if not the greatest," he told Lisa Grainger, a travel writer from *The Daily Telegraph* in London. He spoke to her from the deck of a luxury yacht on the Bosporus. He was there to attend a literary festival and was taken, he told me, "to meet one of the patriarchs of the church, on an island." The Turks, he said, "know how to treat a sultan, and—well, that's what I've become, the Sultan of Savoir."

The writer Derek Blasberg was traveling in Turkey at the time, and happened to meet Gore at a hotel in Istanbul. He recorded his impressions on his blog:

> One late night in Istanbul, after a fancy dinner, we all ended up back at the hotel where many of us were staying, winding up in a room and all sharing (probably too many) drinks. It was fantastic that Gore Vidal was there, propped up in a corner, dropping observant yet crude remarks and setting off on an occasional well spoken tangent. It was hazy and it was hilarious. At one point, he asked my friend Leigh if she were a lesbian, offering a few colorful remarks about girl-on-girl alternative lifestyles. He was provoking us, as he had provoked generations. After he said it, that little grin, the grin of a man who is supremely confident and supremely smart, showed up on his face. Which is I'm sure the same grin on his face now, wherever he has ended up in his afterlife.

Back in the Hollywood Hills, Gore began to fall apart. He was often confused and paranoid. One night, in May 2012, he rang me at three a.m. He said, "Get the next plane to L.A. at once. I need help. There are Somali pirates in my swimming pool." I assured him that this wasn't possible, but he insisted, screaming down the line that I must come. The next week I did go to see him, and we spent a few days in conversation. He was attended by Ernesto Bernal, "Ernie," a youngish man who had looked after other elderly people in Los Angeles. Ernie seemed quite devoted to Gore, even obsessively so. They would often go to the Polo Lounge for dinner, where Gore would eat ice cream and drink and listen to the piano. He had by now almost ceased to eat solid foods. I was, in fact, stunned when for breakfast one morning, he had only a double Scotch. "The amazing thing," he told me, "is that my liver is perfect. My doctor has assured me. The numbers are wonderful."

His nephew Burr grew increasingly concerned, doing his best to help his uncle. But help meant trying to stop him from drinking, and Gore refused this kind of help. The house was incredibly tense because Gore tended to lash out against anyone who refused to condone his self-destructive drinking. Many of his friends stayed away, even Patty

Dryden, who had been a regular visitor for many years. It was not pretty. The morning when I left him, he said, "I just want to die. They should let me die."

There was a last hurrah of sorts: Another revival of *The Best Man* was coming to Broadway in April 2012, starring many of the same actors who had performed in the staged reading of *On the March to the Sea* in North Carolina. He delighted in talking about the play's current incarnation. "It will be a hit," he said with childlike pleasure at the prospect of another success on Broadway at this late stage in his career. One afternoon in March, Gore met in New York with the actors, including James Earl Jones, Angela Lansbury, John Larroquette, and Eric McCormack, to discuss the script. They seemed glad to meet him, but it was obvious that he had very little strength, and it surprised no one when he fell ill with a cough and fever. Ernie wisely decided they must retreat to Los Angeles, where Gore's doctors could look after him.

Gore had, in fact, caught pneumonia, and everyone thought he would die within days. I spoke to him frequently on the phone, but he didn't make a great deal of sense. By summer, he was moving back and forth between Cedars-Sinai and home, closely watched by both Ernie and Norberto, with Burr dropping in for regular assessments of the situation. Alas Burr was seen as the culprit who was trying to keep Gore from drinking, so he was not welcome at Outpost Drive. Even Gore's beloved godson Muzius was not allowed to visit. He had, in Gore's mind, been complicit in the "kidnapping" event in Europe.

I spent a few days with Gore in late spring 2012. By this time, he was completely out of it, awake but scarcely able to talk, mumbling incoherent orders to Norberto. He looked shrunken, attended by a full-time male nurse. A hospital bed had been set up in the living room, and a giant flat-screen television was suspended above the foot of the bed. Gore sat up, semiconscious, watching tapes of himself in various films and interviews, with the nurse alerting him to his various entrances and exits. He did not, by this point, seem to care.

The great empire constructed so meticulously over many decades had crumbled, and Gore was lost, even though any number of visitors came and went, including Shirley MacLaine and—oddest of all—Larry Flynt, who arrived in a gold-plated wheelchair.

I sat by the bed and held Gore's hand, retelling stories he had told me many times with great satisfaction. I recalled how he read to himself in the little alcove on the top floor of his grandparents' house on Rock Creek Park. I mentioned some of his old friends, such as John Latouche and Fred Dupee, Paul Newman and Joanne Woodward, George Armstrong, Barbara Epstein, and Boaty Boatwright. I repeated one of his favorite stories, about the time Edna O'Brien came to Ravello for a visit in the eighties. She ran full of joy onto the filthy beach below Ravello in Atrani, throwing off her clothes, then jumping naked into a stinking cesspool below a drainpipe, her red hair streaming in the redolent sewage that poured into the bay.

Gore smiled once or twice as I spoke. Suddenly he motioned me to move close. In a hushed voice, barely audible, he said, "Howard. Talk about Howard." So I recalled some good times in Amalfi, at Da Zaccaria, their favorite restaurant. I remembered a time in London at the Connaught Hotel when Gore tried to get Howard to like quail eggs, and Howard shouted at him, "I'd like a bagel, Gore! That's what I'd fucking like! A fucking bagel!" I talked about another time at the Goldener Hirsch, a fine hotel and restaurant in Salzburg, when Howard began singing "New York, New York" in a loud voice, "just to irritate the Austrians," as Gore would declare. When the head waiter came over to protest against the loud singing, Gore said to him in his sharpest tone: "I know the lady who founded this goddamn hotel, the Countess Harriet von Walderdorff! So go away!"

Gore looked at me with eyes like cut glass, full of tears. He had wet cheeks as well. This last image of him stays with me.

On the morning of July 31, 2012, I woke up at home in Vermont to this message on my iPhone from Burr: "Jay, I didn't want to call you up in the middle of the night. But I can tell you that Gore's ultimate passing was peaceful—a relief, considering what he's been through in the last months."

Inevitably, Gore's passing led the news on most networks, on NPR, in newspapers around the world. There was even a warm obituary that began on the front page of *The New York Times*, his favorite adversary, with a headline that read: GORE VIDAL DIES AT 86; PROLIFIC, ELEGANT, ACERBIC WRITER.

If there's a heaven, Gore was certainly pissing down from the clouds that morning from a very great height.

Conclusion

"After such knowledge, what forgiveness?" This troubling line, posed by T. S. Eliot in "Gerontion," haunts every biographer. After three decades, Gore stays in my mind, his voice as present now as when he was alive, and I badly miss our conversations. Often I feel the urge to reach for the phone, wishing to discuss with him some outrage on the political scene or something amiss in our foreign affairs. He had a wise and memorable way of characterizing things, and he could formulate an articulate response on the spot. He would have me laughing hard.

Gore understood his strengths and weaknesses as a writer. To Gianfranco Corsini, he once wrote: "The narrative gift is a given: one has it or not. But the gift is often for the ear and eye, for dramatic writing or words on the page. There are not many writers who can do both. Neither Hemingway nor Fitzgerald could write a play or screenplay despite their gift for dialogue to be read. Faulkner, whose dialogue is hard to read on the page, had the gift for dramatic writing, as in *The Big Sleep*. I was always able to do both, in which I resemble Thornton Wilder more than anyone else and, perhaps, Steinbeck. We speak now not of genius but of versatility." Needless to say, he mainly regarded himself as a novelist, not a pundit or wag or wit. Rightly, he considered those terms demeaning.

Of his novels, I prefer *Julian*, *Burr*, and *Lincoln* to his so-called "inventions," yet I suspect that Matt Tyrnauer is right when he says of *Myra Breckenridge* and *Myron*: "They're amazing books, groundbreaking stuff. Gore understood sexuality and sexual politics in ways never before seen—and probably not yet seen. It may take a long time for the culture to catch up with him." I admire some of Gore's lesser-known novels, too, such as *Messiah* and *Kalki*, both of which have imaginative force and ferocity. And *The Judgment of Paris* remains a delicately written and underrated book in which the mature voice of the artist comes into its own.

It's the essays, however, that contain his central work. One can hardly get one's mind, or one's hands, around *United States*, his collected essays. It's a capacious achievement. His voice, whether writing about politics or literature, strikes an irreverent and radical note. That knowing, urbane, and wryly bemused voice was a gift to the late twentieth century and beyond. His anger mattered as well as his humor. The daily injustices at work on this great stage of human folly were painful for him to witness. Writing these essays, he felt his way toward comprehension, even compassion.

That Gore was not always nice to people was noticed. He could be cantankerous, testy, ill-mannered, a terrible snob, a drunken bore. On top of which he had, as Jason Epstein notes, terribly thin skin, and believed a vigorous offense was the best defense. He struck back reflexively at those who criticized him. And he never forgot a slight, however minor. For instance, he disliked a review of *Lincoln* by Joyce Carol Oates in *The New York Times Book Review*—even though it was a fairly positive notice. Unpleasantly (for me, as Oates is a friend of mine), he would make harsh critical remarks about her from that point on, even though I once caught him reading and (as he admitted) enjoying a volume of her essays.

His narcissism skewed his daily life in unattractive ways, as he sought reinforcement wherever he could. His imperial self demanded obeisance and agreement from those around him, and Howard bore the brunt of this black energy. It's no wonder that in the late seventies, Howard was apparently fed up, and friends thought he might actually leave Gore. But Howard could never leave Gore. As Mrs. Micawber famously declares in *David Copperfield*: "I will never leave Mr. Micawber!" Howard was there for the duration, over half a century, and it was—with many downsides as well as upsides for him—a mutually sustaining relationship.

Their sex life was, as Gore frequently said, nonexistent after a year or so. After that, they settled into a loving friendship, and Howard assisted Gore in finding partners, especially in Rome. Gore preferred anonymous sex and had lots of it. Anyone seeking more than I've bothered to detail can pick up a copy of *In Bed with Gore Vidal: Hustlers, Hollywood, and the Private World of an American Master* by Tim Teeman. It's a tell-all book, probably accurate. The extent of Gore's sex life was dizzying, though he gave up sex after a certain point, as he wittily said, in favor of litigation. My impression is that he rarely had much sex after the age of sixty because alcohol made the impulse less urgent, the act itself less possible.

Perhaps the most impressive thing about Gore was his will to power. He understood how the media worked, and he knew how to operate the levers of publicity in ways that got his work before a very large public in many languages. Even when his books didn't quite work, they often sold well. Two of his plays—*Visit to a Small Planet* and *The Best Man*—were bona fide hits on Broadway, even though Gore didn't continue to grow as a playwright. His gift for screenwriting was less than remarkable, with few notable successes, although he kept a hand in the business for decades.

Beginning in the fifties, he fashioned a persona that worked brilliantly on television, and that was no small achievement. His cool manner and clever way of talking, combined with a deep knowledge of world affairs, made him an ideal guest on talk shows. He could drop names as much as he liked, and Johnny Carson, Merv Griffin, and Dick Cavett would never wince. He stood firm before William F. Buckley under the hot lights, and looked on with pity while Norman Mailer tied himself into knots. In countless interviews, he put forward a complex version of himself, exhibiting many sides. The empire grew as Gore added territories, crossing many generic boundaries, including novel, screenplay, television or stage play, essay, and historical treatise. No major sector of the globe was ignored: Washington, Hollywood, New York, and Europe (London, Paris, Rome) all became familiar playgrounds for his expanding self. Even Bangkok and Istanbul were added to the list.

A biographer is not a judge, and I have no wish to do more than describe a man I admired and valued as a friend. He had his faults—not unlike the rest of us. He was both angel and monster, even at the same time. For all this, he was an astonishing man, inventive and shimmering, with a superb linguistic facility and capacious memory. If he could be petty and difficult, that was part of his total being. He was an alcoholic, no doubt. And he had lacked the kind of mother-love that might have encouraged a sensitive young child to grow into a complete and balanced human being. His sexuality certainly complicated his life, as he came of age well before being gay was something one could accept without difficulty. He fought bravely against the stereotypes of gays, of course, coming out publicly in *The City and the Pillar*, breaking ground in American fiction. But he would never feel at ease with his sexuality. As late as 2011, he told me that he wondered if he should have married and had children! "I would have liked a son," he said. But this was just the old imperial self again, never quite happy with territorial limits.

Will anyone remember Gore Vidal in years to come? Will they read him? It's not possible, of course, to answer such questions with certainty. One thinks of his contemporaries: John Horne Burns, Saul Bellow, Philip Roth, Mary McCarthy, John Updike, Truman Capote, Joan Didion, Norman Mailer, and William Styron. Will anyone in a hundred years read any of their books? It's impossible to know. But Gore will certainly be recalled by anyone who lived in his time as a meteor who streaked through the night skies, with a fantail of sparks.

His contribution to the biographical novel might well be his most durable legacy. He took the old-fashioned historical novel in fresh directions with *Julian*, *Burr*, and *Lincoln*, foregrounding the figure in the title, digging into the texture of their lives, examining motives, giving a fully rounded sense of their accomplishments, their needs, their weaknesses, their public self-renderings. It's worth noting that an array of biographical novels appeared in the eighties and nineties, many of them (consciously or not) owing something to Gore's advances in the genre, his willingness to take historical fiction seriously and to move it in unlikely directions. One thinks, for instance, of novels by Peter Ackroyd, Julian Barnes, Bruce Duffy, Russell Banks, Madison Smartt Bell, Michael Cunningham, Joanna Scott, Julia Alvarez, Kate Moses, and many others. A tidal wave of biographical fiction has swept the Anglo-American scene in recent decades, and Gore remains a founding father in this area.

As for his politics, Gore took after his grandfather as a kind of Tory populist. He often sided with the poor and dispossessed, and could summon a proper rage on their behalf, but he had no wish to mingle with them, preferring suites in five-star hotels and good restaurants. He was an anti-Roosevelt Democrat, with a quasi-socialist tinge. The American republic had not lived up to his expectations, and this upset him deeply. His essays and historical novels represent a search for national origins, a decades-long exploration of the disaster (as he saw it) that followed when the drive toward empire began, as far back as the Louisiana Purchase in 1802. As we see in *Lincoln*, he understood that slavery was a wound that would not easily be healed, and he doubted, indeed, that Lincoln himself really meant what he said on this subject.

Gore was a shy man who, when not wearing the elaborately contrived mask of Gore Vidal, could be awkward with people, even frightened of conversations and encounters with those outside of his immediate circle. Having missed out on college because of the war, he became a lifelong autodidact, and one of the most learned men of his time. Like a schoolboy, he often grinned with pleasure in the presence of academics like David Herbert Donald, Isaiah Berlin, or John Kenneth Galbraith, and he actively sought their company.

Gore meant a great deal to me and to many others—as a writer and man of ideas. He was a brave figure on the political scene who would stand up for things that mattered to him, and he made his case eloquently before a wide audience. He was by nature a provocateur and scold, and this quality will not be held against him. The American scene is poorer without him, and one looks in vain for his successors.

Postscript

The obituaries after his death on July 31, 2012, were long and largely admiring, with Gore's face on the front of major newspapers around the world. Many of the leading network programs led with news of his death. But a more intriguing story followed when, two months later, the contents of his will became known. He had, with a single stroke of the pen in 2011, left everything—his manuscripts, his real estate, his money, and all future royalties to his work—to Harvard University. A few paintings were left to the Huntington Library in San Marino, California.

A headline in *The New York Times* read: "For Gore Vidal, a Final Plot Twist." The questions multiplied: Why had he done this, and what did it mean? Had he intended to slight people close to him? Was he seeking posthumous attention?

He certainly cut out of the will those closest to him, including his nephew Burr Steers and half sister Nina, who immediately challenged the will. Many friends (including myself) felt that Gore should have left something to the faithful Norberto, who had devoted himself for many years to looking after him when few others would. I believed that Gore should have created a charitable foundation, not unlike what Norman Mailer had done. It might, for instance, have furthered the cause of literacy and writing in generations to come. Or Gore might have given the money to liberal causes that he had spent so much of his life defending. To my surprise, he dismissed such ideas out of hand when I suggested them. "The gravy train is long enough," he said.

Harvard, of course, welcomed his estate. Needless to say, the estimated $37 million in question would constitute a drop in the bucket of their endowment. Gore's Harvard benefactors—future students and faculty—would scarcely notice his generosity. My best guess is that he wished to associate himself with a great name, such as Harvard. He had been impressed by their invitations to lecture on several occasions, and he thought that his papers—which he had some years earlier transferred to Harvard from the Wisconsin State Historical Society at the University of Wisconsin—had been well looked after. (He had sent me to inspect them, in fact, and I reported that the Houghton Library at Harvard was an excellent place to leave one's papers.)

As mentioned, Gore had bought a small house in the south of France for Muzius Gordon Dietzmann, his godson, a few years before his death. Muzius would get to keep the house. This was perhaps the one aspect of Gore's will that nobody could fault, since Muzius had devoted himself for many years to Gore, helping in any way he could, offering kindness and emotional support during the difficult final decade. The slighting of Norberto and Burr was less forgivable, as both played a major role in Gore's life during the last years. (Gore had always told Burr he would get the house in the Hollywood Hills.)

At various points, Gore asked at least two friends to be his literary executor, including me. Matt Tyrnauer was another. I always hemmed and hawed at the prospect of looking after the rights to his work, suggesting that his vast output would require a good deal of attention, and that he should have a number of knowledgeable and interested parties involved in making decisions about future editions of his work, in various languages. It was apparent to me that he never really wanted me to proceed along these lines, although in public he often called me his executor. I was quite relieved when I discovered I was, indeed, not his literary executor. The problem was that nobody assumed this role. For a man who supposedly cared about his writing and its fate, this was a peculiar lapse of judgment on his part.

Tellingly, Gore said to me in 2011: "I don't really care what happens to my work when I'm dead." Stoicism had given way to nihilism. Nevertheless, his efforts to revise a few of his early novels contradict this statement. At times, he cared a great deal about his literary reputation, and he liked having readers. One has to assume he had mixed emotions about this matter, which isn't perhaps surprising; he had no belief in the afterlife, and was pleased that during his lifetime he had managed to find a wide audience and make enough money from his pen to live in style. His empire of self had expanded well beyond what the young Gore Vidal might have imagined was possible.

Acknowledgments

Most important, I'm grateful to Gore Vidal for suggesting, in the late eighties, that I should write this book and for introducing me to many of his friends over the years, including Alberto Moravia, Graham Greene, Anthony Burgess, Frederic Prokosch, who spoke to me frankly about Gore, with his blessing. I'm also grateful to Howard Austen, who was ever generous with his time, and as much a friend to me as Gore was. Gore has allowed me to quote from his letters and books as I liked, and that has made writing this book possible—it was written in sections over several decades, with many gaps, then completed between 2011 and 2014.

It would be impossible to thank everyone who contributed to this project, as it was under way for such a long time. I acknowledge all of those whom I interviewed in the course of the book, but I want to give special thanks to the following, who in conversations about Gore helped to shape my ideas. These include especially my editor, Gerald Howard; my wife, Devon Jersild; and my agent, Geri Thoma. Gore's agent, Richard Morris, was unfailingly helpful along the way. But I must single out the following as well: George Armstrong, Luigi Bartolo, Ann Beattie, Richard Beswick, Derek Blasberg, Boaty Boatwright, Scotty Bowers, Carl Bromley, Gary Conklin, George B. Cotkin, Patty Dryden, Barbara Epstein, Jason Epstein, Gary Fisketjon, Judith Harris, Anthony Harvey, Shirley Hazzard, Marion Holt, Erica Jong, John Lahr, Gavin Lambert, Frank Lentricchia, Thomas Mallon, Edward Martin, Harry Mathews, Jody McAuliffe, Michael Mewshaw, Alberto Moravia, L. Jay Oliva, Donald E. Pease, Lincoln Perry, Richard Poirier, Thomas Powers, E. Barrett Prettyman, Anthony Quinn, Alastair Reid, Susan Sarandon, Burr Steers, Jean

Stein, Tom Stoppard, Gay Talese, James Tatum, Michael Tyler-Whittle, Matt Tyrnauer, Edmund White, Jon Wiener, and Nicholas Wrathall.

Steven Abbott, Harry Kloman, Heather Neilson, and Will Ray read drafts of this book and offered suggestions for revisions. I owe them a huge debt of gratitude for their generosity, thoughtfulness, and intelligent criticism.

I must also thank Fred Kaplan. His groundbreaking work on Gore has been immensely helpful to me in writing this book. Several critics played a shaping role in my thinking, and these include Dennis Altman, Bernard F. Dick, Heather Neilson, Donald E. Pease, Catharine R. Stimpson, and Ray Lewis White. In addition, I was lucky to have in hand the bibliographical works of Steven Abbott and S. T. Joshi.

Notes

Except where otherwise noted, quotations from Gore Vidal and Howard Austen are taken from interviews with me or, more occasionally, from my diary (cited as JPD). In each chapter, the interviews are noted by date the first time they occur, and the quotations that follow in that chapter, when not specifically noted, are from the cited interview. Many quotations, from the letters or journals of Gore Vidal, are noted as GVP, referring to the Gore Vidal Papers at the Houghton Library of Harvard University.

Chapter One

9 "I always thought it was": Interview with Gore Vidal, May 10, 2010.

11 "Tom Gore had lived": Monroe Billington, "Honorable Thomas P. Gore: The Blind Senator," *The Chronicles of Oklahoma* 35 (Fall 1957): 117.

12 "Unyielding to adversity": MS Am 2350, GVP, 766.

15 "Gore liked to recall": Interview with Judith Harris, April 6, 2013.

16 "I read all twenty-three": Gore Vidal, "Tarzan Revisited," in *United States: Essays 1952–1992* (New York: Random House, 1993), 1129.

16 "Bewitched, I read the play": Gore Vidal, *Point to Point Navigation* (New York: Doubleday, 2007), 13.

16 "My life seemed like": JPD, May 2010.

18 "systematized commercial aviation": Gore Vidal, "Lindbergh: The Eagle Is Grounded," in *The Last Empire: Essays 1992–2000* (New York: Doubleday, 2001), 138.

19 "Early in life, at Yale": Vidal, "Reflections on Glory Reflected," *United States*, 1252.

20 "All of Merrywood's downstairs": Gore Vidal, *Palimpsest* (New York: Random House, 1995), 10.

20 "rain fell in dark diagonals": Gore Vidal, *Washington, D.C.* (Boston: Little, Brown, 1967), 3.

20 "money hedged us all round": Vidal, *Point to Point Navigation*, 21.

20 "Peter admired his father": Vidal, *Washington, D.C.*, 7.

21 "I had no mother": JPD, April 1992.
23 "It was a traditional sort": Interview with E. Barrett Prettyman, September 2, 2013.
23 "We were friends immediately": Vidal *Palimpsest,* 23.
24 "was a multi-sport superstar": Available at http://www.washingtoncitypaper.com/articles/40778/st-albans-pitching-factory-dc-private-school-is-breeding-ground.
25 "You're a queer": Gore Vidal, *The City and the Pillar* (New York: Grosset & Dunlap, 1948), 306.
26 "They were both twenty-five": Gore Vidal, *The Judgment of Paris* (New York: Dutton, 1952), chapter ten.
26 "It was like he came": JPD, June 1998.
26 "She saw poor Jimmie": Letter from Gore Vidal to Val Holley, December 15, 1997, courtesy of Holley.
28 "Rome lay at the center": Interview with George Armstrong, July 29, 1990.
28 "In the Irish Sea": Vidal, *Palimpsest*, 87.
29 "the spindly sons": Ted Morgan, *Literary Outlaw: The Life and Times of William S. Burroughs* (New York: Henry Holt, 1988), 44.
29 "I remember him walking": Interview with Edward Martin, September 3, 2005.
30 "He dropped names": Ibid.
31 "On the rare occasions": Vidal, *Palimpsest*, 88.
31 "I wish that I were": Ibid., 90.
32 "my first beau": Fred Kaplan, *Gore Vidal: A Biography* (New York: Doubleday, 1999), 127.
33 "Night, night black": MS Am 2350, GVP, 761.
33 "Roosevelt knew about the attack": Letter from Gore Vidal to Thomas P. Gore, n.d. 1943, GVP.
34 "He had energy to burn": William H. Tunner, *Over the Hump* (New York: Duell, Sloan, and Pierce, 1964), 19.
34 "His debating skills struck us": Interview with Edward Martin, September 3, 2005.
34 "My grandmother would say": Vidal, *Palimpsest*, 93.
35 "trying to use the war": *The Exonian* (October 28, 1942): 4.
35 "he never failed to hold": Interview with Edward Martin, September 3, 2005.
35 "In this last election": MS Am 2350, GVP, 816.
35 "a lucky ticket": Letter from Thomas P. Gore to Gore Vidal, December 10, 1942, GVP.
36 "Within the first two years": See John McPhee, interview by Peter Hessler, *The Paris Review* 192 (Spring 2010).
36 "You're crazy!": See Vidal, *Palimpsest*, 32–35.

Chapter Two

40 "It was the best": Interview with Gore Vidal, August 20, 1991.
41 "Dearest Gene": Letter from Nina Olds to Gore Vidal, n.d. 1945, GVP.
41 "It's hard to imagine": Interview with Matt Tyrnauer, September 13, 2013.

42 "I met him": Letter from Jean Stein to author, March 19, 2014.

42 "Of course I loved": Gore Vidal, "Remembering Orson Welles," in *United States: Essays 1952–1992* (New York: Random House, 1993), 1196.

43 "Once in bed": Gore Vidal, *Palimpsest* (New York: Random House, 1995), 95.

44 "I think perhaps": Letter from Gore Vidal to Eugene Vidal, January 26, 1945, GVP.

45 "Hemingway was the only writer": Letter from Gore Vidal to Elaine Dundy, n.d. 1972[?], GVP.

46 "I was relieved": Gore Vidal, *Screening History* (Cambridge, MA: Harvard University Press, 1992), 72.

46 "Franklin goes on and on": Gore Vidal, *The Golden Age* (New York: Doubleday, 2000), 167.

46 "The king is dead": Letter from Thomas P. Gore to Gore Vidal, May 14, 1945, in which TPG quotes his grandson's letter, GVP.

48 "Jimmie was more like": Interview with Howard Austen, July 21, 1998.

48 "a sudden unexpected introduction": Interview with Frederic Prokosch, August 10, 1988.

49 "just before New Year's": Letter from Gore Vidal to Bill Gray, n.d. 1945, GVP.

51 "The city was coming alive": Interview with Alastair Reid, October 3, 2011.

52 Her diaries tell only: See Kim Krizan, "Gore Vidal's Secret, Unpublished Love Letter to Anaïs Nin," *The Huffington Post* (September 27, 2013), available at http://www.huffingtonpost.com/kim-krizan/gore-vidals-secret-unpubl_b_4004916.html?page=2.

52 "She constantly reworked": Letter from Gore Vidal to Deirdre Bair, September 1994, GVP.

52 "Nick Wreden was his big supporter": Interview with Jack Macrae, October 6, 2013.

53 "What I see in the homosexual": Anaïs Nin, *The Diary of Anaïs Nin, Vol. 4: 1944–1947*, edited by Gunther Stuhlmann (New York: Mariner, 1972), 125.

54 Lerman's posthumous journals: See Leo Lerman, *The Grand Surprise: The Journals of Leo Lerman*, edited by Stephen Pascal (New York: Knopf, 1997).

54 "I first met Truman": JPD, June 20, 2010. Gore repeated this in a public interview with me at the 92nd Street Y.

55 "the last of Henry James' ": Quoted in Mary V. Dearborn, *Mistress of Modernism: The Life of Peggy Guggenheim* (New York: Houghton Mifflin, 2004), 247.

55 "People wanted to meet Peggy": Interview with Edmund White, June 9, 2014.

55 It is 1946: Vidal, *Palimpsest*, 10.

56 "The air was cool and moist": Gore Vidal, *Williwaw* (New York: Dutton, 1946), 140.

57 "sound craftsmanship": Orville Prescott, "Books of the Times," *The New York Times* (June 17, 1946): 19.

59 "The nice thing": Letter from Gore Vidal to Eugene Vidal, November 1946, GVP.

60 "I recall celebrating": From an inscription to Bill Gray, April 1955, GVP.

60 "central myth of homosexuality": Claude J. Summers, "*The City and the Pillar* as Gay Fiction," in *Gore Vidal: Writer Against the Grain*, edited by Jay Parini (New York: Columbia University Press, 1992), 61.

60 "I wanted to take risks": Gore Vidal, *The City and the Pillar* (New York: Dutton, 1948, revised edition 1965), 246.

61 "It appears on January 9th": Letter from Gore Vidal to Pat Crocker, October 1947, GVP.

61 "The book is now": Ibid., March 1948.

62 "Twenty-two pages": Victor R. Yanitelli, untitled review, *Best Sellers* 7 (April 1, 1947): 7.

63 "must construct this home": *The Diary of Anaïs Nin*, 186.

63 "Your sad Denver letter": Quoted in Krizan, "Gore Vidal's Secret, Unpublished Love Letter to Anaïs Nin."

64 "I never reread it": JPD, April 10, 2010.

65 "self-assurance, which was dazzling": Interview with Dominick Dunne, August 2, 2001.

Chapter Three

69 "And God knows": Interview with Howard Austen, July 21, 1998.

70 "Mailer had obviously suffered": Victor Weybright, *The Making of a Publisher: A Life in the 20th Century Book Revolution* (New York: Reynal & Company, 1967), 234.

70 "Harold had a very nice ass": Interview with Gore Vidal, August 25, 1995.

70 "This hardly bothered me": Gore Vidal, *Palimpsest* (New York: Random House, 1995), 131.

71 "I suppose you're with": Letter from Gore Vidal to Harold Lang, n.d. 1947[?], GVP.

72 "In the late forties": Vidal, *Palimpsest*, 127.

73 "coldly clinical": C. V. Terry, "The City and the Pillar," The New York Times Book Review, January 11, 1948, 22.

74 "Post-adolescent despair": JPD, May 10, 2010.

74 "long artificial speeches": Leslie Fiedler, "The Fate of the Novel," *The Kenyon Review* 10, No. 3 (Summer 1948): 520.

75 "I found Gore surprisingly": Interview with Frederic Prokosch, August 10, 1988.

75 "that unhappy young egotist": John Lahr, *Tennessee Williams: Mad Pilgrimage of the Flesh* (New York: Norton, 2014), 154.

76 "although they never liked": Interview with Edmund White, June 9, 2014.

76 "The idea put forward": Interview with Scotty Bowers, February 17, 2014.

76 "I first met Gore Vidal": Stephen Spender, "Gore Vidal: Private Eye," in *Gore Vidal: Writer Against the Grain*, edited by Jay Parini (New York: Columbia University Press, 1992), 175.

76 "Gore was a handsome kid": Tennessee Williams, *Memoirs* (New York: Doubleday, 1975), 146.

76 "I don't think you realized": Vidal, *Palimpsest*, 152.
77 "It was all spring flowers": Interview with Gore Vidal, September 2, 2006.
77 "Tennessee and I drove": Letter from Gore Vidal to Gianfranco Corsini, n.d. 1974[?], GVP.
78 "wonderfully shady characters": Vidal, *Palimpsest*, 167.
79 "I don't know when": Letter from Gore Vidal to John Lehmann, April 1948, Princeton University Library.
80 "When I was a student": John Weightman, "André Gide and the Homosexual Debate," *American Scholar* 59, No. 4 (August 1990): 591.
82 "American is not English": Fred Kaplan, *Gore Vidal: A Biography* (New York: Doubleday, 1999), 287.
83 "Everybody who was anybody": Interview with Richard Eberhart, June 20, 1990.
84 "You're not a poet!": Vidal, *Palimpsest*, 250.
84 "a short, barrel-chested": Gore Vidal, *The Golden Age* (New York: Doubleday, 285), 281.
86 "He was the single": Interview with Gore Vidal, April 10, 2010.
86 "I am going as fast": Thomas P. Gore to the editor of *The Independent* (Oklahoma City), March 14, 1936; quoted in *Congressional Record*, 74th Congress, 4378.
86 "Vidal apparently intended": John W. Aldridge, "A Boy and His Mom," *Saturday Review* (January 15, 1949): 19.
87 "a variety of poison oak": Letter from Gore Vidal to Pat Crocker, n.d. 1948, GVP.
87 "How is the house?": Ibid., n.d. 1949[?].
89 "I plan to spend": Daniel Rondeau, *Tanger et autres Marocs* (Paris: Gallimard, 1997), 199.
89 "It would be a good idea": Letter from Nina Olds to Gore Vidal, n.d. 1949, GVP.
89 "What nonsense": Letter from Paul Bowles to Gore Vidal, February 22, 1953, GVP.
90 "But Jane Bowles": Vidal, *Palimpsest*, 216.
90 "But I had much less money": Interview with Gore Vidal, August 22, 2009.
92 "The area entered": Gore Vidal, "FDR: Love on the Hudson," *The Last Empire: Essays 1992–292* (New York: Doubleday, 2001), 179.
92 "The house had not been": Interview with Gore Vidal, April 10, 2010.
92 "I should be thrilled": Letter from Gore Vidal to Pat Crocker, n.d. 1950[?], GVP.
93 "thoroughly understood why": Letter from Nina Olds to Gore Vidal, n.d. 1947, GVP.
93 "I need this": Letter from Gore Vidal to Pat Crocker, n.d. 1950, GVP.
94 "When a writer moves": Vidal, *Palimpsest*, 244.
95 "I liked him a lot": Interview with Howard Austen, July 21, 1998.
95 "Who wouldn't": Ibid., June 30, 1994.
96 "I had read *The City and the Pillar*": Interview with Marion Holt, October 20, 2013.
97 "Letters such as yours": Letter from Gore Vidal to Marion Holt, n.d. 1950, courtesy of Holt.

98 "I miss you": Letter from Howard Austen to Gore Vidal, February 10, 1953, GVP.
98 "A little bird": Ibid., n.d. 1953.
99 "a place where lively talk": Interview with Jason Epstein, December 12, 2013.

Chapter Four

103 "It was the first time": Interview with Gore Vidal, April 10, 2010.
104 "He was here at last:": Gore Vidal, *The Judgment of Paris* (New York: Dutton, 1952), 14.
104 "It was Huxley, in fact": Interview with Gore Vidal, April 10, 2010.
105 "I came to Egypt to die": Ibid., 167.
105 "with a subject": John W. Aldridge, "Three Tempted Him," *The New York Times Book Review* (March 9, 1952): 4.
106 "When I implied": Letter from Norman Mailer to Emile Capouya, May 26, 1962, in *Selected Letters of Norman Mailer*, edited by J. Michael Lennon (New York: Random House, 2014), 295.
106 "Gore's reputation was beginning": Interview with Richard Poirier, September 2, 2002.
107 "a talentless, self-promoting": *Selected Letters of William Styron*, edited by Rose Styron with R. Blakeslee Gilpin (New York: Random House, 2012), 195.
107 "The two met at Millie Brower's": J. Michael Lennon, *Norman Mailer: A Double Life* (New York: Simon & Schuster, 2013), 134.
107 "This time": Interview with Gore Vidal, September 2, 2006.
108 "Of all our novelists": Gore Vidal, "Real Class," *The New York Review of Books* 21, no. 12 (July 18, 1974).
108 "I had read Agatha Christie": Interview with Gore Vidal, October 10, 2009.
109 "He could get people laughing": Interview with George Armstrong, July 29, 1990.
110 "the whole thing was a scam": JPD, August 15, 1996.
111 "I am a novelist": Gore Vidal, "Visit to a Small Planet," in *United States: Essays 1952–1992* (New York: Random House, 1993), 1160.
111 "Ideally you need": Letter from Audrey Wood to Gore Vidal, July 18, 1952, GVP.
112 "between the years": Neil Postman, *Conscientious Objections: Stirring Up Trouble About Language, Technology, and Education* (New York: Knopf, 1988), 118.
113 "I am king of television": Letter from Gore Vidal to Pat Crocker, n.d. 1955, GVP.
114 "My dear Mr. Vidal": Letter from Mrs. Thomas P. Gore to Gore Vidal, April 15, 1954, GVP.
114 "You've got to keep popping up": Interview with Gore Vidal, August 20, 1991.
114 "Nothing is easier nowadays": Richard H. Rovere, "Talk of the Town: Vidal," *The New Yorker* (April 23, 1960): 38.

115 "I was maybe fifteen": Interview with Thomas Powers, May 7, 2014.
116 "I faced the efficient vulgarity": Gore Vidal, *Messiah* (New York: Dutton, 1954), 108.
117 "the prolific Mr. Vidal": Jerome Stone, "Frightening Future," *Saturday Review* (May 22, 1954): 35.
117 "*Messiah* is rather a bore": Letter from Gore Vidal to Pat Crocker, n.d. 1954, GVP.
117 "a noble failure": Letter from Gore Vidal to Kimon Friar, n.d. 1954, in Fred Kaplan, *Gore Vidal: A Biography* (New York: Doubleday, 1999), 388.
118 "A novel is all one's own": Vidal, "Writing Plays for Television," *United States*, 1156.
118 "I was just getting into": Interview with Paul Newman, June 6, 1992.
118 "To be frank": Interview with Howard Austen, July 21, 1998.
119 "I knew Joanne": Gore Vidal notes, 1973, GVP.
119 "Shit has its own integrity": Gore Vidal, "The Ashes of Hollywood," *The New York Review of Books* (May 17, 1973): 34.
120 "Gore liked the sexual possibilities": Interview with Scotty Bowers, February 17, 2014.
120 "Scotty was always someone": JPD, June 15, 2011.
121 "We celebrated with much champagne": Letter from Gore Vidal to Pat Crocker, October 1955, GVP.
122 "a tense, smart, glittering": Interview with Elaine Steinbeck, November 3, 1993.
123 "uproarious": Brooks Atkinson, "The Theatre: 'Visit to a Small Planet,'" *The New York Times* (February 8, 1957): 18.
123 "One evening back there": Vidal, "Dawn Powell: The American Writer," *United States*, 306–7.
124 "You will be fortunate": Quoted by N. A. Straight, "On the Other Side of Eternity," *Vanity Fair* (February 6, 2013).
125 "Gore is doing well": Ibid.
127 "For decades now": Unpublished note on a single page in Elaine Dundy file, GVP.
130 Heston, for his part: See Tim Cornwell, "Ben-Hur Gay Slur Drives Heston Crazy," *The Independent* (June 27, 1996): 19.
130 "couldn't stay longer": Letter from Sam Zimbalist to Gore Vidal, June 6, 1958, GVP.
130 "No more movies": Letter from Gore Vidal to Paul Bowles, May 1958, University of Delaware Library.

Chapter Five

136 "I would look into the drawer": Interview with Gore Vidal, August 20, 1995.
137 "both amusing and engrossing": Brooks Atkinson, "The Best Man," *The New York Times* (April 1, 1960): 39.
137 "The play will be": *The Letters of Arthur Schlesinger, Jr.*, edited by Andrew Schlesinger and Stephen Schlesinger (New York: Random House, 2013), 189.

138 When Gore died in 2012: See Jon Wiener, "The Gore Vidal FBI File," *The Nation* (July 29, 1913).
139 "In those days I could": Interview with Gore Vidal, September 2, 2006.
139 "Jackie asked me": Gore Vidal, "Hersh's JFK," in *The Last Empire: Essays 1992–2000* (New York: Doubleday, 2001), 231.
140 "Imagine a guy": Interview with L. Jay Oliva, February 27, 2014.
141 "On the importance of production": John Kenneth Galbraith, *The Affluent Society: Fortieth Anniversary Edition* (New York: Houghton Mifflin, 1998), 100.
141 "dominated the evening": *The Letters of Arthur Schlesinger, Jr.*, 193.
142 "I liked him better": David Pietrusza, *1960: LBJ vs. JFK vs. Nixon: The Epic Campaign That Forged Three Presidencies* (New York: Sterling, 2008), 283.
142 "bachelor . . . who lives": Ira Henry Freeman, "Gore Vidal Conducts Campaign of Quips and Liberal Views," *The New York Times* (September 15, 1960): 32.
143 "If there is anything": Fred Kaplan, *Gore Vidal: A Biography* (New York: Doubleday, 1999), 487.
144 "I liked the play": Gore Vidal, "Comment," *Esquire* (May 1962): 47–54.
145 "a Dostoevskyan ploy": Louis Menand, "Critic at Large: The Norman Invasion," *The New Yorker* (October 21, 2013).
145 "Gore and I were": Interview with Norman Mailer, June 3, 1992.
146 "In August 1961": Gore Vidal, "Washington, We Have a Problem," *Vanity Fair* (December 2000): 35.
147 "Presidential cries for action": Gore Vidal, "The Race into Grace, or the Civilization Gap," *Esquire* (August 1961): 120.
148 "for being drunk": Quoted in Anthony Arthur, *Literary Feuds: A Century of Celebrated Quarrels from Mark Twain to Tom Wolfe* (New York: Thomas Dunn, 2002), 174.
148 "We know what they are": Quoted in Mary Vespa, "Sued by Gore Vidal and Stung by Lee Radziwill, a Wounded Truman Capote Lashes Back at the Dastardly Duo," *People* (June 25, 1979): 38.
149 "I was impressed": Gore Vidal, "Barry Goldwater: A Chat," in *Rocking the Boat* (Boston: Little, Brown, 1962), 39.
149 "The cult of feeling": "Theater," ibid., 83.
150 "Gore would hate to hear this": Interview with Anthony Burgess, February 3, 1990.
150 "a diphthong was able": Vidal, "Ladders to Heaven," *Rocking the Boat*, 130–31.
151 "He came to Athens": JPD, April 3, 1991. Merrill was visiting me in Vermont, and we talked about his various times with Gore.
151 "I have never felt more": Letter from Gore Vidal to A. A. Matsas, July 18, 1962, GVP.
152 "There was something about Rome": Interview with Harry Mathews, January 18, 2013.
153 "Tennessee and I would ride": Gore Vidal interviewed by John Lahr, 2006, courtesy of Lahr.
153 "His damn smoking": Interview with Gore Vidal, October 10, 2009.

155 The response was one: Letter from Harold Hayes to Gore Vidal, March 12, 1963, GVP.
156 "I would see Gore": Interview with Anthony Quinn, October 3, 1992.
156 "I always felt that": Gore Vidal to Irene [?], n.d., GVP.
156 "Rome was a kind of axis": Interview with Anthony Burgess, February 3, 1990.
157 "rugged young men": Christopher Hitchens, *Hitch-22: A Memoir* (Toronto: Signal, 2011), 153.
157 "I visited him often in Rome": Interview with Boaty Boatwright, April 12, 2014.
157 "I was a kid from Arkansas": Interview with George Armstrong, July 6, 1991.
158 "It was rule number one": Interview with Gore Vidal, September 2, 2006.
158 "Fred was the only critic": Interview with Gore Vidal, July 22, 1998.
158 "Gore had been working": Interview with Gavin Lambert, June 10, 2002.
159 "economic apostle": Gore Vidal, "Citizen Ken," *The New York Review of Books* (December 12, 1963): 23.
159 "He was one of the best": Interview with Barbara Epstein, July 15, 1997.
160 "The head-on clash": Bosley Crowther, "The Screen: Gore Vidal's 'Best Man': Stage Play Adaptation Opens at 2 Theaters," *The New York Times* (April 7, 1964): C1.
161 "The breathing actuality": Dudley Fitts, "Engaged in Life and in a Pagan Past," *The New York Times Book Review* (May 31, 1964): 4.
161 "Christianity was established": Gore Vidal, *Julian* (Boston: Little, Brown, 1964), vii–viii.
162 "In a blizzard, we filed": Ibid., 299.
162 "For many biographical novelists": Michael Lackey, ed., *Truthful Fictions: Conversations with American Biographical Novelists* (New York: Bloomsbury, 2014), 2.
163 "With Julian, the light went": Vidal, *Julian*, 502.

Chapter Six

167 "I needed television": Interview with Gore Vidal, August 10, 1993.
168 "Norman imagined himself": Interview with Gay Talese, March 20, 2014.
169 "I had learned a trade": Interview with Gore Vidal, August 20, 1991.
169 "In the mid-sixties": Interview with George Armstrong, July 6, 1991.
169 "Over the next two decades": Interview with Judith Harris, March 9, 2014.
170 He wrote to Fred Dupee: Letter from Gore Vidal to Fred Dupee, September 1, 1965, Columbia University Library.
170 "wreathed in friendship": Ibid., March 8, 1965.
170 "I tried to stay away": Interview with Gore Vidal, September 2, 2006.
170 "Gore thinks distance": Quoted in Boze Hadleigh, *Celebrity Feuds: The Cattiest Rows, Spats, and Tiffs Ever Recorded* (Dallas: Taylor Publishing, 1999), 166.
170 "It was a good life": Interview with Harry Mathews, January 2012.
171 "sex was hugely important": Interview with Thomas Powers, May 7, 2014.
171 "I saw a sign": Interview with Howard Austen, July 21, 1998.

172 "The Italian *character*": Gore Vidal to Judith Harris, available at http://www.i-italy.org/bloggers/34016/gore-vidals-love-affair-italy.
174 "After all, Clay will do anything": Gore Vidal, *Washington, D.C.* (Boston: Little, Brown, 1967), 266.
175 "Kennedy dead has infinitely": Gore Vidal, "The Holy Family," in *Reflections Upon a Sinking Ship* (Boston: Little, Brown, 1969), 161.
177 "I personally find myself": Preface, ibid., xiii.
177 "I just didn't want": Interview with Gore Vidal, August 10, 1993.
178 "The novel being dead": Gore Vidal, *Myra Breckinridge* (Boston: Little, Brown, 1968), 4.
178 "I shall not begin": Ibid., 6.
178 "the cock-worshipping Dorians": Ibid., 6.
179 "Man plus woman": Gore Vidal, "On Pornography," in *United States: Essays 1952–1992* (New York: Random House, 1993), 566.
179 "the midsection of the huge": Vidal, *Myra Breckinridge*, 8.
180 "The sphincter resembled": Ibid., 165.
180 "saddened and repelled": Ibid., 184.
181 "Sympathetic magic": Ibid., 241.
181 "later versions of queer theory": For a clear introduction to queer theory and its evolution, see Sharon Marcus, "Queer Theory for Everyone: A Review Essay," *Signs* (Autumn 2005): 191–218.
181 In fact, three printings: Nicole Moore, *The Censor's Library* (Queensland: University of Queensland Press, 2012), 270.
182 "very subtle psychological self-portrait": Letter from Christopher Isherwood to Gore Vidal, August 12, 1967, GVP.
183 "Sardinia, Venice": Letter from Gore Vidal to F. W. Dupee, September 16, 1967, Columbia University Library.
184 "Gore Vidal's *Weekend*": Walter Kerr, "Ready, Aim, Fire—But at What?," *The New York Times* (March 31, 1968): B1.
188 "Now they're moving in": Quoted on NPR, Ina Jaffe, "1968 Chicago Riot Left Mark on Political Protests," August 23, 2008.
189 "They really sealed the deal": Interview with Matt Tyrnauer, September 13, 2013.
190 "Regularly I think": Letter from Eugene Vidal to Gore Vidal, n.d. 1968, GVP.
190 "A celebrity is simply one": Quoted in John B. Judis, *William F. Buckley, Jr.: Patron Saint of the Conservatives* (New York: Simon & Schuster, 1988), 293–94.
191 "He sued me": Gore Vidal, "Gore Vidal Speaks Seriously Ill of the Dead," *Truthdig* (March 20, 2008); available at http://www.truthdig.com/report/item/20080320_gore_vidal_speaks_seriously_ill_of_the_dead.
193 "It's odd but the older one": Letter from Gore Vidal to Bob Bookman, n.d. 1969, GVP.
194 "Ronald Reagan is a well-preserved": Vidal, "Twenty-ninth Republican Convention, August 5–8, 1968," in *Reflections Upon a Sinking Ship*, 234.
194 "graphic and plausible": "John O'Hara's Old Novels," ibid., 49.
194 "bring what we think about sex": "Pornography," ibid., 98.
195 "The obvious danger for the writer": "Writers and the World," ibid., 11.

195 "Gore told me what he": Interview with George Armstrong, July 29, 1990.
196 "the Black Swan": Gore Vidal, "Black Swan's Way," *The Observer* (May 12, 1994), 36.
196 "resisted reading Nabokov's": Gore Vidal, *Two Sisters: A Novel in the Form of a Memoir* (Boston: Little, Brown, 1970), 230.
196 "People who obtain power": Ibid., 134.
197 "It's a pity that what pleasure": Ibid., 164.
197 "So ends that summer": Ibid., 250.
197 "I read Gore's *Two Sisters*": *The Diaries of Kenneth Tynan*, edited by John Lahr (New York: Bloomsbury, 2001), 141.

Chapter Seven

200 "an insult to intelligence": "Some Sort of Nadir," *Time* (July 6, 1970): 42.
201 "We aren't lovers anyway": Entry from February 26, 1946, in *Mirages: The Unexpurgated Diary of Anaïs Nin 1939–1947*, edited by Paul Herron (Athens, OH: Swallow Press, 2013), 87.
201 "He looks thinner": Christopher Isherwood, *Liberation: Diaries 1970–1983*, edited by Katherine Bucknell (New York: HarperCollins, 2012), 10.
202 "Women are not going": Gore Vidal, "Women's Liberation Meets Miller-Mailer-Manson Man," in *Homage to Daniel Shays: Collected Essays 1952–1972* (New York: Random House, 1972), 391.
203 "he created the most beautiful metaphors": See William F. Buckley Jr., "Norman Mailer: RIP," *National Review* (November 14, 2007): 4.
203 "a prisoner of the virility cult": Kate Millett, *Sexual Politics* (New York: Doubleday, 1970), 314.
205 "Gore was on the *Merv Griffin Show*": Isherwood, *Liberation*, 147.
205 "Gore wanted to run": Quoted in Thomas Maier, *Dr. Spock: An American Life* (New York: Basic Books, 2003), 349.
206 "there were actual bomb threats": Interview with Susan Sarandon, May 12, 2014.
209 "Everyone liked Gore": Interview with Alberto Moravia, August 4, 1988.
210 "a restaurant run by a lay order": Gore Vidal, *Point to Point Navigation* (New York: Doubleday, 2007), 97.
210 "What better place to observe": See epilogue, Roloff Beny, *Roloff Beny In Italy* (Toronto: McClelland and Stewart, 1974), 408.
212 "It was called La Rondinaia": JPD, August 9, 1993.
213 "Coming back from skiing": Letter from Paul Newman to Gore Vidal, n.d. 1973, GVP.
213 "I would visit at Edgewater": Interview with Richard Poirier, September 2, 2002.
213 "I wanted to publish him": Interview with Jason Epstein, December 12, 2013.
214 "Nixon will be out": *The Diaries of Kenneth Tynan*, edited by John Lahr (New York: Bloomsbury, 2001), 163.
215 "I confess to not having": Gore Vidal, *Burr* (New York: Random House, 1973), 58.
215 "spent a comfortable winter": Ibid., 177.

216 "General, we deal with such": Gore Vidal, *An Evening with Richard Nixon* (New York: Random House, 1972), 132.
216 "Colonel Burr was": Vidal, *Burr*, 416.
216 "He was ambitious": Ibid., 351.
216 "misused the Alien and Sedition Acts": Interview with Gore Vidal, July 22, 1998.
218 "Whether or not one thought": Gore Vidal, "Eleanor Roosevelt," in *Homage to Daniel Shays: Collected Essays, 1952–1972* (New York: Random House, 1972), 424.
218 "Although the equality": "Homage to Daniel Shays," ibid., 434.
218 "His essays are almost always": Roger Sale, "Making Gossip into Gospel," *The New York Times Book Review* (December 31, 1972): 7.
218 "It's what they say": Interview with Gore Vidal, December 20, 2010.
218 "Vidal is a writer": Sale, "Making Gossip into Gospel": 7.
220 "We often talked": Interview with Boaty Boatwright, April 12, 2014.
221 "When Vidal visited Australia": Dennis Altman, *Gore Vidal's America* (Malden, MA: Polity Press, 2005), 109.
222 "again at [Myra's] mercy": Letter from Gore Vidal to Richard Poirier, September 1974, GVP.
223 "Myra Breckinridge lives!": Gore Vidal, *Myra Breckinridge and Myron* (New York: Random House, 1986), 220. *Myron* was published by Random House in 1974.
223 "One minute I was fiddling": Ibid., 222.
224 "It is plain that nature": Ibid., 293.
224 "fun-loving, sterile Amazon": Ibid., 279.
224 "Thank God, Myra was not able": Ibid., 416.
225 "Once again, Gore Vidal": R. Z. Sheppard, "Myra Lives!," *Time* (October 21 1974): 119.
225 "worst novel yet": Martin Amis, "Left-Handed Backhand," *The Observer* (April 6, 1975): 30.
225 "a master farceur": Robert Mazzocco, "The Charm of Innocence," *The New York Review of Books* (November 14, 1974): 13.
226 "In one four-week period": Gore Vidal, "The State of the Union," in *Matters of Fact and of Fiction (Essays 1973–1976)* (New York: Random House, 1977), 266.
226 "I would see him struggle": Interview with Michael Tyler-Whittle, August 3, 1993.
227 "Stay close to Vidal": Letter from Norman Mailer to Mickey Knox, March 25, 1974, in *Selected Letters of Norman Mailer*, edited by J. Michael Lennon (New York: Random House, 2014), 441.
227 "I remember Gore in the 1970s": Interview with Edmund White, June 6, 2014.
227 "We were eating pasta": Judith Harris, from her unpublished diaries, courtesy of Harris.

Chapter Eight

230 observed in passing: Richard Zoerink, "Truman Capote Talks About His Crowd," *Playgirl* (September 1975): 50–51, 54, 80–81, 228.
230 "Distortions and lies": Interview with Gore Vidal, September 2, 2006.
231 "I get so monstrously bored": Judith Harris, from her unpublished diaries, courtesy of Harris.
234 "We show him as a nice": Philip Oakes, "Gore Vidal Tells Philip Oakes about the Age of Caligula: Tidings of Bad Cheer," *The Sunday Times* (December 14, 1975): 32.
235 "We are on the dawn": "Blood, Gore & a Whole Lot More," *Photoplay* (March 1976): 46.
235 "sickening, utterly worthless": Roger Ebert, "Caligula," *Chicago Sun-Times* (September 22, 1980): 22.
236 "I liked being in the voice": Interview with Gore Vidal, August 10, 1993.
237 "a married man without glory": Gore Vidal, *1876* (New York: Random House, 1976), 109.
237 "Ships, barges, ferry boats": Ibid., 3.
237 "the lobster salad": Ibid., 87.
238 "I was not prepared": Ibid., 143.
238 "an impressive-looking": Ibid., 361.
238 "Had he the character": Ibid., 285.
238 "the result of a precarious": Peter Conrad, "Re-Inventing America," *The Times Literary Supplement* (March 26, 1976): 348.
239 "Ravello was really Gore's": Interview with Michael Mewshaw, April 3, 2014.
239 "He was a fellow degenerate": JPD, September 20, 2008.
240 "a masterpiece of tender malice": James Wolcott, "Gore Bulls Through Again," *The Village Voice* (May 9, 1977): 77.
240 "At that first meeting": Gore Vidal, "Some Memories of the Glorious Bird and an Earlier Self," in *The Selected Essays of Gore Vidal*, edited by Jay Parini (New York: Doubleday, 2008), 136.
240 "I think that the marked difference": Ibid., 144–45.
241 "He [Williams] is bitter": Letter from Gore Vidal to Bill Gray, n.d. 1976, GVP.
242 "This was the last straw": Interview with Howard Austen, July 21, 1998.
243 "the sort of exuberant badness": Gore Vidal, "The Top Ten Best Sellers," in *Matters of Fact and of Fiction (Essays 1973–1976)* (New York: Random House, 1977), 3.
244 "Acid-yellow forsythia": "Calvino's Novels," ibid., 39.
244 "Calvino has now developed": Ibid., 46.
244 "Because the ambitious teacher": "The Hacks of Academe," ibid., 93.
244 "redskin most at home": Ibid., 95.
245 "Today the first order of business": "West Point," ibid., 204.
245 "Therefore let us remove": "The State of the Union," ibid., 268.
245 "So we are left": Christopher Lehmann-Haupt, "Books of the Times," *The New York Times* (April 20, 1977): C23.

246 "There is no evidence": Gore Vidal, Letter, *The New York Review of Books* (July 14, 1977): 83.
246 "The outskirts of Katmandu": Gore Vidal, *Kalki* (New York: Random House, 1977), 53–54.
246 "What is there": Ibid., 56.
247 "At the most": Ibid., 131.
247 "Vidal's apocalypse": Angela Carter, "Bored Vidal," *The Guardian Weekly* (April 30, 1978): 22.
247 "an apocalyptic extravaganza": R. Z. Sheppard, "Elegant Hell," *Time* (March 27, 1978): 98.
247 "Small things give great pleasure": Vidal, *Kalki*, 253.
248 "Gore said, 'I'm a local icon,' ": Judith Harris, from her unpublished diaries, August 1977, courtesy of Harris.
250 "I butted him": Letter from Norman Mailer to J. Michael Lennon, December 22, 1977, in *Selected Letters of Norman Mailer*, 498.
251 "Howard liked movie people": JPD, October 11, 2008.
252 "$1000 a week": *The Diaries of Kenneth Tynan*, edited by John Lahr (New York: Bloomsbury, 2001), 397.
252 "It was cool": Diary entry for July 25, 1978, quoted in Thomas Powers, "A Conversation with Gore Vidal," *London Review of Books* 36, No. 15 (July 31, 2014).
252 "Such a key period": Interview with Gore Vidal, December 20, 2010.
252 "detested her": Letter from Gore Vidal to Judith Halfpenny, December 1977, GVP.
252 "I agree with Nabokov": Interview with Gore Vidal, April 10, 2010.
253 "I'm very sad about Gore": Mary Vespa, "Sued by Gore Vidal and Stung by Lee Radziwill, a Wounded Truman Capote Lashes Back at the Dastardly Duo," *People* (June 25, 1979): 22.
253 "I shall have to die": Recalled by Michael Mewshaw and others.
253 "Currently, there are two kinds": Gore Vidal, "Lessing's Science Fiction," in *United States: Essays 1952–1992* (New York: Random House, 1993), 380.
254 "I am blind": Gore Vidal, *Creation* (New York: Random House, 1981), 3.
254 "My grandfather in his seventy-fifth year": Ibid., 4.
255 "Personally," he says: Ibid., 142.
255 "I know how perception begins": Ibid., 240.
255 "The absence of purpose": Ibid., 336.
255 "there is never a true account": Ibid., 351.
256 "You know, when I was fifteen": Ibid., 393.
256 "He made himself an expert": Ibid., 529.
256 "I think I felt closest": Interview with Gore Vidal, December 20, 2010.
256 "The next dozen years": Vidal, *Creation*, 503.
258 "Vidal writes with extraordinary": Stefan Kanfer, "Two Cheers for Zoroaster," *The New Republic* (April 25, 1981): 34–36.

Chapter Nine

262 "The Bird had been drinking": Interview with Gore Vidal, December 20, 2010.

263 "The American passion": Gore Vidal, "Pink Triangle and Yellow Star," in *The Second American Revolution and Other Essays (1976–1982)* (New York: Random House, 1982), 168.

264 "What indeed has happened": Midge Decter, "The Boys on the Beach," *Commentary* (September 1, 1980).

265 "so many Max Naumanns": Vidal, "Pink Triangle and Yellow Star," *The Second American Revolution*, 184.

265 "the oligarchs are a good deal": "The Second American Revolution," ibid., 270.

266 "I had seen how much trouble": Interview with Gore Vidal, December 20, 2010.

266 "was written by a man": Christopher Lehmann-Haupt, "Books of the Times," *The New York Times* (April 27, 1982): C13.

266 "a lightweight": Julian Symons, "Fancy Footwork," *The Times Literary Supplement* (August 27, 1982): 916.

266 "No one else": Thomas Mallon, "Catching a Buzz," *National Review* (August 20, 1982): 1035.

267 "He just wouldn't stop": JPD, October 22, 1993.

267 "We drove to the Royal Lodge": Letter from Gore Vidal to Judith Halfpenny, December 1, 1983, GVP.

269 "Thousands of people": Interview with Jonah Raskin in 1985; see "A Life of Reflection & Invention: Gore Vidal (1925–2012)," *The Brooklyn Rail* (September 3, 2012).

269 "The prospect of having Gore Vidal": Robert Chandler, "Putting Words in Gore Vidal's Mouth—a Copywriter Recalls the 1982 Senate Campaign," *The Huffington Post* (August 6, 2012).

270 "I think he was": Interview with Gavin Lambert, June 10, 2002.

271 "I spoke with Vidal": William Bradley, "Gore Vidal: Remembering a Brilliant, Controversial Legend of the Sort We Don't Foster Any More," *The Huffington Post* (August 3, 2012).

271 "I do think he wanted": Letter from Gary Conklin to author, April 22, 2014.

272 "I was of course thrilled": Interview with Gary Fisketjon, March 29, 2014.

272 "laughingly debauches the novel": Peter Conrad, "Not with a Bang," *The Observer* (May 1, 1983): 28.

272 "relishes retailing a brand": Jonathan Yardley, "Throwing Firecrackers Down Main Street," *The Washington Post Book World* (May 15, 1983): 3.

272 "at the console of her word-processor": Gore Vidal, *Duluth* (New York: Random House, 1983), 12.

272 "If, as it has been": Ibid., 3.

273 "August is the month": Ibid., 153.

274 "its mansions and houses": Ibid., 212.

274 "To be sure, Vidal's explicit": Italo Calvino, "Imagining Vidal," in *Gore*

Vidal: Writer Against the Grain, edited by Jay Parini (New York: Columbia University Press, 1992), 35–36.

275 "Gore received honorary citizenship": Judith Harris, from her unpublished diaries, courtesy of Harris.

275 "Howard liked everyone": Interview with Michael Tyler-Whittle, August 3, 1993.

276 "I thought the Baldwin": For a transcription of thirteen letters from Gore Vidal to Jonathan Ned Katz, see http://outhistory.org/oldwiki/Gore_Vidal_/_Jonathan_Ned_Katz_Correspondence:_April_28,_1982_-_2001.

277 "Of the Republic's": Gore Vidal, "William Dean Howells," in *United States: Essays 1952–1992* (New York: Random House, 1993), 194–95.

277 "I lived in Howells": Interview with Gore Vidal, December 20, 2010.

277 "One feels the Great Eraser": Letter from Gore Vidal to Elaine Dundy, July 26, 1997, GVP.

278 "The fact that a novelist": Interview with Gore Vidal, August 10, 1993.

278 "the sweet, insufferable": JPD, April 1998.

280 "the most attractive girl": Gore Vidal, *Lincoln* (New York: Random House, 1984), 253.

280 "the sworn enemy": Ibid., 301.

280 "from a distance of five feet": Ibid., 648.

280 "That was Mr. Davis's chair": Ibid., 633.

281 "the sound of doors slamming": Ibid., 213.

281 "Vidal's imagination": Harold Bloom, "The Central Man," *The New York Review of Books* (July 19, 1984): 5.

281 "The writing in *Lincoln*": Andrew Delbanco, "Gore Vidal's 'Empire' Was a Letdown of Epic Proportions," *The New Republic* (September 21, 1987): 49.

282 "a large man": Vidal, *Lincoln*, 369.

282 "I found so many mistakes": Heidi Landecker, "Gore Vidal's Mistakes Were Mine," *The Chronicle of Higher Education* (August 2, 2012): R5.

283 "more to history": "Gore Vidal's 'Lincoln'?: An Exchange: Gore Vidal, reply by C. Vann Woodward," *The New York Review of Books* (April 28, 1988): 41.

285 "There is nothing quite like": Gore Vidal and George Armstrong, *Vidal in Venice* (New York: Summit, 1985), 11.

285 "I don't know what it was": Interview with Anthony Quinn, June 21, 1993.

286 "Our feud, whatever its roots": Letter from Norman Mailer to Gore Vidal, November 20, 1984, in *Selected Letters of Norman Mailer*, 581–82.

Chapter Ten

288 "gave a dinner for her": Gore Vidal, "Clare Boothe Luce," in *The Last Empire: Essays 1992–2000* (New York: Doubleday, 2001), 92–93.

288 "and Gore was so welcoming": Interview with Susan Sarandon, May 12, 2014.

290 "He is called *lo scrittore*": Interview with Teresa Iridio, February 20, 1986.

290 "I supplied Walter": Interview with Gore Vidal, December 20, 2010.

291 "Let's break a cup": Letter from Norman Mailer to Lucian K. Truscott

IV, November 5, 1979, in *Selected Letters of Norman Mailer*, edited by J. Michael Lennon (New York: Random House, 2014), 483.

293 "Harold Bloom is the only critic": Interview with Gore Vidal, March 11, 2010.

293 "He's just hungover": JPD, May 1, 1986.

294 "Mr. Vidal, who wrote the film": John Corry, "TV Reviews; 'Vidal in Venice,' Two Works on 13," *The New York Times* (June 30, 1986): C1.

294 "Requiem for the American Empire": Gore Vidal, "Requiem for the American Empire," *The Nation* (January 11, 1986): 15–19. This was later retitled "The Day the American Empire Ran Out of Gas."

295 "the most cunning": Paul Berman, "Where Have All Our Racist Aristocrats Gone? A Requiem for Gore Vidal," *The New Republic* (August 3, 2012).

296 "It was a very odd assortment": Interview with Graham Greene, August 20, 1988.

296 "We'd never been enemies": Interview with Norman Mailer, June 3, 1992.

296 "possibly the worst historical novel": JPD, May 5, 2004.

297 an affair with Jackie Onassis: A month later Voznesensky attended a party at Arthur Schlesinger's New York apartment with "a wistful looking Jackie Onassis"; see Alfred Kazin's diary entry of April 14, 1987, in *Alfred Kazin's Journals*, edited by Richard M. Cook (New Haven, CT: Yale University Press, 2011), 535.

298 "It was rather like knitting": Interview with Gore Vidal, August 10, 1993.

300 "he felt that the Administration": Gore Vidal, *Empire* (New York: Random House, 1987), 331.

300 "Why drive poor weak old Spain": Ibid., 25.

300 "Well, I've been to the top": Ibid., 466.

300 "the house which he would never": Ibid., 483.

301 "with its great table": Ibid., 486.

302 "Max knew exactly who": Interview with Gore Vidal, August 20, 1991.

303 "Visitors came and went": Interview with Michael Tyler-Whittle, August 3, 1993.

303 "Gore seemed to know": Interview with John Hay, September 3, 1995.

304 "As the curtain falls": Gore Vidal, "Armageddon?," in *United States: Essays 1952–1992* (New York: Random House, 1993), 995.

304 "A local American heiress": Interview with Gore Vidal, December 20, 2010.

305 "Like you," wrote Dickey: Letter from James Dickey to Gore Vidal, December 14, 1988, James Dickey Papers, Emory University, courtesy of Emory University.

305 "He's in his eighties": Letter from Gore Vidal to James Dickey, January 13, 1989, ibid.

306 "Mr. Vidal's novel was": Harold Holzer, "A Filtered Portrait of Lincoln Comes to the Small Screen," *The New York Times* (March 20, 1988): C3.

306 "the Typhoid Mary": Gore Vidal, *At Home: Essays 1982–1988* (New York: Random House, 1988), 288.

306 "It's nice to be back": Gore Vidal, "Politics Today" (speech, National Press Club, Washington, D.C., March 19, 1988).

307 "adding wings to the mansion": JPD, December 15, 1995.
308 "I'm not an art critic": Gore Vidal, "Fall in the Family," *POZ* (April 1977): 12.
308 "Gore and Howard were": Letter from Steven Abbott to author, August 20, 2014.
309 "bought and revived the moribund": Gore Vidal, *Hollywood* (New York: Random House, 1990), 8.
309 "Although Eleanor blushed easily": Ibid., 19.
310 "to make pro-American": Ibid., 89.
310 "found herself daydreaming": Ibid., 194.
310 "a good deal of Vidal's prose": Michael Wood, "Improvisations on the Fact of Force," *The Times Literary Supplement* (November 10–16, 1989): 1243.
310 "I tell you": Vidal, *Hollywood*, 431.
312 "One billion Muslims": Gore Vidal, "Gods & Greens," *The Observer* (August 27, 1989): 29.
312 "I speak for the nation": "State of the Union Speech," July 7, 1990. See YouTube: http://randomthoughts.club/youtube.php?video=_MJeh8JBDTo.

Chapter Eleven

317 "drug addiction is epidemic": Letter from Gore Vidal to Emma Bonino, n.d. 1991, GVP.
317 "I don't care about sex anymore": JPD, August 15, 1993.
317 "He just had a very": Interview with Jason Epstein, December 12, 2013.
318 "I think one can't emphasize": Interview with Miles Gore, November 11, 2014.
318 "We've become a culture": Interview with Gore Vidal, December 20, 2010.
320 "lecturing his former Exeter classmates": Letter from Steven Abbott to author, August 20, 2014.
320 "Today the public seldom mentions": Quoted in Gore Vidal, *Screening History* (Cambridge, MA: Harvard University Press, 1992), 3.
320 "It had been hard enough": Ibid., 34.
321 "in the end": Ibid., 82.
321 "The English kept up": Ibid., 33.
321 "On both sides of the Atlantic": Ibid., 41.
321 "In life Lincoln wanted": Ibid., 86.
321 "Screen-writing has been": Ibid., 81.
323 "to expose the lies": Noam Chomsky, "The Responsibility of Intellectuals," in *American Power and the New Mandarins* (New York: Pantheon, 1969), 324.
323 a television interview in Boston: The full interview is available at jayparini.com.
324 "This was a prestigious fellowship program": Letter from James H. Tatum to author, May 7, 2014.
325 "Let us dwell upon": Gore Vidal, "Monotheism and Its Discontents," in *United States: Essays 1952–1992* (New York: Random House, 1993), 1051.
325 "Jason Epstein hated it": Interview with Gary Fisketjon, March 29, 2014.

325 "In the beginning was the nightmare": Gore Vidal, *Live from Golgotha* (New York: Random House, 1992), 3.
326 "If he has found": Ibid., 112.
327 "Saint's formula": Ibid., 128.
327 "weighs more than": Ibid., 204.
327 "Saint and I stared": Ibid., 140.
329 "A majority of men and women": Vidal, "The Birds and the Bees," *United States*, 614.
330 "It was not until Mr. Starr": Gore Vidal, "The Birds and the Bees and Clinton," in *The Last Empire: Essays 1992–2000* (New York: Doubleday, 2001), 431.
330 "found him riveting": Interview with Alastair Reid, November 3, 2012.
331 "I am doing my own memoir": Letter from Gore Vidal to Judith Halfpenny, November 22, 1992, GVP.
331 "Vidal's essays go back": Anthony Burgess, "Stating the Case for Gore," *The Observer* (October 10, 1993): 17.
331 "Vidal is the master-essayist": Michael Dirda, "Gore Vidal: Views and Reviews," *The Washington Post Book World* (May 30, 1993): 1.
332 "unmistakably a performance": John Lanchester, "Styling," *London Review of Books* (October 21, 1993): 12.
332 "They'd never been enemies": Interview with Gay Talese, March 20, 2014.
335 "I think he saw me": Interview with Burr Steers, June 10, 2012.
335 "Fear of class war": Vidal, "FDR: Love on the Hudson," *The Last Empire*, 186.
336 "I was an outsider": Ibid., 179.
336 He frequently noted: See his preface to *The Norton Book of American Autobiography*, edited by Jay Parini (New York: W. W. Norton, 1999).
336 "the most charming of men": Gore Vidal, *Palimpsest* (New York: Random House, 1995), 257.
336 "I didn't hear much about Jimmie": Interview with Howard Austen, July 21, 1998.
337 "I have recurring dreams": Vidal, *Palimpsest*, 255.
337 "While I've been here": Ibid., 418.
338 "unflagging brilliance": Hugh Brogan, "Private Faces, Public Places," *New Statesman* (October 27, 1995): 44.
338 "We come to understand": Christopher Hitchens, "After-Time," *London Review of Books* (October 19, 1995): 72.
338 "that much cruelty is present": Christopher Lehmann-Haupt, "Books of the Times: Pithy Recollections and Hints of Revenge," *The New York Times* (October 5, 1995): C21.
339 "thoroughly dissipated": Michael Mewshaw, *Sympathy for the Devil: Four Decades of Friendship with Gore Vidal* (New York: Farrar, Straus and Giroux, 2015), 135.
339 "the recent widow": Vidal, "Clare Boothe Luce," *The Last Empire*, 203.
340 "After Eleanor Roosevelt": Ibid., 208.
340 "I think people don't realize": Interview with Susan Sarandon, May 12, 2014.
340 "To be a lesbian": JPD, September 15, 2010.

340 "We had a friendship": Interview with Erica Jong, May 11, 2014.

341 "Although I've never taken Updike": Vidal, "Rabbit's Own Burrow," *The Last Empire*, 88.

342 "is a writer for whom": James Wood, "Gossip in Gilt," *London Review of Books* (April 19, 2001): 31.

Chapter Twelve

346 "For some reason, Hersh's": Gore Vidal, "Hersh's JFK," in *The Last Empire: Essays 1992–2000* (New York: Doubleday, 2001), 224.

347 "Most Americans of a certain age": "Shredding the Bill of Rights," ibid., 397.

347 "Nothing could justify": Ibid., 416.

347 "Not to worry": Quoted by Vidal in "The Meaning of Timothy McVeigh," *Vanity Fair* (September 2001): 39.

348 "I am about to drop": Fiachra Gibbons, "Vidal Praises Oklahoma Bomber for Heroic Aims," *The Guardian* (August 16, 2001).

349 "I found myself as uncomfortable": Michael Lind, "Gore Vidal: The Virgil of American Populism," *Salon* (August 2, 2012).

349 "dark dried-blood crenelated": Gore Vidal, *The Smithsonian Institution* (New York: Random House, 1998), 4.

350 "Like most teenage mathematical geniuses": Ibid., 20.

350 "The human race will": Ibid., 252.

350 "It didn't sell much": Interview with Gore Vidal, December 20, 2010.

352 "as the curtain falls": Gore Vidal, "Chaos," *The New York Review of Books* (December 16, 1999): 12. This essay appeared, in a different form, as "Chaos" in *The Last Empire*, 379–93.

353 "The academy turned away": Interview with Richard Poirier, September 2, 2002.

354 Tim Teeman: See Tim Teeman, *In Bed with Gore Vidal: Hustlers, Hollywood, and the Private World of an American Master* (Bronx, NY: Magnus Books, 2013).

354 "Gore hated the book": JPD, April 2000.

354 "this dread biography": For example, he said this at the Writers Block on November 14, 1999.

355 "I rarely went to bed": In *Salon*, he mentioned that among his favorite post-war novels were, besides the Mann and Powell, *Good as Gold* by Joseph Heller and *Cosmicomics* by Italo Calvino. Immodestly, he also mentioned his own *Creation*. See "True Gore," *Salon* (May 10, 1999).

355 "But a funny thing happened": See William Bradley, "Gore Vidal: Remembering a Brilliant, Controversial Legend of the Sort We Don't Foster Any More," *The Huffington Post* (August 3, 2012).

356 "amoral mastery of world politics": Gore Vidal, *The Golden Age* (New York: Doubleday, 2000), 458.

357 "He did what no president": Ibid., 459.

357 "As for the human case": Ibid., 464.

357 "modern-day Suetonius": Peter Kemp, "Delusions of Grandeur," *The Sunday Times* (October 22, 2000): Section 9, 47.

357 "enormous task": Zachary Leader, "No Accident," *London Review of Books* (June 21, 2001): 27–29.
358 "I have a hunch": Letter from Gore Vidal to Thomas Mallon, June 16, 2000, courtesy of Mallon.
358 "Gore liked, understood": Interview with Matt Tyrnauer, September 13, 2013.
359 "The last of my U.S. chronicles": Letter from Gore Vidal to Thomas Mallon, June 1999, courtesy of Mallon.
360 "I never thought they'd sink": JPD, June 1999.
360 "Howard's abdominal cavity": Gore Vidal, *Point to Point Navigation* (New York: Doubleday, 2007), 79.
360 "As the nurse opened the door": Ibid., 81.
361 "war with Japan would start": Vidal, "Japanese Intentions in the Second World War," *The Last Empire*, 458.
362 "Having scrutinized all these": Paul Berman, "Patriotic Gore," *The New York Times Book Review* (July 1, 2001): 7.
362 "Wilson questioned the central myth": Vidal, "Edmund Wilson: Nineteenth-Century Man," *The Last Empire*, 7.
363 "It was Dawn Powell's fate": "Dawn Powell: Queen of the Golden Age," ibid., 24.
363 "seems to have dropped out": "The Romance of Sinclair Lewis," ibid., 46.
363 "fancy writing": "Rabbit's Own Burrow," ibid., 89.
363 "Towards the end": "Lindbergh: The Eagle Is Grounded," ibid., 146.
364 "If we so choose": "Time for a People's Convention," ibid., 349.

Chapter Thirteen

368 "The truth on 9/11": See https://www.youtube.com/watch?v=uXJDS_ebv3o.
369 "The supposedly liberal profession": Interview with Carl Bromley, May 29, 2014.
369 "According to the Koran": Gore Vidal, *Perpetual War for Perpetual Peace* (New York: Thunder's Mouth Press/Nation Books, 2002), 3.
370 "The unlovely Osama": Gore Vidal, *Dreaming War: Blood for Oil and the Bush-Cheney Junta* (New York: Thunder's Mouth Press/Nation Books, 2002), 17.
371 "What Chomsky and I have": Ibid., 64.
371 "We hate this system": Gore Vidal, *Imperial America: Reflections on the United States of Amnesia* (New York: Nation Books, 2004), 12.
372 One of the best of these: See http://www.democracynow.org/2004/6/4/imperial_america_gore_vidal_reflects_on.
372 "The book had its genesis": Interview with Gore Vidal, December 10, 2010.
372 "In the fall of 1786": Gore Vidal, *Inventing a Nation: Washington, Adams, Jefferson* (New Haven, CT: Yale University Press, 2003), 1.
373 "I agree to this Constitution": Ibid., 30.
373 "Franklin's blunt dark prophecy": Ibid., 32.
374 "tended to go to the top": Ibid., 19.
374 "He was something": Ibid., 18.

374 "a born political theorist": Ibid., 16.

375 As the historian Joseph J. Ellis: Joseph J. Ellis, "The Right Men, but Not the Real Story," *Los Angeles Times Book Review* (November 16, 2003): R3.

375 "the French fleet came": Vidal, *Inventing a Nation*, ibid., 19.

375 "When he got home": Ibid., 172.

376 "without teeth, without resources": Interview with Gore Vidal, April 10, 2010.

376 "I told him to stop": JPD, October 2003.

377 "euphoric good humor": Gore Vidal, *Point to Point Navigation* (New York: Doubleday, 2007), 83.

379 "That was the day before": Interview with Gore Vidal, December 10, 2010.

379 "The eyes were open": Vidal, *Point to Point Navigation*, 87.

380 "Howard had grabbed": Ibid., 88.

380 "Rebirth? Who knows": JPD, May 2011.

380 "Thanks for the sensitive words": Letter from Gore Vidal to Gerald Howard, n.d. 2003, courtesy of Howard.

381 "This was the culmination": Interview with J. Michael Lennon, June 4, 2014.

381 "Vidal shone as the Devil": Letter from Gerald Howard to author, December 10, 2014.

382 "I could never memorize": Vidal, *Point to Point Navigation*, 90.

382 "I couldn't bear it": Interview with Gore Vidal, December 10, 2010.

383 "Gore meant as much": Interview with Michael Tyler-Whittle, August 3, 1993.

383 "The Civil War just didn't end": Interview with Gore Vidal, July 20, 1993.

384 "Gore arrived in an understandably": Letter from Zannie Voss to author, June 5, 2014.

384 "The hope was that": Interview with Jody McAuliffe, June 3, 2014.

384 "No one wants to admit": Edmund White, *Terre Haute* (New York: Samuel French, 2009), 14.

385 "James scarcely looks": Ibid., 48.

385 "I based the writer on Gore": Interview with Edmund White, June 9, 2014.

385 "Edmund White will yet": Robert McCrum, "Gore Vidal: The Lion in Winter," *The Observer* (June 16, 2007): R3.

386 "I used to chat": Vidal, *Point to Point Navigation*, 27.

386 "The monsoon is early": Ibid., 39.

386 "As I now move": Ibid., 1.

386 "Considering what he ate": Ibid., 120.

387 "a monument draped": Ibid., 44.

387 "a youth at a hotel": Ibid., 112, 114.

388 "I pulled back the sheet": Ibid., 88.

388 "almost alarmingly laconic": Christopher Hitchens, "Leave-Taking," *The New York Times Book Review* (November 26, 2006): 12.

388 "a weary book, fragmentary": Adam Kirsch, "Making It," *The New York Sun* (November 3, 2006): 6.

394 "half-argued and half-written": Christopher Hitchens, "Vidal Loco," *Vanity Fair* (February 2010): 22.

396 "He didn't like the idea": Interview with Miles Gore, November 11, 2014.

396 "Today I have walked": Lisa Grainger, "Istanbul, Turkey: Old City, New Spirit," *The Daily Telegraph* (September 3, 2011): T1.

397 "One late night in Istanbul": Courtesy of Derek Blasberg.

Conclusion

401 "The narrative gift": Letter from Gore Vidal to Gianfranco Corsini, n.d. 1973, GVP.

401 "They're amazing books": Interview with Matt Tyrnauer, September 13, 2013.

Postscript

407 "A headline in *The New York Times*": Tim Teeman, "For Gore Vidal, a Final Plot Twist," *The New York Times* (November 8, 2012): 1C.

Photo Credits

INSERT I

Page 1 (top, left and right): MS Am 4354, Houghton Library, Harvard University
Page 1 (bottom): MS Am 4397, Houghton Library, Harvard University
Page 2: *Gore Vidal: Snapshots in History's Glare* by Gore Vidal. Copyright © 2009 by Gore Vidal. Used by permission of Abrams Books, an imprint of Harry N. Abrams, Inc., New York. All rights reserved.
Page 3 (top): © Corbis/Bettmann
Page 3 (bottom): MS Am 4355, Houghton Library, Harvard University
Page 4 (top): MS Am 4313, Houghton Library, Harvard University
Page 4 (bottom): MS Am 4355, Houghton Library, Harvard University
Page 5 (top): *Gore Vidal: Snapshots in History's Glare* by Gore Vidal. Copyright © 2009 by Gore Vidal. Used by permission of Abrams Books, an imprint of Harry N. Abrams, Inc., New York. All rights reserved.
Page 5 (bottom): Courtesy Los Alamos Historical Society Photo Archives
Page 6 (top, left and right): *Gore Vidal: Snapshots in History's Glare* by Gore Vidal. Copyright © 2009 by Gore Vidal. Used by permission of Abrams Books, an imprint of Harry N. Abrams, Inc., New York. All rights reserved.
Page 6 (bottom): MS Am 4316, Houghton Library, Harvard University
Page 7 (top, left): MS Am 4318, Houghton Library, Harvard University
Page 7 (top, right): MS Am 4357, Houghton Library, Harvard University
Page 7 (bottom): MS Am 4358, Houghton Library, Harvard University
Page 8 (top, left): MS Am 4319, Houghton Library, Harvard University
Page 8 (top, right): Jerry Cooke, The LIFE Images Collection, © Getty Images
Page 9: MS Am 4359, Houghton Library, Harvard University
Page 10 (top): MS Am 4360, Houghton Library, Harvard University
Page 10 (bottom): MS Am 4361, Houghton Library, Harvard University
Page 11 (top): Lisa Larsen, The LIFE Images Collection, © Getty Images
Page 11 (bottom): Karl Bissinger papers, University of Delaware Library, Newark, Delaware.
Pages 12–14: *Gore Vidal: Snapshots in History's Glare* by Gore Vidal. Copyright © 2009 by Gore Vidal. Used by permission of Abrams Books, an imprint of Harry N. Abrams, Inc., New York. All rights reserved.

Page 15 (top): *Gore Vidal: Snapshots in History's Glare* by Gore Vidal. Copyright © 2009 by Gore Vidal. Used by permission of Abrams Books, an imprint of Harry N. Abrams, Inc., New York. All rights reserved.
Page 15 (bottom, left): AP Photo
Page 15 (bottom, right): Courtesy Harry B. Kloman
Page 16: © Corbis/Bettmann

Insert II

Page 1: Everett Collection
Page 2 (top): Wisconsin Center for Film and Theater Research
Page 2 (middle): Everett Collection
Page 2 (bottom): Dick Cavett/Daphne Productions, Inc.
Page 3: *Gore Vidal: Snapshots in History's Glare* by Gore Vidal. Copyright © 2009 by Gore Vidal. Used by permission of Abrams Books, an imprint of Harry N. Abrams, Inc., New York. All rights reserved.
Page 4: Franco Origlia, Getty Images News Collection, © Getty Images
Page 5: Slim Aarons, Premium Archive Collection, © Getty Images
Page 6 (top): Courtesy Jason Epstein
Page 6 (bottom): AP Photo
Page 7 (top): *Gore Vidal: Snapshots in History's Glare* by Gore Vidal. Copyright © 2009 by Gore Vidal. Used by permission of Abrams Books, an imprint of Harry N. Abrams, Inc., New York. All rights reserved.
Page 7 (bottom): Everett Collection
Page 8: *Time Magazine*/ TIME & LIFE Collection
Pages 9–11: *Gore Vidal: Snapshots in History's Glare* by Gore Vidal. Copyright © 2009 by Gore Vidal. Used by permission of Abrams Books, an imprint of Harry N. Abrams, Inc., New York. All rights reserved.
Page 12: Everett Collection
Page 13 (top): AP Photo/Ron Frehm
Page 13 (bottom): Photofest
Pages 14–15: Courtesy Oliver Parini
Page 16: Courtesy Diana Phipps

Index

About the Author

Jay Parini is the Axinn Professor of English and Creative Writing at Middlebury College. His novels include *The Last Station, Passages of H.M., Benjamin's Crossing*, and *The Apprentice Lover.* His volumes of poetry include *The Art of Subtraction: New and Selected Poems*. In addition to biographies of John Steinbeck, Robert Frost, William Faulkner, and Jesus, he has written a volume of essays on literature and politics, as well as *Promised Land: Thirteen Books that Changed America, The Art of Teaching,* and *Why Poetry Matters.* He edited the *Oxford Encyclopedia of American Literature* and writes regularly for *The Guardian* and other publications. He lives in Vermont.